THE
LAST
LIBERTY

THE BIOGRAPHY OF THE SS JEREMIAH O'BRIEN

WALTER W. JAFFEE

THE GLENCANNON PRESS

Dedication

To all Liberty ship sailors, past, present and yet to come.

BY THE SAME AUTHOR:

"The pathway of man's journey through the ages is littered with the wreckage of nations which, in their hour of glory, forgot their dependence on the sea."

Brigadier General J. D. Little, USMC

CONTENTS

ACKNOWLEDGEMENTS

This book would not have been possible without the kind help and cooperation of many people. Among them are: Lisbet Bailey, Dan Bandy, Robert Blake, Bob Burnett, Vincent Carista, Rosario Carista, Nicholas Carista, Bob Crocker, John Crosby, Tom Ender, Francis Erdman, Albert Haas, Judy Hitzeman, Ken Holsapple, Marci Hooper, Charles Hord, Captain George Jahn, Henry Kusel, Ted Martin, Tom McGeehan, Robert Milby, Hector Miller, Harry Morgan, Joanie Morgan, Captain Ernest Murdock, Captain James Nolan, Admiral Thomas J. Patterson, Thora Quackenbush, Norman Robinson, Rochelle Rose, Carl Scharpf, Coleman Schneider, Phil Sinnott, E. Ray Sharpe, Jerome Shaw, Neil Thomson, William Watson and Morgan Williams.

The cover illustration was provided through the courtesy of George Lamuth. My thanks to him for its use and for the other fine photographs he supplied for this book.

The quotes by Bill Boissonneault in Chapter 3 are taken from the book, *Portland Ships Are Good Ships*, by Herbert G. Jones.

The description of Liberty ships in Appendix H is taken from an article which appeared in the April, 1942 edition of *Marine Engineering and Shipping Review*.

Robert T. Young, President of the American Bureau of Shipping, is quoted from his article, "The Lessons of the Liberties," published by that organization in 1974.

The section on the Neptune ceremony appearing in Chapter 13 is adapted from copies of such ceremonies which were conducted during World War II on the *President Polk* and the *Carlos Carillo*.

Many of the quotes by Admiral Thomas J. Patterson in Chapter 15 are taken from an article titled "How We Saved the Jeremiah O'Brien" which appeared in *Sea History* in the Winter 1988-89 edition. I am grateful to the National Maritime Historical Society and Peter Stanford for granting permission to quote from the article.

A special thanks to Albert Haas for providing copies of his diary, Captain De Smedt's voyage letter and other valuable information.

Two people deserve additional highlighting: Marci Hooper for her invaluable suggestions and assistance with the resources of the National Liberty Ship Memorial (NLSM) and Admiral Thomas J. Patterson for his candid and helpful remarks on the manuscript.

Finally, I would like to thank my editor who prodded, poked, cajoled, sympathized and encouraged me to keep on track and finish. Without her help it might never have been done.

Walter W. Jaffee

FOREWORD

The *SS Jeremiah O'Brien* occupies a unique historical berth. She is the last active ship in the world that took part in the greatest sea assault in history — the invasion of Northern France and the liberation of Europe that began on D-Day, June 6, 1944. Of the more than 5,000 ships that supported that epic battle, only the *Jeremiah* remains.

The *O'Brien* also is the first of the World War II merchant marine museum ships. She tested the waters for those to follow. The *John W. Brown*, berthed in Baltimore, Maryland and the *Lane Victory* in Long Beach, California are maritime museums in their own right, but the *Jeremiah* began it all. Her champions conceived the idea, secured support, guided bills through Congress, raised grants and finally established the vessel at a permanent berth, surveying the figuratively unexplored seas so that the ships that followed found themselves sailing through charted waters.

I first met the *SS Jeremiah O'Brien* in 1986. Gene Cleven, Superintendent of the Western Region Reserve Fleet at Suisun Bay, California was invited to attend a function on board but had a prior commitment. As his assistant, the social obligation became mine to fulfill. I boarded her not expecting much. Freighters are freighters. They earn their keep by carrying cargo of all types. In the course of their working lives little time is available for cosmetics — making the ship look clean and nice. Tight cargo schedules, raging seas and tempestuous weather make more than basic maintenance impractical. In addition, I knew she had languished at Suisun Bay for thirty-three years and had been out of "mothball" status for only seven years. So I expected to see a working freighter with rust streaks, more than a few dents and scrapes, a ship well-used but sturdy.

On stepping aboard my first impression was one of surprise at her immaculate condition. You could almost literally eat off her decks. She looked as pristine as she must have on her launching day in 1943. Her deck was spotless, inside and out her brass gleamed, paint was fresh and her engine purred.

Eventually I got to know the ship and her crew and found her pristine appearance epitomized the care, concern, pride and professionalism of her volunteers. They were Liberty ship sailors. They had suffered the rigors of a global war on the oceans of the world. From the Admiralty Islands and the Philippines to Normandy and Murmansk, they knew what it was like to see their shipmates work and struggle and die and wonder if their number would be the next to be called.

The *SS Jeremiah O'Brien* had also been there. She was part of the lore of World War II. She had braved the rigors of "Winter North Atlantic," the submarine-infested waters of the North Sea, the bombing attacks on the beaches of Normandy, the hardships of the South Pacific. And, like many of her volunteer crew, she survived. The *Jeremiah* is not only a museum ship. She is a labor of love and a memorial to all the ships and men who gave their lives. And she is an operating ship. She is alive.

Although not literally the last Liberty ship (the *John W. Brown* is a museum ship in Baltimore and, at this writing, three Liberty hulls are in the James River Reserve Fleet), she is the last unaltered Liberty in existence. The others were modified after the War.

The question is why. Why the *Jeremiah O'Brien* ? Why did she survive when 2,750 of her sisters didn't? Why did she survive when 4,999 of her comrades from World War II went to the scrapyard? What was it that made her special? I hope this book is the answer.

W.W.J.
Menlo Park,
California
1993

INTRODUCTION

T he Greeks had a phrase for it — "the defects of our virtues." In today's parlance it's "the downside." Applied in historical context to the United States, it means we are blessed with a high degree of native intelligence, ingenuity and an abundance of raw materials. Unfortunately, these strengths have caused us to develop a national carelessness, a lack of discipline, a failure to plan ahead. Instead, we trust to luck and rely on our wealth and resources to extricate us from the consequences of our failures. America's maritime policy at the outbreak of World War I is a classic example of this pattern.

Before that war, federal maritime policy stated that foreign-built ships could not be registered in the United States. The intent was to protect the shipbuilding industry. Yet, other than that policy statement, the government did little to encourage shipbuilding. Seeking more immediate profits in other arenas, American businessmen looked to non-maritime investments.

When war broke out in 1914, only 9% of our foreign

commerce was carried on American ships. Almost immediately the foreign flag ships, which carried the other 91% of American cargo, withdrew to their homelands, leaving American piers glutted with ever-growing piles of cargo.

Reacting to this, Congress passed a series of bills and emergency measures allowing American registration of foreign-flag ships and supporting the construction of new American ships. Under the Shipping Act of 1916 the United States spent $3.3 billion to build 2,300 vessels. The number of shipyards increased from 61 to 341 in just one year.

Unfortunately, it was a case of too much too late. Lacking a coherent plan, we reacted in haste, once more without considering the long-term effect of our precipitous actions. First, most of the ships weren't completed until the war was over. In fact, one third weren't even started until after the war ended. Further compounding these errors was the fact that most of our newly-built ships were coal-fired. The international maritime industry, however, was moving towards oil as the fuel for marine power plants. By 1929 the United States was again paying the price for its failure to plan. The backwaters of America's ports became clogged with obsolete, laid-up ships.

There was, however, a value to all this. As the next war approached, it appeared that we had finally learned the folly of simply reacting to events when they occurred, that we now recognized the importance of planning and foresight. In Europe, the rumbles of war could already be heard. Spain was serving as the testing ground as its Fascist dictator practiced the arts of war drenched in Spanish blood while the most monstrous Fascist of all watched and analyzed from his aerie in Berchtesgaden. In the Far East, the Japanese Imperial forces were refining in Manchuria the terrors that would be expanded to all of Southeast Asia.

Santayana wrote, "Those who cannot remember the past are condemned to repeat it," but, for a while in the United States, it looked like the lessons of history had been learned. The United States would be ready for the next war.

1

THE LESSONS OF WAR

And so, the Merchant Marine Act of 1936 was passed. Considered by many as the *Magna Carta* of the United States Merchant Marine, the Act took as its three critical principles:

1. A modern, efficient merchant marine was necessary for national defense and the development of overseas and domestic commerce.
2. The ships of such a merchant marine must be built so that they could be converted to naval auxiliaries in time of war or national emergency.
3. All such ships must be built in the United States and owned and operated under the American flag, and manned by American seamen.

To accomplish its intent, the Act created operating and construction differential subsidies. These allowed American ships to compete in a world market where ship construction costs were half, and ship operating expenses two-thirds, that of the United States.

The average remaining useful life of ships in the American Merchant Marine at the time was considered to be five years. Beginning in 1937, the Act called for a ten-year program in which fifty new ships a year would be built. The new fleet would be made up of fast tankers and three types of freighters (C-1, C-2 and C-3) each powered by economical geared turbines, producing a relatively high sea speed. At the time there were only ten shipyards capable of building ships more than 400 feet long. Containing forty-six slipways, half of these were already occupied with Navy production.

In 1939, before war was declared in Europe, recognizing the importance of controlling our own commerce, the production schedule of the ten-year program was doubled to 100 ships a year. In August 1940 it was doubled again, with construction orders for 200 ships a year being distributed between 19 shipyards.

As country after country fell under Hitler's iron hand, England fought the enemy alone while the United States remained neutral. During the first nine months of war English losses totaled 150 ships, more than 1 million tons. In April 1941 alone, 800,000 deadweight tons of shipping were lost. German U-boats sank ships faster than England could build them.

In desperation, England turned for help to America, with her vast supply of natural resources and unequalled ability to accomplish large-scale projects. In September 1940 the British Merchant Shipbuilding Mission approached the United States about the possibility of building ships for Great Britain. Bringing with them their own plans for a ship design, they proposed a vessel similar to the *Dorington Court,* built in 1939. It had evolved from an old tramp ship design first conceived in England in 1879 and later modified by Joseph L. Thompson & Sons at Sunderland, England. Initially dubbed the "Ocean" class, the ship was rated at 10,000 deadweight tons with a 2,500 horsepower engine that produced a speed of 10 knots. The design was slow, but the construction simple. Driven by an obsolete reciprocating engine with coal burning fire-tube boilers, the vessel had been built, year after year, on the River Tyne and had proven its reliability in trades where speed was secondary to reliability. England wanted sixty of them.

According to Admiral Emory Scott Land, Chairman of the United States Maritime Commission, the quickest way to produce the ships was for Britain to buy them outright, rather than go through the U.S. government. But no construction berths were available. New yards would have to be created in which to build the new ships. To accommodate the sixty-ship order for "Ocean" class vessels, a conglomerate of West Coast construction and engineering firms was called in. Known as the Six Services or Six Companies it included the general contracting firms that built the Hoover and Grand Coulee Dams and was headed by Henry Kaiser. Within months it would include Todd Shipyards Inc. in New York and the Bath Iron Works in Maine, among the oldest and most venerable shipbuilders in the United States.

Even without England's sixty ship order, however, the accelerating construction of new hulls outstripped the industry's ability to provide engines for them. There were not enough turbines to propel the new "C" types, let alone modify an additional sixty ships for Great Britain, and the demand for more tonnage was growing daily. It soon became apparent that the sophisticated, well-made ships envisioned by the Maritime Commission in 1936 would have to wait. Quantity rather than speed and refinement became the overriding goal.

To produce in quantity meant that existing ship designs had to be modified for immediate construction. The time necessary to design and develop a new ship was a luxury no one could afford. With the Battle of the Atlantic already raging, construction timetables were also critical. To reduce production time and costs, it was decided to weld the new ships rather than use the traditional, and time-consuming, riveted method.

The best design available was that brought over by the British for their "Ocean" class. It had adequate horsepower and carrying capacity for its intended purpose. In addition, the *Dorington Court* hull and engine were simplicity incarnate. First, the simple hull lines conformed easily to the new concept of welding, keeping construction costs relatively low and construction time minimal. Second, the reciprocating engine used in the British design was an uncomplicated piece of equipment that could be built in any machine shop. Unlike the high-speed turbines designed for the "C" ships, no special techniques were needed for manufacture and the capacity to produce them was available. The same was true of the engine's steam boilers, especially considering the relatively moderate pressures associated with reciprocating engines. Third, the ship was easy to operate. Operation of the steam reciprocating engine required a minimum of training. Finally, the Navy was fully utilizing the steam turbine manufacturing capability in the United States for combatant ships, making reciprocating engines a necessity for the Libertys.

In early 1941 Admiral Land showed President Roosevelt the plans for the British design with the intent of modifying it to produce a quickly-built, efficient American ship to meet the needs of the war effort. Roosevelt's comment was, "Admiral, I think this ship will do us very well. She'll carry a good load. She isn't much to look at, though, is she? A real ugly duckling." As soon as the press heard the comment, the name stuck. The ships were affectionately known ever after as "ugly ducklings."[1]

The President announced construction of the new emergency class of ship in February 1941 for his "bridge of ships" across the Atlantic Ocean. Describing them as "dreadful looking objects," he set the first construction goal at 200 emergency cargo vessels. This would soon be increased to 2300 vessels totalling 23 million deadweight tons for 1942 and 1943.

Trying to change the public's image of the new emergency ship, which was soon to be the mainstay of American ship construction, Admiral Land referred to the 200-ship order as the Liberty Fleet and declared September 27, 1941 as "Liberty Fleet Day." On that day fourteen "emergency" ships were launched across the nation. The first of these, the *Patrick Henry*, provided the inspiration for the event. It was the ship's namesake who said "Give me liberty or give me death." A month later, on October 15, 1941, the first of Britain's "Ocean" ships came off the ways.

---

[1] To a seaman's eye the ships were smart looking with their raked bow, cruiser stern, and well-designed sheer line.

Prefabrication became an art form during the war. Here a midship section for a C-4 is put in place. Credit NLSM

Named the *Ocean Vanguard,* it was launched by Mrs. Emory Land.

The strategy of building ships faster than they can be sunk would prove to be an effective concept. An equally valid counter-objective is to sink them faster than they can be built, and that was precisely the strategy of the German Navy. In May 1942 German Admiral Dönitz said, "The total tonnage the enemy can build will be about 8.2 million tons in 1942, and about 10.4 million tons in 1943. This would mean that we would have to sink approximately 700,000 tons per month in order to offset new construction; only what is in excess of this amount would consti-tute a decrease in enemy tonnage. However, we are already sink-ing these 700,000 tons per month now." His mistake was in underestimating the ship-building capacity of American yards.

   In the process of gearing up for Liberty ship production the art of shipbuilding was revolutionized. Old-line shipbuilders contributed their knowledge and experience. New organizations developed new techniques, their very lack of preconceived ideas about shipbuilding creating new methods and innovations in an old profession.

   The art of welding had only recently been developed to the point where it could be used in shipbuilding and the first all-welded ship came off the ways in November 1940.[2] With welding came prefabrication. Sun Shipbuilding of Chester, Pennsylvania developed the process of building a ship's bow section on the ground, then adding it to the ship under construction on the ways.

Prefabrication meant reduced construction time. Here a transverse bulkhead is lowered into position. Credit NLSM

---

[2] Welding provided a savings in weight of 600 tons compared to the older method of riveting.

Soon bulkheads and sections of inner bottoms were being built in shops of various shipyards and set on the ways, rather than the old plate-by-plate, frame-by-frame methods. The Bethlehem-Fairfield yard at Baltimore was in the vanguard of this type of construction. In their fabricating shops they assembled materials for eight ships at a time: double bottoms with fuel and drainage pipes already installed, sections of deck structure complete with framing and bulkheads intact. From the shop the complete section was transported to the ways where it was set in place and welded to other sections. Meanwhile, construction began on the next section.

In Oregon, the entire Portland plant was revised to the new prefabricated, assembly-line method of ship construction. Here the sections were prefabricated as completely as possible reaching the point where the entire superstructure, with living quarters and navigation equipment, was built in the shop, lifted by gigantic cranes, and lowered into place as the hull of the already-launched ship floated under the crane. In North Carolina, the Newport News Shipbuilding Company went so far in its newly-constructed Wilmington yard as to preassemble almost the entire sides of their ships. Once assembled, they were cut into manageable sections and the sections were then rejoined by welders on the launching ways. Delivery time, originally expected to be 110 days, averaged about 40 days for the new vessel.

Slowly the new ship caught on. Originally designed to have a life of five years, it was often said during the war that if a Liberty delivered its cargo once, it had paid for itself. Few people would have guessed that the ship would outlast these pessimistic predictions and become the mainstay of the world's merchant fleets for the next twenty-five years. They hadn't counted on American workmanship and know-how — the ability to do the job, do it quickly, and do it well when the chips were down. This unique American quality, harnessed with a national policy and detailed planning, was to be an insurmountable force.

2

A SHIP
FOR ALL SEASONS

Adapting the British "Ocean" design to American standards required some effort. To ensure that the conversion went smoothly and efficiently, the Maritime Commission called on the firm of Gibbs and Cox in New York, the naval architects who had done such a superb job on the original designs of the *SS America.* Their modifications gave a ship suited to the requirements of the times. The simplicity of their design made it easy to weld and facilitated the prefabrication process.

The split house used in the British design was consolidated into one midships house bringing the unlicensed crew into the same structure as the officers rather than having them occupy the fantail area below decks, as they did on the British version. This was considered safer for North Atlantic voyages. It also reduced the amount of piping, wiring and outfitting needed to build the ship.

Because of the extreme shortage of turbine and diesel power plants, the obsolete triple-expansion steam engine was retained.

The original design was altered from coal to oil-burning and from fire tube to water tube boilers, but the engine itself continued to be the triple expansion steam reciprocating type developed in Britain by the North Eastern Marine Engineering Co. Ltd. It was adapted for American construction by Hooven, Owens & Rentschler, a subsidiary of the General Machinery Company of Cincinnati, Ohio. The fully assembled engine weighed 270,000 pounds, stood 19 feet high and was 21 feet long. It turned the four-bladed propeller at 76 rpm, giving the ship a design speed of 11 knots.

The fact that the Liberty burned oil, rather than coal, required other changes. Fixed ballast in the double bottoms was replaced with fuel tanks. Two deep tanks were added in No. 1 hold for water ballast. Without coal bunkers, there was room to lengthen No. 3 hold and single masts replaced kingposts.

Other modifications added to the Americanization of the British model. Steel decks replaced wood in the original design and steel bulwarks were substituted for chain rails. The original canvas wind dodgers on the bridge were replaced with steel. Separate access ladders were provided to the cargo holds so they could be reached without removing the hatch covers. An emergency steering station was included on the stern. The ship was given searchlights, refrigeration for the crew's food and running water in the cabins. The engine, boilers, pumps and deck equipment were all built to one standard specification so that they could be made anywhere in the world and fit on any Liberty.

To facilitate the welding process and mass production, the hull was designed so that most of it could be built with simple hull plating. In other words, because the hull design lacked the twists and turns and double bow and stern curves of a more complex vessel, it was far quicker to build. The only two plates on the Liberty that required special processing were those adjacent to the forefoot.

Welding was a new technology. The process of welding a ship together, however, rather than riveting it, locked a great deal of stress into the hull. When the hull was subjected to the additional stress of freezing temperatures, improper loading and an unkindly sea, something occasionally gave. Some Libertys developed cracks under heavy use. These usually occurred in the unstrengthened square hatch corners and that area of the sheer strake (the uppermost band of plating around the hull, just below the level of the main deck) which was cut to house the accommodation ladder.

Willis "Bud" Hitchcock was third mate on the *Hiram S. Maxim* when she cracked:

"Our route took us thru Bass Straits, between the southern limits of Australia and the island of Tasmania. We found ourselves in terrible Westerly gales. Winds were dead ahead and due to relatively shallow water in this strait the seas piled up into mountainous breaking waves. The ship was barely able to keep her head to the seas. God help us if we ever broached. I remember the sweeping seas caused our deck cargo forward to come adrift and some of it was lost overboard. The conditions were very dangerous for men on decks attempting to resecure this cargo and I know I myself very nearly was swept over. We finally gave up the attempt, as conditions on deck were impossible with large crates grinding away and shifting as the ship pitched and rolled. All of our ammunition lockers for the guns forward were flooded out.

"In the second or third night of this heavy going, at about three in the morning, a loud crash brought all hands up to the boat deck. In the darkness it was impossible to determine what was the cause, had we hit a mine or been torpedoed? I recall in the darkness, on the flying bridge, hearing cargo dunnage boards crashing around our heads as the gale was blowing them from our forward deck cargo like match sticks. It was pitch dark and luckily no one was struck down by these unseen missiles. Soundings were made and we found that we were not taking on water. Further inspection revealed that our deck plates had pulled apart at the starboard aft corner of #3 hatch. As the gale and heavy seas finally subsided somewhat, we broke radio silence and asked the naval authorities if we could make for Melbourne for repairs. We were informed that, due to the higher priority of navy ship repairs, there was no room for us, and we should 'press on.' They did wish us 'good luck.' Well, the ship didn't come unraveled and we secured what was left of our cargo on the foredeck when it calmed down.

"We arrived at Karachi and discharged our cargo and while doing so repairs were made to our cracked deck plate. These repairs consisted of the placement of a 1" thick steel cold patch which was bolted by heavy bolts across the crack. This work was done by a shoreside contractor using nothing but hand tools. It took a week or more to accomplish a job that could have been done in a couple of hours with modern welding and power tools."

James O. Runkle had a similar experience on the Liberty *SS George Weems*, enroute to Molotovsk, then Murmansk, north of the Arctic Circle.

"... the weather was rough. So rough, that the seam between the midships house and the deck was noted to be breaking free at each of the four corners. The split seemed to stop after 5-6 feet and we made port ok in the Firth of Clyde where a crew of welders from Greenock came aboard and re-welded the seams again."

The *John Straub* broke in two and sank in the Arctic. The *Valery Chkalov* broke in two in the North Pacific. Although the two sections were towed to Adak and joined together and the ship successfully finished out the war, the problem was clear. Libertys could crack and in some circumstances break in two.

The ensuing complaints caused the Secretary of the Navy to investigate the design and construction of welded steel merchant ships. Of the more than 2,000 Libertys studied, only one, the *SS John P. Gaines,* suffered structural damage that resulted in casualties. Ten seamen were lost after they had abandoned ship and were in the lifeboat. Another twenty of the 2,000 Libertys had complete fractures of the main deck, and of these, five broke in two. Two of the complete fractures occurred before the ships were placed in service. It was found that if a Liberty ship was going to crack, it would usually occur in near-freezing temperatures or during heavy seas, or both.

The solution was a device known as the "crack-arrestor." By riveting steel reinforcing straps (riveting allows for more "give" than welding) on the main deck the tendency to crack was stopped. In addition the hatch corners were reinforced and gunwale bars were added. Stronger steel was used in areas of stress concentration.

It wasn't all bad news. There were unforeseen advantages to welding. A welded seam is often stronger than the plates it connects. When a welded ship was subjected to the sudden and cataclysmic effects of torpedoes or bombs, it was often more capable of holding together and making port in a damaged condition than its riveted sister. A ship's plating might be torn apart by the force of an explosion but the welded seams generally held. Side plates and bulkheads were often blown in without breaking the welds, and many a welded ship was saved because compartments remained watertight to keep the ship afloat. By contrast, a riveted ship would have sprung rivets and broken seams, with a correspondingly lessened chance of the vessel's reaching port.

The *Ocean Faith* (an American-built, welded "British" Liberty) was hit by a Nazi bomb while on convoy duty. The bomb tore through the ship causing a tremendous volume of water to flood her decks and engine room. Flames burst out from the forward hold, loaded with a thousand tons of bombs and shells. While two of the crew put out the fire, others pumped to keep the twenty feet of water in the hold from rising. The engines were restarted and the ship stayed up with the convoy. Three days later a patch was fitted on the vessel's side. It came adrift twice in the ensuing voyage, but the ship reached her destination and delivered her cargo.

One Liberty was blown in half by torpedoes. The two halves of the ship were towed to separate ports in the Mediterranean and unloaded. They were later welded together again and the ship returned to service. Another ship survived a hurricane after being hit by an enemy torpedo off the coast of North Carolina. She weathered the storm and reached port with no crew casualties and only slight damage to the cargo. The *William Williams* was hit by a torpedo in May 1943. The missile struck the port side near the forward bulkhead of No. 5 hold, shattering plates and frames and blasting a hole through the starboard shell plating. The shaft

ration plant for fresh water, galleys and quarters for the military, heavy lift equipment, strong rooms and equipment storage areas. Of course, extra lifeboats, life rafts and life jackets were supplied.

Four Libertys were converted to the special purpose of carrying war brides and military dependents. Eight ships were converted as animal transports, carrying horses, mules and cattle.

Officially the basic freight-carrying Liberty was an EC2-S-C1 class freighter. "E" represented Emergency, "C" cargo and "2" designated a waterline length between 400 and 450 feet. The "S" meant the vessel was both steam powered and single screw. "C1" referred to the design number. Because of their blunt, box-like appearance, the ships were at first called "Plain Janes" or "Sea Scows" or "Ugly Ducklings." It was only after Admiral Land's speech that the term "Liberty" stuck.

The basic American-style Liberty freighter had an overall length of 441 feet 6 inches, a beam of 56 feet 10 and 3/4 inches and drew 27 feet 9 and 1/4 inches when fully loaded. Her deadweight tonnage (the ship's actual weight in tons) was 10,920, gross tonnage (roughly the internal volume in tons of 100 cubic feet each) about 7,500 and displacement tonnage (the weight in tons of the amount of water she displaced) 14,300.[2] With a full load of fuel a Liberty carried 9,146 tons of cargo when down to her Plimsoll marks, but in wartime it was common to load them deeper than that.

The basic crew complement on Liberty ships was as follows:

Master	1
Chief Mate	1
2nd Mate	1
3rd Mate	1
Deck Maintenance	1
Bosun (Boatswain)	1
A.B. (Able-Bodied Seaman)	6
O.S. (Ordinary Seaman)	3
Purser	1

---

[2] See Appendix A for an explanation of tonnages.

Looking aft about three weeks after the keel was laid, the hull begins to take shape.   Credit NLSM

Radio Officer [3]	1
Chief Engineer	1
1st Assistant Engineer	1
2nd Assistant Engineer	1
3rd Assistant Engineer	1
Deck Engineer	1
Oilers	3
FWT (Firemen/Water Tenders)	3
Wipers	2
Chief Steward	1
Chief Cook	1
Cooks & Bakers	2
Mess Utility Men	5
Total	39

If the ship carried an Armed Guard gun crew, an extra messman was carried. If the ship was designed to carry tanks and planes, an additional Deck Maintenance man was carried. If the ship was a collier, the Deck Maintenance and Deck Engineer were not carried.

To many merchant seamen, Libertys were considered plush billets. James O. Runkle: "Several of us had sailed on older World War I vintage vessels — riveted, rusty, steam steering engines, and worn out ships that still did the job, but were uncomfortably slow and hazardous for the crew. Aboard the new Libertys it felt luxurious and plush, even though the bunks were still mounted thwartships. The plumbing all worked, the triple expansion engine sounded reliable, and she steered predictably."

Captain George Jahn, Senior San Francisco Bar pilot, World War II master of the *SS William Matson* and later master of the *Jeremiah O'Brien* said, "Oh, they were great. You know the first time I went on one I thought, Jesus, here I got hot and cold running water in my room. I never had that before. And they were faster, we made nice time on them."

The Libertys were named after famous or heroic people. Generally, the criterion was that they had to be dead. This held

[3] In some wartime conditions the Armed Guard supplied additional radiomen so the ship's radio could be manned 24 hours a day.

in every case except one. Francis O'Gara was a former sports-writer for the Philadelphia Inquirer and served as purser on the *Jean Nicolet*. The ship was torpedoed by a Japanese submarine in 1944 and went to the bottom with all hands — or so it was thought. The *Francis J. O'Gara* was delivered in June 1945.

In less than a month the main deck, superstructure, masts and gun tubs are in place. Credit NLSM

Four months later Mr. O'Gara was discovered languishing in a Japanese prison camp. He had been picked up by an enemy submarine when the ship was sunk.

With more than 2,700 ships being named after people there had to be a good cross section of American proper names. The *Smith* fleet included *Alfred E., Charles E., Delazon, E. Kirby, Erastus, Francis M., Hugh M., James, Jedediah, Joseph, Junius, Milton H., William L.* and *Winfred L.* There were nine *Jones,* including *John Paul,* seven *Browns,* and six *Johnsons.* Other men honored ranged from Andrew Furuseth, Billy Sunday and F. Scott Fitzgerald to Paul Bunyan and Carl Zachary Webb, a wiper who died while serving on a tanker. The first lady Liberty was the *Amelia Earhart.* Libertys named after other famous women included the obvious such as *Virginia Dare, Julia Ward Howe* and *Pocahontas,* and the not-so-famous such as *Mary Cullom Kimbro,* the first woman merchant mariner killed at sea during World War II when her ship, the *City of Birmingham* was torpedoed on June 30, 1942.

Duplication of first and last names and similarities in names caused some confusion. There were 222 ships with the first name *John* and 193 carrying *William* as a first name. The longest name given a Liberty ship was *Joseph-Augustin Chevalier* and the competition for shortest goes in a dead heat to *Baku, Cebu, Ibex, Lynx, Luna, Lyra, Mink, Niki* and *Oahu.* Eventually those selecting the names ran out of people and chose other appropriate wartime titles: *Stage Door Canteen, Diligence, Faithful* and *Hydra* to name a few.

The first Liberty sunk by enemy action was the *John Adams.* Built by Permanente Yard No. 2 in Richmond, California, she was downed in the Pacific in March of 1942.

Within three years from the day the first contract was signed, fifteen shipyards devoted to the production of Liberty ships had been created, employing over three hundred thousand men and women. They produced more than 2,700 Liberty ships. Each ship contained 52.08 miles of welding, 28,000 rivets, 3,200 tons of steel, 7.5 miles of pipe, 4.75 miles of electrical wiring, was covered with 25 tons of paint and used 900,000 cubic feet of oxygen and 250,000 cubic feet of acetylene gas in its construction.[4]

The Libertys were a great fleet of cargo vessels whose success in supplying our own forces and our allies with the materials of war and with food, fuel and supplies for civilian populations was a major factor in defeating the U-boat and in setting the stage for the downfall of the Axis powers. Of the more than 2,700 built during the war less than 200 were lost.

Only one of the original vessels, the *Jeremiah O'Brien*, is still operating today. Launched in South Portland, Maine, she, with the *John W. Brown*, remains the last of that massive fleet of Libertys. But initially she was just one of many that were "built by the mile and chopped off by the yard."

---

[4] See Appendix B for a complete list of companies that supplied parts for the construction of Liberty ships.

3

A Down East Clambake

The 60-ship order placed by Great Britain almost didn't happen. R.C. Hunter, of the British commission that placed the order, was to return to England with draft contract plans and blueprints. He sailed on an unescorted British liner which depended on speed to avoid submarines. Halfway across the Atlantic, at six in the morning, the ship was struck by a torpedo.

"I was asleep in my cabin when the explosion occurred," he recalled. "The whole vessel shuddered and seemed to drop. I threw on more clothes, grabbed my dispatch case in which were the contracts and documents and rushed up on deck. I scrambled into one of the lifeboats as the ship slid beneath the heavy swell. I pulled an oar with the other passengers for nine hours before we were rescued, with the precious dispatch case at my feet. The papers were sea-sodden and partly unrecognizable and had to be retyped before I could deliver them to the Admiralty."

The order was placed on December 10, 1940 and the contract signed on December 20th. It became the impetus for the creation of two new shipbuilding concerns — both affiliated with Todd Shipyards Corporation, one of the oldest and most respected ship builders and repairers in America. On the West Coast, Todd-California Shipbuilding Corporation was formed with Henry Kaiser as its president and its initial yard in Richmond, California. (In October 1941 the name of the yard was changed to the more familiar Permanente Metals Corporation.) On the East Coast, the Bath Iron Works Corporation joined Todd and the West Coast yards to form the Todd-Bath Iron Shipbuilding Corporation with Richard S. "Pete" Newell acting as president. This yard was to be located on Casco Bay, at South Portland, Maine. Each yard was to build thirty vessels for the British.

While the California yard was to have traditional slanting launching ways, the topography and extreme tidal range of Maine called for something more user-friendly. It was decided to build a basin or graving dock. Ironically, that decision came about because a few years earlier the firm of Gibbs and Cox was asked to build a dreadnought for the Russians. According to M.B. Palmer, in his book *We Fight With Merchant Ships*, it happened this way.

"One day in 1938 (Richard S.) Newell dropped in for a chat at the offices of Gibbs and Cox, New York ship designers. He had nothing in particular on his mind that day, but his eye was caught by a large veiled drawing on an easel. His curiosity piqued, he asked what it was, but was told the whole thing was very hush-hush and just to forget about it. On 'Pete's' promise that he would reveal nothing of what he saw, the architect took off the cloth and the shipbuilder let out a long whistle. There before him was the most fantastic warship he had ever seen, an 80,000-ton monster dreadnought — half battleship and half aircraft carrier — superbly gunned and armored against the heaviest aerial attack. This naval gargantua, Newell learned, had been designed by the New York naval architects on request of the Russian Government.

" 'Why there's not a yard in the country can handle that order!' 'Pete' exclaimed. 'You couldn't find a spot to build her in.' Then, after a moment, he went on, 'But I can tell you where.'

"Gibbs and Cox pricked up its ears. Where did he mean?

Newell answered cryptically by asking for an office boy. To the youngster he said, 'Now, Johnny, you know where such and such a marine store is — go over there and get me a map of Portland Harbor.'

"When the boy came back with the map 'Pete' excitedly pointed out a bit of underdeveloped shoreline in South Portland. There wasn't any shipyard there, not so much as a single way or crane or railroad spur. But Newell knew that strip of land, he said. Twenty feet down through mud and sand was a solid rock ledge. His idea was to shovel down to the rock and build the Russian dreadnought, not on conventional ways, but in an open-water slip. Flood gates on the seaward end would be hoisted up when the job was finished and the ship could be towed right out into the harbor.

"Back in Maine, Newell went forward with his plan. He got a friend in the oil business to secure an option on the stretch of land for five hundred dollars. If anyone heard of the deal, Newell reasoned, he would imagine the oil company had bought it for storage tanks. No one would suspect the shipbuilder. Three thousand dollars he laid out in surveying the land and drilling down to rock. His statement that there was a solid foundation twenty feet down was corroborated. For himself, he was even more convinced than ever that his idea was sound.

" 'I didn't tell anybody what I was doing,' Newell says slyly, 'not even my wife. If she'd known I was spending all that money, she'd be after me. But you know,' the round sparkling-eyed shipbuilder continued, 'it's like some guys to play poker. I had a wonderful time with it — and in the end I got my money back, although the Russian ship was never built.'"

When the British came looking for a place to build their emergency cargo vessels, Washington remembered the insistent man from Maine. Officials from the State Department, Navy, Maritime Commission, British Purchasing Mission, and Todd officials from New York converged on Portland. Totalling 250, they were Newell's guests from morning to night. He recalled, "I took 'em around over thirty miles. We all had a wonderful time, clambake and everything." The result of his Down East clambake was a $50 million contract.

Work started immediately. The area was cleared and construction began. After building a 1,500-foot cofferdam in a mere four weeks, a three-compartment basin 750 feet wide by 450 feet long was excavated. The design was such that seven 441½ foot Liberty ships could be built at one time, any two or three of which could be floated without disturbing the work in the adjacent compartments. Ten months later the yard was complete.

Although, compared to the standard launching ways in California, the process of building a graving dock was necessarily longer, the first British Liberty keel for the *Ocean Liberty* was laid on May 24, 1941, a mere six weeks after the laying of the first keel in the California yard. By the end of June four keels had been laid. The thirtieth ship was delivered 466 days later on November 18, 1942.

At first, few people in the area knew anything about shipbuilding. Bill Boissonneault was "Pete" Newell's nephew and transferred over from the company that built the yard itself. He remembered that, "the work itself was new to me, but hard work was not. We were all learning together. The shipfitters were as green as the rest of us. On Hulls 1 and 2 everything was put together piece by piece like a puzzle.

"After they started welding, I knew I wanted to do that, so I went to the welding school. The welding shed, with twenty-five machines, was between Flat 1 and Flat 2. We had no office. The leadman made out the slips and we went to work. The lines had to go right from there down into the basins. Sometimes it took three or four leads to reach all the way to the other end of the basin. I was a welder's helper at first, so I know what it meant to keep a long line free.

"It's a lot different now (1945), when in the East Area alone we have 439 welding machines and 52 tacking machines. What's the difference? Well, a tacking machine is the same as a welding machine, but by changing the control, five or six tackers can work from one machine, but only one welder can work from a welding machine at a time."

Meanwhile, the need for American ships in the coming conflict grew. In January 1941 Admiral Vickery of the Maritime Commission called on the nation's shipbuilders for increased production. The response was the creation of three new yards: Oregon Shipbuilding Corporation at Portland, California Shipbuilding in Los Angeles and the Houston Shipbuilding Corporation in Texas. Although construction on these yards began at once the Commission soon decided it needed yet more shipbuilding capability. The new yards were expanded and two additional companies were created: Richmond Shipbuilding Corporation to adjoin the Todd-California Shipbuilding Corporation, and South Portland Shipyard Corporation to adjoin the Todd-Bath Iron Shipbuilding Corporation.

The second yard at South Portland came about because Rear Admiral Emory S. Land, Chairman of the U.S. Maritime Commission remembered the persuasive man from Maine, Richard S. Newell. Land asked Newell if he would undertake the building of another yard alongside the Todd-Bath yard for the purpose of building Liberty ships.

"I got one of those aerial photographers," Pete Newell remembered in later years, "and had him photograph the adjacent shoreline in South Portland. Then I took my pencil and marked on the print the location of the proposed machine shops, the piers and the ways, and everything, only where I was drawing it was all water. That didn't matter because I knew there was a good ledge there, too, with only a few feet of mud, then deep water farther out. All I had to do was put in the fill."

As the new site had traditional launching ways, the result was to have two launching systems under one management in South Portland. The Todd-Bath facility with its graving dock was known as the "East Yard" and continued working on the British contract. The South Portland facility with its traditional ways was known as the "West Yard." It built Liberty ships for America under the supervision of the Maritime Commission. It was thought that having the two competing on construction schedules was a good stimulus to production.

South Portland's initial order was for 44 of the vessels. Its first hull was the *John Davenport* launched on May 16, 1941.

When the British contract was completed the East and West yards were combined by the Maritime Commission and on April 1, 1943 the entire organization became the New England Shipbuilding Corporation (N.E.S.C.), an affiliate of Todd Shipyards Corporation of New York City.

At one time South Portland employed 29,680 people in building ships. Because the greatest percentage of their workers were unskilled (85%), they had to be trained and training that many people in a short period of time was a challenging uphill battle against scarcity of materials and lack of suitable yard machinery. An additional factor was the weather. Winter temperatures of 20 to 40 degrees below zero were common. Yet, South Portland achieved a remarkable record. According to Agnes E. Meyer in *Journey Through Chaos*, "the absenteeism and turnover in the N.E.S.C. yards were below that of other yards in the sunny West Coast and the Gulf States."

Among the labor force of nearly 30,000 were 3,700 women, the second largest number of women employed in any shipyard in America at the time. Initially trained as tackers and burners, they eventually became machine workers, pipe coverers, spray painters, even crane operators. Bill Boissonneault, a leadman welder, supervised the first groups of women welders at the yard. "If she's sincerely in here to do the work, a woman is more conscientious than a man on the same job. I never felt that the women were coming here to take jobs away from men. There was enough work for everybody and the women came in just the same as the men — to help with the war effort and do the job that had to be done. Sure, some of them wanted the money ... but so did a lot of the men. And the rank and file of the workers here today (1945), from what I see, are interested in their jobs. I guess they feel about the way I do. I have fifteen nephews in the armed forces. They're doing their part over there and I'm doing my part here. But we're all working for the same thing."

Phil Sinnott, a volunteer on the *Jeremiah O'Brien*, talked with a woman who welded on the ship. "A nice little old lady came on, she said, 'I'm from Portland, Maine. When I was eighteen years old, I graduated from high school. The next day

Women were a significant part of the shipyard workforce during World War II. Janet Doyle, pictured above in 1942 and a present-day volunteer on the O'Brien, *welded on Libertys in Richmond, California. Credit NLSM*

Edna Slocum was California's "Welding Queen." A press release explained how she managed welding and being a housewife. "Her whole family joins in the housework, but she does the cooking, Mr. Slocum does the shopping and their two boys wash the dishes. Each family member cleans a different room of the house. Wash comes from the laundry rough-dry, and Edna squeezes in the ironing. 'And I still have time for a hair wave,' she said." Credit GGNRA

I went to work for New England Shipbuilding and they trained me for two weeks as a welder. They sent me out the first night, on the graveyard shift, and the hull, it turns out, was the *Jeremiah O'Brien*. That was my first job. Well, I got in the little compartment, see, it was either the officer's head or the shower, I forget which, and I got in there and so I got my hood down. I got the stinger out and I started to run a weld up this bulkhead. So I took it off and it had all run down and it looked terrible! I didn't know what to do, I just put my hood down and sat there and cried. I said, I'm too young. I'm too little to do this job. And so I sat there about fifteen or twenty minutes and said well, I'm going to try it anyway. So I worked my way up and lo and behold, I worked my way up to the top and it got better and better all along."

Agnes E. Meyer: "My greatest admiration will always be reserved for the women who work out-of-doors in the Maine shipyards. It is no sinecure to be a welder on the West Coast or in Southern shipyards, but the weather conditions in Maine where the thermometer went to 20 degrees and 30 degrees below zero were a test of character that no other group of workers had to meet. Not in Great Britain nor in any part of our own industrial front have I met war-workers who carry as heavy a load as do these women."

The final output of the South Portland yard was 236 Liberty ships and 30 British "Oceans." This was boosted with a cash incentive program. The government offered a fast delivery bonus of $60,000 to $140,000 for each ship. The average cost for the American Libertys at South Portland was $1,892,000. The first ship took 279 days from keel to delivery. By December 1944 this figure averaged 52.5 days for each ship.

The keel of the last Liberty to survive, the *SS Jeremiah O'Brien*, was laid on May 6, 1943. It was the 30th hull built in the new "West" yard at N.E.S.C and was constructed on launching way No. 1.

4

CREATING A SHIP

When ships are mass-produced to the same design, like Christmas cookies punched out with a cutter, they're indistinguishable until something is done to give them a separate identity. The first thing that marks a ship, that makes her different from her sisters, is the assignment of a hull number. On January 14, 1943 a nameless Liberty hull that existed only on paper at South Portland, Maine, was assigned Maritime Commission Emergency (MCE) hull number 806 and New England Shipbuilding hull number 230. (Like all shipbuilders, New England Shipbuilding assigned its own hull number to the vessel in addition to that of the Maritime Commission).

Little else happened for the next several months but on paper Hull 806 slowly began to take form. Plans, parts and pieces began to be designated as being for hull 806. Then, on May 6, the keel was laid. With substance, the laying of the first piece of the keel, comes reality and a name -- in this case, *Jeremiah O'Brien*, after the first naval hero of the Revolutionary War. With

The SS Jeremiah O'Brien *just before launching. Credit San Francisco Maritime National Historic Park.*

the assignment of a name, things began happening with increasing speed. The hull was quickly assembled on the launching ways -- double bottoms, frames, hull plating and decks.

The first official record of the ship occurred on May 20, 1943 when the Master Carpenter's Certificate, also known as the builder's certificate, was delivered to the Treasury Department. In it the vessel *SS Jeremiah O'Brien*, hull No. 230, is valued at $1,750,000.

Having a vessel on the ways and soon to be launched meant an operator must be selected. On May 26, 1943 the War Shipping Administration (WSA) advised Grace Line, Inc. that the new ship was allocated to them under their Service Agreement, (Contract 363) dated January 1, 1942.[1]

The Irish say that luck is something you're born with. If so, the O'Brien's luck must have started with the laying of her keel, for she seemed protected by good fortune throughout her career. It started with her naming. The omen of her namesake, a good, lucky, Irish name, bode well for the new ship. Then she was assigned, not to some fly-by-night newcomer started up to take advantage of the war, but to Grace Line. Of the dozens of steamship companies operating in the United States at the time, the one selected to operate this vessel had been in the business since 1869. The O'Brien was one of two dozen ships eventually operated by Grace for the WSA. When Grace Line was notified of the new ship, it was thought the vessel would be ready for delivery on June 27, 1943. Grace was advised to obtain the necessary insurance and send copies of the policy to the WSA, to become effective when the first crew member was placed on board.

On June 3, 1943, the vessel was assigned official number 243622 and call letters KXCH, and the number and letters registered with the Collector of Customs. At the same time, the home port of Portland, Maine was designated.[2] The WSA also instructed Grace to have the master and chief engineer report aboard "on or about June 12, 1943" (15 days prior to scheduled delivery on June 27). The clerk-typist or purser was to be aboard 10 days in advance, or about June 17. So that he would have time to learn Grace Line's operations, he was also allowed time to train in the company office.

The following ratings were assigned five days prior to delivery of the vessel, about June 22, 1943: Chief Mate, First Assis-

---

[1] The Service Agreement called for Grace Line to operate a ship or ships to be named at future dates. This way a separate agreement wouldn't have to be drawn up for each new vessel.

[2] In peacetime the port of registration is the city in which the owner (usually a corporation) resides. Hence many American ships are registered in the little-known seaport but well-known corporate headquarters of Wilmington, Delaware. In wartime, however, the government, which technically owned the ship, elected to use the port in which the ship was built as the port of registration rather than Washington, D.C., its residence.

Mrs. Ida Lee Starling, whose husband was head of the White House Secret Service, launches the SS Jeremiah O'Brien *on June 19, 1943.   Credit San Francisco Maritime National Historic Park*

tant Engineer, Second Mate, Second Assistant Engineer, Third Mate, Third Assistant Engineer, Radio Operator, Chief Steward. The WSA allowed each of the newly-assigned crew members a subsistence rate of $4 per day to cover their meals and lodging while they waited for the new ship to become habitable.

Because the ship was government-owned and because the government had just established a new United States Merchant Marine Academy at Kings Point, New York, arrangements were made for a maximum of two deck and four engine cadets but in any event no less than two deck and two engine cadets, if available, to be part of the first crew.

On Saturday, June 19, 1943 the *Jeremiah O'Brien* was launched. The sponsor was Mrs. Ida Lee Starling, wife of the head of the White House Secret Service. Handing her bouquet of roses to her matron of honor, she tightly grasped a champagne bottle and took her place at the bow of the ship.

The launching ceremony, laden with tradition, comes from a time when the first seafarer pushed his modest ship into the sea with the knowledge that he had fearful things to face. Sudden, strangling death lurked in the high waves and strong winds, a slow, painful death could come with a dead calm and a mirror sea or the swish of a giant fish tail could imperil his ship, his cargo and his crew. And there were a thousand ways he could lose himself in the uncharted waters. Sailing was a deadly venture and the sea a brutal lord.

With their lives and goods at stake, seafaring people learned to bargain with the gods that controlled the Deep. The gods demanded sacrifice, so blood was offered in the beginning, in exchange for later protection. Launching ceremonies, then, began with an invocation to the great destructive forces and ended with the sacrifice of a beautiful maiden or a brave seaman. With blood on the prow of the new vessel, she slid into the water with as much assurance of luck as her builders could procure. In the North, where Norse gods hurled icebergs in freezing seas and thick fogs, the Vikings were driven to harder bargains. They launched their galleys on rollers down an inclined way to the water's edge. Between the rollers, bound captive slaves were ground to a pulp by the moving ship.

In later centuries, greater knowledge of the ships and seas banished monsters and angry gods into books of ancient lore. Christianity spread through Europe, and launchings took on a religious aspect. Even now, devout French fishermen launch their boats with the celebration of the full sacrament.

Launching ships with a toast of wine began in Protestant England with the building of the first great British fleet during the reign of Henry VIII. When a ship was floated, the King or some member of his family rose from a throne on the after-deck. He sipped wine from a golden goblet, prayed for luck and divine protection for the ship and spilled a little wine on the new deck, marking carefully the four points of the compass. Then he threw the cup into the sea.

In the nineteenth century the first woman sponsor christened a British man-of-war at the invitation of the Prince of Wales.

Sliding down the ways, the SS Jeremiah O'Brien *makes contact with her new element, the ocean, for the first time.* Credit NLSM

Before that, naming the ship in a flying spray of wine had been a masculine prerogative. Until champagne became generally available, red wine, with its similarity to sacrificial blood, stained bows of ships at launchings. But champagne, sparkling and seemingly alive, had more meaning to the builders and sailors of proud new ships. In early launchings in the United States, a ribbon-bound champagne bottle was thrown at the sliding ship, the thrower taking careful aim and hoping for a good "hit." But so much of a ship's good fortune depends on the christening, seamen say, that surer methods were soon adopted.

Mrs. Starling held the bottle by the neck and awaited the first movement of the vessel before beginning the ritual. A ribbon-covered chain secured the bottle to the deckrail of the ship. At a signal, she crashed the ribbon-bound bottle against the steel bow and in a spray of white foam, the *Jeremiah O'Brien* was on her way. Christened with a name, imbued with a spirit that would

Just launched and moving toward the fitting out berth, the SS Jeremiah O'Brien *shows the fine lines of a well-made Liberty ship. Credit San Francisco Maritime National Historic Park.*

conquer oceans, the new vessel slid into the channel. Whistles from the ways, from the harbor and the yard roared a salute as the ship cocked gently, then settled with poise and confidence in her new element. With wartime efficiency uppermost in everyone's mind, the first piece of keel for the next ship was probably set in place on launching way No. 1 of the new West yard that same day.

Demands of war and the production of so many ships made christening ceremonies brief and simple but to the men who built the ships and those who sailed them, there was always dignity in the rites of launching. For they, more than all others, sensed the miracle of birth when dead tons of steel became a living, floating ship.

The yard's tugs carefully shepherded the new vessel to the fitting-out berth where she would spend the next few weeks. The crew began arriving before the ship was ready. Purser Tom Ender remembered: "I spent a few days at the Eastland Hotel before all the finishing touches were wrapped up."[3]

After a week at the fitting-out berth, the *O'Brien's* engines were operated for the first time on June 26 when the Builder's Dock Trial was held. This important first testing of the main engine and auxiliary machinery consisted of running the main engine ahead for 2 1/2 hours at 68 rpm and 1/2 hour astern at 60 rpm. At the same time all the support machinery -- pumps, motors, circuits, plumbing and hydraulics -- was tested. To be sure everything was up to specification, indicator cards were taken showing operating readings. These were compared with standard readings for Libertys to ensure proper operation. The engines were balanced and all was proven satisfactory to the Inspectors and Trial Board Engineer. The *O'Brien* was ready for the next set of tests, the official trials.

The official dock trial was conducted on June 28 between 0600 (6 a.m.) and 1300 (1 p.m.), EWT (Eastern War Time)[4]. The engine was run six hours ahead at an average of 68.8 rpm and one hour astern at 60.8 rpm, developing 1597 IHP (Indicated Horse Power) ahead and 945 IHP astern. Indicator cards and all data were taken every half hour. The evaporator and distiller capacity was measured at 360 gal. per hour. These devices were critical for the former created fresh water for the engines while the latter made potable water for the crew. Each main feed water pump and fuel pump was run one-half the time of the trial (there are two sets). The soot blowers were tested and the three steam driven electric generators were run in parallel.

Official Sea Trials were held on June 29 and June 30, 1943. During these trials a bevy of officials had to pass judgement on the capabilities of the new vessel. Representing the Maritime

---

[3] See Appendix C for a complete listing of the *Jeremiah O'Brien's* crews and voyages.

[4] Just after the United States entered the conflict the country was put on War Time. It was the equivalent of double daylight savings time. In other words, all the clocks were moved ahead two hours. This allowed for more daylight working hours and increased productivity and efficiency. War Time was a year-round condition and stayed in effect until the war was over.

Commission was a Trial Board consisting of F.J. Mann, Chairman, T.A. Goodson, Machinery Inspector Member, and F. P. Waite, Hull Inspection Member. Attending for the builders, New England Shipbuilding Corporation were: Capt. P. Laury, W. Ashburn, Assistant Superintendent of Machinery and C.E. Sherman. Grace Line was represented by the master, Capt. O. Southerland and the chief engineer, R. G. Montgomery. The American Bureau of Shipping representative was J. Stewart and the Coast Guard had two officials in attendance: Lt. E.A. Holmes and Lt. B. Hays.

The vessel was ballasted with fresh water so that the propeller would be submerged deep enough to get a good "bite" yet maintain a realistic trim. Ballast water was carried in reserve feed water tanks, port and starboard, and in the after peak tank. The fuel oil settling tanks had approximately 500 barrels, and No. 3 Port and Starboard tanks were partly filled with fuel oil.

One of the first tests was of the emergency steering gear. Located aft, on the deck above the gunners' quarters, it contains a wheel that enables the ship to be steered from that location. There is also a magnetic compass to mark the ship's course and a telephone to communicate with the engine room. Should the navigation bridge be destroyed by enemy action, the emergency steering station could be manned to steer the vessel. This was an important safety measure in the submarine-infested North Atlantic. The emergency steering gear was satisfactorily tested at the dock on June 30, 1943 in the presence of the American Bureau of Shipping surveyor, USCG Inspectors, U.S. Maritime Commission Inspectors and the Resident Trial Board Member.

Once the vessel left the dock, other tests could be conducted. One of the first of these was the anchor windlass. Both anchors were lowered until thirty fathoms of chain were out. Then the windlass was engaged and the anchors raised. Both anchors came up from 30 fathoms to 0 fathoms in four minutes with a chain speed of 45 feet per minute, well within specifications.

Certain other facts about the new ship had to be determined beyond question before she could be delivered. Could she withstand the shocks and stresses, the heavy structural strains that come in an emergency when her engines must be suddenly reversed from full speed ahead to full speed astern? Was she easily maneuverable? To find out, the engine and main steering were tested. Running ahead at 72 rpm, with steam pressure at 80 pounds (the *O'Brien's* steering gear is steam-operated), the steering wheel was swung to hard left. It took seven seconds for the rudder to reach that position. From hard left to hard right took 15 seconds and from hard right to hard left, 14 seconds. Returning the rudder from hard left to midships required six seconds.

Once it was established that the ship answered properly going ahead, it then remained to discover if she was equally responsive going astern. With the engines running 60 rpm astern at a steam pressure of 82 pounds it took six seconds to go from midships to hard left, hard left to hard right, 14 seconds, and hard right to hard left, 14 seconds. Finally the wheel was brought to midships from hard left, with the rudder following in six seconds.

Many a collision has been avoided by a quick response of the ship's engines. Recognizing this, one of the basic tests required by regulatory agencies is the Emergency Ahead and Astern Test. The *O'Brien's* engines were reversed from 72 rpm ahead to 60 rpm astern in 21 seconds. The propeller shaft stopped in four seconds. Then, once the ship was well underway astern, the engines were put ahead. Reversing direction from 60 rpm astern to 72 rpm ahead required 14 seconds with the shaft stopping in the first four seconds of the maneuver.

Being made of steel, a ship has a lot of built-in magnetism. In fact, the direction it's pointing when it's built determines the residual magnetic field it will have. The wiring in a vessel also adds to this magnetism. Sending a ship, carrying its own magnetic field, to the coasts of Europe or the islands of the Pacific, both areas strewn with magnetic mines, was a recipe for disaster. Two methods were used to neutralize the ship's built-in magnetism: first, it was constructed with a built-in degaussing system, a cable network mounted just inside the hull plating that was controlled by a panel in the wheelhouse; second, it was sent over a degaussing course. To do this the chronometer and other sensitive instruments were removed from the ship, the outer hull was wrapped in deperming cables and the vessel sent over a grid of electrically-charged underwater cables. This had the effect of negating the ship's natural magnetism. Once that was completed, the magnetic compass could be adjusted and the radio direction finder calibrated. Incoming radio signals were also subject to deflection, and subsequent erroneous readings, by the vessel's built-in magnetic field. Knowing what the deflection was allowed the ship's officers to accurately predict the margin of error when they took readings.

The Official Sea Trials were complete at 0905 (9:05 a.m.) on June 30 when the *Jeremiah O'Brien* returned to the dock, a broom proudly flying at her truck indicating a clean sweep of all tests.

A few formalities remained. A complete inspection of the vessel was made and unfinished items were noted and referred to the builder for completion. The Navy Armed Guard crew had arrived before the ship was finished. Billeted ashore, they helped with the trial runs and even in putting the finishing touches on the ship.

Morgan Williams was a newly-assigned Gunner's Mate Third Class. "She was brand-new and we joined her in Portland, Maine. She'd just been launched and we had to help finish the painting, then get all the guns ready. One of the boilers had trouble in the trial cruise. But they got that fixed and she was fine after that."

With all tests complete and all paperwork filled out, the ship was delivered at 1400 (2 p.m.) E.W.T., June 30, 1943. It had been just 56 days since her keel was laid.

Technically, several things happened simultaneously: the ship was transferred to the new owners, the Maritime Commission; the Maritime Commission gave title of the ship to its operating division, the War Shipping Administration (WSA); the War Shipping Administration transferred possession of the vessel to Grace Line, Inc. under Service Agreement, Form GAA (General Agency

Agreement).[5] All of this occurred at 1400, E.W.T., June 30, 1943. At the time of transfer consumable stores, fuel and water on board were valued at $6,607.67.

The *Jeremiah O'Brien* was ready. Her machinery hummed, her decks swarmed with people, she was an entity. Built to last one voyage, five years at the most, she began what would be a long, long life. Named after a Revolutionary War hero, she embodied the spirit of her namesake -- Jeremiah O'Brien of Machias, Maine.

---

[5] The General Agency Agreement is a device still used by the government for the operation of merchant ships during wartime. Basically it authorizes a steamship company, because of its expertise in operating ships, to receive the ship from the government and operate it on their behalf. The steamship company provides all the same services its other ships receive -- manning, maintenance, insurance and so on -- and receives a daily cost-plus payment for doing so. Initially the payment was based on the amount of deadweight tonnage assigned to an operator with rates of 50 cents a ton for the first 50,000 tons, 40 cents a ton for the next forty thousand tons, and so on. This was changed in December 1943 to a flat rate of $65 per day per ship plus $15 per day per ship to cover accounting costs. Fixed rates per ton of cargo handled were also paid. Ninety percent of all amounts over $15 per day per ship were subject to recapture by the government.

5

JEREMIAH O'BRIEN

A Scots-Irish lumberjack from Machias, in the "Province of Main," Jeremiah O'Brien was the offspring of a family that settled in the area in 1765. For ten years the O'Briens peacefully made their living logging the pine forests of the northeast, providing lumber for the local colonists' needs.

In 1775 long-festering problems with the British Crown reached the breaking point. In the spring of that year a shipment of Machias pine was loaded into two sloops belonging to Captain Ichabod Jones. Normally the lumber would be sold in Boston for the account of the townspeople of Machias but being firmly pro-colonist and unsure of the situation there, they instructed Jones to sell the lumber along the coast. Captain Jones, however, had another agenda. His family lived in Boston. Anxious to move them out of harm's way, he ignored the instructions and sailed directly into Boston Harbor. He sold the cargo and made a deal with the British. In exchange for the promise that he would return with another load of lumber to build barracks for British troops, he was allowed to move his family.

Loading his sloops with badly-needed supplies for Machias, Captain Jones sailed for Maine. Admiral Graves of the British Navy, wanting to be sure the colonist kept his word, instructed the armed schooner *Margaretta*, under command of Captain Moore, to escort Jones' ships.

On June 2, 1775 the people of Machias were angered to see the *Margaretta* enter their harbor escorting the two sloops, *Polly* and *Unity*. Captain Jones tried to talk the townspeople into supplying lumber in exchange for food. The good people of Machias had a mere three weeks' rations left, but they knew the lumber was for Boston which had recently fallen to the British and they wanted no part of the deal.

Refusing to be bullied, the townspeople erected a Liberty Pole as a symbol of their defiance. When Captain Moore of the *Margaretta* saw it he was incensed. Moving his ship into position to fire on the village, he ordered the Liberty Pole taken down and demanded that trade begin immediately. A few of Machias' more influential (and cautious) townsfolk agreed to the trade and the sloops' cargo was discharged and loading began. Others were less fearful and more determined. On June 11, while the commander of the British schooner was ashore attending Protestant services in the local church, they decided the timing was right to put the British bully in his place. As he looked out the window of the church, the commander of the schooner saw several colonists swimming toward the *Margaretta* on logs. Quickly returning to his vessel, he weighed anchor and sailed farther downstream, threatening again to burn the town if anyone interfered with the loading of the sloops. Firm in their resolve, the men of Machias located the schooner at its new anchorage. They began a small arms fire from a bluff whose elevation was too high for the ship's cannon to reach. The ship was forced to up anchor again and look for safety still farther downstream. In the haste of departing, with musket fire raining down from above, the ship's main boom snapped, seriously crippling her.

The following day the *Unity* was commandeered at anchor and brought alongside the town dock. Rapidly loading the ship with arms and ammunition (there was no time to remove the cargo of lumber) the ship sailed with the idea of capturing the *Margaretta* anchored downstream.   Jeremiah O'Brien, a young man of 31, was chosen captain.   His crew of 35 included his five brothers.   For victuals they carried one loaf of bread, a few pieces of pork and a barrel of water.   Their weaponry consisted of 20 shotguns with three rounds of ball and powder each, a small cannon, a few axes and swords and some 30 pitchforks.   What they lacked in provisions and arms they more than made up for in conviction.   As the *Unity* rapidly gained on the *Margaretta,* which had weighed anchor and was now running slowly toward the safety of the open sea, young O'Brien shouted, "Now, my brave fellows ... our first business will be to get alongside of the schooner yonder; and the first man to board her shall be entitled to the palm of honor."

Ordering the cargo of lumber to be placed as a breastworks around the vessel for protection, O'Brien quickly gained hailing distance.

"In America's name, I demand you surrender," he shouted.

The British answered with a volley from the stern gun that killed two men.   A backwoods moosehunter by the name of Knight manned the *Unity's* gun and picked off the British helmsman.   This cleared the quarterdeck leaving the vessel wallowing out of command and caused her to broach.   As the two ships crashed into each other, Capt. O'Brien lashed them together.

John O'Brien, younger brother of Jeremiah, with 49 year old Joseph Getchell, was the first to set foot on the *Margaretta.* They were met with heavy small arms fire from the British captain and crew.   Leading a select group of 20 pitchforkmen, they boarded the British vessel and fought hand to hand for a full hour.   At the end, O'Brien personally hauled down the British Ensign, winning the first naval battle of the Revolutionary War. Following this battle, Jeremiah became known as Colonel O'Brien.

Subsequently the *Unity* was outfitted with the armament from the *Margaretta* and became the armed cruiser *Machias Liberty,* the first American armed cruiser of the Revolution (and, in a sense, the first true Liberty ship).

In mid-July 1776, Colonel O'Brien, in command of the *Machias Liberty,* with the aid of Capt. Benjamin Foster on the *Falmouth Packet,* captured the British vessels *Diligent* and *Tapnaquish,* both of which had been sent for the express purpose of bringing "... the obstreperous Irish Yankee in for trial."

Following this success, Jeremiah O'Brien patrolled the North Atlantic in the *Machias Liberty.* Later he commanded the privateers *Little Vincent, Cyrus* and *Tiger.* After a year and a half he was given command of *Hannibal* mounting twenty guns and manned by one hundred and thirty men and brought many prizes into Machias.

Two years later the *Hannibal* fell in with an English fleet of merchantmen off New York, sailing in convoy. She was immediately chased by two British frigates and, after a forty-eight hour running battle, taken. Jeremiah O'Brien was captured. Following detainment in the famous guard ship *Jersey,* O'Brien was transferred to Mill Prison in England. His brother, John, in a memoir written several years later, recounted what happened next.

"He purposely neglected his dress and whole personal appearance for a month. The afternoon before making his escape he shaved and dressed in decent clothes, so as to alter very much his personal appearance, and walked out with the other prisoners in the jail yard. Having secreted himself under a platform in the yard, and thus escaping the notice of the keepers at the evening round-up, he was left out of the cells after they were locked for the night. He escaped from the yard by passing through the principal keeper's house in the dusk of evening. Although he made a little stay in the barroom of the house, he was not detected, being taken for a British soldier. In company with a Captain Lyon and another American who also had escaped from the prison and were concealed somewhere in the vicinity, he crossed the English Channel to France in a boat and thence came to America, just about the time the hostilities ceased."

During the War of 1812, when the British again threatened to take Machias, Colonel Jeremiah O'Brien, still dauntless despite his advanced years, defiantly brandished the same sword he so capably used in the Revolutionary War.

Seemingly imbued with the same spirit and determination, the *SS Jeremiah O'Brien* lives, honoring her illustrious name-sake, as our nation enters the 21st century -- a name -- and a ship -- for all time.

6

BREAKING IN

With the war on, Grace Line lost no time in getting the ship outfitted and ready. In fact, many of the crew arrived before the ship was delivered. Among them were three brothers, Rosario "Russ", Nicholas "Nick" and Vincent "Vinny" Carista, who signed on as messmen so they could sail together.

Russ Carista: "My two brothers and I sailed on that. We were messman. Those were the only jobs that were open where we could all be on the same ship. So my brother Nick was the gun crew messmen, I was the crew messman, and Vinny was the officer's crew mess.

"The ship, they were finishing it up. They put us up in some hotel there. We were there about a day. Fixing it up and cleaning it up."

Nick Carista: "They put us up in the Eastland Hotel for a week 'cause they were still stocking the ship. It was exciting because everything on this ship was brand new."

Vinny Carista: "Those Liberty ships, everyone used to want one. They'd say I'm going to get me a Liberty ship, a new Liberty."

The day after the *O'Brien's* delivery the first crew signed on for voyage No.1. Comprised of some 44 merchant seaman and a gun crew of 28 Navy sailors, their commander was Captain Oscar Southerland. The shipping articles were a far cry from those issued in peacetime which typically said: "...now bound from the port of New York to a port or ports of loading in the continental United States if so ordered or directed by the U.S. Government or any department, commission or agency thereof, thence to (or as may be ordered by the U.S. Government or any department, commission or agency thereof) such other ports and places in any part of the world as the master may direct and back to the final port of discharge in the United States, for a term of time not exceeding twelve (12) calendar months." But this was wartime and the articles were terse: they were signing on for twelve months and the final port of discharge would be in the "U.S.A." Leaving Portland, the articles were a technicality for the coastwise voyage to Boston. Once there and ready to sail to a foreign port, a new set of articles with the same brief wording would be signed.

On July 2, 1943, while the merchant crew readied the ship for sea, the gun crew loaded ammunition. Ordinance for the two 3" cannons and eight 20 mm anti-aircraft guns included: three hundred 3"-50[1] anti-aircraft projectiles; one hundred fifty 3"-50 common projectiles; two 3"-50 short projectiles for firing out lodged projectiles; two auxiliary fuze setting wrenches, 30 seconds each; 13,500 20 mm cartridges, high explosive, anti-aircraft, tracer; 27,000 20 mm cartridges high explosive, anti-aircraft, incendiary and two hundred forty 20 mm cartridges, target projectiles. In addition there were eighteen snowflake rockets with cartridges and one hundred twenty .38 caliber ball cartridges. The ship departed Portland, Maine at 2230 the evening of July 2nd.

At this stage of the war, the threat of enemy submarines was everywhere, even along the coast of Maine. Despite the fact she

---

[1] Three inches in diameter by 50 millimeters in length.

was only going coastwise from Portland to Boston the ship sailed in a blacked-out condition. Coast Guard Regulations were very specific about blackout during wartime. They stated:

> "Blackout enforcement. On ocean and coastwise vessels the master shall, when the vessel is at sea, maintain a complete blackout of his vessel from dusk until dawn except for the display of running lights in such area and under such conditions as may be directed by competent naval authority.

> Luminous marking. All ocean and coastwise cargo and tank ships of 3,000 gross tons and over and all ocean and coastwise passenger vessels shall be provided with interior marking in the accommodation, machinery, and working spaces of the vessel in the form of an approved luminous cloth or tape. Such markings shall be sufficient in character to clearly show in darkness the location of exit doors, ports, ladders, companionways, the location of emergency lights, control valves, if necessary, and similar vital locations or accessories."

Wartime seafaring called for various conditions of readiness on the part of the Armed Guard. As defined in The General Instructions for Commanding Officers of Naval Armed Guards on Merchant Ships, 1943, Third Edition, issued by the Navy Department, these were:

> Condition 1--General Quarters.
> Showing disposition of naval personnel at the ship's armament, with all hands at battle stations, including the merchant crew."

> Condition 2--
> In areas where submarine, surface, or air attack is imminent and contact with the enemy may be expected at any moment, the entire Armed Guard will stand watch and watch. Each of the 2 watches under this condition may be divided into two sections. This will provide sufficient men for each section to stand 2 hours' lookout duty each 4-hour watch. The standby section will be stationed at the guns ready for instant action. If conditions warrant, the standby section shall also be stationed on lookout duty.

> Condition 3--
> During normal steaming at sea, the Armed Guard will be divided
> into not to exceed 3 watches. The Armed Guard lookouts shall
> stand their watches at the guns at all times. When anchored in an
> unguarded anchorage or roadstead, condition 3 shall be maintained.

As the ship departed Portland, the Armed Guard posted sea watch condition III (3). In the months ahead, they would set Condition III while the ship was underway between sunset and sunrise and Condition I while underway during daylight hours.[2] At 0900 on July 3, 1943 the *Jeremiah O'Brien* arrived at Boston, Massachusetts and anchored. She remained at anchor through the following day, then, at 1730 on July 5, she went to the Bethlehem Steel Docks. There she loaded a partial cargo of steel for England.

Purser Tom Ender: "I remember going ashore in Boston. My wife came up from New Jersey. We stayed at the Statler Hotel and since her train got in late we didn't get to the ball room until near midnight. We were all set for a night of fun when to our disappointment they invoked the 'Blue Law' and cut off all drinks at midnight. It was the first time we had encountered such a law."

It isn't difficult to imagine the feelings of most of the crew at this time. Made up of midwest farm boys who had never seen the ocean before, young men from New England and the deep South, veteran seamen and "first-trippers," some were excited, looking forward to the adventure to come. Others were afraid. Still others, those who had served before, looked on it as routine. A few certainly thought it might be their last voyage and were determined to live life to the fullest before they sailed. So it was that on July 6 one of the Armed Guard Seaman First Class reported aboard after being AWOL. The log does not document what, if any, discipline was administered to the miscreant who felt his time ashore was more important than reporting on board on time.

---

[2] See Appendix D for a complete list of Armed Guard responsibilities.

While longshoremen loaded the cargo, the Armed Guard crew was occupied with stowing a secret experimental anti-submarine device known as the Mark-29 gear. Basically a combination sonar/anti-torpedo device it was designed to detect propeller noise and explode approaching torpedoes. It consisted of two paravanes[3] equipped with explosive charges and sensors which were towed behind them and to the side of the ship. When armed, the sensor detonated the explosive charge when it detected an approaching torpedo. In addition, a hydrophone was towed off the stern. Electric wiring ran from it to a listening panel on the bridge which allowed an operator to detect the sounds of enemy submarines or torpedoes without the interference of the ship's engines. Because it was a secret device, the listening panel was guarded by a sailor carrying a sidearm while the ship was in port. The crew of the *O'Brien* didn't know it yet, but Fate had just put aboard a device that would prove to be a "shield" against an unusual turn of events. But that was in the future. In the perverse way such things often work, the *O'Brien's* good luck was bound up in what her crew quickly came to consider a very rotten deal, indeed.

On July 9 the cargo of steel was on board and the ship shifted to the grain elevator at Charlestown, in Boston Harbor.

Russ Carista: "The trip we made, we left out of Charlestown, Mass, loaded up with grain."

Britain was in a state of siege. Rationing came into effect in 1940 on most foodstuffs and the amount each person was allowed steadily diminished. Eggs were unobtainable and worst of all, for the English, tea was limited to two ounces per person per week. By 1942 the United States had committed itself to supplying Great Britain with one fourth of its food supply. This translated to 500,000,000 dozen eggs, 18,000,000 pounds of chicken,

---

[3] Shaped much like airplane wing tanks, paravanes are usually towed in pairs by a wire rope fastened to the bottom of the stem of the ship. At the stem the wire rope is mounted to a fastening called the paravane skeg. Paravanes have tail fins which give them direction, causing them to swing out toward the sides of the ship rather than being towed directly behind. A more common use of paravanes was to sever the anchor lines holding mines to the bottom of the sea.

759,000,000 pounds of pork and lard and canned fruits and vegetables. Beef was high on the desired list but as America had no surplus, 9,000,000 hogs were substituted resulting in new foods such as "Spam fritters." Powdered egg omelets became the subject of a major British publicity campaign. By March of 1943, because of the U-boat menace, Britain was consuming 750,000 more tons of food, oil and military supplies than it was importing.

As the grain came aboard during the following days the merchant crew spent their time stowing gear and learning the intricacies of their new ship. The Armed Guard spent most of their time stowing ammunition, painting the new Mark-29 gear and cleaning guns.

Jerome Shaw, Seaman First Class: "The grain was dusty, they had dust all over the ship when they loaded. The ship was very dirty when they finished."

The ship's crew was paid off and coastwise articles were terminated on July 10. Simultaneously articles were signed for the coming foreign voyage.

Coleman "Coke" Schneider was the newly-assigned Deck Cadet from the Merchant Marine Academy at Kings Point. "We were assigned the ship out of the ATR (Area Training Repre-

Cadet Coleman Schneider's Certificate of Service, issued at the U. S. Merchant Marine Academy, qualifies him to serve as a deck cadet in the merchant marine. Credit NLSM

sentative) office at 39 Broadway in New York. So we went downtown in Manhattan and got our assignment, then took the train, the New Haven Railroad, up to Boston and then got a taxi that dropped us on the ship. There was this movie, 'Action In The North Atlantic,' with Humphrey Bogart and Raymond Massey, all about the merchant marine, that had just come out and was very popular among seamen at the time. One of the characters in this movie was the cadet and his name was Parker. So I'm walking up the gangway to the *O'Brien,* in uniform, of course, first ship and everything, and this mate hollers down to me, 'Hey, Parker. Come here.'

"Well, that was the second mate, Pellegrino was his name. So after I got my gear stowed, the first thing he tells me is to go down to the engine room for a bucket of steam. I wasn't <u>that</u> green, you know."

On July 12, with all cargo on board and the hatches battened, the ship shifted to the Mystic coal docks. This was simply a staging area, a place for the *O'Brien* to wait while enough ships were gathered for a convoy.

The Armed Guard had their hands full learning how to operate the guns that many of them had never seen before. On July 15th they bore-sighted the 3" guns. This is a process whereby the accuracy of the guns is set. By sighting through the bore at a fixed target, the guns' sights are adjusted for accuracy. Although they didn't do any shooting, they did become accustomed to the hard metal sounds of the guns' breeches, springs and mechanisms, and the smell and feel of the oil and grease.

On July 17, the Armed Guard went through anti-aircraft training on the Polaroid trainer. This is a shoreside simulation of shipboard anti-aircraft firing. The crew was placed in a large room with a 20 millimeter gun emplacement in its center. As each member of the gun crew sat at the gun, silhouettes of enemy planes flew past which they shot at. The effect was realistic and three-dimensional with mock tracers darting from the barrels and "kills" recorded automatically. It was an effective way to hone the crew's skill, both in coordination and plane recognition.

July 19, 1943. One of the last merchant crewmembers to join the ship was Frederick C. Warren. He signed on as Fireman Water/Tender. His career in the merchant marine began just over a year earlier with a letter from the Coast Guard Recruiting Office in Portland, Oregon. It was the maritime equivalent of a draft notice.

> Dear Sir:
> You are hereby instructed to report to this office at 8:00 a.m., Saturday morning, May 2nd, to be sworn in as an Apprentice Seaman in the U.S. Maritime Service.
>
> Completion of your enrollment papers will be made and you will be sent to the training school at Port Hueneme, California next day, Sunday, May 3rd.
>
> Upon receipt of this letter, please inform us by phone or in person of your intentions to be here on that date.
> Respectfully,
>
> > L. H. Painter
> > Officer in Charge
> > U.S. Maritime Service

Russ Carista. "The reason I shipped out is I didn't pass the physical in the Army so I decided to ship. I figured I'd go to sea. Vinny was a seaman already. I wanted to see some of that action. I was curious. They started dropping them bombs [on his next ship, which was on the Murmansk run], and I realized they wanted to kill us. Those guys were trying to hurt us. That's when I first realized it."

Nick Carista: "I was underage. I was going to be drafted. I used to meet my older brother at the coal works when he came in from sea. I shipped out, I went through the union hall. You know, they assign you to a ship and that was it. It was probably safer than being in the Army."

Vinny Carista: "I didn't want to join the army again. I did one hitch in the Hawaiian Islands, and I didn't want to work in a bake shop 'cause my father was a baker. But I had a little skill with my father and he used to give me the jobs. When I got back from the army my father had a job waiting for me. I said, 'Shit. I went in the Army to get away from this.'

"The Italians were looked down on in Boston. So I joined the Army 'cause I couldn't get a job. So when the war came in, my cousin said, 'You want to get in the union and go to sea.' It was the best job I had in my life."

Ken Holsapple, Seaman First Class in the Armed Guard joined after having already been torpedoed and losing an earlier ship. "I was only 18 or 19 at the time. Something like that you just kind of tried to forget it. When I first went aboard the *O'Brien* somebody asked about losing the ship. I just walked away from him."

Jerome Shaw was making his first trip to sea. "I guess I was just a gung-ho kid. Everyone wanted to do their part. I had to get my father and mother to sign me, when I went in. I was only seventeen. Number one, I didn't want to go in the Army. My family was Navy in both wars and it was kind of a family tradition."

Other ships gathered as time drew close for departure. On July 20, 1943 the captain, radio operator and Armed Guard officer attended a convoy conference.

On July 21, the Mark-29 gear was laid out on deck in preparation for streaming. As the crew took in the lines, the *Jeremiah O'Brien* slowly eased away from the wharf and glided out of Boston Harbor. Departure was taken at 1618. In this first convoy were 23 ships and three escorts. The speed was set at 8 knots.

Captain Ralph "Buck" Wilson, second master of the *Jeremiah O'Brien* after she became a museum ship, recalled his wartime convoys. "We sailed 400 yards apart. No lights. It was pitch-black at nights. We were supposed to run at a certain speed, but sometimes in the engine room they'd let the rpms build up."

Traveling in convoy was a nerve-wracking experience. A sharp watch had to be kept on all four sides to ensure that no ship drifted out of its "slot" in the convoy. Four hundred yards' separation between 440+ foot ships is a figurative "arm's length" with little margin for error. If the master or mate on watch saw that his ship was creeping up on the one ahead, he had to adjust. Coleman Schneider recalled, "... heavy seas and fog. I would see the mate on watch yelling in the voice tube down to the engineer on watch to say, 'down 5 revs or up 5 revs,' to try to keep the proper distance from the ship ahead. I don't know if the engineers made all the changes as the bridge called them because sometimes we would call every 10 minutes during the whole watch. Occasionally we would get a little excited and yell a little louder. Of course, the ship ahead of us was most likely doing the same thing since he was also following a ship who was doing the same thing."

Occasionally ships carried mascots. Coleman Schneider: "There was a pet on board, a cat. We left Boston and were on our way to Halifax. So the cat was walking along the gunwale, on the starboard gunwale, and it was wet and everything and it just disappeared. One minute it was there and the next it was gone. It turned out it was the Chief Engineer's pet. And because I happened to be nearby when it happened, he blamed me! The Chief didn't have much use for me after that."

Russ Carista: "They didn't want no pets on that ship. The Old Man, he considered them bad luck."

For the Mark-29 gear to work as an anti-torpedo device it had to be able to explode an approaching torpedo. To do this required that the lines trailing from the paravanes have detonators and booster charges called armed covers. Through an oversight these weren't sent on board. The result was that although the Mark-29 devices were on deck and ready to run, they weren't put over the side.

Although the anti-torpedo section of the Mark-29 gear couldn't be streamed, the hydrophone could. After dinner that first day, the crew, struggling with unfamiliar equipment, got it rigged to tow 500 feet astern of the ship. The listening panel and hydrophone were tested and found in good working order. After a thorough two-hour test the gear was brought back on board by the exhausted crew.

Jerome Shaw: "It was some kind of a sounding device and the radio man monitored a listening device on the bridge."

During the night fog set in. The normal anxiety of night convoy travel was exacerbated by the fog. The morning of July 22nd the fog was so thick that none of the other ships in the convoy could be seen although they were traveling within a few hundred feet of one another. Each ship in the convoy had been assigned a position number at the convoy conference and throughout the day the sound of foghorns permeated the air as ship after ship periodically sounded its number on the whistle.

The morning of July 23 was dark and thick again, the fog persisting. At 1330 the *O'Brien* received radio orders from the convoy commodore to heave to. Normally, fog wouldn't be a deterrent to a single ship. But somewhere ahead lay Nova Scotia. The commodore didn't want to risk running his 26 ships aground because of thick visibility. In the afternoon the fog broke. The *O'Brien* found herself separated slightly from the rest of the fleet and increased speed to half ahead to regain her convoy position. At 1820 the ships arrived at the pilot station at Halifax, Nova Scotia only to find that no pilots were available. The *O'Brien* hove to for the night. After waiting all night and most of the next day, July 24, a pilot finally came aboard and directed the *Jeremiah O'Brien* to an anchorage.

That evening a conference was held ashore for all the captains of the ships in the convoy including those that were joining at Halifax. Captain Southerland returned to the ship with orders to leave two hours ahead of the main convoy in order to allow time to stream the Mark-29 gear. Apparently the missing equipment for the device was on its way. The *O'Brien* was the only ship in the convoy with such an apparatus and everyone was anxious to see it work. After streaming the gear, the ship could take her position in the assembled convoy.

On July 25, 1943, before sailing from Nova Scotia, three explosive streamers and six armed covers (detonators and booster charges) were brought aboard for the Mark-29 gear. The *O'Brien* sailed, official departure from Halifax being taken at 1116. They sailed into a fog again with 32 ships and two escorts. Speed was set at 10 knots.

At 1300 that day, in a thick fog and with a rough sea throwing spray on the main deck, the Armed Guard crew began launching the Mark-29 gear. It was miserable work, straining on slippery decks, their hands numb with cold, as they wrestled the bulky gear. Because of the constant pitching and the wet deck, the port and starboard sides of the gear were streamed separately. Then they noticed that the port gear wasn't working. It couldn't be retrieved without slowing the ship down and dropping out of the convoy. Rather than risk losing sight of the other ships, Captain Southerland decided to leave the gear out all night. Chilled to the bone, the crew retreated to their cramped quarters.

Jerome Shaw: "We had that Mark 29 gear on there. When we went into a convoy they always put us in the 'coffin corner,' in the back right or left corner, so we could stream that gear. We'd have to slow down to put it out and then the convoy was over the horizon. Then we'd try to catch up and about the time we caught the convoy we'd have to slow down again to take it in. We spent a lot of time out there by ourselves, watching that convoy disappear.

"That was a real doozey to put out. The paravanes run almost parallel to the boom they came off of. And each one had a sensor and three detonators running back, all the same length, almost as long as the ship. They were heavy, they were extremely heavy and it was back-breaking work. They had a rubber coating, I don't know what was inside, but the outside was heavy black rubber. The idea was when a torpedo went over the sensor the detonator charge would blow it."

From Morgan Williams' personal diary: "Pulled port side in July 26 and launched it again and it still doesn't work."

The next day the fog cleared and the Halifax group joined a fleet of ships which came up from New York. The full convoy was an impressive sight. A total of 73 ships and 10 escort vessels now proceeded across the North Atlantic toward England at a speed of 10 knots.

At 1030 the *O'Brien's* speed was reduced to 4 knots. The Mark-29 gear on the port side was partially retrieved and the armed cover on the inboard explosive streamer was changed. By the time the gear was relaunched it was noon and the *O'Brien* was six miles astern of the rest of the convoy. The streamer on the port side still wasn't operating. The rest of the afternoon and evening were spent catching up. The following morning Captain Southerland requested permission from the convoy commodore to decrease speed again to four knots in order to repair the Mark-29 gear. The commodore granted permission by flashing light but also signaled that he had no idea what a Mark-29 gear was! The device was so secret that few people were aware of its existence. This would cause a great deal of frustration in the coming days.

The *Jeremiah O'Brien* again slowed down and at 1000 started the retrieving process. When the gear was pulled in it was found that the faired[4] towing line and several electrical conductors had breaks in them. A spare faired towing line was substituted and the gear relaunched. By 1130 the gear was once again out and the ship had dropped eight miles astern of the convoy. This time they were successful. The Mark-29 gear operated perfectly.

Unfortunately, the convoy commodore had become increasingly impatient with the lagging ship. At 1400 a blinker message was received from the convoy escort saying the *O'Brien* would be placed in a slower convoy next time. It was impossible to explain why the ship was out of position since the escort commander had never heard of Mark-29 gear and conditions didn't allow for a lengthy explanation by blinker light. Breaking radio silence was out of the question.

It took until 2300 to regain the proper position in the convoy. In the back of everyone's mind was the knowledge that a favorite U-boat tactic was to shadow convoys and pick off stragglers.

With so much time spent on the Mark-29 gear the Armed Guard crew had little time to organize and practice responding to an attack, but on July 30, 1943 at 1300 the first gun drill was held. The ship's general alarm bells were used to signal a surface attack. The crew's response was enthusiastic and eager. The gunnery officer was so impressed that he made the following entry in his daily log: "Ship's crew participating and showing considerable interest."

Nick Carista: "The gun crew, they were teaching me to clean the 20 mm."

Kenneth Holsapple: "I was on the twenty-millimeter. I just shot for parctice."

---

[4] Faired in this sense means streamlined. The towing line offered little resistance to the water it was being towed through.

Jerome Shaw: "I was just a wet-behind-the-ears kid, I was only 17 years old. I was pointer on the forward three-inch fifty, the guy that pulled the trigger. The big heavy guys they would make the loaders 'cause they could handle the stuff."

For berthing, the Armed Guard was divided between the midships house and the after deck house -- the least kindly area on the ship in a storm. To help pass the long hours off watch, they were issued an entertainment kit consisting of a punching bag, boxing gloves, a medicine ball and several games including chess, checkers, cribbage and dominoes.

As the voyage progressed, personalities became established. Tom Ender recalled Captain Southerland fondly. "Captain Southerland was a fine man of Scandinavian descent. Whenever something hit him as being out of the ordinary he would use his favorite expression, 'Great Scott," dragging out the word 'Great.'

Coleman Schneider: "Southerland was medium height with light hair. I think he was of Scandinavian descent. He was soft speaking and well-spoken, very competent and knowledgeable. Christianson, the Chief Mate, was Norwegian, in his mid-twenties or early thirties. The Third mate, Morgan, came from Matthews County in Virginia. They were all nice guys."

Other reminiscences were less fond.

Russ Carista: "I'll tell you what it was, I was the crew messman and John Gird was the bosun. And he tried to act tough with the gloves hanging out the back and a deep voice and everything. We're out at sea and he put a quart of beer in the refrigerator. And Chips (the ship's carpenter) was his brother-in-law. He used to grind his cigarettes out on the deck. Just to get at me. So, anyway, he put the quart of beer in there and he was going to show everyone he had a beer. He was going to drink it with Chips. And my brothers and I snuck it out and drank it. Was he surprised. He opened the refrigerator and no beer." He laughed, recalling the incident as the funniest thing that happened that trip.

Apparently the escort ships were still puzzling over the strange equipment the *Jeremiah O'Brien* carried. The following evening a blinker message was received from one of the escort vessels.

"Senior escort commander requests 'What is Mark 29'?" A quick reply was flashed back, "An anti-torpedo device."

On August 1st a signal was received from the commodore of the convoy that guns might be test-fired. With so many ships traveling close together it was prudent not to fire the guns unless everyone knew it was going to happen otherwise someone might think an attack was taking place and respond accordingly.

From the Armed Guard Log: "Gun crew, ships crew who were assigned gun stations, and ships officers firing guns."

The 20 mm guns were test-fired with a total of 330 rounds of ammunition being shot. Since these were machine guns, this was not much firing, but it was enough to ensure that everything was in good operating condition. There was, however, a problem. From Morgan Williams' personal diary: "We fired all the guns today for the first time except the 3"-50 forward. It wouldn't fire with the electric firing so they tried it with the percussion firing trigger and it still didn't fire. They worked on the gun all afternoon and got it fired."

Liquor was at a premium and technically forbidden on merchant ships. The ship's articles clearly state that "no grog" shall be allowed. "Grog" is interpreted to mean any alcoholic beverage. But where there are thirsty seamen, there will always be found a way to improvise.

Russ Carista: "They used to get dried apricots and prunes and stuff and use a crock pot, you know. Put it somewhere warm for a couple of weeks and let it stew."

Vinny Carista: "We had these guys, they used to make this 'kickapoo juice' they used to call it. I had my birthday. They used to get fruit and make booze out of it."

As the crew got to know one another friendships formed and idle time was spent speculating about the war.

Nick Carista: "Well, going over we used to go out on deck on the after part of the ship and talk after lunch, at number four hatch. I enjoyed that. It was a good crew."

As the convoy neared the coast of England the threat of attack became more real and excitement grew. On August 2, 1943 at 0930 eight of the ten escort vessels were seen sweeping astern of the convoy. Two white flares went up. Although no depth charges were heard, the gun crew went to battle stations. At 1200 two more white flares were shot from an escort vessel astern of convoy. Just after four in the afternoon roaring sounds were heard on the Mark-29 hydrophone. The panel was armed in case it was a submarine attack but after nothing happened it was decided that the sounds were depth charges. These incidents, nevertheless, were an ongoing reminder that the convoy was in a war zone and helped keep everyone alert. Statistics on sinkings weren't released until after the war, but during the month of July 1943, 61 ships totaling 350,000 tons were sunk by enemy action.

Coleman Schneider: "On the way across on the first voyage the captain and mate set up a schedule for teaching. So I was supposed to work with the bosun. Well he gave me a mop and a bucket of red-lead and said, 'Paint the deck from bow to stern.' So that's what I did. With red lead and a mop."

On August 4 at Latitude 55-45 North, Longitude 10-11 West the Loch Ewe (Scotland) portion of the convoy consisting of 18 ships, including the *Jeremiah O'Brien,* and two escort vessels left the main fleet. Seas grew increasingly rough with the ship pitching heavily and taking water over the bow. It became so rough that at 1400 the sailors on watch at the forward 3" gun were pulled off the guntub and stationed on the bridge. At 2000 the ship's speed was decreased to four knots and the Mark-29 gear was retrieved. It was a difficult process because of the heavy weather and took three hours to accomplish. Morgan Williams noted in his diary, "We pulled in the Mk. 29 gear. It was quite a job. The sea was coming over the side. We were all drenched to the bone by the time we were through. My opinion of the Mk. 29 gear isn't very good."

Finally the gear was in and speed was increased to 10 knots but it still took until 0800 the next morning for the *O'Brien* to regain her position in the convoy.

Coleman Schneider: "Three of us were ordered to secure a number of barrels on the forward deck. The weather was extremely bad and we donned our slickers, boots and so on. There were about thirty to forty barrels lashed together, these lashings

Loch Ewe on the west coast of Scotland as seen from the boat deck of the SS Jeremiah O'Brien *in 1943. Credit Coleman Schneider*

were getting loose. As we worked with the deck heaving up and down in about twenty to thirty foot seas, all of a sudden the bosun put his arm over my shoulder and yelled into my ear, 'Hold on!' as a huge wave broke over the port side forward completely covering us all. I think we secured them pretty fast after that and returned to the safety of the deck house."

Just after noon on August 5, 1943 the *Jeremiah O'Brien* arrived at her first foreign port, Aultbea, Loch Ewe, Scotland. Despite the fact that the German submarine U-33 had mined the area in late 1939 and the battleship *Nelson* was seriously damaged by a magnetic mine off Loch Ewe that same year, the harbor was entered without incident.

Situated on the northwest coast of Scotland, across from the Outer Hebrides, Loch Ewe was described by James O. Runkle (when he saw it from another ship) as "... a beautiful but barren bay with but a single shepherd's croft showing on shore."

Tom Ender liked it, too. "I will always recall our dropping anchor in Loch Ewe, Scotland. It was the first of many visits there and although I never got ashore it impressed me as being just a little bit of heaven, so beautiful and peaceful. One was hard put in that atmosphere to believe there was a war going on -- and not so far away at that."

Coleman Schneider: "Loch Ewe is a big inlet with a big island in the center. It's big enough that part of the convoy could lay at anchor."

While anchored in Loch Ewe, the ship was fitted with a barrage balloon. Filled with helium, the blimp-shaped balloon floated on a wire tether above the ship. The theory behind it was that enemy planes would avoid low-level attacks for fear of colliding with the balloon or its wire.

That same evening the *O'Brien* departed with 16 merchant ships and two escort vessels at a speed of nine knots. Proceeding northeast and then east, the convoy rounded the northern tip of Scotland. At two in the morning the fleet was illuminated by a flare dropped in greeting from friendly planes flying overhead.

At 0745, August 6, the convoy arrived at Methil, near Edinburgh, in the Firth of Forth, Scotland. This wide bay was mined by the German submarine U-31 in late 1939. One of its mines sank the brand-new cruiser *Belfast*. Fortunately the area was well swept and several other ships were peacefully at anchor.

A convoy conference ashore took up most of the day. William G. Shofield, in his book *Eastward the Convoys* described these meetings. "In British ports the convoy conferences almost always were held in some dark and depressing backroom down a waterfront side street. There you sat, in a cloud of thick tobacco smoke, drinking lukewarm tea, watching the rain stream down the dirty window panes, staring at bare patches where green paint had peeled from the walls, and trying to pay attention to the Royal Navy Admiral in charge as he mumbled his instructions and information in a monotone that nearly put everybody to sleep. When you left, you felt drowsy and lethargic and indifferent."

Convoy conferences were a source of information for the ship's crew. Captain Southerland brought back the news that there was an air raid over Hull the previous evening and that the convoy ahead of the *O'Brien's* was attacked by German E-boats[5]

---

[5] The E-boat or *schnellboat* was a motor torpedo boat used by the Germans as an escort and a combatant against British naval units, merchant ships and aircraft and, eventually, against the Normandy Invasion shipping.

with only two ships surviving. The crew fell silent as the reality of just how close they were to the war sank in.

That evening the convoy, now consisting of 37 ships and one escort vessel, sailed at a speed of 7.5 knots for London and arrived just before noon on August 9, 1943 with the ships disbursing to various docks and anchorages.

Coleman Schneider: "As we entered London we could count literally hundreds of planes flying south out of England. They were mostly American planes. In London we kept going through areas to docks that were like canals off the Thames. I didn't know there were so many of them. I was surprised to see all the buildings where we discharged our cargo were basically new."

The *Jeremiah O'Brien* found herself tying up at Victoria docks just before midnight.

Russ Carista: "We went to Victoria docks in London. In England it was blackout. We'd go up to Piccadilly Circus and play 'feel in the dark.' The merchant marine, they had a uniform, and the chicks thought we were officers -- pea coat, black leather jacket, black navy pants, black navy shoes, and sometimes the pea coat and sometimes the leather jacket. And an officer's hat with just the gold braid, no insignias or nothing."

Ken Holsapple added: "When you went ashore in the summertime you had to wear the blues, not the whites, because the whites would show up in the night."

Inevitably, some seamen on leave will get into trouble. On August 13, late in the evening, one of the Armed Guard, a seaman first class, was reported to the officer in charge for being in a fight with a civilian ashore while under the influence of liquor. An hour later he returned to the ship. Still drunk, he threatened the third assistant engineer with a knife. But there was more to it than that. Tom Ender recalled in later years, "This took place on Friday the 13th. Some of us visited Lord Nelson's Pub in Canterbury, England -- either a suburb of London or a nearby town to the dock area. At 'closing time' I, along with several other unsuspecting crew members became involved in a brawl outside the pub. A fight had started between a member of the Armed Guard

Coleman Schneider poses on the rail of the Jeremiah O'Brien, *alongside the dock in London, ready for attack or come-what-may. Credit Coleman Schneider*

and an English civilian. We tried to step in but wound up getting a severe licking."

The three Carista brothers remembered the incident vividly.

Russ Carista: "A fight ensued in the Lord Nelson Pub, and this young fellow from Texas cut this Englishman across the stomach because he wanted to make his wife. Meanwhile there was a lot of soldiers there. Nick and I had slipped out to a bombshelter there with two nice little Air Force girls. So we missed most of it."

Vinny Carista: "Well they had a kid from Texas and this kid, you know he used to get drunk and he used to say, 'Don't fool with me, I'll cut your pants off.' So we went ashore and we met in a pub. So I had another girl, and she's a clean-cut girl and I says, 'I'll stick with her.' And we're fooling around in there and then we're outside closing the pub. And I saw Tex and I says, 'Hey Tex, what's the matter with you?' This English guy says to Tex, 'Hey Yank. Leave that girl alone.'

"Tex, he turned around and swung at him. That son of a gun, that crazy bastard. And before you know it, I was going to cross the street and this guy about six feet tall comes at me. I seen these guys getting cut up so I ran away. Then he caught up to me and I dodged and he went head over heels. And these two sisters said, 'Don't bother him. He's all right.' So I got a hold of him and they calms him down."

Nick Carista: "Our radio man was all cut up. One of our sailors pulled a knife."

Russ Carista: "And the bosun got hit in the back of the head and lost an eye because of that."

Vinny Carista: "The bosun, he got a piece of glass in his eye."

Russ Carista: "He was from Chelsea. Then you had the second officer on there, Pellegrino. He was the one that tried to keep order. He locked the navy gunner in the chain locker."

The following afternoon the seaman was taken ashore with six others and the gunnery officer. A line-up was held so the civilians involved could pick out the assailant.

Vinny Carista: "And this sister of one of the girls picked him out of the crew."

The seaman was taken ashore under armed guard. He returned the morning of the 15th with three Lieutenants and a chief petty officer who conducted a court martial. The seaman was detached from the ship.

Ken Holsapple: "They wouldn't let us go ashore after that. We put Tex in the brig. They tried to hide him so the bobbies wouldn't get him. They gave him a DD [Dishonorable Discharge] a carton of cigarettes and ten dollar fine."

Tom Ender: "I think of that every August the 13th as the Battle of Lord Nelson's Pub."

Everyone seemed to remember the incident.

Gunner's Mate Third Class Morgan Williams: "I wasn't involved in that but when one of the boys knifed somebody the bobbies came aboard and took him ashore."

Jerome Shaw: "I wasn't there but I heard about it. It was a real donnybrook."

Eventually, though, there was more shore liberty and as always, girls were uppermost on the crew's mind.

Nick Carista: "Eggs for the girls. They'd do almost anything for fresh eggs. One time I brought some eggs. You had to hard boil them first."

Russ Carista. "After awhile we couldn't afford to go ashore. I got a bag of lemons from the steward, chicks liked the lemons. Any kind of citrus was scarce. Better than nylons. Citrus fruits. If you brought them ashore in England, you was king. If they was susceptible ..."

Ken Holsapple: "Cigarettes and watches, silk stockings and whatever you could get your hands on. We got six dollars for a carton. Soap was another thing they used to like. White sheets, too, but soap more than anything."

Coleman Schneider: "On the ship we could get cigarettes for 60 cents a carton. So I stocked up on those and I got a lot of candy. Customs came around marked an 'X' on the closet in your cabin to show it had been inspected, but they never looked inside it. So I sold all these cigarettes to a longshoreman right there on the ship. The candy I took ashore and gave to some kids I found on the street. Made some kids very happy for a while."

Even Captain Southerland entertained.

Vinny Carista: "The captain, he thought I was the greatest. I used to set up the table for him. And he brought a girlfriend on board in England and asked me to set up the ship. He says, 'Vinny, how about setting up a table for me?'

"So I says, 'Yeah, I can do that.'"

There were other diversions.

Nick Carista: "I did like England 'cause they spoke our language. The parks were beautiful, with flower decorations. The English people I found to be very good people, very friendly.

Vinny Carista: "Ah, I liked the English. I almost was going to marry an English girl but she wasn't going to leave her mother. In England they have a lot of history and I like history. I saw a Roman fort in Cardiff and they had a Roman statue there. The Romans was really up to date and they had tunnels and they used to knock the shit out of the English and they tunneled up underneath and behind them."

Ken Holsapple: "I got treated good by the English. They were good people."

Jerome Shaw: "There wasn't a heck of a lot to see there. Everything was blacked out but the English people were very nice to us."

Coleman Schneider: "We saw the results of bombs dropping in London, and I saw the people with all their bunks sleeping in the subways. And of course you know in the merchant marine you got a bonus if the port was bombed. We never got a bonus."

At 1410 on the afternoon of August 14th the ship left Victoria docks and dropped anchor at Southend, England. On August 16, at 0710 the anchor was weighed and the ship departed London at 1135. Coleman Schneider: "As we left we saw the planes coming back again. Maybe it was because of the time of the day."

The *O'Brien* was one of 30 ships in convoy with two escorts, proceeding at a speed of 7.5 knots. The course was north, to pass over the top of Scotland and then west toward the United States. All the ships were in ballast.

The reality of war was never far away. Although a different ship in a different convoy, this Liberty with number 2 hold on fire is a vivid example of what the crew often feared would happen to the O'Brien. *Credit National Archives*

With the cargo discharged at Victoria Docks and the vessel homeward-bound it might be thought the worst was over with. In fact, danger loomed just over the horizon and set in quickly. Late that evening, while passing offshore of Great Yarmouth, the firing of big guns and loud explosions on shore were heard, raising speculation around the ship. Morgan Williams recorded in his diary, "We can hear some bombing tonight ashore. Can also see the flashes. We are sailing pretty close to land." The crew would later learn the port of Hull was under air attack.

The next morning brought the first incident of the *O'Brien's* Irish luck, a near-miss. A loud explosion shook the ship bringing everyone to battle stations. There were no submarines or planes around but minesweepers were working the area the convoy traveled. They had detonated a mine directly in the *O'Brien's* path. An hour later planes were sighted overhead. Again the crew manned their stations. The planes didn't attack and it was decided they were friendly.

The following evening the convoy arrived at Methil. Here the ships were separated according to destination and new convoys assembled. The *Jeremiah O'Brien*, along with 23 other ships and four escorts was assigned to a northbound convoy that traveled at an agonizingly slow speed of 4.5 knots. The crew settled in for the evening.

One traditional form of recreation, even in these dangerous waters, was poker.

Tom Ender: "The second mate, Frank Pellegrino, I remember as being full of self-confidence and a great card player. The latter for sure, since he won a bit of my money during the voyage."

Russ Carista. "Pellegrino, he was well-liked by everybody. He was a lady's man, good looking man, tall, well-liked. Always bringing women on board before we sailed, showing them around."

Vinny Carista: "Pellegrino, he come up from the ranks, and he was a good guy."

The morning of the 19th came peacefully with the ships plodding their way northward. At 1030 friendly planes flew over, giving everyone a feeling of confidence. Then, just as supper was over and the convoy was off the Buchan Ness Light near Aberdeen, a periscope was sighted. Three depth charges were dropped by the escort vessels, "about 6 hundred yards out," according to Morgan Williams' diary. The *O'Brien* made a 45 degree emergency turn to starboard as general quarters was sounded on the ship's alarm. Ten minutes of anxious watchfulness followed but apparently the submarine was frightened off and the convoy returned to base course.

At 2050 the same night the escort vessel's signal lights began flashing across the water. Enemy aircraft were in the area. The convoy commodore ordered all ships to man their guns. General quarters was again sounded on the general alarm and the Armed Guard crew manned their guns. At 2150 the "all clear" was received from the escort ships on the radio-telephone. By this time even the young novices were getting used to the mentally demanding routine -- long hours of boredom punctuated by card games, messroom conversation or paperback books, broken by hours on watch which could also be boring unless they were on the Mark-29 detail, interrupted by occasional alarms, which most hoped wouldn't be "for real."

Coleman Schneider: "I remember passing the northern tip of Scotland and seeing a Liberty ship piled up on rocks there."

On the afternoon of August 20 the convoy arrived at Aultbea, Loch Ewe, Scotland. Lt. Marshall, Naval Control of Shipping Officer (NCSO) of the U.S. Navy came aboard with routing instructions for the return voyage to the States. When the subject of the Mark-29 gear came up he said he had no orders regarding it. In the end it was decided not to stream it because the convoy was to travel part-way unescorted and the time involved in rigging the device would slow everyone down too much to reach their rendezvous on time. On August 21, 19 ships without escort departed Loch Ewe at a speed of 10 knots. Early during that first night, to help in holding convoy position, running lights were shown although in a dimmed condition. At 2230 caution prevailed and they were ordered extinguished.

The next day the Loch Ewe ships joined a larger convoy comprised of ships from the Mersey and Clyde Rivers. This took place six miles off Oversay Island and created an armada of 52 ships with seven escort vessels. They traveled eastward at a speed of 10 knots.

Coleman Schneider: "We put out for one day and had boiler trouble. Then we had to go back to Glasgow by ourselves."

To this point, the *O'Brien* had performed admirably. Except for the problems with the Mark-29, her maiden voyage had proceeded remarkably smoothly. Then her luck changed. At 1830 Captain Southerland received a call from the engine room. Both boilers were leaking badly, the ship couldn't maintain speed. This was transmitted to the convoy commodore who signaled, "Return to port now." The *Jeremiah O'Brien* slowed down and came about. The captain's sealed sailing orders had specific instructions for such eventualities. Stragglers were to proceed to the Firth of Clyde. As an escort couldn't be spared for a single ship, the *O'Brien* sailed back alone. Fortunately it wasn't far. In the morning of August 23, 1943 the *O'Brien* arrived at Gourock, on the Firth of Clyde, Scotland.

Morgan Williams: "We went into Glasgow and sat there for several days until they got her going again. It was a nice city. It was inland and it was pretty, real pretty there."

Coleman Schneider recalled with some embarrassment, "I got rolled for the first time in my life in Glasgow. We went ashore and met these two girls. They said give us the money and we'll get a bottle of good scotch and meet you upstairs, on the fifth floor of a certain building. So we went up there and of course it was just some old guy who never heard of them and he chased us off. You only do that once. We did take the train into Glasgow and saw the castle and some of the other sights."

Morgan Williams: "I remember one time they were loading cargo off another ship right next to us in Glasgow, Scotland, and the net broke or something. All that scotch whiskey broke and the kid on the net grabbed four or five. We had a party in our quarters aft and we were making a lot of noise. Real nice party. So Ensign Foote came in and took what was left and broke all the bottles."

While the boilers were being repaired, a conference was held concerning the Mark-29 gear. The Armed Guard Gunnery officer and Captain Southerland met with LTJG Thompson, United States Navy Liaison Officer (USNLO) and Capt. R. C. Crooks, Royal Navy, Naval Gun Control Service Officer. They discussed the problems the ship had with the gear and made tentative arrangements for streaming it while in convoy. The conference resumed the following day. The Royal Navy was especially concerned with knowing the difficulties encountered in streaming the gear while in convoy. Tentative plans were made for the ship to have a rear flank position in the next convoy so the gear could be put to use in such a manner as to protect the bulk of the ships in the grid.

On August 27, 1943 a three-hour convoy conference was held. Captain Southerland received the following instruction regarding streaming the Mark-29 gear:

To: Master, S.S. Jeremiah O'Brien
From: N.C.S.O., The Clyde

You are to await streaming your Helm Apparatum (MK-29) gear. If not received by the time you reach 10 degrees west then ask permission to go ahead and stream gear.

Strange things can happen when people are confined in relatively close quarters with little to break the monotony between watches. Idle chatter and desultory conversations can take on a life of their own. Add in the pressures and propaganda of wartime and every unusual or inexplicable action on the part of a shipmate indicates a potential spy. Someone apparently thought the Chief Engineer was aligned with the Axis. He was reported to Naval Intelligence for communicating with an enemy agent in Northern Ireland. The afternoon of the 27th a Lieutenant from the Office of Naval Investigation came aboard looking for Chief Engineer Robertson Montgomery. After lengthy questioning it came out that the chief's wife and family lived in Northern Ireland. The "coded messages" he was sending to this spy were simply letters written home.

Sailing that evening, the *Jeremiah O'Brien* accompanied ten other merchant ships without escorts at a speed of 9.5 knots. By prearrangement the Royal Air Force (R.A.F.) held a dummy air raid on the convoy. Six bombers conducted the raid, dropping flares and simulating attacks on individual ships. The raid ended at midnight. This was the most excitement the young seamen had yet seen and good practice for possible future encounters.

The early morning of the following day saw ships for the new convoy converging from three areas: Loch Ewe and the Mersey and Clyde Rivers. It took three hours to form a broad front and get all the ships in their proper convoy positions. Once again this took place off Oversay light. The result was a gigantic square of 60 ships and five escort vessels sailing at 9.5 knots for the east coast of the United States.

Losing convoy position made a ship a "sitting duck" for Nazi U-boats. The intensity of the fire on this Liberty would indicate something burning at a high temperature, such as manganese. Credit Smithsonian Institution

After supper that evening the chief engineer reported that despite the repairs made in Gourock, four tubes in the starboard boiler still leaked. He thought it significant but not serious enough to prevent the *Jeremiah O'Brien* from maintaining convoy speed without difficulty -- providing the weather held.

It didn't.

By August 29 the ship was pitching and rolling badly in a very heavy sea. Captain Southerland decided not to stream the

Mark-29 gear since the ship's speed could not be decreased and still allow it to retain position in the convoy. At 1400 that afternoon a message was relayed from the convoy commodore.

> From Comm.
> To: 1-6 (the *Jeremiah O'Brien's* position in the convoy)
> Have you special gear in operation. If not stream it at your convenience and warn other ships regarding apparatus.

Captain Southerland sent an immediate reply:

> From: 1-6
> To: Comm
> Gear not in operation at present will stream gear as soon as sea moderates."

After supper the chief engineer told the captain that the boilers were leaking badly and if weather moderated by 0600 the next day, repairs could be made to the boiler tubes while they were underway. The next morning Chief Montgomery reported that as long as full speed was maintained and no fires extinguished under the boilers, the leaking of tubes could be held to a minimum. Apparently the fires were hot enough to vaporize the water as soon as it leaked out of the tubes. He planned to continue the voyage without attempting repairs.

The convoy commodore signaled that convoy speed would be reduced to 6 knots at 0800 so that ships with net defenses might stream nets.[6]

The *Jeremiah O'Brien* didn't have nets, but she did have the Mark-29 and at 0800 the Armed Guard crew began streaming it. But in lowering the paravane on the starboard side, the faired towing line was torn so badly as to render it useless. Abandoning the starboard gear, the crew rigged out the port paravane. Two

---

[6] Some ships were equipped with nets that could be rigged over the side. The idea was for the nets to catch and/or deflect any torpedo that was fired at a ship. For the nets to function the ship was forced to travel at a slow speed which made it more susceptible to submarine attack as submarines had a relatively slow underwater speed at this time. It was questionable whether or not the reduction in speed was a worthwhile trade-off.

hours later the gear was out and running. But when the circuits were tested it was found that it didn't work. Fortunately, because of the slow convoy speed, the ship had not lost position.

That quickly changed. Fifteen minutes later the convoy increased speed to 9.5 knots. The *O'Brien* tried to stay with the group but finally, at 1300, Captain Southerland decided to reduce speed to pull in the useless Mark-29 gear. Engine speed was decreased to four knots and the Mark-29 paravane on the port side was retrieved. The faired towing line was found to have several torn sections that had filled with salt water. All the Mark-29 gear was stowed on deck, engine speed was increased to maximum and five hours later the ship regained its position in the convoy.

Jerome Shaw: "We'd pull it in and the rubber coating had all these scars on it."

Morgan Williams' diary: "When we got all the streamers rolled up on the spools it was 5:00 p.m. This Mk-29 is one hell of a mess."

The bad weather continued. On August 31 the conditions were logged as "Very heavy sea. Ship rolling badly." It was so rough the watch on the forward 3" gun was again repositioned on the bridge for their own safety. Morgan Williams' diary: "Sea is plenty rough. We are rolling about 40 degrees."

Nick Carista: "In this storm the strainers in the galley was screeching and everything. The ship was rolling twenty-five degrees. It was scary."

Vinny Carista didn't blame the sea alone: "There was this wise guy from Boston and he used to steer and sometimes he'd make the ship roll on purpose."

By 1100 the weather abated slightly and the seas were calmer. But this was the North Atlantic and calm weather is short-lived. By 1400 it was again blowing a moderate gale with the wind at a Beaufort force of 7-8 (28-40 knots) and the ship was again rolling severely. From the Armed Guard Log: "1900. Difficult for ship to make headway. Became separated from main body of convoy. Placed 2 men on wings of navigational bridge and 2 men on main deck below after 3" gun platform. Difficult for men to maintain footing on wet decks."

Nick Carista. "Yeah, I had a good gun crew. They did everything for me. We had a big storm you know. They had all the jams and peanut butter on the tables and they fell off in this storm and made a big mess. They cleaned it up. The gun crew, they took care of everything for me. There was about twenty in the gun crew and they cleaned it all up for me."

Russ Carista agreed: "Nick, he had that gun crew trained. They did everything for him."

By the following morning the *O'Brien* found herself in company with four other ships who were unable to keep up. Fortunately, an escort vessel spotted them and signaled that the main convoy was just ahead over the horizon. By 1000 the main convoy began to appear, the sea moderated and the wind dropped to a force of 3 (7-10 knots) on the Beaufort Scale. In the mid-afternoon Chief Montgomery informed everyone it would be necessary to ration water since the boilers were using more than twice the regular amount.

On September 4, just after midnight, two white flares were spotted on the starboard side of the convoy. An emergency turn was made. Apparently a ship had been torpedoed somewhere forward of their position for, an hour and a half later, the *O'Brien* went through a heavy oil slick. Due to radio silence, the crew was left to wonder what had happened.

Jerome Shaw: "They never told you anything. That was frustrating, they never told you anything. Usually that would happen when it was dark, too. That just made it worse."

Just after noon the same day a heavy fog set in. Once again the air was filled with the sound of ships' whistles as each vessel periodically sounded its convoy position.

After days of pitching, rolling and being battered about in heavy seas and hellacious winds, a weather advisory was received on September 5, 1943 and the commodore obediently relayed it to all the ships in the fleet: a hurricane warning had been received. It was about four days too late.

Vinny Carista: "These pots kept falling out of the rack. So I was an experienced guy, and they let me go down in the engine room and they let me make things and so on. So I used to get stuff and junk and whatnot and I made a hoop so when the ship rolled the pot never fell off again. I did a pretty good job of being a good messman."

The *Jeremiah O'Brien* was known as a "feeder."

Russ Carista: "The food was good. The Chinese cooks were good. Twice a day. Two meats on a menu and three vegetables. And breakfast either bacon or sausage or hot cakes and fried eggs any way you wanted."

Nick Carista: "We had a good crew there. We had some Chinese -- very good people. Good food, excellent. Good galley. The steaks were wonderful, you could eat all you want. The three of us used to eat with the Chinese cooks. They made some things you wouldn't find in a Chinese restaurant."

Tom Ender: "The second mate used to take white bread at mealtime and ball it up in his hand to show you how it lumped up in one's stomach. 'Bad for you,' as he said."

Ken Holsapple: "The food was good. We ate good on there."

Morgan Williams: "We had a couple of Chinese cooks and, by golly, they were good. They put out some good stuff."

Jerome Shaw: "The food was great. We never had a problem with food and sleeping quarters. They gave us clean linen and fed very well, excellent."

On September 6, at suppertime, the fog set in again. Although there was no wind, the ship was rolling badly in heavy swells. On September 7, fifteen ships detached themselves for Halifax, Nova Scotia but in the fog no one saw them leave.

Cadet Schneider: "Going into New York they decided they wanted to oil all the rigging. And, being the cadet, they figured I'd be scared, first trip and everything. So they gave me a rag and bucket of fish oil and put me in a bosun's chair and hoisted me aloft. I had a great time, it didn't bother me at all. After that I became kind of a hero because I wasn't scared to go aloft."

Finally, on September 10, 1943, just after midnight, the convoy and the *Jeremiah O'Brien* arrived at New York City. At 1800 she docked at Pier 57 in the North River. Nick Carista:

"We paid off in New York. I didn't want to leave. Southerland was a nice captain, very good man."

Tom Ender remembered, "Many of the crew on the first voyage were Boston Irish and they signed off when we arrived back in New York."

Russ Carista agreed: "Mostly from Boston, the crew was mostly from Boston. They knew each other from their past trips. They never had any dissension on the ship. They might fight on the beach but they got along on the ship. They were true sailors. They were professionals."

Vinny Carista was less nostalgic: "After that trip I said I'd never sail with brothers again. My brother Russ used to give some of the crew a hard time. I didn't get along with that. But if one brother gets into a fight you got to defend him."

The *Jeremiah O'Brien's* first voyage was over. It was one in which the ship was literally broken in. Her future voyages would have fewer problems but no less danger.

7

THE MARITIME PARADOX

At Pier 57, North River, New York City, the *Jeremiah O'Brien* immediately began preparing for a load of general cargo and ammunition. Having completed their first voyage to the war zone successfully, some of the crew were naturally inclined to celebrate their survival. Unfortunately, some celebrated too much and had to face the consequences. One of the Armed Guard third class petty officers was restricted to the ship because of drunkenness and disorderly conduct the previous evening. His performance must have been extraordinary for on the following day he was removed from the ship and reassigned.

On September 14 the *O'Brien* shifted to Pier F, Jersey City, New Jersey to load explosives[1], then shifted back to Pier 57,

---

[1] It was common practice at that time to load explosives and ammunition in the upper 'tween deck on the square of each of the hatches. This allowed for quick access when discharging, thus almost immediately removing the hazard from the ship when it arrived at its discharge port.

North River the following day to finish off her load with a deck cargo of vehicles and general cargo.

The crew continued to decompress. Purser Tom Ender: "Ensign Foote was in charge of the Armed Guard and I recall he was a likeable man, well thought of by his crew." To Ensign Charles Foote, Armed Guard Commanding Officer, fell the not inconsiderable task of maintaining discipline in the Armed Guard. On September 19, one seaman was absent at morning muster. He reported aboard the following day and was restricted to the ship and given extra duty. Another seaman returned aboard 5 hours late. He was placed on report for being absent over leave (AOL). Most of the Navy gunners didn't seem to resent the discipline. It was simply the price one paid for not following the rules.

As on the previous voyage, the crew signed 12-month articles for a foreign voyage with final discharge port once more being simply "USA." A number of new crewmembers were on board. Robert Milby, newly-assigned radio operator on this voyage, was enthusiastic about Liberty Ships. "When I came on the first Liberty ship, boy, it was like heaven. It was really something. Man, I thought I'd died and went to heaven.

"I shipped out because there was a war and I thought I could be in it. I went down to San Diego right away, to join the Navy. Couldn't pass the physical, because of my eyes. So I couldn't get in the Navy. I guess if I'd stayed around longer I'd have been drafted into the Army, I don't know. So then I went to work in the shipyard and I found out that these ships do a lot of things and they don't make you take a physical. So I went to radio school and became a radio operator."

Tom Ender: "I didn't want any part of the Army and I knew I'd get drafted. I had to get my father's signature on the papers for the Navy but they rejected me for color blindness. I got a call from Waterman [Steamship Company] and I jumped on it and I figured I'd get a chance to get home once in a while in the merchant marine. Later I went with Grace Line."

By September 21, 1943 the deck cargo had been loaded and lashed in place with chains. From Gunner's Mate Third Class Morgan Williams' diary: "We took on some incendiary bombs

Statistically, convoys meant fewer ships were subject to attack. Unfortunately the weather was rarely as depicted in this photo.   Credit National Archives

and a tank, also some deck cargo." Deck Cadet Coleman Schneider: "I was really awed by the point of the Plimsoll marks. They loaded us below the waterline, below the marks."

In the early morning the *O'Brien* shifted to an anchorage off the Statue of Liberty to await the formation of a convoy. That evening five Navy men came aboard as passengers. They were assigned as crew to the *USS Augusta* and were to join her in England.[2]   Official departure from New York was taken on September 22 at 0630. The *Jeremiah O'Brien* left in a convoy of 48 ships with speed set at 10 knots.   Four escort vessels accompanied the group as they headed into the open sea bound for England.

Robert Milby: "Well, getting in the Atlantic, we always went in convoy. And it was real protected. We had a lot of protection,

---

[2] The *USS Augusta* would be Rear Admiral A. G. Kirk's flagship leading the American Task Force in the Normandy landings on D-Day.

even a small, what they called a 'baby' aircraft carrier, and you had plane support and warships."

The practice of ships sailing in convoy dated from World War I when England was losing one out of every four ships to submarines. They organized the convoy system in 1917 and found it reduced their losses by 80 per cent. When aircraft were added to the protection, the losses became negligible. The effect of sighting an airplane, civilian or military, by a surfaced U-boat, was an immediate dive to deep water with the accompanying loss of opportunity for the submarine and the disclosure of its location to the plane and, shortly thereafter, to the naval escorts.

During World War II the convoy system was refined. After lengthy analysis, the British concluded that the number of vessels lost in any convoy was proportional to the number of attacking submarines and the size of the escort, not to the number of ships in the convoy. That is, if a wolf pack attacked a group of 25 ships it might sink 12, yet if the convoy contained 75 ships it would still only sink 12. The result was larger convoys with more escorts. The strategy proved effective. Of the 215 merchant ships sunk during the first nine months of the Battle of the Atlantic, only 21 were escorted.

Basically, a convoy sailed in a square of rows and columns. Typically a group of sixty ships would have a front consisting of a row of twelve ships across with each ship having a column of four ships behind it. Put another way, there would be a grid measuring 12 ships across by five ships deep. A ship presents the largest target from the side, therefore having only five rows of ships minimized the number of targets.

The convoy commodore, normally a U.S. Navy senior captain, would be in a merchant ship responsible for the other merchant ships in the convoy. Located in the center of the front row, he also had to see to it that the ships stayed in position. The merchant ships traveled 500 yards apart fore and aft and 1,000 yards apart side to side. Ammunition ships, troop transports and tankers would be placed in the center of the grid with the provision that ammunition ships were never placed side by side or next to a tanker or trooper to eliminate the possibility of a chain reaction or a large loss of life should one be hit.

Five thousand yards diagonally off each point of the rectangle of ships would be a destroyer or corvette.[3] With their great speed and armed with "ash cans" or depth charges, they patrolled in an elliptical pattern protecting the front and back of the convoy. In addition, two or more escorts patrolled the convoy's flanks, 10,000 yards out, in long rectangular patterns. The distance between the two flank escorts was about 18 miles with the convoy halfway between them. The escort commander was usually the senior Naval officer of the escorts in the Naval vessel patrolling the left front corner of the convoy. When under attack he took charge of the entire convoy, including the merchant ships.

Keeping station in a large convoy, often sailing through stormy weather, heavy seas, in darkness or blinding fog was a formidable enterprise. In addition to the difficulties of keeping position, shipmasters had to be sure their ships didn't show smoke by day or lights at night. They were warned not to throw rubbish or garbage overboard or pump bilges during the day so that floating waste or oil slicks wouldn't betray the convoy's route.

That first morning, the *O'Brien* ran ahead of the convoy, the crew preparing to launch the by-now-accursed Mark-29 gear. Its reputation had run before it and even the new crew knew about all the problems it caused on voyage No. 1. But the submarine danger in the North Atlantic was increasing and every possible anti-torpedo device available, flawed or not, had to be employed. With grim determination the Armed Guard began streaming the paravanes, faired lines and hydrophone just after noon. They finished at 1400 only to learn the paravane on the starboard side

---

[3] At the beginning of the war Great Britain was short on escorts, the basic defense of the convoy system. Prime Minister Winston Churchill ordered fifty-six escorts based on a whalecatcher, the *Southern Pride*, then in use by Smith's Docks Ltd. of Middlesborough. These became the "Flower Class Corvettes," and quickly filled a serious need. Although three knots slower than the U-boat's surface speed, the design existed and could be produced cheaply at £90,000 with only slight modification for armament. Eventually 288 corvettes were built in England and Canada and accounted for the destruction of fifty U-boats. Churchill referred to them as "Cheap and Nasties."

In 1943 a corvette signals the SS Jeremiah O'Brien *while negotiating a rough sea in the North Atlantic. Credit Coleman Schneider*

had broached and needed to be pulled in. Finishing that task, the crew hoped they were through for the day and enjoyed a warm supper, anticipating a well-earned rest. But the rest was short-lived. During the night it was discovered that the gear retarded the speed of the ship to less than the speed of the convoy so they were called out and the remaining paravane was taken in. The log does not detail their state of mind nor the remarks that were made, although Morgan Williams recorded the following in his personal diary: "I sure don't think much of Mk-29 and neither do the other boys or even the Ensign."

Because of the need for radio silence, communication between ships was difficult. Most messages were transmitted by flashing light, flag hoist or semaphore. This method of "pass it along" was slow, inefficient and prone to errors or misunderstanding. Situations frequently occurred in which the escorts simply couldn't stay up with what each ship was doing at any given time. This was sometimes frustrating and at other times comical. For example, the following morning one of the escorts called by blinker.

"Take in your special gear and take your position in convoy."

One can envision Captain Southerland on the bridge, "Grr-r-r-r-e-e-a-tt Scott. What do they think we've been doing for the last twenty-four hours?"

But the official reply went out immediately.

"Gear has been retrieved and we are proceeding at utmost speed."

The hydrophone was allowed to stream from the stern and a continuous watch was kept at the listening panel. This was the only component of the system that performed to expectations and it didn't slow the ship down, unlike the paravanes with their additional paraphernalia of faired towing lines and explosive charges. Nonetheless, it took until mid-afternoon to regain position in the convoy.

At this time almost the entire North Atlantic was a figurative minefield. In addition to stationery mines planted by both the Allies and the Axis at every harbor entrance, German U-boats prowled the ocean in wolfpacks, loaded with enough torpedoes to sink entire fleets. Add the dangers in the depths to those on the

This British tanker, exploding after being hit by a German torpedo, vividly shows the full impact of the Nazi U-boat menace. Credit U.S. Naval Historical Center

surface -- bitter cold, blinding fogs, fierce storms and wild seas -- and the Atlantic run was a perilous one, indeed.

Every seaman's greatest fear was of being torpedoed. The freezing water temperatures were as great a threat to life as any bomb or torpedo. As the war progressed, stories of days, weeks and months in lifeboats on cold, fog-bound waters added to the lore of Atlantic mariners -- stories like that of the Liberty ship *Stephen Hopkins* which, sailing alone westbound in the South Atlantic in 1942, sighted what appeared to be two cargo vessels. One of the ships stripped away its disguise, raised the Nazi flag and revealed its true identity as a merchant raider, the *Stier*. Armed with six 5.9 inch guns and two torpedo tubes the raider and her supply ship, *Tannenfels*, ordered the Liberty to surrender. Captain Paul Buck, the *Hopkins'* skipper, raised the American flag and turned his ship with its single 4 inch gun mounted aft, away from the Germans and for twenty minutes the ships exchanged fire.

The lone Liberty sank the *Steir* and was sunk herself, the 15 survivors from the *Hopkins* spending four weeks in a lifeboat before reaching the coast of Brazil.

To enhance survival, the Coast Guard issued new regulations based on the lessons learned in earlier sinkings. Part 153 of Coast Guard wartime regulations created new standards based on the "Unlimited National Emergency" proclaimed by President Roosevelt on May 27, 1941. In addition to the standard requirement that a ship carry lifeboats on each side for 100% of the crew, ships were also required to carry a minimum of four rafts, each capable of holding between 15 and 20 persons. These had to be carried so they would float free if the ship sank. In addition to the standard requirement of one life preserver for each member of the crew, ships were now required to carry additional life preservers on the boat deck equivalent to 25% of the crew. These were also to be stowed so they would float free if the ship sank. Lifeboats were carried at the boat deck railing and griped in or held there for immediate lowering although wise masters in heavy weather kept their boats swung in to keep them from being battered and lost overboard by heavy seas. Air tanks were required so that the boat would float, even when filled with water. Made of metal, these were strapped or otherwise fastened to the undersides of the thwarts.

Because of the severe weather conditions more than two-thirds of those who survived a vessel sinking in the Atlantic usually died of exposure. So the equipment list for lifeboats was adjusted to enhance survival at sea over long periods of time in cold and adverse weather. This included:

Blankets. At least six woolen blankets in waterproof covers.

Chart. A current Hydrographic Office Pilot Chart of the waters navigated, in a metal container.

Drinking cups. At least three drinking cups, marked in one-half ounce graduations, with lanyard attached [so they could be tied to something and not lost overboard].

First Aid Kit. Containing the usual compresses, bandages, and ointments.

Flashlight batteries. Three extras.

Canvas hood and sidespray curtain. Made of No. 8 yellow duck
(canvas), the hood extended from the stem to the mast with 12
inch spray curtains carrying from the mast aft to the stern.

Lamp wicks. Two extra wicks for the kerosene lamps in a
waterproof container.

Massage Oil. One gallon of a type suitable for massaging the feet
and legs.[4]

Mast and sail. A mast, mainsail and jib were carried. They were
colored red or chrome yellow to make them more visible.[5]

Matches. Two boxes of friction matches.

Provisions.[6] Fourteen ounces for each person, of biscuits known
as "Type C" ration covered by U.S.Army regulations. Each
biscuit to measure approximately 2-9/16 inches square by 5/16
inch thick. The biscuits to be packed and heat-sealed in
moisture- and grease-resisting wax glassine paper. Additional
provisions shall include: fourteen ounces of pemmican covered
by specifications for U.S. Navy Aircraft Emergency Ration
Pemmican; fourteen ounces of chocolate tablets in waterproof
packages or containers or an additional 14 ounces of biscuits
"Type C" rations covered by U.S. Army specifications, and;
fourteen ounces of malted milk tablets in waterproof packages
or containers.

Signal Flag. One yellow or bright orange bunting flag (4' 6" x 8')
to be attached to a boathook pole, for tricing up to mast head
to attract aircraft.

Water containers. At least ten quarts of fresh water for each person
in the boat stowed in four separate tanks equally distributed in
inboard and outboard tanks. In addition, small wooden casks
of fresh water were slung under the boat's thwarts.

Signal pistol. An approved signal pistol outfit consisting of a
pistol with lanyard, and 12 approved parachute red signal
cartridges, all contained in a watertight metal case properly
marked.

---

[4]   One of the negative effects of sitting in a lifeboat for long periods of time
was a condition similar to the trenchfoot of World War I, known as "immersion
foot." The massage oil was designed to combat this.

[5]   Rowing tires people quickly, making them more vulnerable to exposure. A
sail was considered the best means of propulsion over long distances.

[6]   Traditionally, hard bread or equivalent is carried in lifeboats. The emergency
regulations were very specific in defining what would be substituted.

Fishing kit. One for each boat. It contained a pair of gloves, a knife designed to be capable of floating, an assortment of sinkers, a stone for sharpening hooks, 12 pork rinds for bait, an assortment of hooks, instructions, a dip net, cord, line, winders and a bib. The kit was required to be marked, "EMERGENCY FISHING KIT. OPEN ONLY FOR ACTUAL EMERGENCY USE"

Daytime distress signals. Four self-contained smoke signals of an approved type, designed for attracting aircraft.

Portable identification boards for identification in friendly ports.[7]

Life preserver covering. Life preservers were covered with a fire resistant, slate-colored cloth.

Life Preserver Light. A life preserver light of an approved type was provided, attached to the preserver and showing a red light.

Lifesaving suits. One for each person on board.[8]

Whistles and jackknives. Each person on board to be provided with a police whistle and a jackknife.

Abandon-ship kit. Each ship shall be required to carry at least two kits. They consisted of: 20 one-quarter grain syrettes of morphine, 48 one-half gram tablets of sulfadiazine in a bottle, 10 Navy type, watertight packages containing 2 1/2 grams of crystalline sulfanilamide, 4 ounces of approved oil cleaning solution in a bottle having a screw cap, 5 four-ounce tubes of 5 percent sulfadiazine -- tannic acid 10 percent jelly, 2 chemical heating pads of approved type, and three copies of the directions for using the above.

Lifesaving nets. At least ten feet across and long enough to reach from the rail to the light load line.

Signal mirrors. Two stainless steel or other suitable polished mirrors having approximately 20 square inches of reflecting surface.[9]

---

[7] In peacetime ships are required to show the vessel's name and home port on each lifeboat and on the bow and stern of the ship itself. These were painted over in wartime.

[8] A modern version of these is now required on merchant ships traveling in certain colder latitudes. They are known as "exposure suits."

[9] The wartime requirements for lifeboats are abbreviated in the interest of conserving space and reducing boredom. In addition, many of the items routinely carried in lifeboats in peacetime are not included on the assumption that the reader is familiar enough with them.

Of course, if your ship sank and you were bobbing at sea in a lifeboat, you had to know what to do with all the equipment, provisions and paraphernalia. To this end the Coast Guard issued the following dated January 2, 1942:

Subject: Advice to Officers or Persons in Charge of Life Boats.

A list stating the quantities of water and provisions with instructions for rations should be provided in each boat. The officer or person in charge of the boat should check the provisions and water at frequent intervals to insure the quantity and quality are complete and satisfactory and ready for instant service. The person in charge of the life boat or life raft should check this equipment as soon as possible after abandoning ship to determine its condition and quantity that may be serviceable. He should consider all the circumstances in the case and prepare to ration the water and provisions to the best advantage bearing in mind the possibility of being adrift for an extended period of time. The rationing should begin with the first issuance of food or water. The provisions and water breakers should be shifted to the after end of the boat, stowed and guarded to prevent pilferage. Extreme care should be exercised when issuing drinking water to account for every drop without wastage.

The emergency rations will better serve their purpose if taken several times a day in small quantities rather than if taken seldom and in larger quantities.

Drinking water is of utmost importance in sustaining life. Drink the ration slowly, savoring each sip. Heavy rain in calm weather will afford an opportunity to replenish your water supply. Be sure that the canvas or other cloth used for catching rain water is free of salt before putting the water into your tanks.

Biscuits are best used with small amounts of the other foods. Eat slowly, and chew thoroughly.

Pemmican should be eaten with biscuit and may be dissolved in water. Empty pemmican tins should be used for drinking cups.

Milk tablets should be allowed to dissolve slowly in the mouth. They may also be dissolved in water.

The chocolate should be dissolved slowly in the mouth or may be eaten with biscuit.

Care of feet is an important matter. Much sitting with dangling legs causes painful swelling. To combat this condition, massage them frequently with the oil. Feet constantly damp and cold become "trench feet", so keep them dry if possible. In any case, rub them well with oil and combat frostbite of feet and extremities with similar massage.

MORALE: The man in command of each boat should get his boat's company settled down without delay. In any but the finest weather, all must sit low in the boat. In order to prevent moping, the boat commander must set watches and assign each person a regular job. He must also arrange a routine for meals at which a fair distribution is vital. In cold weather spells of exercise with oars are valuable if not too prolonged.

In rough seas, it is essential that the boat be kept head-on to the sea. For this purpose, the sea anchor will be of real assistance, but a strong man, or two men, must also work the steering oar constantly to steady the boat. Constantly means constantly, both day and night. Any let-up at an unfortunate moment may result in swamping and probably capsizing.

The evidence of men who have been many days adrift in life boats has helped much in giving you this advice.

A copy of these instructions should be issued to each person in charge of a life boat or life raft and a copy should be placed in each airtight provision receptacle.

A copy of the: "Manual for Lifeboatmen and able Seamen", August 1941 edition, should also be placed in each life boat for the information of the person in charge."

Ken Holsapple, Seaman First Class: "I know it was cold on almost every trip we made. We had to wear that foul weather gear all the time. We didn't take our clothes off, slept in our lifejackets when we got in close [to England]."

John Crosby, third mate on voyage #6 of the *O'Brien* recalled his Atlantic crossings in later years: "I never showered and always slept in my clothes out of fear of being hit and not adequately dressed for the cold weather in the life boat. The North Atlantic was always high winds, heavy seas, 150 ships in convoy and constantly under submarine and air attack."

In the early evening of September 24, 1943, sixteen ships from Halifax joined the convoy off Sable Island making a total of 64 ships traveling together. Little happened for the next few days. On September 28, the 20 mm guns were test fired. Two days later, chief engineer Montgomery reported that the boiler tubes were leaking again and using excessive amounts of water. The weather grew worse and by supper time that evening the seas were heavy. The *O'Brien* was forced to drop two miles astern of the convoy in order to lash down some of the deck cargo of military vehicles that had worked loose. It was difficult scrambling around the pitching deck dodging loose cargo, trying to refasten lashings in what dim light they were allowed, punctuated here and there by the eerie glow of luminous tape. Eventually they got the job done and caught up with the rest of the ships.

That same evening an aircraft carrier and several additional escorts joined the convoy, bolstering the crew's confidence. There was something very reassuring about having the might of a carrier in their midst. In the morning of October 1, the carrier sent up two planes which searched the water ahead for submarines. During the day, for unknown reasons, it left the convoy, but rejoined it that evening. The next morning the carrier again dispatched several planes. The ships were closer to Europe now and the danger was growing greater. Nine escort vessels now protected the convoy.

A convoy as viewed from the stern of a Navy destroyer. Note the depth charge racks in the after end. Credit National Archives

Two days later the Loch Ewe portion of the group broke off, heading for Scotland. The remaining ships formed into three columns.

Late in the evening of the 4th of October, forty-three depth charges were heard exploding off Tory Island, Ireland. After launching the Mark-29 hydrophone, the Armed Guard manned their guns, ready for action. Although another false alarm, it was a reminder that the crew was in waters that could at any moment spit up a torpedo that would send those that survived scurrying to the lifeboats.

In the early morning of October 5 the Mark-29 hydrophone was retrieved. As usual it was difficult work. The crew had been at battle stations most of the night and the seas were heavy, so heavy in fact that many of the ships had difficulty maneuvering. Several ships signaled the convoy commodore for instructions. None were forthcoming.

It was one of the ironies of wartime crossings that although ships were surrounded by scores of convoy sisters, most had little or no idea what might be occurring around them. Each ship was a virtual island, sufficient to herself and knowing only what was happening on her own decks. Explosions, alerts and alarms, the appearance and disappearance of carriers, escorts, and planes and even members of the convoy were only to be conjectured at with no answer forthcoming. The more curious or persistent might find out some information later, but after awhile, each ship's crew simply settled into their own world and looked after themselves.

Coleman Schneider: "On the second voyage, they're going along and they're playing cards. Pellegrino and Morgan. And these guys beat the hell out of me. I only played a couple of times because they cleaned me out. But I wanted to buy a sextant in Liverpool, but I didn't have the money. So I asked Captain Southerland if I could have an advance on my wages and the captain said, 'O.K.' Anyhow I did a lot of sights with that sextant on the way back."

The *Jeremiah O'Brien* arrived at Liverpool, England on October 6, 1943 at 0730, anchored awaiting a berth and docked the same afternoon at Gladstone dock #1. With the ship safely in port, the crew's interests quickly turned to the enticements ashore and the following afternoon six of the Armed Guard seaman were discovered drinking whiskey and restricted to the vessel.

On October 8 the five Navy passengers departed the ship. The crew would see them again as the *O'Brien* passed the *USS Augusta* off Land's End, a few hours before the invasion of Normandy.

Coleman Schneider: "I took a train to Blackpool with a bunch of guys. Just to see the sights. The English people were fantastic, really great. And in the blackouts, if I lit a cigarette at that time I got hell from the street warden. Everyone stayed together. There was lots of cohesion there."

The next several days were occupied with the routine discharge of cargo and some of the gun crew was sent ashore for training. Ken Holsapple remembers: "I went to school in England for the 20 millimeter gun."

Ensign Foote was called to London to explain the problems with the Mark-29. From the Armed Guard Log: "Conference in London concerning Mk-29 gear, at Technical Section, U.S. Naval Forces in Europe, U.S. Embassy."

A ship is a microcosm of the human condition. Eventually, most things that happen to people ashore will happen aboard ship. One of the Armed Guard Seamen First Class complained of stomach pains. After diagnosis he was sent to the local Royal Navy Hospital with appendicitis. Another Armed Guard Seaman had a more delicate problem. He reported the first signs of gonorrhea and was treated with Sulfa-thiozole. It was the same sailor who was AWOL in New York before the ship sailed.

The last of the cargo was offloaded on October 18 and the *O'Brien* departed from Liverpool in ballast. So many ships were running in and out of English ports they no longer steamed at night in the nearby waters in blackout. This was partly because the R.A.F. had won the battle of the British skies and was carrying the attack into European airspace, giving the homefront a measure of security. As the *O'Brien* proceeded through the North Channel she was allowed to show her running lights. Then, in the relative safety of English waters, an unexpected disaster struck. The morning after departure, as the convoy tried to get into their assigned positions for the voyage home, two ships collided and one ship caught on fire. Why or how the collision occurred was never determined. Presumably it was from the intricacies of too many ships maneuvering too closely together. It was another reminder that there were other dangers besides U-boats and mines and that a high state of alertness had to be constantly maintained. There was just too much going on to take things for granted or accept them as routine.

The convoy finally formed off Oversay Light, on the Northwest coast of Scotland, a total of 68 merchant ships with 6 "close" escorts all traveling at a speed of 9.5 knots.

Crews on board merchant ships lived in an atmosphere of suppressed danger. There was the constant fear that at any moment they might be bombed by enemy planes or struck by a torpedo and if this happened they had to be ready to abandon ship on a moment's notice. But on a "lucky" ship such as the *Jeremiah O'Brien* the reality of day-to-day life was long stretches of routine watchstanding and boredom spiced with the unpredictable sounds of depth charges and the general alarm signaling "G.Q." The paradox was that life aboard ship continued in a relatively normal manner, yet one always had to be ready because the next alert might very well be for the torpedo with "O'Brien" written on its nose.

As the convoy pushed north the barometer fell and the seas rose -- the curse of North Atlantic weather again bedeviling the ships. The crew groaned as the ships rolled heavily homeward. On the *Jeremiah O'Brien* the men staggered across the heaving decks and the engine room floor plates as if drunk, the constant rolling making the simple task of getting from one place to another almost impossible. Sometimes soup and sandwiches were all that could be prepared for meals. Pots and pans wouldn't stay on the stove long enough to cook anything. At night the crew cursed the sea, wedging themselves into their bunks with lifejackets under the mattresses as they tried to get a few hours' fitful sleep. In extreme rolls, the brittle sounds of crockery breaking, punctuated by the reverberant clang of falling pots and pans, echoed throughout the midship house.

Tom Ender: "A Liberty was completely different from what I expected. I didn't expect anything that would roll so much. They rolled terribly. It was a little scary when you came into a foreign port and saw the bow or stern of one sitting there on the beach."

Ken Holsapple: "We had one guy in the gun crew, Lamonica. He was sick all the time. Couldn't help it, just his nature. Even when the weather was nice, he was sick."

An aircraft carrier joined the convoy, taking position in Column 6. Whatever sense of security the massive warship's presence gave the *O'Brien's* crew was short-lived. Heavy seas made it impossible to hold position and the convoy was forced to scatter. During the night the weather abated enough to regroup. Early in the morning of October 21 a signal came by convoy light[10] for all

---

[10] All ships carried a "Christmas Tree" of convoy lights on a mast on the

Even approaching the east coast of the Untied States a convoy couldn't let its guard down. U-boats could strike anywhere, any time. Credit National Archives

ships to execute three 20 degree turns to starboard. Had a submarine been spotted? Again, communications were almost nonexistent and there was no way of knowing. The ships did as they were ordered and the turns were made quickly, one after the other. The following day a second aircraft carrier joined the convoy. At this time, standing on the flying bridge, Captain Southerland counted 50 ships around the horizon.

---

flying bridge. Three red and three green lights were displayed in a vertical line, side by side. Various turns and directions were indicated by the combinations of red and green shown at any given time.

By October 23 the seas had moderated. Eleven escort vessels were visible in the vicinity of the *Jeremiah O'Brien*. During a two-hour period from 0900 to 1100, three changes of course were made. Again there was no communication or observable cause. Perhaps a sub had been spotted by one of the carriers' planes. A flying boat was seen circling the convoy while the turns were made and conjecture was that it had spotted something in the water. A message was sent to the convoy commodore:

"Please advise if we should stream our special gear?"

The reply was: "No, not now."

Later in the afternoon a high whining was heard on the Mark-29 listening panel. The sailor manning the device thought it was a torpedo and sounded the general alarm. The crew manned their battle stations. The sound persisted, unchanging, for about 10 minutes and in the end it was decided it was again probably due to a mechanical defect in the hydrophone. The disgust of the crew was obvious. Every time the Mark-29 malfunctioned, they had to go to general quarters, yet the danger of attack was so real that every alarm might be the last one.

When they awoke on the morning of October 25, the crew discovered that one of the aircraft carriers had left the convoy during the night. Where had it gone and why? No one knew. The remaining carrier dispatched planes at intervals throughout the day. A flying boat was seen patrolling over the convoy during the morning. The following day, in the early afternoon, the seaman at the listening panel of the Mark-29 heard sounds resembling exploding depth charges. Some 60-70 sounds were heard during the afternoon. The escorts were in position. None of them was dropping depth charges. As there were no other indications of activity Ensign Foote decided the sounds were probably due to mechanical defects in the hydrophone. It was another cry of "wolf" by the mechanical monster.

A signal was sent from the convoy commodore to all vessels for "New Defense" ships to stream nets at 1500. The *O'Brien* signaled "Shall we stream our Mk-29 gear at 1500?"

The reply was "No," with no explanations.

By now most of the crew had given up on the Mark-29 gear as being any kind of help. Robert Milby: "We sort of disregarded it. Because it didn't work."

That evening two white flares were seen, apparently from a ship on the forward port corner of the convoy, followed in quick succession by three sets of two white flares fired together and a Roman candle fired singly. The general alarm was sounded and the gun crew went to battle stations. No explosions and no depth charges were heard. An hour later the crew secured from battle stations. Once more, it was the old complaint, "Hurry up and wait."

On October 27, after discussing the matter, Ensign Foote and Captain Southerland decided to stop listening to the Mark-29 hydrophone. The constant mechanical noises coming through the listening panel were more of a distraction than a help.

Little happened the next two days except that the weather deteriorated and on October 30 the ship was pounding badly from heavy swells coming from dead ahead. Morgan Williams recorded the effects of head seas in his diary. "Every time we would hit a big wave the screw would come out and what a vibration it makes. Didn't sleep much the rest of the night." The weather continued to worsen and soon was so bad the ship had to reduce speed to avoid pounding and fell astern of convoy most of the day, regaining her position in mid-afternoon.

Coleman Schneider: "The crew were getting mad at me by this time because I never got sick. So they sent me up to the forepeak to mix paint in 55 gallon drums. So I went up there and climbed down into the forepeak and started mixing this paint. And the bow was going up and down, and I'd mix and then hold on for dear life, and then mix some more and then hold on some more. So after about fifteen minutes of this, I said, 'What the hell am I doing here?' I came up and went back to the messroom and the crew all starts laughing. They had a big laugh over that, but I never got sick."

Finally, they approached the east coast of the United States. The convoy of ships formed into long columns as they approached New York to negotiate the narrow approach area which was constantly patrolled and swept for mines. For the first time in days the running lights were turned on, dimmed, during the night. The Atlantic seaboard of America was still a shooting gallery for Nazi submarines at this time, however, and even this close to home there could be danger. In the time that the *Jeremiah O'Brien* had plied the seas since her launching in June, 134 Allied ships totalling 750,000 tons had been sunk. Apparently a sub or subs were spotted for numerous depth charges (Morgan Williams counted "around forty") were heard exploding throughout the morning of November 3rd. Again, of course, no one knew for sure.

The *Jeremiah O'Brien* took official arrival in New York at 1400 that afternoon and at 2100 she docked at Pier 58 North River. Voyage No. 2 ended at midnight on November 2, 1943.

Cadet Coleman Schneider: "I think my pay as cadet was $60 a month. So between what I lost in the poker game and my advance to buy the sextant, I didn't have anything coming. When we got into New York my payoff was $1.29. If we had arrived a day earlier I would have owed the company money."

The daily expenses for voyage No. 2 were: Deck, $15.68, Engine $29.91 and Steward $9.77. These figures include all expenses except wages. The engine department figure was high because of the continuing problem with the boiler tubes.

The *Jeremiah O'Brien's* next voyage would be both more economical and more grueling.

8

WINTER NORTH ATLANTIC

Voyage No. 3 should have started at one minute after midnight on November 4, 1943. Instead, several days passed
with the ship tied up to Pier 58 in the North River, New York
City. This was significant for during wartime there was seldom
a wait for cargo to be loaded. Delays were common in unloading,
especially in Europe or the South Pacific where a ship might have
to wait her turn at a berth but a delay in loading in a U.S. port was
rare and a source of speculation. By now, though, the ship's
officers and crew were used to being the last to learn of new
developments or changes in plans, which could be altered from
hour to hour.

The first sign of any kind of action was on November 10 and
was most unwelcome -- additional Mark-29 gear was brought on
board including a complete new instrument rack assembly, a new
angle indicator panel, four detector streamers, two faired towing
lines and four paravanes. Apparently the ship was being prepared
for another run.

Meanwhile, in the Grace Line main office across town, a message was received withdrawing the ship from the company's list of GAA vessels! Further, it was to revert to the War Shipping Administration which was, in turn, planning to lease it to the War Department on a bareboat charter basis. The WSA ordered the *O'Brien* shifted to Section 10, Erie Basin, Brooklyn, a shipyard. As word filtered down, the crew turned to, amid much speculation. Obviously something was up and the ship became a hotbed of rumor and question -- why had they put aboard the extra Mark-29 gear? Why was the ship taken off charter? Was the ship being "punished" for all the problems with that anti-torpedo device? What would happen to the crew? The next day Captain Southerland received a message that the ship was going to be taken to Boston and transferred to the Army for conversion to a hospital ship. The news was received with consternation. Conversion would take some time. What would happen to the crew in the meantime? Those making their first trip were just settling in. The veterans of the *O'Brien's* earlier voyages had become good friends and felt they were part of a team effort. Conversion to a hospital ship would require them all to uproot and start again on different ships.

But other forces were at work. Grace Line didn't want to lose the lucrative contract it had on the vessel any more than the crew wanted to lose their ship. The company's port director met with the WSA. He explained that the *Jeremiah O'Brien* was one of the few merchant vessels operating that was equipped with the experimental and highly-secret Mark-29 gear. It would be more important to the war effort and less costly to continue operating the ship as it was rather than outfitting another ship. Any Liberty could be converted to a hospital ship, but why go to the time and expense of outfitting another ship with Mark-29 when the *O'Brien* already had it? It took some talking and more than a few calls to Washington, D.C., but in the end the *Jeremiah O'Brien* was returned to Grace Line's list of ships. To formalize it, the WSA immediately issued Grace Line a letter canceling allocation of the ship to the War Department. The vessel would remain with Grace Line under Service Agreement, Form GAA. The crew breathed a sigh of relief. They would have a "home" for the next few months after all.

That evening the ship shifted from Pier 10, Erie Basin to Pier 58, North River where it began loading a cargo of trucks, tanks and mail. The gunnery crew was sent ashore to hone their skills on their weapons and for the next week they practiced at 3" and 20 mm mounts. On November 18, 1943 foreign articles for 12 months were signed. The voyage, which began at one minute after midnight of November 19, was to be from "a point in the Atlantic Ocean to the Eastward of New York and thence to such ports and places in any part of the world as the Master may direct or as may be ordered or directed by the United States Government or any department, commission or agency thereof." The crew was pleased to sign their articles. Foreign articles are the final contract, before sailing, between the master of the ship and his crew. At least they wouldn't have to worry about the ship being yanked out from under them for awhile.

It was increasingly clear that an Allied invasion of Europe would occur some time in the near future. There were obvious signs -- the cargoes being sent to England consisted more of military equipment and less of civilian commodities than earlier in the war. England was surviving, now she needed to be fortified. On board the *O'Brien* discipline and security measures tightened and the rules for standing watch were strictly enforced. The watchstander was required to literally stand and watch for strangers loitering, for unusual incidents, for anything out of the ordinary. It comes as no surprise, then, that on November 19, one of the Armed Guard crew was restricted to the ship for five days for standing watch improperly. This could have been as simple as sitting down to rest or talking to someone or reading a magazine. Whatever it was, the watchstander was not devoting his full attention to his duty.

Although New York was far from the battlefields of Europe, everyone was constantly aware of the war. Sabotage by the enemy was a prime concern. Every merchant ship received a list of security instructions from the Captain of the Port on arrival. These covered every eventuality from swimmers in the water to saboteurs to direct attack and fire.[1]

The safety of the ship was not the only concern. It was especially important that the enemy not learn what cargoes were loaded on which merchant ships nor their destinations. "Loose lips sink ships," was the credo of the waterfront. Most cargoes were crated and marked in code. A person could not tell from the outside what was in a given container.

Tom Ender: "We didn't really know what was in the holds. Nothing was marked."

Sealed sailing orders were given to the master to be opened only after the ship was at sea. When the O'Brien finished loading her cargo on November 24, the Army restricted everyone to the ship.

The following day was filled with pre-sailing conferences: at 0900 the gunnery officer attended a Gunnery conference, at 1000 the gunnery officer, ship's master and radio operator attended a Communications conference. At 1100 the gunnery officer and captain attended a Master's conference. They were given verbal orders NOT to stream the Mark-29 Gear. In view of the fact that the O'Brien had just been saved from conversion into a hospital ship because she was equipped with the Mark-29 the men were surprised to receive this order.

In his book, *Eastward the Convoys*, William G. Schofield described the convoy conferences: "The personnel makeup was always the same, with the merchant captains and the Armed Guard commanding officers sitting together while some Admiral in charge introduced the Escort Commander and the Convoy Commodore, and outlined the routes, destinations, and special emergency tactics.

"In New York or Boston or Norfolk or Halifax, there was an electricity to those conferences. They were held in well-lighted surroundings, amidst great wall maps and marine charts, where mock-up convoy formations were moved about and where late reports on the location of submarine wolfpacks were illustrated by lights and models. When you left to return to the ship and await

---

[1] See Appendix E for a detailed listing of the wartime regulations for the port of San Francisco.

departure time, you went out feeling the way a well-trained football team does when it runs from the locker room onto the playing field for the start of the second half. You felt alive and confident and ready for hard action."

Despite the orders restricting the crew to the ship, the Captain let the two cadets go ashore for Thanksgiving.

Deck Cadet Coleman Schneider: "So, after we're loaded, we tied up in Staten Island to await the convoy. We were supposed to leave on Thanksgiving Day to form the convoy. They changed the sailing time and I asked the captain if I could go home. So the other cadet and I got off and caught a bus and rode fifteen miles home. The bus was full of Italian prisoners, they let them out on their own at that time. My mother held up Thanksgiving dinner until we got home and then we had dinner and took the bus back. She gave me a big package that said, 'Do not open until Christmas' on it to bring back to the ship. We got back that night in time to sail the next day."

Bill Watson had just signed on as Third Assistant Engineer: "It was my first Liberty. I can't compare it with the *Mooremac Moon*, a C-3 I just got off of which would travel at 16 knots. Libertys were slow but were about as reliable as anything you can get. They were kind of like an old Ford. You could open the hood and there was nothing fancy. But I would say that the Liberty was as reliable as the Model 'T' in all those years."

The *Jeremiah O'Brien* finally set sail on voyage No. 3 on November 26, 1943, departing from New York at 0845 in a convoy of 37 ships. Her assigned position was #91, meaning she was the lead ship in column number 9. There were four escort vessels and the convoy speed was set at 9.5 knots. That evening the *O'Brien* received radio instructions reiterating what had been made clear at the conference: she was NOT to stream her Mark-29 gear. Now that the Navy knew the Mark-29 gear existed, they wanted nothing to do with it. It is probably unnecessary to relate that the crew concurred with the Navy and received the news without any expressions of disappointment.

Just after midnight ship No. 81, in the column next to the *O'Brien* in the convoy, developed steering engine trouble and fell out of position. Fortunately the *O'Brien's* mate on watch saw the other ship swinging closer and took quick evasive action. It was a near miss. Still fresh in everyone's mind were visions of the two ships colliding and burning off Scotland on the previous voyage. The strict rules surrounding watchstanding were clearly and dramatically impressed upon the crew.

Because of coastal traffic and the size of the convoy, running lights were shown continuously during the first night. In the next three nights they were either shown continuously or for two minutes every half-hour, depending on the whim of the convoy commodore. Rarely able to learn the reasons behind events, the crews took to explaining things as "the old man's idea." In this case the "old man" was the convoy commodore, not Captain Southerland.

On November 29 the fleet was joined by 23 ships from Halifax, Nova Scotia, making a total of 60 merchant ships. As they proceeded eastward the weather, as usual, deteriorated. The difference was that, with winter coming on, the usual bad weather could be expected to be even worse. The North Atlantic did not disappoint. The next day the beam seas were extremely rough causing the ship to roll heavily. There was so much water on deck and footing was so difficult that the sea watch was secured from the forward gun and posted on the flying bridge.

Gunner's Mate Third Class Morgan Williams noted in his diary, "November 30, Tuesday. I didn't get a bit of sleep last night."

Bill Watson, Third Engineer. "They rolled a lot, no doubt about that. Many times they rolled so much you'd walk on one bulkhead and down the engine room floor plates and up the other bulkhead."

The heavy seas continued. By December 1 the *O'Brien* was separated from the main body of the convoy. Only five other ships were in sight. A hurricane warning (more timely than those on previous voyages) was issued. The sea watch on the after gun was secured and brought to the flying bridge and at 1000 everyone in the quarters aft (the Armed Guard gun crew) was moved amidships because of heavy seas. With saltwater coursing from one end of the ship to the other, Captain Southerland feared for their safety and he was right. Only a few hours later the wooden catwalk built over the after deck cargo of tanks and trucks washed away. Morgan Williams' diary: "Heavy sea came over and took away our catwalk. We have to go down through the shaft alley to get back aft." By the following morning the seas had moderated enough that watches could be posted at the forward and after guns and the gun crew was allowed to return to their quarters. But now they faced a new problem. There wasn't a ship in sight, the convoy was lost. Such contingencies were covered in the sailing orders. If separated, a ship was to sail to a rendezvous position. However, due to an error in the rendezvous position the *O'Brien* found only empty ocean at the appointed time and place. A second contingency called for a ship to take a "straggler's route" to her destination. The *O'Brien* set course on this route and at 1630 sighted a plane and one ship, hull down (only masts and superstructure showing above the horizon).

Coleman Schneider: "From Halifax across was just fantastic. The North Atlantic was wild all the way. A couple of times we lost the whole convoy because of fog or bad weather. I remember one day we logged sixty-four miles backward."

On December 3 two merchant ships and an escort vessel were sighted. Receiving word from the escort that the convoy was astern, the *Jeremiah O'Brien* slowed down to let the bulk of the fleet catch up and eventually she regained her position.

On December 6, a warning was received from the convoy commodore via flag hoist that enemy submarines were known to be operating in the vicinity. At this time there were 37 ships in the convoy with nine escort vessels; twenty-three vessels had scattered to parts unknown. The following day a radio warning was received that submarines were shadowing the convoy. Stragglers were ordered to proceed immediately to the straggler's route while the *O'Brien* received an individual message that her first port would be Loch Ewe. The day was filled with confusion. For some reason the convoy commodore kept changing the *O'Brien's* assigned position. At 1000 she was shifted from position #92, to which she had been assigned when the Nova Scotia section joined the convoy, to position #34. At 1100 she was shifted from position #34 to position #21. The following day she was shifted to position #22. Finally, at 1600, the *O'Brien* and seven other ships were detached from the main convoy to continue on their own. They had one escort vessel as they entered the areas of heavy ship traffic near Great Britain, sailing through The Minches.[2]

On December 10 the escort vessel left the convoy and shortly thereafter the ships arrived at Loch Ewe, Aultbea, Scotland. As on previous trips, a barrage balloon was put aboard. The *O'Brien* and Convoy #29, now consisting of 11 ships and two escorts, departed from Loch Ewe traveling northward around Northern Scotland towards Methil.

Early on December 11 loud explosions were heard and eleven flares seen astern of the group. The crew went to general quarters. Six more white flares were seen astern of the convoy. Nothing else happened so the crew could only watch and wonder what was going on. On December 12, 1943 the ships arrived at Methil in the Firth of Forth, Scotland, picked up 17 merchant ships and two escort vessels and departed maintaining a speed of 7.5 knots. The next evening the *Jeremiah O'Brien* left the main convoy for the Humber River and at 2000 she arrived at Immingham dock (across the river and downstream from Hull).

Merchant seamen are allowed an advance against their wages when they arrive in a foreign port. Called a "draw" because the advance is drawn against their earnings, it gives them money for excursions ashore. The crew was given a draw against their wages the following day at the official rate of exchange of one British pound = $4.035 (American). The captain received £286 and 10 shillings from the ship's agent for this purpose, and the crew was soon off to enjoy themselves ashore.

Bill Watson: "We had to take a tram into the town. The English people were real fine. They were hospitable and we had a good time in all the ports."

Coleman Schneider: "I met a girl I fell in love with and I swear my wife looks just like her. She was a British W.A.F. (Women's Air Force). We went out for dinner one night and had

---

[2] The Minches are that area of the ocean between the west coast of Scotland and the Outer Hebrides.

pheasant under glass. We'd go out to a pub at night with some of the guys and some of the girls. I was seeing her off on the last night and several people saw us. She called me the next day and said everyone wanted to know who the British officer was she was with. I guess I sort of picked up the accent."

Cargo work went slowly because there were more ships in the harbor than there were berths and cranes to handle them. Civilians were augmented with U.S. Army personnel and the following week was spent discharging cargo and loading dunnage lumber as ballast.

Air raids were a constant threat. The bombing of Hull was seen from the ship on the first voyage. If the crew was ashore when an air raid came, they were instructed to return immediately to the ship, ready to sail on short notice. Ken Holsapple: "When they had the air raids we had to go back aboard ship." There was always the danger that an air raid might be a precursor to a German invasion.

Bill Watson: "I remember we were there Christmas Day."

Coleman Schneider: "I took out that package my mom gave me at Thanksgiving. It was up in the back of my closet. Well, I guess she never thought I'd wait until Christmas to open it. It was full of fruit and cake and things and it was all Eeeyuchh! It had all rotted. There was some clothing and other things in there that was all right though."

On Christmas Day the *O'Brien* left the Immingham docks. Anchoring just inside the submarine nets[3] in the River Humber, she awaited the formation of a convoy. On board was a cargo of sand ballast and 150 tons of dunnage lumber. Two U.S. Army security officers were aboard as passengers to the United States. Christmas dinner included turkey, mashed potatoes, peas, dressing, cake and fruit. As the ship proceeded up the coast running lights were shown at intervals during the night. On December 27 the

---

[3] Submarine nets were made of steel cable. With a mesh of about one foot between strands or links, they were suspended across harbors from buoys. At times of scheduled ship arrivals and departures a boat called a net tender would open the net by towing one end clear of the entryway. Many nets were equipped with acoustical devices to detect the approach of submarines.

ship arrived again at Methil, Scotland to await orders. Sailing shortly afterward, eight merchant ships in convoy with two escort vessels, she made a peaceful run over the top of Great Britain. On December 31, 1943 the *Jeremiah O'Brien* arrived at Loch Ewe in the morning and departed just after noon with 14 other merchant ships and one escort vessel. On New Year's Day, 1944 they joined the main convoy from the Clyde and Mersey Rivers off Oversay Light. There were now approximately 50 ships spread in a broad grid eighteen miles across returning to the United States, shepherded by seven escort vessels and one aircraft carrier, speed set at 9.5 knots. They immediately ran into heavy weather. Being in ballast, the ship rolled badly. After consulting with Chief Engineer Montgomery, Captain Southerland ordered No. 3 tank filled with sea water to dampen the effects of rolling.

The chief engineer was popular with the crew. In the close confines of a freighter, battling weather, enemy submarines, fear and boredom, the personalities of the men were magnified, some had a depressing effect while others helped lighten the tension. The chief engineer was one of the latter.

Bill Watson remembered him almost fifty years later. "Chief Montgomery. Yeah, he was short and fat, Irish. Full of jokes. Always telling jokes. He had a good sense of humor. I don't remember discussing too much personal with him, but he was a likeable guy. Probably in his forties at the time."

Coleman Schneider: "The Chief was Irish, he was basically a happy-go-lucky kind of guy, despite the incident where he thought I had something to do with the disappearance of his pet cat." Laughs.

The weather moderated slightly for the next two days. During that time aircraft, bombers and carrier-based planes were seen over the convoy at intervals. It was both reassuring to see so much protection on that side of the Atlantic and anxiety-inducing because it indicated a stepped-up level of submarine activity. Frequent changes of course were ordered by the commodore, adding to the tension. Fifty-seven ships of various tonnages and differing configurations, sailing in relatively close formation, trying to change course simultaneously while rolling in heavy seas was a real navigational challenge.

On January 5, the commodore suddenly became aware of the Mark-29 gear. At 1100 a message was received "Are you equipped with Mark-29 gear?"

The *Jeremiah O'Brien* replied "Yes."

After digesting this news for a few hours the commodore signaled at 1430, "What time would you require to stream gear?"

The *O'Brien* replied "2 hours' time at least."

This resulted in another two hours' rumination. Then at 1630 the commodore flashed, "Take station 125. I will reduce speed of convoy if necessary."

The *O'Brien* signaled back, "Are we to stream our Mark-29 gear tomorrow morning? Can not get ready before dark today. Our orders were not to stream gear. Have these orders been changed?"

The message traffic was interrupted at 1700 when a flag hoist went up indicating that enemy submarines were in the vicinity. The crew went to battle stations. Escort destroyers made wide sweeps, sonar pinging in all directions, trying to locate the elusive U-boats. Crews scanned every sector of the horizon searching for the small but tell-tale appearance of a periscope.

But the commodore was not to be diverted from his discovery. At 1710 he continued with what, to him, was the new, more interesting business at hand. "As regard the last part of your signal are you allowed to run this now and who changed the orders?"

The ship replied, "Orders from Port Director, New York, on Nov. 25. Also Nov. 26. 'Do not, repeat not, stream Mark 29 gear until further orders.' We are not to stream gear."

That gave the commodore an all-night pause for reflection. On January 6 at 0730 he signaled, "Have read message to which you referred. You are not to stream gear. Take position 125, now."

The *Jeremiah O'Brien* took position 125.

A day later the weather came up again. Seas were heavy and the convoy was forced to reduce speed. By January 9 the ship was pounding heavily. From Morgan Williams' diary, "We have swells about 30 feet high and the screw is out of the water half the time. When the screw comes out of the water the whole ship vibrates." At 1745 the same day the bridge discovered that the ship wasn't answering the helm. Fortunately for all concerned position 125 was at the back right hand corner of the convoy. By reducing speed, the *O'Brien* was able to avoid colliding with anyone else. Running quickly aft, Chief Engineer Montgomery found that an oil line connecting the telemotor to the steering engine had broken. It would take time to repair. Worse yet, it meant dropping out of the convoy to make repairs. Working frantically, they repaired the line in only an hour, but by the time the *O'Brien* resumed her course the convoy was out of sight and she had to travel through the night alone. Once again there was the fear of being a lone duck target for an enterprising Nazi submarine.

The next morning, ship #122 was contacted by blinker light. She signaled that the commodore was to her port. The seas were still heavy and with the dawn came driving rain and a low barometer. Visibility fell to .25 mile. Despite the weather, convoy position was regained but the steering gear again went out. Lagging astern for 45 minutes while repairs were made, the ship once again had to play catch-up.

Ken Holsapple: "The weather was terrible. The ship rolled and pitched quite a bit. We had a line we had to hold on to to get across the deck. And it was so cold. We had masks on our faces to protect against the cold, you could only see your eyes. It was really cold, miserably cold up that way."

The miserable weather continued and the pounding on the ships took its toll. The morning of January 11 found three ships showing breakdown lights and dropping astern of the convoy. The seas were too rough to maintain speed without damaging the ship's hull and it became increasingly difficult for the *O'Brien* to maintain steerageway, not because of mechanical problems, but because of the weather. As dawn broke, she had once again lost the other ships. That afternoon four vessels were sighted, two ahead and two astern. Apparently the convoy was scattered all over the ocean. The *O'Brien* plowed on relentlessly, shuddering as her bow plummeted into wave after wave, spray and saltwater making her decks and superstructure glisten and shine in the sun.

The following afternoon one of the escort vessels came into view, giving a course to steer to find the rest of the convoy and by sunset the ship was once more in her assigned position. But the weather was unremitting and the *O'Brien* soon began to lag astern again because of the heavy head seas and strong winds. After another day of miserable pounding, the commodore flashed a welcome signal, "Your destination is St. John's, New Brunswick." This was happy news. It meant the voyage was almost over. Just to assert herself and remind the captain not to become too complacent, however, the *O'Brien's* steering engine acted up briefly again that evening.

On January 15, the *Jeremiah O'Brien*, with seven other ships and one escort vessel, left the main convoy as the escort vessel signaled, "Proceed unescorted to St. John, N.B." Departing from the Halifax-bound ships, the *O'Brien's* group found themselves in a blinding snowstorm. Then disaster struck. In the early morning of January 16 an SOS was received. "Collision - ship in sinking condition."

From 0200 to 0900 a series of radio signals were received from the distressed ship. After an initial hesitation the *O'Brien* broke radio silence and transmitted messages so that the sinking ship could take bearings on them. At 0900 the scene of the collision came into view. Two ships and one escort vessel were sighted, the escort standing by a British vessel in distress whose bow was caved in and who had a pronounced list. The *Jeremiah O'Brien* stood by the *George Westinghouse*, a U.S. Liberty Ship, which had a full load of cargo and was taking on water badly. She had been hit in number 1 hold and was listing badly by the bow. That afternoon the *Westinghouse* was taken in tow by a Canadian corvette and the *O'Brien* was released from standing by.

The trials and travails of ships on the North Atlantic supply runs were not unique. The route to Europe via Nova Scotia was by no means the only "highway" on the ocean. Other ships and convoys went to the North African ports of the Mediterranean and above the Arctic Circle to Murmansk. Convoys meant safety and protection. They were the state-of-the-art when it came to getting supplies across the oceans. Supplies to support military and civilian operations were not the only cargo. Hal Rubin recalled his Liberty ship convoy experiences in an article for Oceans magazine in 1979.

"I can testify that riding one [a Liberty ship] in no way resembled a pleasure cruise. Most of the bomber crews in my B-17 group flew their planes to the combat zone, but extra crews and all of the ground personnel sailed on Liberty ships. One of the holds on the ship that carried my squadron was jammed with about 500 men, stacked up in tiers of bunks. The other holds carried aerial bombs and assorted munitions. We boarded at a port of embarkation in Virginia on a gray February afternoon in 1944, but our convoy did not leave until the next day.

"Seasickness was a serious problem for the hundreds of servicemen locked below decks, many of whom had never before seen the ocean. During our month-long voyage we encountered frequent heavy storms. In the midst of one of the worst blows, a huge tub of butterscotch pudding overturned in the galley. The cook and several of his helpers lost their footing in the gelatinous mass, and were being thrown back and forth as the ship rolled and pitched. We barely saved them from being hammered into pulp.

"One enlisted man became seasick within minutes of boarding; he remained that way for the next thirty days. We carried him ashore in Naples more dead than alive. He swore he would never set foot on another ship, even if it meant spending the rest of his life in Europe."

Hal Rubin gives us a glimpse of daily life on the North Atlantic run. "Feeding several hundred men from a galley designed for forty, meant that the passengers -- those who were well enough to spend several hours daily in a chow line -- subsisted mainly on sandwiches and stew. Water for bathing was rationed and a quick, once-a-week shower was a luxury. In bad weather the troops were restricted to their bunks or to a few open spots in the overcrowded hold. On infrequent calm days we were allowed on deck in small groups for exercise and a breath of fresh air. During one smooth spell we staged some boxing matches, with a wooden hatch cover as the ring. Otherwise, the tedium was lifted only by floating crap and card games. The available pocketbooks were worn out long before we reached port."

The scale of the convoy operations was always impressive.

"A few times I wandered up to the captain's bridge. From there it was possible to sense the drama of a sixty-ship convoy moving through hazardous waters. Destroyers raced back and forth searching for evidence of enemy submarines. As we approached Europe, there was added danger from enemy aircraft. At least twice during the crossing our Navy escorts tossed depth charges at real or imaginary pursuers.

"It was no imaginary attack that caused the convoy to suddenly reverse direction after we had entered the Straits of Gibraltar. There we encountered a convoy heading in the opposite direction. For an hour, collision was a far greater threat than enemy torpedoes. Later we learned that when the antisubmarine net at the mouth of the Straits had been raised to admit our convoy, some German submarines also sneaked in and began to play havoc with the tail-enders. Hit and sinking, a Liberty ship radioed the convoy commander for instructions. 'Africa, turn right,' was the terse reply."

As dangerous and miserable as the North Atlantic Run was, it was a "pleasure cruise" compared to the 'Murmansk Run.' Russia was gasping for her life, isolated behind German lines, and her people were dying in the millions from cold, hunger, war and disease. Supporting the Russians and helping them to survive and keep the "Second Front" open was a critical concern of the Allies -- almost an overriding preoccupation. Whatever the cost, Russia had to be kept alive to fight Hitler's armies and keep them pinned on the eastern front. In so doing, the Allies forced Hitler to violate one of the oldest and most basic of military maxims: Never fight a war on two fronts.

Russia's lifeline was one supply route over the top of the world -- the storied, dreaded "Murmansk Run." Every seaman who survived the trips ever after carried the tales as a talisman of

This photo, taken north of Norway, shows a ship of the ill-fated convoy PQ-17 being torpedoed by a German U-boat. Note the barrage balloon. The photo was taken from the submarine that fired the torpedo. Credit U.S. Naval Historical Center

maritime valor. And justifiably so, for the Murmansk Run was the icy parallel to hell.

Hal Rubin: "Throughout the war, the roughest run was to Murmansk, Russia, in the high latitudes north of Norway. In winter, drift ice slowed ships down to two or three knots, and the Liberty ships were bombed, strafed, and torpedoed without mercy. JU-88's and Heinkels cruised overhead, striking quickly. When the bombs missed, they raised tall white mushrooms. When a bomb found its mark, the ship disappeared into orange and black smoke. Escort vessels nosed around abandoned boats and wreckage, picking up survivors. The remaining ships closed up formation and plowed on."

A first-hand account of one Murmansk run comes from James O. Runckle on the *George Weems:*

"After a night at anchor, 20 of us formed up again and with six small escorts of corvettes and one destroyer headed North. The date was about December 18th, and daylight lasted only about 3 to 4 hours as we went around Norway's North Cape, and most of that was twilight. The ships were either American or British style Liberty ships and the escort was all British or Canadian. Each evening as we approached farthest North we noted a blinker on the Northwestern horizon. About 12 hours out of Murmansk there were depth bombs. Up until this time the ships complement was getting pretty tense. Life preservers were worn or carried constantly. The "Old Man" especially was having a hard time, sleeping in the wheelhouse and having all his meals brought up. It had been just a year previous that a convoy had been decimated with a lot of losses by submarine and aircraft attack, and convoys before that had also really suffered, so the tenseness was pretty well justified.

"The depth bombs were perhaps a false alarm for there was no note of any action or loss. The next morning we awoke steaming alone, along a frozen white coastline with no trees or shrubs in view. We were entering the White Sea. Floating sea ice abounded..."

Convoy PQ 17 sailed from Iceland in June 1942 with 33 merchant ships, four cruisers, two submarines, two battleships, and a carrier. Then the British pulled all of the escorts and ordered the convoy to continue alone. Subjected to massive air attacks and the threat of assault by enemy battleships, the convoy scattered with only 11 ships of the 42 finally reaching Russia.

Convoy PQ 18 fared slightly better. Consisting of 40 merchant ships, 29 destroyers, a heavy cruiser, an escort carrier and a screen of patrolling submarines, it arrived at Murmansk in September of 1942 with a loss of 13 merchant ships. One of those to make it was the *Patrick Henry,* the first Liberty launched.

Richard Braithwaite's experiences on the Liberty *Richard Bland* were typical of the run. His notes were transcribed a few months after the event.

"... left Archangel, Russia, in the early part of March, 1943; ... torpedoed the first time on the 5th day of March 1943; from then until the 10th day of March, 1943, the ship was kept afloat and struggled on; ... at 3:43 P.M. on the 10th of March, 1943, the ship was torpedoed a second time which stopped the engines and threw the rafts overboard; ... the weather was rotten; the seas were rough and the gale winds were blowing with air temperature of 22 degrees F and water temperature of 28 degrees F; ... soon afterwards two lifeboats were lost leaving sixty-one men and only two more lifeboats, which meant terrific overcrowding; ... at 6:38 P.M. on March 10, 1943, the final torpedo broke the ship in half, killing some men in the explosion. ... (Braithwaite) succeeded in launching his lifeboat and carried twenty-seven men safely through the night until rescued, but the other boat was swamped in launching and to the best of his knowledge went down with the ship. The deck cadets, the captain, five other officers and twenty-seven crewmen were missing.

"...the destroyer which rescued his lifeboat full of men searched for two days at the scene of the sinking,--searching back and forth; ... another destroyer was also present; ... the destroyer then had to leave so as to search for the survivors of another ship sunk under similar conditions."

Ninety-seven ships in all were sunk on the runs to Murmansk. But the Allies accomplished their objective, although at a fearful price -- Russia's perseverance on the Eastern Front exacted a heavy, and ultimately fatal, toll on Nazi Germany's armies.

On January 17, 1944 at 0200, the *Jeremiah O'Brien* arrived at the Pilot Station for St. John's Harbor and that afternoon the ship was docked at Pier 5, West St. John.

Coleman Schneider: "In St. John's the tidal range is extreme. So I went ashore and had to walk down a steep gangway. And because of the tides when I came back to the ship I again had to walk down a steep gangway."

Seaman First Class Jerome Shaw: "The biggest surprise I had was the tides. They were twenty-four feet or better. When we was tied up at the dock we had to walk down to get off and then we came back and the ship was gone! We thought they had sailed without us. But the tide was so great the ship had just dropped down where we couldn't see it. We had to go down the gangway to get on again."

As usual, the captain issued a draw to the crew, at the official rate of exchange $1.00 (Canadian) = $.909 (American) and as usual some of the crew celebrated too much. On January 19, a radioman third class was brought aboard by the Canadian Shore Patrol. He had been admitted to St. James Military Hospital. His story was that he had been drinking and apparently slipped on the icy streets. In the process of drinking or slipping or both he reported the loss of $45 cash, his identification card, his Partial pay card, and a Bulova wristwatch. The following day a radioman second class was brought aboard by the Shore Patrol, reporting he had been in the brig for 3 hours.

But these were exceptions. Most of the crew didn't get into trouble but passed the time the way sailors do everywhere, drinking, chasing girls, going to movies, having a quiet dinner ashore or just walking the streets, making an occasional purchase of books, magazines or candy.

The remainder of the month was spent loading a cargo of grain, explosives and general cargo.

On January 20, Captain Alfonse Adolph De Smedt took command of the *S.S. Jeremiah O'Brien*, relieving Captain O. Southerland, and Lieutenant Allen R. Memhard, Jr. relieved Ensign Foote as the Officer in Charge of the Armed Guard on January 27.

Ken Holsapple remembered Ensign Foote: "The officer in charge was a nice guy. I liked him. With his help I made gunner's mate third class on the third voyage."

Lieutenant Memhard quickly earned the respect of his crew. Years later, Daniel Bandy, Armed Guard Coxswain, remembered the new officer: "Lt. Memhard was one of the nicest Navy officers that I ever sailed with."

Captain De Smedt, on the other hand, was a dramatic change from the soft-spoken Captain Southerland.

Coleman Schneider: "Captain De Smedt. He was a tall guy, about five-ten I guess, tall with a prominent slim straight nose.

Sea water froze on the main deck. Ice was so thick you couldn't get your hands around the railings.   Credit Coleman Schneider

The O'Brien *arrived at St. John's looking like an ice palace. The ice was so thick she was in danger of capsizing. Credit Coleman Schneider*

He was a strict guy. All of a sudden we were only allowed to enter the lounge with a hat and jacket. Stern guy."

Normally, deck officers wore khakis and engine officers might wear coveralls, a boiler suit or khakis. Cadets were expected to wear uniforms but usually adopted the style of dress set by the ship they were on. Captain De Smedt's dictum may or may not have carried over to the other officers. The cadets, however, being mere students and unprotected by a union, would be the first to come under the captain's fierce gaze. Apparently Captain De Smedt was also more of a disciplinarian than Captain Southerland. On January 31, the new commanding officer of the Armed Guard mustered his crew and informed them that weekly inspection would now be a formal one conducted by the master of the ship and himself. He also stressed that "Attention" was to be sung out on entering crew's quarters and that any symptoms of a venereal disease were to be reported to him immediately. The crew was suitably impressed for fifteen minutes later one of the seamen first class reported that he had been exposed to a reputedly infected woman. He was given six sulfa tablets and instructed to take two more every six hours.

The Armed Guard commanding officer received new instructions on aiming the guns, based on recent experiences from other ships, and passed them along to his crew at their daily muster: at night the range would be set to 800 yards and during the day a range of 2000 yards would be used for the 3"-50's. In addition, if torpedoed at night, convoy position permitting, the 3"-50's were to open fire in the direction from which the torpedo came.

Just before sailing on February 1, 1944, Albert Haas replaced Tom Ender as purser. The *Jeremiah O'Brien* left St. John's, bound for the convoy rendezvous at Halifax with a full load of grain, general cargo and explosives. The weather was freezing-cold with snow and biting wind. Once again the forward lookouts were moved to the flying bridge and later in the day the aft lookouts were also put on the flying bridge because of the weather. Morgan Williams' diary: "Was cold all day, so we didn't do any work. Sea is coming over and freezing on everything."

Weather was the driving force on the voyage. Every plan and action -- convoy instructions, the shipboard schedules, the watches and practices, the daily routines -- all revolved around the weather. Fifty years later, the weather stories were still dominant in the mariners' recollections.

Coleman Schneider: "Going from St. John's to Halifax, it was completely fogged in. So to get the ship's position they kept calling shore stations to get a radio fix. The shore stations would take bearings and sent us our position and that was the only way they could get in."

Ken Holsapple: "It was so cold we stood 15 minutes on 15 minutes off. They had a line you had to hold on to to go from

It took hours to chop all the ice off. Here two of the gunners work at it with long-handled deck scrapers. A major effort was needed to just stand upright on the slippery decks. Credit Coleman Schneider

one place to another. Sometimes you couldn't stand watch on the bow. Sometimes you couldn't see one ship from the other. And sometimes they'd come close to you and you could almost read the names on the ship. Sometimes the weather was so bad you only made four miles during the day."

Coleman Schneider: "The water temperature was 28 degrees and the weather was not that great. We were taking spray all the way over the stack. When we pulled into Halifax we had six inches of solid ice on the foredeck."

Dan Bandy: "One of the things I remember so clearly going into Halifax was all the ice. Ice everywhere. That ice was six inches thick all right and thicker than that in some places. Well, conditions all the way across was perfect for that ice to build up. The standing rigging was full of ice. It was more than six inches thick in places. There was no question of anyone going out on deck. For a while it didn't look like the old ship was going to make it. The ship was so heavily coated with ice that people were concerned about it capsizing or not making port. There was just an unbelievable amount of ice on that trip. She must have been a well built old Liberty to survive that."

Arriving in Halifax on February 3 the *O'Brien* looked like a fairy-tale ice palace. The anchor was dropped and the crew put to work removing ice. It wasn't an easy task. Slipping and sliding across the deck, there was nothing to hold on to. The gunwales and rails were so thick with ice the men couldn't get their gloved hands around them to hold on. The Armed Guard spent the afternoon breaking ice off the guns and cleaning the forward guns which had received the brunt of the weather.

Jerome Shaw: "We had already been loaded and had this ice and stuff and cargo tied down on deck, airplanes. That's why we were chopping this ice. The water was up to deck level. Normally the merchant crew did that, but this was so bad even the gun crew assisted. We used axes, hammers, anything to get it off."

Dan Bandy: "We had to clear the ice first thing. I went up to one of the twenty millimeters. It had a canvas cover on it. And the ice was so thick I had to break it off with an ax, just a big mound of ice. But when I got the ice off and took the cover loose, the gun was all ready. In perfect condition, ready to fire."

Coleman Schneider: "When we went into Halifax on Voyage 3 we were anchored and this boat came alongside. It was about 40 foot long and they called me to help them out. It was from the Canadian Red Cross and they came alongside and gave us turtleneck sweaters, heavy socks, and scarves and toilet articles. Mittens, gloves all kinds of cold weather gear, enough for the whole crew."

The following day the Mark-29 gear was removed from the deck of the ship. The veterans in the crew watched with mixed feelings. The gear had been a royal pain to stream and retrieve, required constant maintenance, had caused the *Jeremiah O'Brien* to get a reputation as a slowpoke and never seemed to work properly. On the other hand, the fact that it was on board had saved the *O'Brien* from being converted into a hospital ship.

The next day, just as when she was first launched, the ship weighed anchor and sailed across the degaussing range, realigning her polarity against magnetic mines for the voyage to come. This prevented the ship's magnetic field from reacting with the mines' magnetism, causing the mine to explode. Sailing on February 7, the harbor's submarine nets were towed out of the way and the *O'Brien* cleared the entrance at 1000. She was in a convoy of 65 ships, six corvettes, 12 destroyers and three aircraft carriers.

On February 8 each member of the Armed Guard crew was given another present, thanks to the Canadian Red Cross -- six pounds of chocolate and five packages of chewing gum. The Armed Guard had perhaps the hardest, most uncomfortable duty aboard the *Jeremiah O'Brien* and no one begrudged them the gift.

As always in an outward-bound convoy, a great deal of time was spent in practice and preparation. On February 9, on instructions from the convoy commodore, the master of the *O'Brien* rang the general alarm to indicate the convoy was going to have target practice. By the end of the afternoon all but six columns of ships had fired. The following day the gun crew fired six rounds of common ammunition from the after 3"-50. Their target was the windward edge of a smoke float dropped by one of the escorts. Lieutenant Memhard proudly recorded in his log: "Opening range 3000, closing 3800. 5 of 6 shots right on target, 6th being slightly off in deflection. Good shooting; favorable comments from master and other ship's officers. Gun OK."

Jerome Shaw: "Red flags used to go up all over the convoy for practice. Some times we'd send balloons up, helium filled. We'd set the fuzes to go off at a certain range."

The convoy sailed on, gunnery practice and watches alternating with hours off spent reading, writing letters, telling war stories and, of course, playing poker.

On February 15 a flag hoist was raised warning of an enemy submarine in the vicinity. Some of the crew came on deck to watch. Two of the carriers and several escorts were seen congregating about six miles broad off the port bow (the *O'Brien's* position was #11) and three planes were observed covering the area between the carriers. Depth charges were seen by the crew but not heard or felt. At dusk, the escorts left the area and one carrier returned to its convoy position.

As always, when the convoy drew closer to England the watchfulness increased and tension levels grew high. Jerome Shaw: "We used to start out four [hours] on and eight off. Then as we got closer to Europe it was four and four [also referred to as "watch and watch."]."

On February 17, a warning was received that aircraft were approaching, possibly enemy. The escorts closed around the convoy for protection. Five planes from convoy carriers went up searching and Condition II was set until general quarters was called. All the 20 mm's were kept cocked and loaded. During the night more planes flew around the convoy and the jittery crew braced for an attack. None came and it was decided they must be from the convoy carriers which routinely sent up planes on patrol. The following day English bombers flew overhead, covering the group at intervals. This time there was no doubt. The crew could clearly see the markings and they welcomed the sight.

Through all this the poker games continued. Bill Watson: "The two mates, Pellegrino and Morgan, took me for about two grand in cards on there. We played every night. Nothing big, but it accumulated. They were a little better than I was, that's all." Although poker was king, other card games such as cribbage and pinochle went on during off hours. Those who didn't play cards passed the time reading, telling stories, writing letters or simply stared thoughtfully out to sea.

On February 19, at 1050, three loud explosions were heard, close enough to shake the ship. The weather was foggy and there was no way to know what they signified. Although by now experience should have taught them that communication and information was not to be expected, the speculation and rampant rumors never ceased. Each explosion, every maneuver of the escorts, every course change started a fresh wave of conjecture as to what was happening. No one questioned the importance of maintaining radio silence but being "kept in the dark" was a constant source of grousing among the crews.

John Crosby, third mate on the *Jeremiah O'Brien* on voyage #6 had this to say about North Atlantic convoys: "All the radio traffic was incoming. We could never send a message, ever. Messages from the commodore would be by code flag and semaphore flags. If a ship was out of control in a convoy, they would put up a couple of red lights. That was havoc when you'd see that and try to avoid a collision. Between the U-boats and the bad weather and the fog and the ships out of control, it was horrible. You never knew what happened, you never knew anything. The only thing you could do was assume and maybe talk to somebody on the other ships when you got into port."

The perspective from the engine room was even worse than up on deck. At least the deck crew could sometimes see what was happening. Bill Watson: "You're closed up and you're below water and every time an explosion or depth charge goes off outside, the hull of the ship acts like the skin of a drum. It just vibrates and magnifies the sound and scares the hell out of you, especially the first few times it happens. Eventually you just get so you wait for it to get over with."

Two hours later the fog lifted a little and, to their horror, the crew saw two floating mines only 1500 yards away. Attempting to explode the mines, one of the escorts dropped eight depth

Cadet Coleman 'Coke' Schneider standing anchor watch awaiting a berth in Edinburgh, Scotland. Credit Coleman Schneider

charges at the same time signalling the nearby ships to disregard its actions. The ships in the immediate vicinity, for once knowing the cause, could "disregard" the explosions. But for the rest of the convoy, the depth charges were just another source of concern, tension and unanswered questions.

In the evening the *O'Brien* and her sisters arrived at Oban, on Scotland's west coast in the Firth of Lorne, anchored overnight, then proceeded around the northern tip of Scotland to Methil, on Britain's east coast, where they arrived in the morning of February 23. At 1315 that afternoon the ship took arrival at Leith (now part of greater Edinburgh). With the aid of Capt. W. Lyle, a harbor pilot, they tied up to the East End of the Imperial Dock. The crew eagerly prepared for shore leave, took their "draws" and went out on the town.

Rowdiness, fights and drunken episodes were not the only concerns when crews went ashore. Venereal disease was a serious problem. The Armed Guard crew was mustered at 1000 on February 27 and warned that each man going on liberty was to have sani-tubes and safeties (condoms) and, further, that the gangway watch was to check each man going ashore to be sure he had them. Lieutenant Memhard also noted that each man was to be checked for exposure when he returned on board. Just how this was to be accomplished isn't stated in the Armed Guard Log. The merchant crew was left to their own devices.

Bill Watson: "In Edinburgh we had a hell of a good time. It was really a lovely place up in Scotland, beautiful country."

Coleman Schneider: "I hung out mainly with the engine cadet. Leith was quiet. Going to the pubs was about the only thing to do."

Jerome Shaw: "We were in Edinburgh and it was a beautiful place. Nicest place I ever was. And the Scottish people were even nicer than the English. They had a club up there we were invited to, and we enjoyed it."

On March 2 the lieutenant held mast, the traditional Naval Board convened to hear reports of violations of regulations and to "award" punishment. A seaman first class was seen the previous evening coming aboard with several bottles of beer, having first left the ship without permission. The sailor was given a warning, fifty hours' extra duty and restricted to the ship. This was the only incident logged -- not too bad a record for a Naval Armed Guard ashore in wartime. In general, however, the merchant and Naval crews of the *Jeremiah O'Brien* were not given to bad behavior ashore. The logs record some incidents of drinking, unruly behavior, some fights, but,only to a relatively minor degree.

Although much of the time ashore in Edinburgh was spent visiting pubs, the deck cadet did manage to have this photo taken in native costume. Credit Coleman Schneider

The *O'Brien's* crews were professionals, deeply concerned with the serious business of the war -- supplying the Allies, being ever alert -- carrying a strong feeling of patriotism and responsibility. As many of them said in later years, "We just wanted to get the job done."

After unloading, the ship sailed in ballast from Leith on March 5, anchored in Leith Roads overnight, and proceeded to Methil where she arrived at 1030 the following morning. That afternoon the *O'Brien* departed Methil in a convoy of 11 vessels, arrived at Loch Ewe just before midnight the following day and a few hours later departed to join an ocean convoy home. Continuing standard convoy procedures the starboard 20 mm guns were practice-fired during the following day, shooting 190 rounds of ammunition. All the guns worked properly.

The submarine menace never abated. On March 11 the convoy commodore signaled, "Submarines have been sighted and one sunk in area we are approaching. Shore based aircraft on anti-sub patrol may be seen. Keep sharp lookout and do utmost to make as little smoke as possible."

At 1800 on March 10 a black pennant, signifying contact with a submarine, went up on one of the escort ships and two depth charges were dropped. Condition I was set.

Bill Watson: "Oh yeah. The escorts would go through flying the black pennant and they would be throwing depth charges right and left. And when those things went off they'd lift you about two feet off the deck in the engine room and you'd land on your fanny on the deck plates. You never knew if it was you that got hit or what. After a while you got used to it."

On March 13 one of the escorts just ahead of the convoy hoisted a black pennant. Where normally this meant a submarine was sighted, in this case no depth charges were dropped. It indicated the escort was having target practice. Then a hoist was raised for fog buoys to be tested.

Cadet Coleman Schneider: "In bad weather when ships in convoy lost sight of the ships in front or back of them, they would put over the stern a buoy which was easily sighted by the ship astern. As it was drawn forward, the buoy, because of its design,

From left to right, gunners Serra, Smedley and Shaw. Taken just after arrival in New York. Credit Jerome Shaw

March 27, 1944. Gunners Serra and Shaw aboard the O'Brien in New York harbor. Credit Jerome Shaw

would cause a spout of water to shoot upward which was easily seen by the forward lookout on the ship astern." Occasionally, anxious lookouts mistook the fog buoy's plume of water for that thrown up by a submarine's periscope.

On March 14 the message was received: "From Commodore. *Prince Rupert,* one of our escort vessels, yesterday sank a sub and picked up a few survivors." The crew was pleased to finally be getting some information.

As the *O'Brien* neared the East Coast her built-in degaussing was turned on. The convoy was slowed to 6 knots and arrived at New York on the 22nd. It had been a long, cold, bitter voyage, crossing the Atlantic twice in each direction and the crew were glad to be home, yet the sense of patriotism that pervaded the country was also aboard ship.

Armed Guard Coxswain Bandy on the left, gunners Serra in the middle and Shaw on the right.   Credit Jerome Shaw   *Jerome Shaw, armed, at his gun and ready to do battle. Taken in New York City, March 27, 1944. Credit Jerome Shaw*

Bill Watson: "I didn't care about getting off. In fact I made another trip. We all had a job to do and just did it. And regardless of the odds against us we had a good time. We were lucky. Better than some guy laying in the mud. At least we had three squares a day and a warm bed."

Coleman Schneider: "Well, there was a book by Studs Terkel called, 'The Good War.' And that's what it was for me. We never got bombed or torpedoed or shot at. I had a lot of fun. Of course I had to get off and go back to Kings Point."

Cadet Schneider then completed an additional nine months of advanced training which allowed him to graduate with a third mate's license, a commission as an ensign in the Naval Reserve and a commission as an ensign in the U.S. Maritime Service. He would also be issued a complete officer's uniform allowance.

Average daily expense of consumable stores for this trip by department were: Deck, $2.58, Engine, $4.20 and Steward, $3.12.

9

PRELUDE TO AN INVASION

V oyage 3 ended at midnight on March 24, 1944; Voyage 4 began one minute later. The *Jeremiah O'Brien* was at the Bethlehem Steel Shipyard, Pier 57 in Brooklyn. According to Captain De Smedt's voyage letter, "The bottom was painted, strainers removed and cleaned, and the hull and screw inspected and found to be in good condition."

Just across Long Island from Brooklyn, at Great Neck, stands the United States Merchant Marine Academy at Kings Point, at the time the newest federal service academy. The shipbuilding industry had risen magnificently to the challenge of building ships faster than they could be sunk and merchant vessels were rolling down the ways on both coasts. As many as three ships a day were being launched with an output that would total more than 2,700 Libertys and more than 500 Victorys. All those ships needed officers and the function of the new academy was the training of those officers. The Merchant Marine Academy at Kings Point was established in the same manner as the earlier federal academies at West Point (Army), Annapolis, Maryland (Navy) and New London, Connecticut (Coast Guard), drawing its student body from the nation through nominations by U.S. Senators and Representatives. It required a rigorous course of study including cargo stowage, ship handling, navigation, marine engineering, chemistry and physics and culminated in a license as a merchant marine officer. But during the war its student body did not have the luxury of four years to complete the course. Mirroring the urgency to get the job done in the shipyards, the four-year course was compressed into eighteen months (3 months of preliminary studies, 6 months at sea and 9 months of advanced training) combining academia with military discipline and producing more than a thousand merchant marine officers every six months (in some periods, two thousand). Part of the training included sailing as a cadet on board active merchant ships.[1]

Tom McGeehan was one of the newly-assigned deck cadets from Kings Point. "I was assigned as cadet in March of 1944. I picked her up in Brooklyn and after a few days we shifted to Staten Island. It was my first Liberty. I was on the tanker *Delaware* for Texaco before that. I liked the *O'Brien*. She was homely and small compared to the tanker, but I liked my quarters on there. They were comfortable."

Henry Kusel was the other deck cadet. "I had a job in the South Portland shipyards. I was building these ships so I was interested because I was working on them. There was a strong feeling of patriotism. So when I heard they had a hard time to find the men to man these ships and I learned about Kings Point, I signed up. I didn't want to go in the Army. I had some friends who went in the Army. They were the same age as I was and they didn't go over for a year or more until they were trained. I was over there a month and a half later."

Captain A.A. De Smedt was an enigma to the new cadets. Tom McGeehan recalled, "Well, I didn't have much to do with the captain. I remember Captain de Smedt as being very elegant

---

[1] Because of the requirement to sail in the merchant marine as part of their education, Kings Point cadets are the only students from federal academies to face battle as part of their training. The Kings Point battle standard lists 142 cadets lost at sea in World War II.

and arrogant. If I met him on the ship's ladder and I was going up and he was going down, I had to back down the ladder, to let him pass. He would have walked right over me. He didn't say hello or good-by. But, of course, I was only the cadet and he was the ship's master."

Henry Kusel shared his feelings: "The captain was not too sociable with cadets. He didn't have much to do with us and I didn't have too much to say about him."

Shifting from the shipyard to Grace Line's pier in New York on March 29, the ship loaded stores and fuel and trimmed her ballast. The *Jeremiah O'Brien* was given deck and engine stores for six months and four months' worth of commissary stores. At the same time fifteen hundred tons of ballast previously loaded in Great Britain was trimmed and leveled off in the lower holds: 350 tons in No. 2, 550 tons in No. 3 and 600 tons in No. 4. A three-inch plank floor was laid atop the ballast on which to stow cargo.

Francis Erdman joined the ship in New York as an oiler. "The *O'Brien* was almost loaded. We left very soon after I got aboard. A couple of days I guess. I kind of liked her from the start. For one thing she was only eight months old."

On April 1 deep tanks #1 and #2 were loaded with a cargo of 3952 barrels of diesel oil weighing 515 long tons. The consignee was the Petroleum Division of the British Ministry of Fuel and Power. April 4 found the ship loading army cargo at Pier 16 on Staten Island. As the ship neared completion of her loading, a convoy conference was called. The *Jeremiah O'Brien* was assigned to Task Unit W-1, HXF 287 consisting of eighty-one ships.[2] Her position was #132 (column 13, row 2).

Robert Milby, Radio Operator: "The radio operator at the beginning of the trip was a little bit of a celebrity. Before you left, they had convoy meetings. And the captain and the armed

[2] Convoys were assigned prefixes and numbers according to their routing. HXF indicated a convoy originating in Halifax (HF) bound for England (X). The number indicated it was the 287th convoy to emanate from Halifax since the war started. Other prefixes were OA (outbound from the Thames or east coast of England), OB or ON (outbound from Liverpool or the west coast of England), HX or KJ (inbound from Halifax), OG (outbound from Gibraltar), HG (homebound for Gibraltar) and SL (Sierra Leone).

guard officer and the radio officer would go to these meetings. Three people from every ship and the Navy would conduct this meeting, telling us different things about the upcoming convoy, but not where we was going. So we'd go back to the ship and all the guys wanted to know where we were going. So I'd always tell them Murmansk." He laughs.

"They'd give us stuff that wasn't to be opened until we were out at sea. And then when we were out at sea, we stood guard, or watch, and if a message came to us it was coded. The captain had the code book and either he or I would decode it."

As the war continued, the orders became more stringent. Lieutenant Memhard returned from the conference with new instructions for his crew: in the future, any airplanes between 36 degrees west longitude and 7 degrees west longitude should be regarded as suspicious. East of 7 degrees west longitude all aircraft should be regarded as enemy. They were to open fire on any unidentified plane approaching within 1500 yards of the ship regardless of where it was encountered.

At 1330 that afternoon the ship's degaussing was turned on. The degaussing system consisted of a circuit of copper wiring mounted throughout the ship. When energized it had the effect of demagnetizing the hull so that magnetic mines would not be attracted to it. This was in addition to the practice of running the ship through a degaussing range in some ports. The heavily-mined coastal waters of the United States could be as treacherous as those of Europe.

Tom McGeehan: "I remember we took a lot of deck cargo and had to build catwalks across the fore and after decks. We were below our Plimsoll marks when we sailed."

Plimsoll marks are the lines on the side of a ship that indicate the maximum depth to which she can be legally loaded in peacetime. The marks are calculated according to prevailing weather conditions and whether the ship is loaded in salt or fresh water. They also vary from trade to trade and ship to ship, but generally the highest mark, indicating the greatest load, will be marked "TF" for tropical fresh water. Below it may be "F" for fresh water, "T" for tropical below that, followed by "S" for salt water and "W" for winter. The lowest mark, indicating the lightest load, is "WNA": "winter, North Atlantic." During World War II Plimsoll marks were frequently ignored.

Tom McGeehan: "We left April 12, 1944, in a convoy of what seemed like a hundred ships. The weather was heavy for the first seventy-two hours."

Robert Milby: "To me one of the scary things was the fog. We were going out in the ocean in fog. You couldn't see anything. The way they kept the ships in line, the ships were periodically blowing on their whistle, whistling their position, their convoy position."

For the first few days, the voyage was relatively quiet. The merchant crew settled into a seagoing routine of four hours on watch and eight hours off -- 12 to 4, 4 to 8 and 8 to 12. Breakfast was served from 0730 to 0830 in the morning to catch those going on and coming off watch. Lunch was served from 1130 to 1230 for the same reason. Dinner would run from 1700 to 1800 with a sailor, officer and black gang[3] member called out to relieve the watchstanders so they could eat supper. The Armed Guard easily fell into their routine of Condition I and Condition III, day and night, respectively. The Mark-29 hydrophone listening device, the only part of the maligned gear remaining on board, was streamed and put into operation.

Tom McGeehan: "The bosun was a rough, tough character but he was good to me. I learned a lot from him. He had me working on these fenders made out of manila line most of the way across. I completed two of them.

"I wanted to show them that Kings Pointers were afraid of nothing. So when he wanted to send someone aloft to work on the mast, I'd go up. A lot of the regular seamen were afraid to do that."

Although the long-anticipated assault on the European continent was cloaked in deepest secrecy, it was becoming increasingly obvious that it was imminent. The convoys from America and

---

[3] The unlicensed engine department crew is normally referred to as the "black gang." This comes from the days when ships' engines were coal-fired and the crew traditionally came off watch covered with soot and coal dust.

Canada had been delivering supplies to England in a never-ending stream and British ports and warehouses were overflowing with millions of tons of food, medicines, ammunition, and vehicles of all types including tanks, half-tracks, armored cars, trucks, jeeps and even thousands of railroad locomotives and tanker and freight cars. The level of alertness was raised, discipline and order were stepped up and enforced, practices and precautions against gas and other hazards were increased and became part of the routine. Helmets and gas masks were distributed to the Navy crew and the anticipation of the impending campaign grew daily.

On April 16 the *O'Brien's* merchant crew held a meeting. There was a great deal of discussion and conjecture as to what lay ahead and what could be done to ensure the safety of the ship. Sixteen men volunteered for gun stations to back up the Navy Armed Guard and watchfulness increased. A muster of the Armed Guard crew was also held to discuss how to prepare for the expected escalation of the war. The two leading petty officers were given morphine syrettes to sew into their lifejackets for use in emergency, another indication of the mounting danger.

A few days later another meeting was held and both the ship's crew and the Armed Guard crew were given instruction on the effects of liquid and spray mustard gas. This was the first of many meetings regarding precautions against a gas attack, how to wear the protective clothing they had been issued and other information.

On April 19 a series of explosions, presumably depth charges, were heard on the amplifier for the Mark-29 hydrophone. The ship's position was approximately 46° 40' North, 39° 30' West Longitude. As always, the crew had no way of knowing what the explosions signified -- torpedoes, mines, depth charges -- but training practices intensified. The following day, on instructions from the convoy commodore, the entire convoy test-fired its anti-aircraft guns. The *Jeremiah O'Brien* shot 6 rounds of AA, Mark 23, with a fuze setting 2 seconds[4] from each of its bow and stern

---

[4] Fuzes are set so that the projectile isn't armed until it's a safe distance away from the ship. In this case, two seconds would put the shell several hundred yards out before it became armed and could explode.

3"-50's. But even practice had its dangers. The fifth round shot
from the bow gun misfired. In the process of loading the shell
into the breech of the gun, the projectile became separated from
the powder casing. When triggered, rather than going out the end,
the projectile lodged itself in the gun's bore. Fortunately, the
crew was well-drilled. The first loader immediately called
"Silence" and threw the powder case overboard. The gun captain
closed the breech and used a short case (a special shell designed
for this purpose) to fire out the lodged projectile. To everyone's
great relief it worked and things returned to normal. The constant
practices had paid off and the crew needed no urging to continue.

The starboard 20 mm guns, numbers 3, 5, 7 and 9 each fired
two magazines of 60 rounds each. While doing this the merchant
crew volunteers and gunners from the port side were allowed to
shoot, one group getting used to the sound and feel of the guns
while the other honed their skills. The merchant crew was
enthusiastic enough to turn out for gunnery practice the next day.
Now accustomed to the sound and feel of the guns, they, too,
improved their accuracy.

Coxswain Dan Bandy, Armed Guard: "I was the senior Navy
rated man on board. And one of my gunners was J. Hardin. He
had to be the youngest man in the Navy. He was fourteen when
he enlisted, lied about his age, and he was the highest rated man
in gunnery school. When they found out, he had to get his parents
to give permission for him to be enlisted. So the Navy said, 'All
right, but no sea duty.'

"So he ended up in the Armed Guard. See, a merchant ship
wasn't considered 'sea duty' like a Navy ship. Hardin was a real
good seaman."

Seaman First Class E. Ray Sharpe: "I remember another fella,
Donald O. Weeks. He was a tall farm boy from Virginia or
someplace. Someone asked him what his initials, D.O.W. stood
for. He said, 'Duration Of the War.'"

On April 21, at latitude 51° 07' north and longitude 29° 45'
west an escort ship flying the black contact pennant dropped four
depth charges about 500 yards, one point (11 1/4 degrees) on the
port bow. The alarm was rung for general quarters and the crew

manned their battle stations. Less than an hour later the crew saw four depth charges dropped by the escort 2000 yards away, two points forward of the port beam. Lieutenant Memhard wrote in his log that all the charges were heard on the Mark-29 amplifier, indicating the device was operating correctly.

While most of the focus was on the dangers of the North Atlantic, routine shipboard life continued but the underlying tension sometimes made people act strangely. E. Ray Sharpe, one of the gunners, remembered an incident with one of the gun crew. "We had a big Swede in the gun crew, Swanson was his name, and I do mean huge. He wanted some clean linen for his bunk one day, so he asked the Chinese steward to give him some clean sheets. But the guy was a little bit slow to give him any. So he picked him up by the collar of his clothes and held him over the side of the ship. We were in the North Atlantic. So it didn't take him long to change his mind to get all the sheets he wanted."

"We used to stand watch together, Swede and I. And they gave us these chocolate bars. Well you were only supposed to eat about one-third of a bar at a time, they were too rich. He'd eat three or four bars a night. I don't know how he survived."

The threat of sinking and the dangers of war were never far off. On April 22, at 0600 two emergency turns were ordered by the convoy commodore. From Albert Haas' personal diary, "While on the high seas, Naval escort vessel dropped depth charges a few columns to our port side." That evening a series of depth charges was heard on the Mark-29 amplifier. Escorts were seen working the area on the far side of the convoy. Their actions, combined with the sounds, indicated they had a probable submarine contact. But the crew could only guess, based on what they saw and heard.

April 25 found the *Jeremiah O'Brien* passing over the north coast of Ireland and into the Irish Sea.

Tom McGeehan: "We rounded what they call the North Channel between Ireland and Scotland, came down the Irish Sea, and separated into two lanes as we came into the Bristol Channel."

E. Ray Sharpe: "Some guy told me one time a Liberty ship would roll in drydock. A lot of times we ate cold cuts cause it was so rough. The food was great most of the time. What you missed more than anything else was sweet milk. You forget all about it at sea, you wouldn't think you'd miss milk that much. You'd get to port and they'd bring about forty gallons on board and we'd demolish it in about two days."

The following day Lieutenant Memhard again gave instructions to his Armed Guard concerning their arrival at the next port. Customs officers routinely searched crew quarters to be sure that no items were brought into England without the proper duty being paid on them. To avoid paying the duty, seamen commonly hid goods such as cigarettes, nylons and fruit in various places around the ship. The Lieutenant was afraid some of his more naive sailors might be taken advantage of so he issued orders that no merchant crew items were to be kept in Navy quarters to evade customs.

There was a high rate of venereal disease and everyone was advised to avoid contact or take precautions. As usual, the crew was ordered to carry safeties and sani-tubes when going ashore.

E. Ray Sharpe: "We really liked that ship and the Lieutenant, he was good, real good to us."

Dan Bandy: "If we did our jobs, Memhard, he dismissed a lot of the regulations. There just wasn't much to do. We weren't to use our guns in port. We had two-thirds liberty and one-third on board. I talked to some of the Armed Guard on other ships and they were standing watch and watch, you know, port and starboard. They said, 'Two-thirds liberty! I never heard of that.' They were jealous of us. But it made a very happy bunch.

"Memhard's home was Grosse Pointe, Michigan. Well-to-do family. He was educated in England, but there was no put-ons, no airs about the man."

Tom McGeehan: "Memhard was a ninety-day-wonder. He used to borrow my naval traditions book. He used that to read up on navy regulations."

On April 27, the ship arrived at Newport, South Wales, at fifteen minutes after midnight. Tom McGeehan: "Because of tides the port had locks. There's a great tidal range and the ships can only go in at high water slack and come out at high water slack."

Francis Erdman: "We discharged at Newport and lay tied up there some time. Newport is in the west of England, not far from Bristol. We were there long enough to get acquainted ashore, friendly townspeople. It was my first foreign port. An old fashioned looking place, the buildings built of stone, old pubs. I had my first experience drinking warm beer -- and bringing my own cup along."

E. Ray Sharpe: "Cardiff, Wales, yeah, real nice. We enjoyed the fish and chips. That was about all we could find to eat. We got to where we liked those."

May Day, a traditional British festival day, came with the advice that safeties (condoms) should be used with "good judgement" since there was a limited supply in Great Britain at the time. Although the ancient dances for village lads and lasses "around a Maypole on the green" were not often seen, the celebrations were prominent in every port and the advice was timely.

Dan Bandy: "The English people treated us very well, very well. I liked England very much. There was a little friction because sometimes the women would pick out an American seaman. But overall we were well treated. I had the greatest respect for those people. They put up with so much with the blitz and everything. And toward the end the Germans developed those V-weapons."

Henry Kusel: "Cardiff was a nice port. It was heavily protected by big barrage balloons and they were manned by female battalions in that particular port. About all I had to do at night was visit the pubs. It was a nice place but it was a busy port."

Tom McGeehan: "I was raised among Welsh people in Pennsylvania. I liked very much being in Wales, it was beautiful and a beautiful time of year. It was so nice. May was a very nice summery month. I remember coming back to the ship on a street called Corporation Road. We were always told we had to be in uniform, so I was walking in my dress blue uniform and white cap. A couple was walking along the road and the man said to his girl, 'Look at that Yank. Isn't he nice?'"

From the Armed Guard log: "30 April 1944. Began to get feeling that we were going to be used in a coming invasion or some kind of special mission -- procedure for special training course being outlined."

On April 30 the *O'Brien* gave some equipment to the *SS J.W. Marshall*, a previously bombed and gutted ship being outfitted for a special mission. She would later be encountered as one of the block ships at the "Omaha" beachhead.

Twelve smoke generators[5] were placed on board the *O'Brien*. The Armed Guard crew was informed there would be an intensified training schedule with classes on air recognition, plane spotting and practice abandoning ship. Air recognition consisted of identifying silhouettes of airplanes shown with flash cards or with slides through a projector. Being wartime, projectors weren't easily available. The crew of the *O'Brien*, however, was resourceful. During this class a projector they made themselves was successfully used for the first time. It was built with a pineapple can, a grapefruit juice can, two 500-watt bulbs, one magnifying glass and miscellaneous other bits and pieces of wood and metal. The results, according to Lt. Memhard were, "excellent for both photos and silhouettes, of which collection over 200 shots. Noticeable increase in interest on part of men thru projection of planes."

Other practice procedures were instituted. Dan Bandy: "Lieutenant Memhard, he called me to his quarters and asked what I thought about close-order drilling. And I said, 'Well, Sir, as long as you asked, I don't think shit about it.'

"He laughed and said, 'Well, I think we'll try it anyway.'

"We went to aircraft identification several times a week. And he wanted us to march there, to aircraft I.D. So I mustered the men on the fantail and we practiced all this close-order drilling. And we drilled and drilled and drilled on the dock every morning and we got pretty good. Lo and behold the guys got where they liked it. So everyday, sometimes a couple of times a day, we'd march off to aircraft identification and we'd march back. And it

---

[5] With smoke generators a smokescreen could be created. This made it difficult for shore batteries to pinpoint the ship as a target.

got to where people would come out of the offices and buildings to see us march by. So he was right and I was wrong."

Tom McGeehan: "Bandy was quite a good guy, a good leader. His men respected him and he knew how to control them."

The last of the cargo came off on May 8 and, according to Captain De Smedt's voyage letter, "the vessel was turned over to the U.S. Army to be outfitted and equipped for special operations." Three days later the ship shifted to mooring buoys just outside the harbor.

Gas training became the order of the day. May 12, 1944 found the crew engaged in gas and gas mask drill and instruction. Each man's mask was checked for adjustment and all hands told they would be required to have their masks on within seven seconds from hearing the order "gas." Everyone except those on watch went ashore for special training in gas warfare, first aid, air recognition and abandoning ship.

The tempo of preparation increased. Five hundred twenty-five life jackets were placed on board for Army use. On May 14, the Armed Guard crew was mustered and advised that when troops came on board they would have added responsibilities. In addition, they were now to carry gas masks and lifejackets at all times. May 14th to May 16th was designated as a practice period to get in the habit. In the afternoon a life boat was lowered for the Navy crew to practice rowing and boat handling. Nine men spent two hours rowing back and forth across the harbor. Later a class was held on identifying signal flags and semaphore.

The war was never far off. From Purser Albert Haas' personal diary, "Air raid in vicinity of Cardiff, Barry, and Bristol." Flashes of light were seen and the muffled thud of bombs heard throughout the night.

The intensity and urgency of training continued to increase. Now, daily classes were held in air recognition, flag and semaphore. Practice was conducted on the shoreside firing range and the ship's guns were operated daily. The crews didn't know it, but they were being prepared for their date with history.

Tom McGeehan: "They put two signalmen in with me. They were part of Lieutenant Memhard's crew. G. Ward. and Bob

Something, he was the senior. They rotated with the ship's radio operator so the radio would be manned 24 hours a day."

On May 19 a waiver was obtained from the U.S. Coast Guard at Cardiff. According to Captain De Smedt's voyage letter this was to enable the ship to carry "troops and cargo, out of compliance with law, for the duration of military operation in which we were about to engage and to be effective until the return of the vessel to the United States."

At noon that day the degaussing was turned on and the *Jeremiah O'Brien* left Newport at 1840 that evening.

Oiler Francis Erdman: "The *Jeremiah O'Brien* was ordered to proceed to Gourock, Scotland. Gourock is on the South Shore of the Firth of Clyde[6]. Here the crew was sent to 'gas school.' We were taught about the different kinds of poison gas, the characteristics of each kind, how to contend with the stuff if it leaked, and so on. There was a strong feeling that the Germans would use gas."

Albert Haas noted that the "harbor was full of Liberty ships and warships."

There was also the growing certainty that the great invasion was now close at hand. From the Armed Guard Log: "We had training in military preparedness. What was happening was that we were preparing for the invasion of Europe -- but we didn't know it. However, we drew our own conclusions." The crews practiced uncomplainingly, with great mental concentration, knowing that their fate -- and that of the ship -- could depend on how well they learned the lessons.

But there were lighter moments, too. Gunner's Mate Morgan Williams: "Waiting to go into Scotland, we were at anchor and we had a deck light hanging over the stern of the ship. And you looked down and you could see all these salmon just rolling under the light. They came right up to that light. So we rigged some lines and you put a hook down with a rag or meat or anything on

---

[6] According to Webster's Geographical Dictionary, "During World War II debarkation point for U.S. forces (in 2 1/2 years after May 1942, about 1,317,000 Americans landed here).

The Germans were expected to use gas during the invasion. Here Radio Operator Robert Milby dons his full gas regalia for the camera. Taken in 1944. Credit Robert Milby

it and they'd bite it. We loaded up the whole ship, galley and everything with eight to ten pound silver salmon."

The ship went to the dock at Gourock-the-Clyde on Sunday, May 21. The first order of business was a "short arm inspection" for the Armed Guard crew by Army medics. Fortunately the results of this check for venereal disease were negative.

Francis Erdman: "Gourock was another very old town -- very old. Quiet. The only way to pass your time, really, was take long walks in the Scottish countryside."

Three days later 25 additional lifejackets were placed on board for the Army by the Army. The Armed Guard crew was given a class in 30 cal. rifle instruction, including field stripping. June 1, 1944, came with more instructions on fighting the enemy. Under multiple air attack each man and unit was to act independently of bridge control. Instructions were issued on how to act under various circumstances and with reasons why. Each gun was assigned a sector, for example, from dead ahead to 45 degrees on the bow, and they were told to concentrate on covering their sectors while under attack. They were cautioned not to be distracted by what was going on in adjacent sectors.

Another class in air recognition was held. Dan Bandy laughingly recalled those sessions: "Aircraft identification classes on board ship, well it was dark and some of the guys would fall asleep. But Memhard, he solved that by once in awhile throwing in a slide of a naked woman. That kept the guys up."

The classes continued. A fire and boat muster was held for the merchant crew. At the same time the Navy gun crew mustered on the aft gun platform in complete gas protective clothing for inspection by Lt. Memhard. Every man wore rubber boots, oilskin gear, gloves, mask and Army protective headgear.

One of the greatest fears on the part of the Allied Command was a poison gas attack and, as we have seen, crews were heavily drilled on the use of gas suits and masks. Training included developing a familiarity with the different types of gas they might encounter. A document titled "GAS-DEFENSE" succinctly categorized the potentially lethal weapon.

LACRIMATORS
CHLORACETOPHENON(CN)
Tear Gas Solution (CNS)
Brombenzylcyanide (CA)

LUNG IRRITANTS
Chlorine (CL)
Phosgene (CG)
Chlorpicrin (PS)

VESICANTS
Mustard Gas (HS)

Lewisite (M-1)
Ethyldichlorasine (ED)

IRRITANT SMOKES
Adamsite (DM)
Diphenylchorazine (DA)

SCREENING SMOKES
TITANIUM (FM)
Sulphur Trioxide
Solution(FS)
H.C. Mixture (HC)
White Phosphorus (WP)

INCENDIARIES:
Thermite (TH): Iron, Aluminum, Magnesium.

Iron oxide and aluminum mixed in a granulated powder make Thermite, which fills the magnesium casing of the bomb. Set off by a flash of priming powder, both thermite and casing combust in intense flame that burns through metal and cannot be smothered or put out by water or chemical extinguishers.

OTHER POSSIBLE AGENTS:

Carbon Monoxide

Hydrocyanic acid (in solution with arsenic trichloride) called vincinite. It is about 30 times as toxic as chlorine or carbon monoxide.

Both of these agents affect the nerve and blood functions of the body.

Carbon monoxide reacts with red coloring matter of the blood and renders the blood incapable of taking up oxygen and distributing it to the body.

Hydrocyanic acid paralyzes the nerves and prevents the use of oxygen by the blood.

A number of substances which act in a more or less similar manner to these two substances are known, but none of them seem to have properties requisite in a chemical agent.

A practical part of the training for gas warfare included demonstrating several of the gasses by detonating small quantities in the field for crewmembers to smell. These were mustard, lewisite, phosgene and chlorpicrin. In addition chloracetaphemone, adamsite and diphenylchlorarsine were opened in the classroom for sniff identification. The crew was carefully cautioned to <u>sniff, don't smell</u>. The odors of these gasses were distinctive:

Mustard	Garlic, horseradish
Lewisite	Geraniums.
Phosgene	Cut corn or silage, depending on concentration.
Chlorpicrin	Sweetish-like licorice.
Chloracetaphemone	Locust or apple blossom. Ripe fruit.
Adamsite	Odorless.
Diphenylchlorarsine	Like shoe polish.

Robert Milby: "I do remember we was up at the Clyde River in Gourock. And we went to a school up there for gas equipment. Gas protection helmets were to be with the men at all times."

Now, seemingly all of Great Britain was buried in war matériel. Everywhere were lined up jeeps, tanks, trucks, half-tracks and ambulances. Rations, canned goods, cannons, machine guns, rifles, pistols, ammunition, bombs, hand grenades, mines, mortars, uniforms, clothing, medicine, dental fillings, bandages, ointment, plasma, drugs, gasoline, kerosene, diesel fuel and hundreds of other necessary items were stacked in cans, boxes, barrels, drums, kegs and cartons in the streets and alleys of the cities, along the highways and byways of the countryside, on the moors, in the valleys and hidden in the forests. The fortress called Great Britain was stockpiled with equipment and literally covered with supplies.

Third Engineer William Watson remembered, "There was so much material over there. 'My God,' we used to say, 'if they cut the barrage balloons loose, England would sink all the way to China.' Material stacked up everywhere."

On the left radio operator Robert Milby, on the right third assistant engineer William Watson. Taken on board just before Operation Overlord. Credit Robert Milby

Now all Petty Officers in the gun crew were advised of the necessity for special attention to proper lookout and the possibility of E-boat attack in the unspecified area the ship was leaving for. The latest advice from the British was that an E-boat attack was practically a certainty. Special instructions were given for E-boat fire control[7] and probability tactics.

The Navy gun crew were advised of the type of attack to be anticipated in the next few days and given special instructions. The men were again reminded that gas masks and helmets were to be carried at all times.

By this time the status of the civilian merchant convoy had subtly changed.

Tom McGeehan: "The army assigned us Army Transportation Service number MT 267. We were basically under the U. S. Army. We had lots of training there, lots of gas mask training. They put some extra guns on board ship. Army 40 millimeter

---

[7] Fire control in Navy parlance refers to the aiming and firing of guns, not, as a civilian might think, to controlling something on fire.

mobile guns were put on deck. They tied them down and they were for extra protection on the invasion.

"The *Jeremiah O'Brien* departed Gourock-the-Clyde, Scotland, on June 2nd. We sailed on down the Irish Sea toward Land's End. And as we went we picked up an escort of naval vessels. So the mate on watch sent me back to the fantail to do the normal courtesy of dipping the flag. I saw the *Augusta* pass by and I dipped the ensign and watched as she lowered her ensign and raised it again. Then I raised ours. I found out in later years this was Admiral A. G. Kirk's flagship. So then a battleship came by and I dipped the ensign again and then another battleship, and then some cruisers and so on. I just kept dipping. I was at that for two hours before they all went past."

Saturday, June 3, 1944. The *Jeremiah O'Brien* and her convoy were covered by a heavy escort of ships and, in the air, by an umbrella of Spitfires, Hurricanes, B-24's and Mosquitos.

Robert Milby: "Four or five ships started down between the islands and ships kept coming and joining us and then we went around Land's End towards Southampton. And, my God, you never saw so many ships. Thousands, just thousands and thousands. It was incredible. The water level of the ocean must have gone up twenty feet with all those ships there."

William Watson: "It was an Armada. There was just ... the whole water was just covered with ships."

Albert Haas: "There was a huge fleet of Allied warships that passed our convoy. It looked like a two ocean navy."

Francis Erdman: "The *Jeremiah O'Brien* was at the head of the convoy -- in the first wave of ships in the convoy. As we steered down the west coast of Great Britain, passing ports large and small, we picked up ships at each one until there were so many vessels that there was no end to the procession. As we passed around Land's End, entering the English Channel, different ones of us would go up on the flying bridge and use the mate's telescope. As far as you could see, for mile after mile in the distance, ships, ships, ships! The *O'Brien* was in the vanguard of perhaps the greatest flotilla ever assembled in history."

Dan Bandy: "There was over 5000 ships as far as I know."

Part of the cargo and a few of the troops the Jeremiah O'Brien would carry to Normandy wait on the dock at Southampton as she prepares to load. Credit Robert Milby

Tom McGeehan: "It was the biggest thing that any human being could ever see in the history of the world. There were so many ships that the curvature of the earth prevented you from seeing it all. It was just stupendous!"

Monday, June 5, 1944. At 0658 the *Jeremiah O'Brien* anchored in Poole Bay, outside the Solent of Southampton (at Bournemouth). Tom McGeehan recalled it 50 years later: "We got to Southampton around June 4th and there we loaded army troops, it seemed like 5,000 troops. It was either the First or the Twenty-Ninth division, I'm not sure which."

E. Ray Sharpe: "We carried troops. It looked like millions of them in Southampton. We spent all our time carrying troops."

Francis Erdman: "Finally we started loading troops. No equipment. Just troops. I can only guess at the number of troops that came on board -- they overflowed the ship. There were soldiers everywhere, crammed and crowded in. As I remember, they each carried their rations. No other provision was made for feeding them."

Heavy gunfire was observed in the distance from about 2300 on throughout the night. Allied bombardment of the French coast had started.

Albert Haas recorded in his diary, "Hundreds of aircraft passed overhead, enroute to the continent. Hundreds of small craft and some transports in the area. It looked like an invasion practice. Warships seen in distance of English Channel and seemed to be heading toward continent. Glare from gunfire over the horizon of the Channel was visible."

Robert Milby: "I distinctly remember the night before the invasion. We were sitting there in the harbor and thousands of planes went overhead. And two searchlights coming up in a V right over us. Squadrons of planes went overhead all night long. Hundreds and thousands of planes.

"Where we were at, you could see the explosions, ninety miles away or whatever. It was the bombs they were dropping. The whole area was lit up."

E. Ray Sharpe: "You know, we saw the first salvo fired over there. We were in Southampton and we could see that all the way across the Channel."

It was early morning, Tuesday, June 6, 1944.

10

NORMANDY

Operation Overlord began at fifteen minutes after midnight with the dropping of two battalions of British and American pathfinders into the moonlit sky over Normandy. Their job was to light the drop zones on the French coast, roughly between Cherbourg and Le Havre, for the paratroopers and gliders filled with infantry who were soon to follow. Once landed, the airborne soldiers fought their way through the swamps and hedgerows toward their assigned sectors. Offshore, more than two hundred thousand soldiers rode more than five thousand ships across the Channel toward five beaches across 60 miles of French coast. The Americans landed at "Utah" and "Omaha," on the western shores of the coast, with the British and Canadians taking "Gold," "Juno" and "Sword," farther to the east.

By breakfast time news of the invasion sent an electric pulse of excitement throughout the ship. The *O'Brien's* crew and troops anxiously passed the day with one ear to the radio and the questions, "What's the latest?" and "When do we go?" on everyone's

lips. A torrent of Spitfires, Hurricanes, Thunderbolts and Mustangs flew in thunderous waves overhead toward France. Across
the globe, newspapers carried the momentous news in giant black
type and millions held their breaths, glued to their radios, listening to the bulletins from England. It was a day never to be
forgotten -- the skies dark with aircraft, ships stretching to the
horizon and beyond -- the invasion of Europe was unparalleled in
scope, at once bold and magnificent, yet ominous with an "awful
grandeur." In some cases the beaches and inland areas were
quickly and easily taken, in others every inch of ground had to be
wrested from fierce defenders, captured with perseverance, sacrifice, blood and guts. By the end of what author Cornelius Ryan
called "the longest day in history" the Allied forces, under Commanding General Eisenhower, were firmly back on European soil
and the liberation of the continent from Nazi domination had
begun.

On the *Jeremiah O'Brien,* the deafening roar of the planes and
the sight of the greatest armada in history raised a fevered desire

Part of the Armed Guard on the SS Jeremiah O'Brien *before they shaved their heads for the assault on Normandy. Credit Robert Milby*

in many who saw it to rush out and be part of the historic day. Others were pale with fear. Some sat, silently writing letters or alone with their thoughts. Others exchanged names, addresses and messages for the folks back home, "just in case." Priests and chaplains walked among the troops reassuring, counseling, taking messages and doing what they could to encourage the men, many of whom were young homesick soldiers, not long out of school. The gun crews checked and re-checked their equipment. The radio operator strained every sense to hear the traffic crashing over the airwaves, almost drowned out by the constant drone of thousands of airplane engines overhead. Captain De Smedt paced the bridge. The *Jeremiah O'Brien* waited for her orders.

The paratroopers who jumped behind the beaches of Normandy on the night before D-Day had cut their hair into "Mohawks," bald heads with a narrow brush of hair running from front to back. When the Armed Guard crew heard about this, they responded with a strong sense of camaraderie and *esprit de corps*.

Coxswain Dan Bandy: "We all had Lone Eagle haircuts [Mohawks] or baldies. And it caught on. First one gun crew and then another and pretty soon all the merchant gun crews did it. We just wanted to do it."

Gunner's Mate, Morgan Williams. "Yeah, shaving heads. They started out, we shaved to a Mohawk and then some of the guys went bald-headed. It went from ship to ship."

Seamen First Class E. Ray Sharpe: "All the guys shaved their heads for D-Day, they had a Mohawk haircut or something similar to it."

Once the beachhead was established it was vital to keep a constant stream of troops and supplies supporting the advancing front line. There could be no interruption in the flow of men and matériel flooding the Normandy coast. This meant that some ships were scheduled to unload on the first day, others were scheduled for the second day, third, fourth and so on. The success of the whole great enterprise rested on this unbroken stream of men and supplies.

D-Day+1, June 7, 1944. A Royal Navy officer came aboard with an exclusive radio receiver for the assault area. Labeled

*After they shaved their heads the Armed Guard called themselves "baldies."
The crew on one merchant ship shaved their hair and soon almost all the
Armed Guard crews in Southampton sported shaved heads. Credit Dan Bandy*

*Gunner's mate Morgan Williams opted for the Mohawk haircut favored by
many of the paratroupers landing behind the beaches at Normandy. Credit
Dan Bandy*

"Reception set R-109," it was tuned to special frequencies to receive warnings of impending attacks, instructions for crossing the Channel and mooring at Normandy. There was always a large crowd gathered around it, listening to the developing news.

While they waited, twenty Army men volunteered and were assigned to back up the *O'Brien's* gun crew and assist with the extra guns tied down on deck. The Navy Armed Guard crew were given assault area instructions from a brochure called "The Cross Channel Pamphlet," issued to those involved in the invasion, and signalmen were given special instructions on communications for the assault area -- frequencies, code words, flag identification.

To relieve the tension and pass the time waiting for the coming battle the troops diverted themselves. Oiler Francis Erdman: "The night (before we left) the troops in the hold had themselves a jam session. Several had brought instruments -- there were ten or twelve musicians. They played all night, partly out of fear, I guess. When they disembarked, the instruments were left on board. 'We won't be playing those any more!' they said."

In a different hatch, Dan Bandy watched G.I.s boxing. "Those soldiers of ours were outstanding. We all heard what great fighting men the Japanese and Germans were, but the men that we had on the *O'Brien* the evening before we sailed were the best in the world. They were having elimination boxing matches in the square of the hatch! They'd have kept it up all night, but we finally turned the lights off on them. Those were soldiers. I will tell you, they would make you proud."

Cadet Tom McGeehan: "They were magnificent soldiers, wonderful fighting men. We carried the first bunch to Omaha."

Cadet Henry Kusel: "We carried troops. They consisted of a ranger battalion and they were very organized, cool, under control."

At 2210 on D-Day+2, the *Jeremiah O'Brien* left the dock at Southampton and anchored in the Solent. On board the several hundred Army troops checked their equipment one more time. This was the springboard for their assault.

Tom McGeehan: "We had hundreds of sand bags aboard for D-Day, for extra protection. There were all kinds of sandbags piled around the guns. Captain De Smedt's quarters were on the starboard side of the bridge deck, just under the flying bridge. He had these sandbags stacked above his quarters two or three high. There must have been a hundred of them, just over his room. The rest of the deck was bare. Then, in August one day, after it was safe, he had the crew throw them over."

The following day, D+3, the *Jeremiah O'Brien* sailed at 2220.[1] Weighing anchor with hundreds of other vessels, she pointed her bow toward the assault area off the coast of Normandy -- a place code-named "Omaha Beach." She had on board 10 officers, 563 troops, 135 armored vehicles and 161 tons of explosives.[2] At midnight the Armed Guard set Condition II. No one slept.

From Albert Haas' personal diary, "Friday, June 9, 1944. Sailed from Southampton enroute to France. Left about dusk."

The war zone was on the horizon and quickly came out to meet them. In the early morning darkness of June 10, two mines were seen on the port side, less than 100 yards from the ship. Then a mine was seen on the starboard side less than 50 yards off. A ship a few miles away on the starboard beam suddenly exploded and burned brilliantly for several hours.

At 0330 the general alarm was sounded. Tracer fire was spotted about 4000 yards away on the port side. The Germans had mustered an E-Boat attack and the ships on the perimeter of the convoy were shooting at them. Twice more during the dark-

---

[1] Dan Bandy, Morgan Williams and Francis Erdman insist that the *Jeremiah O'Brien* sailed for Normandy on June 7. The Armed Guard log, Captain De Smedt's voyage letter, Purser Albert Haas' personal diary and other sources show the vessel departing Southampton on June 9 and arriving at "Omaha" on June 10. The author elected to use the written data with the thought that during the fifty years since the invasion, some memories may have played false.

[2] There are three sources for the number of troops carried, the captain's voyage letter, the Commander's Condensed Log and a personal itinerary prepared by purser Albert Haas. Mr. Haas' figures appear to be based on the Commander's Condensed Log. I choose those on the captain's voyage letter simply because they are higher and give the operation a slightly greater sense of importance. Author.

A line of 'gooseberry' ships, sunk to create an instant artificial breakwater, assured the success of the supply side of Operation Overlord.   Credit Robert Milby

ness of that early morning, tracers were seen firing at surface targets. Flares dropped frequently throughout the night, giving the scene an eerie, surreal quality.

Francis Erdman: "Before we got to Omaha beach we encountered barrage balloons -- hundreds of balloons up there to discourage air attack on the shipping. But the enemy was there and their planes had flares -- it was as bright as noonday at three o'clock in the morning. We steamed on, toward the shore. It was a low coast line with hills and scattered in the hills, although we couldn't see them very distinctly, were numbers of pillboxes. But they didn't open fire right away."

At 0830 June 10, 1944 the *Jeremiah O'Brien* arrived at "Omaha." The Channel waters had been rough and many of the soldiers were seasick. The first sight of their objective was not comforting.

Albert Haas' personal diary, "Saturday, June 10, 1944. Arrived at the 'Omaha' beachhead. Thousands of ships were in the

To create the "gooseberry" breakwaters ships were put to a use for which they were never intended -- resting on the bottom of the ocean. Nonetheless the concept was quick and effective. Credit Robert Milby

harbor, of all types. Warships (mostly destroyers and D.E.'s) provided a semi-circle of protection."

Among the major difficulties that had to be overcome was getting the troops and cargo safely ashore. There were no piers or ports as such in that part of France. This meant troops and supplies had to be off-loaded from ships into amphibious craft which would then run the cargo ashore. The amphibious ducks (DUKW) and landing craft were necessarily small and vulnerable to the rugged sea and swell coming in from the English Channel. To quickly create a safe harbor where none was before, the idea of sinking several ships to form an instant breakwater was conceived. Known as the Gooseberry or "block" ships, they were sunk in rows to form breakwaters which provided protection for the unloading of troops and supplies. In the Omaha Beach area seventeen American-flag ships were sunk: *George S. Wasson, Benjamin Contee, Matt Rasnon, David O. Saylor, Vitruvius, West Nohno, West Cheswald, West Honaker, Victory Sword, James*

Iredell, George W. Childs, Artemus Ward, J. W. Marshall, Wilscox, Galveston, Courageous and *West Grama.* As some of these broke up during ensuing storms others were added: *Alcoa Leader, Exford, Illinoion, Kentuckian, Kofresi, Lena Luckenback, Pennsylvanian, Robin Grey, Sahale* and *West Nilus.*

Commander J.E. Taylor of the Royal Navy was part of the group responsible for setting these instant breakwaters. In his book, *The Last Passage,* he described what it was like putting ships to a use for which they were never intended.

"A ship is designed to serve its life afloat and those who man her are trained to keep her in that state. A beach means only shipwreck and stranding to sailor minds. There were many who expressed surprise at (ships) sitting upright on a beach. They did not know that a merchant ship is a vessel of flat bottom, perfectly capable of sitting upright on a flat sandy shore. Sometimes when the bottom on which they settled wasn't level, frames were strained, but few suffered major hurt. We passed one coaster that waited, and her captain leaned over the wing of his bridge and waved to us. He presented a vast and cheerful countenance that reflected a schoolboy relish in the unorthodoxy that had been brought into his life. This was no way for a master to treat his ship, not to have crowds of soldiers swarming over her; but he had no need to worry, everything had official sanction."

The process of lining up the Gooseberry ships and sinking them went with clock-work precision. Among the vessels was a French man-of-war, the battleship *Courbet.* "High up, from the top-most point, a gigantic flag of the Free French flaunted its colours. At the stern a huge tricolour flew."

"The *Courbet* came on, persuaded steadily forward by four tugs. Around her dozens of ships busied themselves with the purpose that had brought them there. Yet the progress of that old battleship seemed to dwarf all other activities into insignificance. One felt that there ought to be a crashing of military music to accompany that flaunting Cross of Lorraine. And that last passage seemed too easy of accomplishment. Without a hitch or apparent difficulty the *Courbet* came right in, was turned with slow dignity, and pushed into position. Her bow came to rest on that of another ship already sunk. There was a great rending and tearing of steel as one bow scraped past another, and there was a strange unconcern in watching that buckling and tearing of a ship's bow, because it no longer mattered. No court of enquiry on the collision would follow. Then the *Courbet* was in position and once there she just stayed still as if conscious that this was the end and compliant in the matter. The explosion was sudden--just a dull thud and brief tremor, and then a quick settling of the three feet that separated her keel from the sea bed."

Of course the explosive charges designed to sink the gooseberry ships didn't always go off as intended. Commander Taylor was on the *Durban* when she was planted. "And when the *Durban's* life ended in a sudden disruption it was a vast explosion that for a moment threatened collapse of the topmast. Instead of forcing its way outward through holes blown in the ship's side, the blast went inwards then sought escape by every possible egress. Up through vents and gratings rushed the force of explosion taking all movable debris with it. In its path it found a bundle of old clothing supplied for cleaning rags, and draped the rigging with an unseemly display of ancient and ragged underclothing. The ship's company had been moved to the empty gun platforms, and some did not escape. Those near the boiler-room vents emerged from the thinning cloud of dust like coal-trimmers from the bunkers. In five minutes the *Durban* was on the bottom and we waited to be taken away. There was an aimlessness about those who awaited on her upper deck. There was no further purpose in their presence on board, for the reason behind it had ceased. Like uncertain children they waited for the next move."

A newly-sunk ship had an other-worldly quality to it. Commander Taylor recalled boarding another vessel in which "... the water lapped at an upper deck and one could step aboard straight over the rails. Only twenty minutes ago she had been planted, and there were still signs of her dying. I walked along the deck and looked in at the galley. Food still simmered there for the mid-day meal that was never eaten. That galley had a strange empty look, for who sees a galley without its cook when the food is ready for dishing up? A long cube of corned beef waited for slicing, and the pots simmered on the stove. I almost expected the cook to burst in at any moment with a wrathful injunction to get out of his galley, and when lifting the lid to examine the contents of a pot there was a guilty feeling of trespass. But the authority had gone, and there was clear evidence of this in the 'midships house. The saloon was wrecked and on the deck half a dozen counterpanes torn from a cupboard, were strewn. In the pantry, the captain's cabin and officer's quarters it was the same. I felt a sudden anger at those who had despoiled her. It was like robbing a body that was not yet cold.

"I looked in at the engine-room, and stepped on to the upper grating. Water was just lapping around the tops of the great cylinders in the gloom below. The engine room was full of sound, not great sound, but the tiny sounds of unseen movement in the water below: faint gurgles and bubblings and occasional plops, last dying murmurs where for years there had been the steady thud, thud, thud of massive machinery, and constant suppressed murmur of high pressure. There was the funereal atmosphere of church beneath the blacked-out arch of the skylight. It was a place of departing souls that murmured in their passing. The sunlight outside was blinding in comparison."

Third Assistant Engineer William Watson was less poetic: "I remember all the ships that were sunk to make the breakwater. A friend of mine was on one of the ships that they towed out there and sunk. And his job was to get in there and sink it and get out of there."

With the breakwaters in place, large, prefabricated sections of piers called Mulberrys were towed into position and partially submerged to facilitate the unloading process. Tom McGeehan: "I remember seeing the Mulberry harbors being towed across. They looked like the Empire State building lying on its side. They had railroad tracks already built into them so when they got there they just sunk them and they were ready to use."

The *O'Brien* anchored off "Omaha" beach and discharging of cargo began. The crew secured from general quarters. The Armed Guard set Condition II.

The Normandy beachhead. Note the barrage balloons, the number of ships at anchor and the road already established parallel to the waterfront. Credit National Archives

Francis Erdman: "LSTs came out to meet us and take the troops off. The weather was very rough, swells that I recall as from fifteen to twenty feet. This made it very hard unloading the troops. All along one side we hung cargo nets and the soldiers scrambled down."

Throughout the day (D+4) air protection over the beachhead was excellent. Spitfires, Mustangs, Thunderbolts, Lightnings, Hurricanes and Typhoons were on constant patrol. At 2000 that evening the R-109 receiver came alive with the information that heavy German air attacks were expected as soon as weather permitted. At 2316 anti-aircraft firing broke out. Hostile planes were near the outer edges of the landing force. Although they weren't near enough to the ship to open fire, the general alarm was sounded and the crew went to general quarters.

Francis Erdman: "Before long, all hell broke loose. I could never be sure where the shells from those pillboxes went. Over

Not long after the initial landing, equipment offloaded from the ships in the background, is lined up ready for the march inland and the liberation of Northern France. Credit National Archives

us? God knows, they really cut loose. The *O'Brien* was positioned close to the battleship *Texas* on one side and the cruiser *Augusta* on the other. The *Texas* was shelling the beach without let-up. The sounds of war were coming from all directions -- the pillboxes, machine guns on the planes -- the *Texas* was enough all by herself to deafen you."

Morgan Williams: "The coastal guns really raised heck at first."

On June 11 at 0345 the general alarm again sounded. The *Jeremiah O'Brien* and the ships around her were under attack. According to Lt. Memhard's log: "On 11 June 1944, at 'Omaha' beachhead, the USN Gun Crew was called to battle stations at 0345. Enemy planes were circling overhead and some ships in the vicinity opened fire with 20 mm's and larger AA guns. Following assault area instructions, since it was too dark to see clearly this ship withheld fire. The enemy planes appeared to be

A line of LSTs unloads troops, equipment and supplies at one of the Normandy beachheads shortly after D-Day.   Credit National Archives

flying over the anchorage at about 10,000 feet. At 0400 three planes came down lower and one was heard to go into a dive, in the direction of this ship. Two men on the aft 3"-50 saw it briefly as it passed from bow to stern, and the undersigned also observed it -- the plane being identified as a JU-88. Four bombs were dropped, one splashing about 200 yards away on the port bow and the other three just the other side of another Liberty. About 0425 one FW 190 was seen flying from shore toward and over us, first at about 14,000 feet and subsequently lower -- for'd and aft 3"-50's opened fire and expended two rounds each. About 0500 at least three groups of FW 190's, three planes to a group, were seen coming in from the shore (the dark side) toward the ships at anchor. Heavy AA fire was thrown up. All guns on this ship opened fire, 12 rounds of 3"-50 and 500 rounds of 20 mm ammunition being expended. No hits were observed by the undersigned, although several people on board said they saw a plane go down in smoke several miles out to sea."

The view from a slight elevation just beyond the beach proper, looking seaward. Just a few of the 5000 ships which took part in the initial landing can be seen in the background. Credit National Archives

Albert Haas recorded the evening's events in his personal diary. "During the evening, enemy aircraft came over the beachhead area, two planes diving (supposedly) at our ship, releasing bombs to the starboard (aft) and port (fore). Gun crew opened fire on all guns (10 guns). Fortunately no damage of any sort. Shrapnel heavy, lifeboat damaged. Terrific gunfire ashore all evening. Front two miles from anchorage."

Captain De Smedt, in a letter to Grace Line described it: "Shortly before dawn on June 11, while at the 'Omaha' beachhead, the vessel was attacked by enemy dive bombers. Bombs fell wide of their mark and the vessel, though shaken, was undamaged. The gun crew, commanded by Lt. Memhard, USNR, put up a heavy AA barrage and drove the enemy away preventing a second attack by the promptness and accuracy of their fire. An inspection of the vessel during the day revealed that the only damage was to No. 4 lifeboat which had been hit by shrapnel."

Francis Erdman: "I ran back and forth across the ship to see it all. But I gave that up. There was just too much. German planes were strafing whatever they could get their sights on. Our side was offering such a target that they could hardly miss, it seemed to me. But I really think that the barrage balloons on their long wires seriously hampered their planes from closing in. Something kept them away from the O'Brien."

At 0530, with the coming of dawn, the enemy planes disappeared, although Albert Haas noted that battleships were still shelling shore batteries.

Francis Erdman: "Now another astonishing scene was unfolding before us -- within half an hour of our men hitting the beach we could see graders and bulldozers (ours) building roads." The military engineers performed miracles, building roads and bridges with lightning speed over impossible terrain, often under murderous fire.

The crew secured from general quarters. Condition II was resumed. More troops and equipment were sent ashore.

Robert Milby: "We had a lot of soldiers and equipment. There was firing ashore and things like that. Some of the poor G.I.s were petrified. They had to beat them to go down the side of the ship. You know, the ropes. Not many, but some of them. And I felt so sorry for them. They were beating their hands, step by step as they were going down. Otherwise they just froze."

Henry Kusel: "Except for the rangers, many of them were disorganized and scared. They got sick and some of them wouldn't go over the nets."

Dan Bandy: "All the Navy men painted our hometown on the backs of our jackets so the soldiers could see it. That way if they were from your home town, they'd come over and talk to you. Well, one guy I remember saw 'Columbus, Ohio' painted on my back and he came over and talked to me. I knew where he lived, too. So he asked me to go see his folks when I got back home. Then he went over the side. I never did see him again. I know that he got killed that day."

Francis Erdman: "I think it was three or four LSTs that came alongside to take on our troops. A couple of LSTs would be alongside and a couple of others standing by to take their place. It was all done very rapidly. No delay -- none."

On June 13, with the coming of darkness, the menace from the air resumed. But, unlike the previous evening, the enemy, with one or two exceptions, stayed at a safe distance, circling just out of range. Again from Lieutenant Memhard's log: "During general quarters 13 June between 0345 and 0515, there were two alerts. On the first occasion three enemy planes were seen in the immediate area at about 8000 feet; later a single plane at the same height. The single plane flew directly overhead and was tracked, but fire was withheld since it appeared to be very unlikely that this ship or the others in the vicinity could be seen due to haze."

Normally, the Navy Armed Guard log entries were short, limited to simple fact. But on this occasion, the Lieutenant, recognizing the historical significance of the landing, added his observations.

"In general, it was surprising that more determined and heavier enemy plane attacks were not encountered, particularly so soon after "D" Day and since enemy-held territory at this point was only a few miles inland. During the day excellent Allied plane coverage was maintained, mainly by Spitfires of several types, Mustangs, Thunderbolts, Lightnings and Typhoons in this area. At night, from dawn to dusk, enemy planes were always about and dropping flares, but practically no damage to Allied shipping was observed by the undersigned. "E" boats also made frequent attempts to penetrate the destroyer protective ring. On one occasion it appeared that a combination plane and "E" boat attack was being made on the protective ring outside the anchorages."

Dan Bandy saw it this way, "At the time of the invasion, the German air force was in bad condition. We fired our guns several times. I was on the flying bridge and watched it through the glasses. It was very bad."

Albert Haas watched "terrific gunfire ashore, giving the impression of a terrific electrical storm."

At 1035 on the morning of June 13, the *Jeremiah O'Brien* weighed anchor and left the "Omaha" beachhead.

Francis Erdman: "We had our orders -- we hauled up the anchor and headed back to England, to Southampton, to get another load. This time it was equipment and ammunition in the holds, and we loaded quite a bit of food, field rations."

The ship would know the beaches of Normandy well in the weeks ahead.

Tom McGeehan: "Just outside Southampton harbor is the Isle of Wight. Going to Normandy we'd go out the starboard [west] side of the island and coming back we'd go in on the other [east] side, the port side. There was so much traffic it had to be one-way. By far the biggest amount of ship traffic for Normandy came out of Southampton. It was just continual."

Dropping anchor in the Solent just before midnight, the *O'Brien* was fetching up on her chain when a ship appeared out of the darkness. The *SS Thomas Wolfe* grazed the port side, knocking the #2 lifeboat davit around and causing minor damage to the superstructure. Captain De Smedt thought the *Wolfe* was probably going too slow and lost control. Neither ship was appreciably damaged. In his voyage letter to Grace Line, he explained what happened: "On June 13, at 2359 B.D.S.T. (British Double Summer Time), the *SS Thomas Wolfe* struck us a glancing blow on the port side while we were anchored in the West Solent, Southampton. Slight damage was done to the bridge superstructure. The *Thomas Wolfe* was approaching the anchorage with a pilot on board at the time and there was nothing I could do to avoid the accident."

The next morning the *O'Brien* was alongside the dock loading for Normandy. Her cargo was 12 officers, 453 troops and 217 vehicles. The repairs took place while the ship was loading.

William Watson: "I remember one time that we had to go in for temporary repairs. I think we were in the Bristol Channel and I guess someone ran into us and they opened up a couple of plates on the side. Hit us hard enough that they opened up a little bit of the side. It was nothing serious. They repaired it right there at the dock."

Loading finished in the early morning of June 17. Part of the cargo was 50 cal. quadruple machine guns. Four of these were left on deck as additional armament for the ship and fire control

Two of the SS Jeremiah O'Brien's Armed Guard prepare one of the 3"-50's for action. They were called to general quarters several times a day while the ship was anchored on the coast of Normandy. Credit Dan Bandy

Seaman First Class Swanson (with back to camera) and seaman First Class Murphy at right, loading the 3"-50. Credit Dan Bandy

Seaman First Class Swanson completes loading just before firing.   Credit Dan Bandy

procedure was explained to the gun crew on these weapons. Leaving the dock at 0645 the *O'Brien* anchored in the Solent, waiting for the convoy to form, and sailed at 0850. As on the previous voyage, 20 U.S. Army soldiers were given instructions for helping on the ship's guns.

Henry Kusel: "On those trips across the Channel we were full of officers and Army personnel. Some of the officers slept in our cabin. The troops were in the upper 'tween deck. We had heads for the troops on deck so that they drained over the side."

At 1400 the general alarm was rung. An escort ship about a mile off on the starboard beam dropped several depth charges. Then four other escorts closed in, two of them flying black pennants indicating contact with a submarine. At 2025 the evening of June 17, the *Jeremiah O'Brien* arrived for the second time at "Omaha" beachhead, which had become the most active port in Northern France. From D-Day to June 18th 197,444 troops, 27,340 vehicles and 68,799 long tons of supplies were landed.

There was no respite from the heavy weather and to the weary crew the Channel was just another extension of the North Atlantic.

E. Ray Sharpe: "That Channel was rough. One time we had a barrage balloon and it blew away from us. And we had a railroad engine that got loose and broke in on somebody."

William Watson: "They [Liberty ships] rolled a lot. When we went across that Channel we took some pretty heavy seas. We went across on one trip and had wave crests about seventy feet high. When she came down the ship shook like a string on a violin."

Robert Milby: "The second trip they had a tremendous storm. Couldn't unload and everybody got sick, I'm sure. The ship was pitching. We dropped anchor and it was pitching so hard we had to pull up anchor and move farther out because it was hitting ground. And we finally did unload there. I think we were there four or five days before we could leave."

That same evening the crew had their first experience with the V-1 rocket. Just before midnight, an object was seen coming in from seaward over the ship. It zipped overhead on a straight course, flying very fast, looking like a ball of fire in the night sky.

Dan Bandy: "We were on general quarters right off Normandy. Memhard was on the flying bridge and I was aft on the 3" and I saw this thing coming and he located it and he said it was a buzz bomb. It was pretty low, flying at about 2,000 or 3,000 feet. It looked just like a little airplane. Later on, the Germans used the V-2's. They were demoralizing 'cause you never saw them coming. By then the Germans knew they had no chance, but they used them anyway."

E. Ray Sharpe: "We saw a lot of flying bombs come over. They sent a lot of those over. We saw them at the beachhead. They couldn't change direction or speed. They just went."

Albert Haas' personal diary: "Saturday, June 17, 1944. 'Flying bomb' was seen going across anchorage area. Flares were dropped by enemy planes, illuminating entire harbor. All ships except ours opened fire on approaching bomb and aircraft."

By midnight the crew had secured from general quarters. There was some firing by other ships but none by the *O'Brien*. During the remainder of the night enemy planes were seen overhead but they merely dropped flares and fired from a distance. The crews were on duty virtually around the clock. They stood their assigned watches and spent the rest of the time in a perpetual state of watchfulness.

On June 18 at 0410 general quarters was again sounded. Some enemy planes came in closer only to be repulsed by the firing of the gathered merchant and navy ships. The crew secured from general quarters at 0500.

Cadet Henry Kusel: "There was a lot of action from the anti-aircraft guns. A terrible amount of noise. And we had lots of shrapnel falling on deck."

That night additional passengers came on board, Lt. (j.g.) Webber who was Armed Guard Commanding Officer of the *SS West Grama* with 13 men, and 12 men from the *SS Alcoa Leader*. These were sunken "block" ships and the crews were being evacuated from the beachhead. Through most of that night Allied shore batteries and some of the ships fired at enemy planes overhead.

Having discharged her cargo and loaded her passengers, the ship left "Omaha" in the early afternoon of June 19, 1944. She arrived at her Solent anchorage just after midnight and went alongside the dock in Southampton in the early afternoon of June 20th.

Francis Erdman: "Southampton was my first British city; I was favorably impressed by it. While we were loading we had a chance to visit and to make other excursions. We went up to London. Every night after dinner in Southampton we would sit on the after hatch covers and watch the B-26's setting out across the English Channel to do their nightly bombing. On occasions, we counted fourteen hundred of them -- this by counting the number of planes in a squadron and then the number of squadrons. There was some argument over these counts, but fourteen hundred was about right.

"Later on in the night you would have the enemy's retaliation -- self-propelled bombs, buzz bombs. As long as you heard the motors you were all right -- they were still coming. When the motor stopped you knew they were descending. But they were targeted for manufacturing plants, railroad marshalling yards and other targets inland. For some reason none of them landed in the Southampton Docks."

Captain De Smedt vividly recalled the buzz-bombs flying over. "On the night of June 20, while at anchorage at Southampton, a heavy raid by flying bombs was experienced. A total of 18 flying bombs passed directly over the vessel at high speed, in a northerly direction. Only one of these bombs fell in the Southampton area and caused damage, all others landed far inland. This was the last raid on this port as these bombs were launched from the Cherbourg Peninsula, which our troops captured soon afterward."

Robert Milby also remembered the "buzz-bombs": "They started shooting these V-I rockets over to Southampton and they were pretty exciting. We learned to expect them. They had a chain sound in them, rattling chain, and when that quit, then they were going to dive down."

Deck Cadet Henry Kusel was detached from the ship on June 21 and transferred to the *SS Pearl Harbor* as third mate. "Something happened to the third mate on the *Pearl Harbor* and they were short an officer. So I had to go to the WSA office at the embassy in London. I think both captains were there because they had to agree to the transfer. I was supposed to go back to Kings Point because I had my time in, but I got stuck out there. I became what they called a special cadet afloat. In the end, my sea time ran over the tour of duty. So rather than returning to the academy, I went to take the exam directly after I got back."

On June 22, just after breakfast, the *O'Brien* again sailed from Southampton, this time as flagship of the convoy. But rather than going south to Normandy, the destination was West. Captain De Smedt: "We proceeded to Belfast, Ireland on June 22, from Southampton. I was appointed Commodore of the convoy."

Cadet Tom McGeehan: "Captain De Smedt said his name was Flemish. I think his father was an executive for Grace Line. He used to smoke these big long expensive cigars. He had a good voice like a radio announcer. Somebody, it might have been Pellegrino, nicknamed him 'The Nose,' because his nose was rather prominent. One time the chief engineer heard me say that. He said, 'If the captain ever hears that, you'll get in trouble.' I never used that nickname again."

The short trip passed without incident although there were several small alerts. An escort ship about 2000 yards on the port beam hoisted a submarine contact pennant and dropped six depth charges. The alarm was rung for general quarters. Albert Haas noted in his diary, "During afternoon, escort vessel dropped depth charges about a mile on our port side, causing entire vessel to rumble and vibrate." Nothing further happened and the crew secured from general quarters. Later one of the escort vessels signaled that subs had been sighted and were moving towards the entrance of the English Channel. Again the evening passed without incident. On June 24, the ship arrived at Belfast, Ireland and anchored outside. The following day a fleet of American ships -- two battleships, three cruisers and ten destroyers -- entered the harbor.

Francis Erdman: "The chief engineer went to visit his parents and relatives in Belfast while we were in port. He was an Irishman."

Dan Bandy: We had a "cargo net liberty" there. We laid out a week or two. So when the guys finally did get ashore, they had to be back at midnight. At any rate some of the guys went ashore and when they came back they couldn't make it up the gangway so Pellegrino hauled them aboard in a cargo net."

Away from the front, the poker games resumed. Morgan Williams: "We got along good with all the crew. Pellegrino was friendly. Good card player. I could always lose but I could never win much. I spent a lot of time in the mess galley playing poker."

E. Ray Sharpe: "We had a fellow named Potts on there. He used to play poker all the time. We used to bet French money and English money, anything we had. The soldiers got invasion money, French Francs. Anyway, he got a good hand and he says, 'I'll bet a pound,' English money, see?

"And one of the other guys had a better hand, a real good one, and he says, 'Well, I'll bet a ton.'"

Constant attention to the armament ensured that it worked when needed. Here Seaman First Class E. Ray Sharpe cleans one of the 20 mm's. Credt Dan Bandy

After cleaning, the guns must be oiled and greased. Here Seaman First Class Helbing lubricates a partly-assembled 20 mm. Credit Dan Bandy

Assembled, this 20 mm is loaded and ready to defend the ship.   Credit Dan Bandy

Poker wasn't the only game. According to Third Engineer William Watson, the First Assistant was an expert at chess and checkers. "Lauritsen was his name. He challenged the captain to play chess and at the same time played two games of checkers with two other crewmen."

Belfast was pleasant after the Normandy trips. James O. Runkle recalled visiting the port on the *George Weems:* "We anchored in the bay off Bangor, near Belfast in North Ireland. It was good to see green land, feel warm air, and receive mail."

On Independence day, July 4, 1944, after waiting at anchor for 11 days, the *O'Brien* went alongside the dock. On this same day, 29 days after D-Day, several hundred miles away, on the beaches of Normandy, the one millionth Allied soldier stepped ashore.

Tom McGeehan: "We got up to Belfast and anchored and went in on July 4th. There we picked up Patton's army. It was the first I ever heard about Patton."

The Allied offensive was now well underway, moving rapidly inland toward Germany. General George Patton's Third Army would play a major role and throw the term *"blitzkrieg"* right back into the faces of the Nazi Command.

Seaman First Class "Bob" Robichaud: "I think we took the 5th Division out of Belfast. They were put in 4 and 5 'tween deck in bunks stacked five high. We carried some kind of cargo in the holds, I don't know what. They had army tanks on deck, though."

Tom McGeehan: "I got ashore there. We weren't supposed to go ashore but I took the first engineer to a Navy hospital ship in our lifeboat. This was in the morning and they said to come back at two, so we went back into Belfast and we tied up to a marina. We walked around a bit, but the Northern Irish weren't too friendly."

After all the waiting, the loading was done almost instantaneously. Captain De Smedt received a briefing and the *O'Brien* sailed the following morning at 0825. On board were 23 officers, 386 troops, 227 armored vehicles and 160 tons of explosives. The soldiers were part of General Patton's Third Army, Fifth Division.

Cadet Tom McGeehan: "We picked up a mascot in Southampton, a little terrier.

Morgan Williams: "He was a little brown short-haired dog."

Tom McGeehan continues: "Well, De Smedt and the pilot are on the bridge and all the lines are gone and the pilot is backing off from the pier and someone sees the dog on the pier. So one of the crew hollered up, 'The dog. Go back for the dog.' Pretty soon the whole crew and the Armed Guard is hollering, 'Get the dog.' We had all those soldiers on board and then they took up the cheer. You could hear it all over the harbor, 'Get the dog.' So Captain De Smedt talked to the pilot and they brought the ship back alongside. Someone put a jacobs ladder over and one of the navy guys went over and grabbed the dog and brought him on board."

After waiting a day at anchor outside Belfast a convoy was made up. Captain De Smedt: "The vessel was loaded with troops and armored vehicles and we proceeded to the assault area in convoy on July 6."

All was quiet on July 7 as the convoy worked its way toward Normandy. An escort vessel dropped a target and the ship's Armed Guard had 20 mm gun practice, firing 240 rounds from the starboard guns. As the ship drew near the French coast, Captain De Smedt called the crew together to tell them what to expect. Numerous subs had been sighted and were active in the area from Land's End to beyond Portsmouth. In addition, the enemy had also recently laid several new mine fields in the area. At ten-thirty that night the convoy commodore advised by signal light that the ships could expect an enemy air attack by dawn.

In the early morning of July 9 one of the escorts dropped several depth charges nearby. It was too dark to see what she was after but the alarm was rung for general quarters. So far, the *O'Brien* had been lucky. Through all the Atlantic and Channel crossings, despite the mines, submarines, air attacks and V-1 rockets, she had not been in harm's way. But no one took this good luck for granted or relaxed their vigilance. At every sighting or unexplained event the crew went to general quarters, ready for anything that might happen. Far better to stand down from a score -- or a hundred -- false alarms than to risk not being ready in an emergency. A member of one crew remarked, "I'd rather have a false alarm any day than the real thing."

That evening, the convoy arrived at the "Utah" beachhead. They were part of the typical group of nine transports, 20 LCIs, 25 Liberty ships, 40 LSTs, 75 LCTs and 38 British coastal freighters to arrive at the Normandy assault areas during any one day. The total number of supply ships arriving from D-Day to the end of June was 180 troop transports, 570 Liberty ships, 372 LCIs, 905 LSTs, 1442 LCTs and 788 British coasters. Albert Haas noted "hundreds of ships in the harbor." The daily tonnage handled at Normandy was equal to one-third of the normal import capacity of the United Kingdom.

Tom McGeehan: "We carried them [Patton's army] back to Utah and we arrived there a few days later. Then Eisenhower activated the 3rd Army."

"Chow time." A typical load of troops and vehicles with the soldiers using the hatches as mess tables. Credit Dan Bandy

The day was spent discharging men and equipment. Here they were closer to the action than at Omaha but it still was relatively quiet -- the front had moved inland. One man was posted at each 3"-50 with battle phones while the remaining men on the Armed Guard watch were assigned to the 20 millimeter guns on the bridge. The tension on these was alternated during the day to prevent metal fatigue in the springs. The *O'Brien* continued unloading her cargo. Enemy planes were heard overhead during the night but not seen due to a low, overcast ceiling. The crew stayed inside. Shrapnel from shore batteries went whizzing past the ship, some of it falling on the deck.

"Utah" was known for the ferocity of its German air raids. The historian Samuel Elliot Morison described it in one of his books[3]: "The really brisk time off Utah was the small hours of the morning, which the Luftwaffe chose for raiding. Plenty of warning was given to the invasion fleet by radar. The Luftwaffe ritual was to have a reconnaissance plane drop a line of float

---

[3]   *The Invasion of France and Germany, 1944-1945.*

lights as a guide to the bombers. As soon as the first flare was seen, patrolling PTs began to shoot them out one by one and every vessel that could make smoke did so. In a few minutes the bombers were overhead. The Army ashore and the ships afloat opened with anti-aircraft fire, tracers crisscrossed the sky, burning planes plummeted into the ocean, exploding 1000-kilogram bombs sent up immense geysers. After half to three quarters of an hour the pandemonium ceased and the amphibious forces tried to grab a little sleep before unloading was resumed at daylight."

The *O'Brien's* crew performed valiantly. Nominally civilian, the merchant marine served with distinction and devotion to duty. They became indispensable to the military services. They faced the same dangers from the air and sea, persevering under every condition, doing their duty and giving their lives in service to the nation. Few considered themselves heroes. Their heroes were those who went into battle. The merchant crews worked, sometimes around the clock, on what they began to call the "bus runs" to Normandy -- routine, undramatic, unglamorous. No journalist covered their trips, no historian chronicled their quiet determination, but their role in the war and final victory was crucial.

At noon July 12, having finished her discharge, the *Jeremiah O'Brien* hoisted anchor and left the "Utah" beachhead. With the beaches secured, the supply effort increased in geometric proportions. Albert Haas noted in his diary, "During our passage, we passed six convoys enroute to France."

The *O'Brien* arrived at the Solent at 2200 that evening and anchored. It was early evening on July 13 before she tied up to the Southampton dock. During that night and the next, flying bombs (V-1's) were seen passing overhead.

Captain De Smedt: "Upon completing discharge, we returned to Southampton on July 14, at which time I was appointed Commodore of all E. M. P. convoys in which my ship sailed."

With her next cargo of 13 officers, 271 troops and 135 vehicles successfully loaded, the ship departed Southampton July 15 arriving at the "Utah" beachhead just before seven that evening.

The next day was spent discharging what must have been a

partial load for the ship was empty by 1900. She sailed and anchored at a rendezvous fifteen miles to sea known as Capetown, awaiting orders to cross the Channel. The morning of July 17 was thick with heavy fog that didn't clear until afternoon and the *O'Brien* couldn't sail until 1530, which put her in the Solent the following morning at 0230. Weighing anchor early on July 20, the ship went to Southampton dock, loaded all day and night, and sailed the morning of July 21st, back to "Omaha." While alongside the dock Captain De Smedt obtained a new Mark XIV gyro and three repeaters from the War Shipping Administration and had them installed. They were from the *SS John Troutline* which was torpedoed in the English Channel on her maiden voyage.

Tom McGeehan: "I was in the chartroom one time and he started talking to me about the gyro that just came on board. He was quite excited about it. I hadn't had any courses on the subject yet, but he blabbed about that as if I knew what he was talking about. It was one of the few times he talked to me."

The rough Channel waters continued taking their toll on the men, especially the troops. E. Ray Sharpe: "Seems like all the soldiers got seasick. Some of the guys, the soldiers, not knowing any better, would vomit into the wind and the wind would blow it back on them. It was awful."

The *O'Brien* arrived at the "Omaha" beachhead an hour before midnight on the 21st and spent the next day at anchor doing nothing. The barges used in unloading had been damaged in a recent storm and were unavailable. The early morning of July 23 found the *Jeremiah O'Brien* in the fallout of a battle between German planes in the sky and Allied guns ashore. As the planes circling overhead neared the anchored ships, shore batteries opened fire with 40 mm and 90 mm guns. The shrapnel from the shore batteries' exploding shells rained on deck, creating a hazard for everyone on board.[4] The general alarm was rung to scatter the

---

[4] Anti-aircraft fire usually consisted of proximity shells. These explode at set altitudes. The theory is that the likelihood of a plane being damaged flying into the debris of an exploding shell is greater than it is of being directly hit with a shell. If the shell explodes and doesn't hit a plane, the shrapnel falls into the sea below. If there are ships underneath these explosions the shrapnel falls on them.

On each trip to the beachheads the O'Brien *took several hundred troops and several hundred vehicles.   Here an Army truck is loaded in Southampton. Credit Dan Bandy*

At the beachheads the O'Brien's *heavy lift gear was used to off-load heavy equipment into landing craft alongside.   Credit Dan Bandy*

The DUKW was an agile amphibeous craft that could drive up the beach or into the water. This one heads toward the beach with a full load. Credit National Archives

The Rhino barge was large, bulky and unwieldy, but carried big loads. This one is only partially loaded. Note the large number of ships in the background, typical of the Normandy beachheads. Credit Robert Milby

gun crew in case of a hit and to stand by in case flares were dropped and the ship directly attacked.

E. Ray Sharpe: "We were over there one day and a plane came over and every ship there opened up. A piece of shrapnel fell and hit me on the shoulder. I was wearing a heavy coat and it didn't go through or anything, but I felt it. Didn't hurt me. He dropped one bomb and sunk a barge. I don't know if anyone was on it or not."

Morgan Williams: "There was so much shrapnel we had to wear helmets. A kid on the next ship got killed by falling shrapnel. We saw him buried at sea the next day."

E. Ray Sharpe remembered the incident: "We saw a burial at sea on the ship behind us while we were in the Normandy Beach area. We were anchored at the time. It was a sad sight to see..."

Tom McGeehan: "After we had all that shrapnel falling, an order was issued that only Navy ships were to fire. Another problem was a lot of these young navy gunners weren't watching where they shot and they'd shoot the rigging away on other vessels. So these ships had to go back to Southampton for repairs, to have their cargo gear re-rigged."

William Watson: "A little bit later we got some activity. Some German Air Force came over and did a pretty good job. We were up all night with the searchlight, with the guns... the 3-inch and the twenty millimeters and the forty millimeters they left on deck..."

To everyone's relief it was quiet during the daylight hours. Then, on the following evening, again, pandemonium. From the Armed Guard log: "0100 Enemy planes overhead -- heavy fire from shore batteries." On July 25, "During early morning hours -- beginning about 0030 -- enemy planes overhead several times -- heavy barrages from shore batteries."

The *Jeremiah O'Brien* finished her discharge and sailed once again for England. It was a repeat of the earlier shuttles. She arrived at the Solent on July 26 and anchored. On the 27th she tied up at the Southampton docks. This time there was a slight delay while the cargo was assembled. Most of the weary crew tried to rest but some managed to get ashore.

In general, the English and Americans got along well. Cooperation between the services was outstanding and the civilian population was friendly.   But after several stress-filled years, everyone was getting weary of the crowding, the discomfort and the inevitable jealousies that arose.   American servicemen and sailors are often noisy and boisterous and the more reserved British found this irritating.   Even more irritating to the English men was the attraction the Americans had for many English women.   So, while the English people continued to be friendly and welcoming, often there was no love lost between British and American soldiers, sailors and seamen.

Morgan Williams: "My buddy Bandy and I went into a pub in London one time and Bandy said, 'Look at all the Limeys.'

"They all started grabbing chairs, and we decided we better get out of there and we left."

The wartime rules and precautions continued.   E. Ray Sharpe: "We went ashore one night in Southampton and everybody went to a bar.   They had to carry their gas masks ashore and one guy ended up taking about 20 of them back with him.   He looked like a porcupine."

It wasn't until August 1 that the ship was loaded.   Again it was a light load consisting of 23 officers, 296 troops and 137 vehicles.   An unusual part of the load was 14 police dogs, being shipped to France.

Dan Bandy: "The *O'Brien* carried over to Normandy the only K-9 outfit in the cross-Channel operation.   Several dogs and their handlers.   They were mostly German shepherds, but there was one airedale and one doberman.   The Army sergeant in charge told me they were the only K-9's in the invasion.   I think he said they were a scouting outfit.   One man, one dog.   They respected and obeyed no one else."

Morgan Williams: "The K-9 corps ...   They sent a few German shepherds.   The had them in a cage kind of a deal and they did a lot of barking.   The dogs didn't like it.   They took them off at Normandy and used them for scouting for whatever they wanted to get.   They'd put them on a scent and follow the trail."

Semaphore, now no longer used in the merchant marine, was a common means of communication. Seaman First Class Hardin "wig-wagging" to another ship. Credit Dan Bandy

The *O'Brien* left the same night for the Solent anchorage, sailed the following morning and arrived at "Omaha" beachhead that evening but was unable to discharge due to fog and limited visibility. There was some anti-aircraft firing during the night.

Seaman First Class E. Ray Sharpe: "One night, I was on watch with Swede Swanson and they were shooting these tracers on the beach. Swede looks over at this firing and he says, 'You know, a fellow could get hurt over there.'"

On August 4 unloading started and finished the same day. Tom McGeehan: "After a couple of trips, we'd unload into rhino barges. These were a series of tanks welded together. They measured about two hundred fifty feet by two hundred fifty feet and they had two auxiliary engines in the back. They loaded them and they could hold as many as twenty trucks with the men sitting on top. Of course the decks were awash then. Rhino, they were called. Very much in evidence after the first few trips.

"Each one had a navy chief in command. These guys never shaved or bathed or anything and they were really dirty and looked almost like pirates. They'd come aboard looking for something to eat or just to pass the time and everyone was afraid of them, they looked so bad."

By this time, the main thrust of the invasion had moved far inland -- across France towards Germany. The *O'Brien* crews were eager to get ashore and see the scenes of the recent battles, perhaps collect a few souvenirs.

Dan Bandy: "A week or so after that first trip it wasn't too much of a problem on the beach."

Tom McGeehan: "I snuck ashore one trip. The army medical people were unloading ambulances. So a couple of us told them what we were going to do and we snuck inside one while it was down in the hatch. They unloaded us and we got ashore and we roamed around the beach and picked up souvenirs. Everyone was really nice to us. So when it came time to go back, a beachmaster just ordered a duck to take us back to the ship. We came in under the stern and climbed up a jacobs ladder I had left out and nobody knew we were gone."

On August 5, the ship departed the beachhead and arrived at the Solent anchorage a half hour before midnight that evening, but it was August 9 before she was able to go alongside.

The invasion had been underway for more than two months and the Allies now knew much more about the hazards of crossing the Channel and how to handle them. On August 12 the crew was gathered and given the results of the latest findings. Practically all casualties to Liberty ships on cross-Channel operations were from acoustic mines or torpedoes and the most serious and greatest number of injuries were to men on the stern. These occurred to lookouts whose hips were shattered when an explosion went off under them while they were standing in a rigid position. Captain De Smedt ordered that when underway on the cross-Channel shuttle, everybody was to keep out of the stern quarters and only the lookouts on the gun platform aft were to be allowed. These men were told to sit on the gun or lean in such a way as to be completely relaxed, not in a rigid upright position. Wearing life jackets at all times was stressed.

There were additional instructions for the Armed Guard. The two leading Petty Officers would be stationed on the bridge so that there would be no loss of sector coverage due to the stern lookout arrangement. Also, there had been several cases reported of Germans at the beachheads using so-called "infernal machines" which were snipers disguised to resemble boxes, debris, etc. The Armed Guard was advised that two rifles would be kept on the flying bridge with an extra man, in case of a need to fire at suspicious objects. The gunners were told that Bureau of Ordinance (BuOrd) findings proved it was no longer necessary to change the tension on the gun springs as they had in the past.

As the *O'Brien* got underway for Normandy on Sunday, August 13, the usual church services were held -- mass for Catholics with Church service for Protestants following immediately afterward. The anxiety of the earlier Normandy runs having passed, the urgent requests for spiritual assistance and divine intervention had abated and the communicant population reverted to the pre-invasion few. On this trip the ship carried 21 officers, 296 troops and 137 vehicles.

Captain De Smedt's voyage letter: "On August 14, I arrived at 'Utah' beachhead with troops and vehicles and commenced discharging. A storm broke and the wind reached gale force from the N.E. Heavy swells were experienced and at 0245 August 15, the vessel touched bottom at low water. Soundings taken showed 8 fms. water forward and five fms. aft. The draught aft being 21' 06". Though she only touched bottom once, I pumped 150 tons water overboard from the after peak and transferred fuel oil from No. 6 double bottom to No. 2 double bottom as a precautionary measure. I was unable to shift anchorage before daybreak because of numerous small craft anchored in vicinity."

That evening at 1920 an enemy plane was shot down in flames from a very high altitude. The crew watched the dramatic sight as the blazing plane plummeted, finally falling into the sea between the ship and the beach.

The next few days were spent unloading with little of note happening. The Armed Guard log referred to them as "routine days." Tom McGeehan: "One time I came into the captain's office, he wanted me to do something. He and the chief engineer were sitting there with an expensive bottle of scotch on the desk between them. I lost my balance and dumped the bottle of scotch. He caught it without losing too much, but he gave me one of those dirty looks."

Robert Milby was matter-of-fact about the trips. "I think we averaged about four hundred troops a trip, sometimes more. One time it was just a few. And tanks and trucks and jeeps and supplies and all kinds of things." On this particular trip it was 21 officers, 251 troops and 143 vehicles of the 28th Infantry Division.

Robert Milby: "Once you were unloaded then you pulled anchor and got out of there. I don't know how many ships there was making this back and forth deal. It must have been quite a few 'cause there was constant ships going across."

Just before noon on August 16 anchor was weighed and the ship left the beachhead, arriving at the Solent just before midnight. After waiting three days for a berth, she went alongside the Southampton dock on August 20 and spent the day re-loading for

A woman was a rarity at Normandy. This unidentified WAC lieutenant made one of the O'Brien's crossings. She's pictured with Lt. Memhard, C.O. of the Armed Guard. Credit Dan Bandy

The same WAC lieutenant pictured with Captain De Smedt, the O'Brien's *master. Credit Dan Bandy*

Gunner's Mate Second Class Dan Bandy and Seaman First Class Hardin with the WAC lieutenant. Credit Dan Bandy

Normandy. The load included 20 officers, 308 troops and 158 vehicles.

Sailing again on August 21 she was underway for three hours when a blinker message was flashed calling back all Libertys in the convoy to the Solent anchorage because of bad weather. It was just too rough to unload into the small landing craft and barges at Normandy. After waiting two days for the weather to lay down, they got underway again on August 23. Suddenly, at 1235, the now-complacent routine of crossing the Channel was no longer so.

Captain De Smedt: "On August 23, I was Commodore of convoy E.P.M. 42W. While crossing the Channel, the *SS Louis Kossuth* struck a mine about 250 yards on my starboard quarter. A heavy concussion was felt on my vessel. I turned the convoy over to the Vice Commodore and came about, ready to remove the troops from the *Kossuth* if necessary. Her master signalled that she was in no danger of sinking, but her wheel and rudder was disabled. A tug was ordered to tow her back to Southampton and three escort vessels remained to guard her. I then proceeded to rejoin my convoy."

Tom McGeehan was on the flying bridge at the time. According to him, the ship sank before the tug arrived. "We also had a degaussing device inside the vessel which was supposed to set up a magnetic charge which would keep magnetic mines away. I was up on the bridge at high noon, it was a warm day in August. We felt fairly safe. I felt a thud under my feet and looked around and sure enough there was the ship behind us, a Liberty, sinking. She sank within a matter of minutes. She had a couple of thousand army people on board which the destroyers picked up."

Lieutenant Memhard happened to be looking at the *Kossuth* when she hit the mine and he, too, recorded the event in his log, "A large geyser of water thrown up, fringe of explosion circle appeared to be somewhat discolored, as though from mud. Explosion from my view appeared to take place about under counter of ship. Escort later signalled she had requested *Kossuth* to be towed back to Southampton. General alarm rung. No torpedo wake observed. 1255 Secured from GQ."

Left to right, Captain De Smedt, master of the SS *Jeremiah O'Brien, Frank Pellegrino, chief mate and an unidentified Army officer. Taken during one of the shuttles to the Normandy coast.   Credit Dan Bandy*

Albert Haas recorded the incident in his diary, "ship hit an acoustic mine (or torpedo) causing terrific rumble throughout convoy. In all probability, our ship just missed making contact with enemy weapon."

William Watson was not reassured: "The only other thing that worried me was the mines. They were set to go off after the third or seventh or eighth or tenth ship went over. Saw a lot of them go down. You just never knew." But the *O'Brien's* luck was holding.

That evening they arrived at the "Utah" beachhead and the next two days were spent discharging with the ship sailing on the evening of August 25. She anchored at 2030 for the night at the beachhead anchorage, known as "Capetown," then returned to the Solent anchorage.

From Albert Haas' personal diary: "Enroute to England, Channel became very foggy and upon coming out of the first fog bank, we lost the convoy but still had escorts. It is supposed that the other merchant ships failed to sight the buoy and make a starboard turn at Cherbourg. After coming out of the second fog bank, the escort vessels were no longer with us and we proceeded to Southampton alone. Also, while in one of the fog banks, a Liberty ship missed ramming the stern of our vessel, and at another point our vessel just missed ramming a destroyer escort vessel."

The *Jeremiah O'Brien* went alongside the Southampton dock, loaded 15 officers, 145 troops and 127 vehicles, which took one day and night, then anchored in the Solent on the morning of the 30th for her ninth trip to Normandy. The crew were beginning to feel like yo-yos.

The shuttle runs having become relatively routine, the crew's interests returned to life on board and "Chow" resurfaced as a prime topic. During the excitement of the invasion it had momentarily slipped down the list of priorities but as the trips became ordinary, it resumed its rightful place.

Dan Bandy: "The food on the ship was very good until we got low on supplies in the U.K. because of the invasion and because we'd feed some of the army people when they were on board."

Dan Bandy: "We got to taking on the English supplies and they weren't too good. Then Williams, with his mechanical ability, made a key and got us into an Army supply of rations. Nothing was said about it. We'd go in and take these Army rations. Williams and I had quarters to ourselves, aft, just two bunks in our room. We had a small burner and we'd get these Army rations and heat them up and they were pretty good."

Morgan Williams: "Most of the time the food was real good. But toward the end they ran out. We had to eat K-rations with the soldiers. They furnished plenty of those. For awhile we had some English rations and sometimes the mutton was so rank you couldn't eat it."

Tom McGeehan: "As I remember the food wasn't too great. Toward the end we'd sneak into the Army depot and get Army rations. We were eating a lot of things from the Army, and by the time we got to New York we were pretty well cleaned out."

Some of the crew got ashore while the ship was discharging on her last shuttle. This pillbox is one of the fortifications used by the Germans to defend the Normandy coast.   Credit Dan Bandy

Crewmembers from the O'Brien's Armed Guard inspect a German gun emplacement on the beach at Normandy.   Credit Dan Bandy

Captain De Smedt's voyage letter phrased it more diplomatically: "Commissary stores were supplemented from time to time as needed."

Tom McGeehan had another interest: "From D-Day on, we fed the ranking officers on board. In the officers' mess you have three tables across the front and one separate table aft and off to one side. Well I ate at that separate table in the mess room. It was for cadets and visitors. And they were just magnificent soldiers. I remember a Brigadier General sitting at my table. Normally the captain dominated the conversation in the officers' mess. He always talked to the senior officers. But somehow this general sat with me. He was interested in Kings Point and asked me questions about it and told me all about West Point. I was stunned to have this general eating with me and talking to me."

The crews generally had a high regard for the troops they came in contact with. Especially during the first weeks of the invasion, recognition of the great undertaking, the critical responsibility of the soldiers and the dangerous sacrifices and horrors they would face forged a bond of admiration, sympathy and understanding between them.

But not all the soldiers were as impressive as those on earlier trips. Dan Bandy: "Later, there were different kinds of soldiers. There was a bird colonel that kept talking to me and buttering me up. And he was just scared. I didn't like it 'cause I had seen all these great fighting men on earlier trips. After a while I got tired of this and finally I just let go and I told him off. I said things were quiet on the beaches there, but the enemy had left snipers behind that were just after officers. He really got scared then. So I went to Memhard and told him what I told this guy and the Lieutenant, he tells him the same thing."

Sailing from the Solent on August 31, there was a minor mishap. At 1415 the general alarm was rung as a fire was reported in #4 hold. Vehicles in the hold had been stowed in a hurry and broke loose, smashing together due to the ship's rolling in choppy seas. Each time they hit, they threw sparks. As the vehicles were loaded with gasoline and some of it had spilled, the potential for fire was extreme. The captain had the ship heave to while the cargo was secured.

September 1 was spent unloading at "Utah" and all the cargo was off before midnight. The ship left the beachhead, anchored at the "Capetown" anchorage for the night, crossed the Channel again on September 2, and arrived at the Solent just before 11 in the evening. Again, there were too many ships and not enough berths and it was September 6 before the *O'Brien* could go alongside the dock.

Tom McGeehan: "Pellegrino had been a seaman and worked his way up and he was only in his thirties. He was kind of my mentor. At Southampton we raised the anchor and it had a turn in it so it wouldn't seat properly. To get the turn out you have to send someone over the side, fasten a wire rope around it and turn it with that. So Pellegrino sent me over the side. He put me over in a bosun's chair with this line to fasten to the anchor. It's something you shouldn't do underway. If I fell I would have been sucked right into the propeller. So the captain and the pilot were on the bridge and Captain De Smedt could see something was going on, but he couldn't tell what. He hollered through the bull horn, 'What's going on up there.'

"Pellegrino told him and he hollered back, 'Get that boy up God damn quick or I'll hang you from the yardarm.'

"I came up, but I already had the line secured and we did get the anchor turned."

After one day of quick loading the ship left the dock and anchored in the Solent, awaiting the formation of a convoy. On board were 4 officers, 230 troops and 128 vehicles. As though playing a game of battledores and shuttlecocks, the ships once more left the Solent and arrived at "Utah" in the early evening. It was the *O'Brien's* tenth trip. After three days of unloading, the *O'Brien* left the beachhead on September 12, anchored at "Capetown," then crossed the Channel and arrived back at the Solent. This time the berth was vacant and the cargo ready and the next morning the ship was alongside the Southampton dock.

With all the danger seemingly on "the other side," it was natural to relax while in England, in the relative safety of a well-protected port. But ships and docks are inherently dangerous places with narrow passageways, steep ladders and hard, unforgiving metal and concrete surfaces. While returning from shore with a sack of mail, one of the Armed Guard Gunner's Mates Third Class was seriously injured. At the head of the gangway, just where one steps on to the main deck of the ship, a guy (wire rope holding a cargo boom in place) extended from a boom at #3 hatch starboard and was made fast to an eye on the rail in such a way that it stretched across the gangway. A person coming on board had to duck under or climb over the guy to step to the ship's main deck. The sailor was just bending to go under the guy when he lost his balance and toppled over, falling 25 feet to the cement dock. Fate was not entirely against him. By chance, a hospital unit was being put on board just at the time. The Army doctor set the man's broken arm and took him to an Army hospital in an ambulance. Later Lieutenant Memhard took the sailor's gear and personal effects to the U.S. Navy hospital at Netteley outside of Southampton, where he had been transferred. It was learned his condition was serious, a probable a skull fracture, but fortunately he was not in great danger.

September 15 found the *Jeremiah O'Brien* once again anchoring in the Solent and on the 16th she sailed for "Utah" once more. It was to be the last time. She had on board 23 officers, 467 troops and 205 vehicles. The evening before sailing, a farewell dinner was held aboard the *O'Brien* and attended by Army and Admiralty officers and the American Consul General, Mr. F. Willard Calder. The vessel, her officers and crew were commended for their good work in bringing the mission to a successful conclusion.

After three and a half months, the beach was well secured. According to the Armed Guard Log, the Navy gun crew was allowed ashore at "Utah" beachhead, in the beach area only, for four hours at a time. But this entry was only for the official record. In reality the crew had been going ashore since after the first few shuttles.

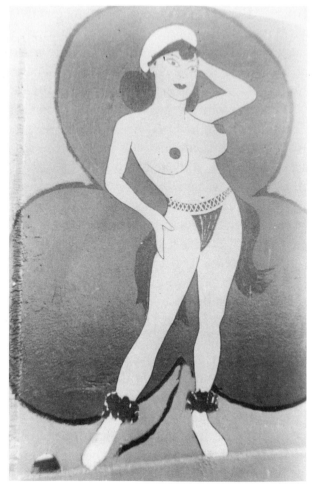

Miss Jerry O'Brien, the ship's pinup, had to be painted over before arrival in the United States. Fortunately she was found intact (under grey paint) and resurrected when the ship became a museum. This photo was taken in 1944. Credit Dan Bandy

Dan Bandy: "We did not get ashore at first. We got ashore later, we would go on any kind of little old DUKW or landing craft. We got ashore as we wanted to after the first few runs."

Going ashore also did not mean simply visiting the beach area. E. Ray Sharpe: "I went ashore in France. We caught a ride with a fellow on a half track. We went to St. Lô." Located twenty miles inland, St. Lô had been headquarters for the German 84th Corps.

Morgan Williams: "The last trip, Memhard let us take turns going ashore. A couple of us went through a minefield. We saw all these trip wires and everything, but you could see where the soldiers had walked there before us and we just walked where they did. So we got to the other side and some soldier yelled at us that two or three guys had been killed there just the day before." What the inexperienced men did not know was that some mines are set to go off after a set number of passes -- the fifth, tenth, etc. So, walking in another's steps was not necessarily proof that the path was not mined. Fortunately for the *O'Brien* gun crew, no mines exploded.

Morgan Williams: "We saw some big bunkers and we did get some souvenirs. I got a potato masher [hand grenade] and different shells and so on. I still have them. So we went about ten miles into France, then caught a ride on a Sherman tank and he brought us back."

Tom McGeehan: "We were thrilled when we found out we were going home. The merchant crew and the navy crew were elated. We had forced down the danger, but we knew it was there. The Germans were still mining the Channel. And the food was bad. That was demoralizing. All K-rations, no fresh milk, no fresh vegetables and we were just about out of everything. We went to Southampton, it was a cold night, and I remember looking at Cherbourg, through the glasses, knowing we were going there. We sailed from Cherbourg to Milford Haven and went in the convoy from there."

The cargo was discharged by September 23 and that morning the *O'Brien* sailed for Cherbourg, France where she arrived in mid-afternoon. During her eleven trips to the assault area the ship carried 3492 troops, 1746 vehicles, 14 police dogs, 117 tons of special cargo and 341 tons of dynamite. On September 24, the *O'Brien* left Cherbourg and the next day arrived at Mumbles Point, off Swansea, Wales.

At about this time Grace Line received an unusual letter in its New York office from the U.S. Coast Guard.

"This office is in receipt of a confidential report from a reliable source, which states that a member of the crew of the *SS Jeremiah O'Brien*, under your operation, made the written statement that there is a still in the engine room of that vessel where the crew draw their own alcohol." The not-exactly-startling allegation was calmly acknowledged by Grace Line which promised to look into the matter.

William Watson remembered it in a very vague way: "I seem to remember hearing something about that. It was a fact, but I don't remember too much about it. I know that somewhere along the way I think I even got a shot of the alcohol."

The ship and crew had been out almost six months, working hard in dangerous conditions in the greatest military maneuver in history. They looked forward to returning to their families and loved ones at home. They were overjoyed to sail just after midnight on September 29. The ship was homeward-bound at last in a convoy toward New York.

Tom McGeehan: "The last thing we saw, we went through St. George Channel and the Irish Sea and all we could see of that was the loom of a light on the Irish Coast. Pellegrino and I were on the flying bridge, and he said, 'Well cadet, that's the last thing of Europe you'll see.'"

The crossing was uneventful except for some minor incidents. On October 6, at 1115, ship #46 of the convoy, the *SS William Ellery*, suddenly opened fire. No flag hoist was up, nor was one put up until 1120. They seemed to be having firing practice. Lieutenant Memhard noted in his log, "Opening fire in such fashion a particularly annoying violation of Mersig's (signaling instructions for merchant ships), since other ships in convoy initially can only go on assumption that firing is at a hostile target."

And there was always the North Atlantic weather. Tom McGeehan: "There had been a hurricane that had passed through a few days earlier and done damage to the East Coast. I don't know if it was the aftereffects, but we were in mid-Atlantic and the ship was rolling terribly. The Chinese cooks were crying and wailing down below. Pellegrino said, 'I never heard of one of these ships rolling over but let's go up on the flying bridge and see.' So we went up and the wind was blowing like hell, and of course up that high you really feel it. She was rolling really bad, probably forty degrees each way. It was all we could do to hold on."

As the ship neared the East Coast the crew relaxed visibly. Wartime precautions and military rules gave way to civilian concerns. What had happened while they were gone? Had their friends changed? Had <u>they</u> changed? Would their homecoming be welcomed? Helmets and gas masks were collected from all personnel. A bulletin was posted advising the ship's company of federal ballot particulars and setting October 10th as voting day. Franklin D. Roosevelt was running for his fourth term with Harry Truman as his Vice-President.

The North Atlantic weather was, as usual, foul. The fog set in so thick that the gun crew didn't stand general quarters in the morning. Visibility was zero. On October 10, the crew voted by Federal ballot. Lieutenant Memhard, who was the ballot officer for the ship, recorded that only two members of the Merchant crew voted. Perhaps the others planned on voting after they got ashore.

Coming back to home port required that one final detail be attended to. Gunner's Mate Morgan Williams: "Miss O'Brien was a painting we had on the forward gun tub. Kind of a pin-up, like on the planes. Well, she was naked, bare-breasted and everything and there was a chance we'd get into trouble, so we had to paint her over with gray coming back into New York."

Finally, on October 12, at 1800 the ship arrived at the Ambrose light ship, marking the approach to New York Harbor. The voyage was over. The ship had made it through. Seemingly protected by a lucky charm, she had triumphed over the worst the North Atlantic could give, braved the Nazi bombs, torpedoes and shelling barrages, delivered her cargo, and brought her crew safely home.

Tom McGeehan: "We got back on Columbus day October 12, 1944. I remember we took arrival and the pilot came aboard and the captain made the remark that we had been out six months to the date."

Dan Bandy: "I would have said it was a happy crew, the merchant crew got along good. Captain de Smedt was a good man, he was very accommodating, very good with the Navy crew. I would say at that time he was in his early forties or mid-forties. All the way through we had a good crew on that ship. She was a good old happy ship." It was high praise.

On the day of payoff the crew filed through the saloon, collecting their wages. In the passageway outside, plans were made, good-byes were said. One by one or, in some cases, in groups of two or three, seamen walked down the gangway, their belongings in a duffel bag slung over their shoulders or carried in suitcases. Some were happy to be getting off, others were sad at losing friendships. As they reached the end of the dock they turned for one last look at the ship, their home for the previous six months, a never-to-be-forgotten voyage.

Tom McGeehan: "Lieutenant Memhard was the last guy I saw. I was walking down the pier and he was going the other way. Of course I was in uniform, so I saluted and he saluted back. He said, good-bye, it had been nice sailing together and so on. We talked a little and the last thing he said was, 'Keep smiling, Cadet.'"

As usual, when in port...

E. Ray Sharpe: "Al Helbling, from Ohio. He was young and heavy set. He and another guy went ashore in New York. They went up to this bar and there was all these Coastguardsmen in the place. You could tell them 'cause they had a shield on their uniform. So Helbling and this other guy says, 'Move over shallow water, let the deep blue sea in.' Well they moved over all right. All over them. They came back to the ship with the biggest shiners you ever saw. The shiners lasted about two weeks and every time we'd see one of them in the passageway we'd tell them, 'Move over shallow water.'"

Voyage four was not completely history. The Coast Guard still had a score to settle. William Watson: "I remember when we came into New York they searched the ship. Someone from the Coast Guard made a look-see through the ship trying to find that still they got the letter about. But it was a happy ship, everyone was good friends with everyone else. All friendly and helpful."

Francis Erdman: "We arrived in New York and dropped anchor in the outer bay. A launch came alongside and we paid off -- and I took off. The last time I saw her, looking back, the *O'Brien* was lying quietly, rusty sided and war-worn -- but a good ship that had seen us through."

11

IN THE SHADOW
OF THE ANDES

W e rejoin the ship several days later at the Bethlehem Dry
Docks in Hoboken, New Jersey, where she has just been
given a "shave and a haircut." This is maritime slang for a quick,
routine drydocking. The ship was showing the effects of the
heavy duty. Gunner's Mate Morgan Williams: "When we was
over in Normandy, she got where she needed painting pretty bad."
No major repairs were necessary. All she needed was the barnacles scraped off her hull and several coats of fresh paint.

On October 20 the *Jeremiah O'Brien* moved to Pier #3 on
the North River in New York to load a mixed general cargo of
trucks, foodstuff and machinery for the Canal Zone. After the
long, eventful voyage No. 4, many of the crew needed a vacation
and the ship received almost an entirely new complement. The
replacements came from many different backgrounds.

Gunner's Mate Third Class Robert Crocker: "I joined her in
New York. When you come to port, you'd get two weeks ashore.
Marieko and Doyle and I had been on the previous ship together

and we met up at the Armed Guard Center on First Avenue and Fifty-Second Street, Brooklyn, New York. There was also one in New Orleans and another one in San Francisco. It was a busy place. There would be survivors coming in and new crews going out constantly. When I got out of boot camp, they sent me there immediately. Anyway, Marieko and Doyle and I were all there together and we all had the same rating, gunner's mate. So they were looking for a crew for the *O'Brien* and we said, 'Let's take this one and we can ship out together again.' So we told the guy making the assignments, 'Here's your three gunner's mates for that crew.' And he put us right on board."

Ensign Norman Robinson, Armed Guard Officer-in-Charge: "I was slated for the *PC1158* as a pharmacist's mate. I shipped out of Boston, transferred to a destroyer *DE683*, again as a pharmacist's mate. We ran convoys between Trinidad and Gitmo [Guantanamo Bay, Cuba]. We had no trouble, it was nice duty. Then I was sent to "90-Day Wonder" school in Princeton and ended up on the *O'Brien* as an officer."

Third Assistant Engineer Carl Scharpf: "I graduated from Johns Hopkins with a mechanical engineering degree in June of 1940. I went to work for an aircraft company, testing aircraft engines. So in early January of forty-two they put me on an engine test stand, testing experimental bomber engines, working midnight to ten a.m. six nights a week. It was noisy as hell. I was exhausted and fed up with the long hours. I'd been at sea in the summer when I was in college and had five months sea time as a wiper. So in the spring of forty-two I realized I had five months of time in the engine room, and with another month and my degree I would be eligible for a marine engineer's license. The Maritime Commission put me on the *American Seaman* as a fireman and with my month on there I was able to go to Fort Trumble in New London and get my license."

First Assistant Engineer William Wallace: "Before I got on the *Jeremiah O'Brien* I had been working on a Grace C-2, the *Santa Barbara*. I was third assistant, then second. The boilers leaked all the time and that was a real headache. I worked on her for two years with hardly a day off, so I got off the ship in New

York. I wanted to raise my license to chief and I was planning
to come home for a vacation. So I was in the company office
collecting my vacation pay and I ran into Montgomery. He and
I were very good friends and he said he was looking for a first
assistant. I says, 'No, I'm going home.'

"He said, 'Well, the ship is going down the west coast of
South America and she'll be back before Christmas.' So I said,
'O.K. I'll go.'"

Captain De Smedt went on to become Port Captain in Grace
Line's New York office and was replaced by Captain Arthur J.
Gunderson. Ted Martin, Seaman First Class, recalled Gunderson
as, "about two hundred pounds with a rough complexion and
thick, wavy hair. He was Norwegian, no accent but rough-look-
ing. He was a hell of a nice guy, but don't do him wrong. He
was very stern with the crew. He wasn't social at all, very confined, stayed to himself a lot on the ship. He was a rough-spoken
man. When he said something, you got on your heels."

Norman Robinson: "Captain Gunderson, he was Norwegian. He was a fine man. He was strictly business. He handled
us well. He might have been called severe by some people, but
he was all right. We got along fine."

Voyage 5 began at midnight on November 1, 1944. Casting
off her lines, the O'Brien passed through the submarine nets to
New York harbor at 2034. For the first time in her career, she
was traveling independently. According to the Secret Log[1] her
course was s/c [steering course] 144 T. [true]. This is south-
southeast from New York and toward Florida. As if in reward for
her valiant service on the storm-lashed North Atlantic, the O'Brien
was heading for warmer climes.

Norman Robinson: "We went down for a load of copper ore
in Chile and Peru."

---

[1] Secret Logs were carried on all merchant vessels during the war. Information relating to course steered, speed made good and prominent landmarks
were entered in this log and not in the deck log as peacetime tradition dictates.
The Jeremiah O'Brien's secret log for earlier voyages was not available as of
this writing. See Appendix F for information regarding filling out the Secret
Log.

Carl Scharpf: "We made a special trip down there to get war materials. I got my first exposure to the Spanish language on the *Jeremiah O'Brien*. I went below and my fireman was from Chile. He couldn't speak English and I couldn't speak Spanish, but we got along."

William Wallace: "I heard this story that on the previous voyage some of the crew were hard up for something to drink so they concocted some kind of mixture and made a still out of a fire extinguisher. The chief heard about it and someone offered him a drink and he took it down straight and it was so raw that he could hardly keep it down. Then, when they got into New York, somebody came aboard the ship and inquired of the chief about the still. The chief said very loudly, 'I don't know anything about any still.' That tipped the crew off."

The Armed Guard set Condition III the next day, normal watchstanding at sea. Robert Crocker: "I was gunner's mate in charge of the eight 20 mms. We also had a 3"-50 on the bow and a 5"-38 on the stern.[2] We had one gunner's mate on the twenties and one on the bow gun and one on the five inch aft. Then there was one coxswain who the gunner's mates reported to."

According to the Secret Log, at noon the first day out, the ship had steamed for 15 hours and 26 minutes since departure for a distance of 178 miles, making good a speed of 11.4 knots. Although it was November, the weather was warm and pleasant -- a welcome change from New York's leaden skies and cold winds.

Carl Scharpf: "I spent my twenty-fifth birthday on there. We made a trip of seven or eight weeks. It was very comfortable and we had a pleasant crew. They were all nice people, I enjoyed it very much."

William Wallace: "Being first assistant I had the four-to-eight in the morning and afternoon. When I got off watch I

---

[2] The standard armament for a Liberty ship was eight 20 mm machine guns, one 3"-50 on the bow and one 5"-38 on the stern. Because of this and the fact that some of the gun crew sailed on other Libertys they recall (after 50 years) the *O'Brien* having a 5" gun aft. This was not the case. The shipyard records show a 3"-50 was installed at each end of the ship. In addition, Navy records show that 5" ammunition was never carried on board.

wanted to take a shower and read a little and go to bed, but Montgomery wanted somebody to talk to and he would catch hold of me when I came off duty and I'd visit with him for a while."

On November 3, a Liberty ship was sighted on the port side on the horizon, travelling parallel to the *O'Brien*. The crew watched with interest as the other ship kept the same position all day long, mirroring the *Jeremiah O'Brien's* course. Just as the four-to-eight watch came on on November 4, a signal light flashed through the dark. It was a British Destroyer Escort. She identified herself as (D.E.) *K 377* and asked for the *O'Brien's* radio call sign. The call letters KXCH were flashed and acknowledged. After checking her vessel lists, the British ship flashed back an acceptance and continued on her way.

Fifty years later Robert Crocker still remembered, "KXCH was our call sign. A funny thing, I was a gunner's mate but I was probably one of the very few gunner's mates in the Armed Guard who did signalling by light. Normally we had a signalman for that. So sometimes I would get up there and shoot the breeze with ships that were going by."

Ted Martin: "Crocker spent all his time on the bridge working the signal light. He was always up there, six or eight hours a day. He knew more about the flasher than the signalman did. He could send and receive faster than anyone."

The daily entry in the Secret Log was, "Noon St. [steaming] Time 24h 00m, dist. 281 miles, speed 11.7 knots, departure to noon, st. time 2d 15 h 26m, dist. 724 miles, speed 11.4 knots. Lat. 28-44N, Long. 73-57W, Base Course 187 T." By comparison the deck log for the day contained only weather observations and the names of the men on watch. No other information was allowed.

On November 5 six ships at varying distances were seen, some on the horizon and some closer at hand. Three of them were in a small convoy consisting of a large cargo vessel traveling with a troop transport and a single destroyer for escort. They came up from the stern and quickly overtook the *O'Brien*. As they passed they asked for identity signals. In the course of a

On the Atlantic seaboard and in the Caribbean challenge by blimp, as well as military vessels, was common. In this photo a Navy blimp checks the identity of two merchantmen.   Credit National Archives

lengthy signal light conversation with Bob Crocker, these were given and accepted.

By November 6, the ship was in the Caribbean. The icy grey waters of the Atlantic had given way to a deep rich blue with pastel green shades in the shallower areas close to shore. Cuba was sighted off the starboard bow, a verdant green island mass, covered with lush foliage. The off-duty crew basked in the warm sun, glad to be away from the cold of the eastern seaboard. The war seemed far away. But it could not be completely forgotten. Here, the challenges to the ship's identity came from the air. At 1105 the ship was challenged by a Navy patrol blimp. The answer was given by flag hoist. The blimp acknowledged the signal and quietly drifted away, continuing her patrol.

November 7, 1944. "Secret Log: St. Time 24h 00m, dist. 300 miles, speed 12.5 knots[3], departure to noon st. time 5d 15h 26m, dist. 1599 miles, speed 11.8 knots."

---

[3] This was the fastest day's run recorded in the Secret Log for the *O'Brien's*

Because the *O'Brien* was traveling alone in the still-potentially-dangerous waters of the Caribbean, she was required to zig-zag, a series of frequent course changes designed to confuse any submarine that might be lining the vessel up in her crosshairs. Once released, torpedoes travel in a straight line until they hit their target or run out of fuel and sink. Zig-zagging was thought to improve a ship's chances by either confusing the submarine commander enough to make him reluctant to fire or turning the ship out of the path of an already-fired torpedo. The Germans had developed an acoustical torpedo that homed on the sound of a ship's propeller but zig-zagging was continued because not all U-boats had the newer device.

For the Armed Guard crew it was easy duty. Robert Crocker: "We didn't have anything to do but take care of the guns. The twenties always worked fine. If something went wrong you'd have to help them, find out what was wrong. Sometimes we kept four guns loaded and four unloaded. We'd rotate the tensions, there was 60 pounds of tension on each drum, each held 60 rounds. One man to a gun.

"They were not easy to load. We would have like a steel rope attached to the gun and the pedestal. You'd have to pull it up to get the tension. Then you'd toss the sixty rounds on. There's a clip up along the top of the barrel. You load and it's cocked and you're ready. When you shoot the sixty rounds, you have to load another."

November 8, 1944. Secret Log: "Noon St. time 24h 00m, dist. 236 miles, speed 9.8 knots. Dep. to noon st. time 6d 15h 26m, dist. 1835 miles, speed 11.5 knots. Lat. 12-14N, 79-30W, Base Course Var's."

As they neared the Panama Canal Zone, security became tighter. On November 9, despite very heavy rain and very low visibility, they were challenged by a Patrol boat which signalled for the ship's International call sign. The *O'Brien* answered quickly. The "G" flag, requesting a pilot, was hoisted. Another Patrol boat challenged, again asking for the ship's Secret

---

early years. She was probably being helped along by one of the coastal countercurrents from the Gulf Stream.

Recognition signal and speed.   Again the ship answered.   At 1250, just outside Limon Bay the pilot came aboard and the "G" flag was exchanged for an "H" indicating a pilot was on board.[4] As he guided the ship through the breakwater, the crew had their first glimpse of Gatun Locks, the entrance to the Canal itself. This soon disappeared behind a lush, green hill as the ship eased to her left toward the commercial section of Cristobal.   By 1530 the *O'Brien* was alongside the dock and tied up, preparing to discharge her cargo.   The air was thick with the smells of the jungle, light perfumes from tropical flowers, the richness of growing plants and the underlying heavier miasma of decayed vegetation.

Secret Log: "1017 Arr. Cristobal, noon to arrival st. t. 22h 17m, dist. 166 miles, speed 7.44 knots, New York to Cristobal, st.t. 7d 13h 43m, dist. 2001 miles, speed 11.0 knots.   Arrival Cristobal 1417 G.C.T. [Greenwich Coordinated Time] -- 1017 l.t. [local time] 1248 Pilot abd.   1329 let go port anchor 30 fms. Awaiting docking order.   1436 docking pilot on board & heave anchor.   1530 tied up to dock, FWE [Finished With Engines]."

German submarines were still operating on the Atlantic Coast and the United States was urgently aware of the potentially crippling effects of a successful attack on the Canal, the "crossroads of the world."   The Allies (in reality, primarily the United States) were fighting a two-ocean war and the Canal was the supremely-critical and extremely vulnerable, link, conduit and supply line between the Atlantic and the Pacific. Damage to the Canal would force ships to take an almost 8,000-mile journey around Cape Horn, subject to conditions that were even worse than on the notorious North Atlantic.   Security -- total, absolute and impenetrable -- was required to safeguard this passage.

One of the first people on board after the *O'Brien* tied up was a Navy officer.   Before escorting Captain Gunderson ashore for a routing interview, he briefed him on rules and regulations for ships in the Canal Zone.   The briefing was lengthy,

---

[4]   At this time the "G" and "H" flags stood for "George" and "How" respectively.   In later years the international phonetic pronunciation would be changed with "G" and "H" standing for "Golf" and "Hotel."

encompassing updating codes and publications, what to do under various attack or alert conditions and the types of wartime blackouts used in the area.[5]

An alert was called for the nights of the 15th, 16th and 17th of November and all hands were ordered to remain aboard ship during the hours of the alert. Cargo unloading proceeded slowly due to frequent and heavy downpours. Rainfall for the Atlantic side of the Canal is 130 inches each year.

Alerts notwithstanding, shore leave was granted but on a limited basis. A memo from the Port Captain of the Canal Zone to all shipping agents stated:

> In the interest of security every vessel at any dock or mooring within Canal Zone waters shall be ready to move at all times on a moment's notice. At least one third of the ship's officers and crew must be kept on board at all times so that the ship may be ready to move on a moment's notice. The captains and crews of vessels should be on board at least 12 hours prior to going to sea or transiting the Panama Canal.

The humid air combined with the tropical temperatures gave Cristobal a pleasant, "shirtsleeve" atmosphere. The docks were in the heart of town and the *O'Brien's* crew, when allowed ashore, enjoyed brief excursions to the nearby restaurants and bars. These were either built without fronts or had large paneless windows to let the customers enjoy the balmy air and watch the passersby on the sidewalks. The overall feeling was one of pleasant lethargy, an oasis from the battles in the far reaches of the Atlantic and Pacific.

Norman Robinson: "Panama was very exciting. We had shore leave at night that was very good. It was very different from Massachusetts. I just stayed up as long as I could. It was very impressive and very colorful. The color of the water in that part of the world was so absolutely gorgeous. It was so different from the dark grey Atlantic."

---

[5] See Appendix G for more detailed instructions given to merchant ships in the Panama Canal Zone.

William Wallace: "It seems that in the Panama Canal it's always hot and humid and rainy."

The Canal transit was scheduled for November 17, arranged in advance by Grace Line. The ship left the dock in ballast at 0628 that morning, dropped anchor in the stream at 0715, took on a Canal pilot and approached the first lock. In addition to native linehandlers, a detail of U.S. Marines was placed aboard. This relieved the Armed Guard crew of their duties and allowed them to watch the process of going through the locks. Many of the off-watch merchant crew also came out on deck to observe the fascinating procedure.

The first set of locks separate the Atlantic Ocean from Gatun Lake and, appropriately enough, are named Gatun Locks. As the *O'Brien* approached the open gates and eased into the lock, the linehandlers threw heaving lines to compatriots on the concrete walls on either side. These were fastened to eyes in wire rope cables which in turn ran off constant tension winches fastened to the "mules" running on tracks along both sides of the locks. The "mules" (named for the animals used to pull barges on the Erie Canal) were actually electric locomotives, each one weighing more than 50 tons and having more than 35 tons of pull or braking power. Once the heaving lines were fast, the linemen pulled the cable ends to the *Jeremiah O'Brien's* bow and stern. The ship was now held in place in the center of the lock basin with a mule on each side of the bow and stern keeping her in place with their constant tension winches. The floating gates, each weighing 720 tons, yet so finely engineered that they were moved with a 40 horsepower motor, were then closed. Fresh water from Gatun Lake was pumped into the basin until the *O'Brien* floated at the same level as the water in the lock in front of her. The gates separating the two locks were opened and the mules carefully guided the ship into the next basin where the process was repeated. Exiting the final basin of Gatun Lock (there are three), the mules were cast off and the *O'Brien* found herself floating on Gatun Lake, 85 feet above the Atlantic. To their right the crew could see the top of the spillway to Gatun Dam. One and a half miles long and one-half mile wide at its base, it was the largest earthen dam in the world when built as part of the Canal project that opened a new era in global shipping on August 15, 1914.

The water in Gatun Lake is fresh and very pure. Merchant ships often take advantage of passing through the lake to fill their tanks and, if time allows, to wash down the ship with fire hoses.

Approaching the Canal proper, the *O'Brien* passed the largest island in the lake, Barro Colorado. Here, capuchin and howler monkeys chased each other through the treetops, ignored by the alligators and iguanas sunning themselves below. Then, as lush green hills and mountains rose abruptly on either side, the ship entered Gaillard Cut, the most difficult section of the canal to engineer. Evidence of the 674 million yards of earth removed to dig the eight mile-long "ditch" was obvious in the broad sweeping cuts and terraces rising on either side, partially covered with meadows and groves of trees. From the banks of the encroaching jungle could be heard the lazy singing of the striped cuckoo, "Tres, tres, tres, pesos, pesos, pesos." Tiny birds, blue-black grassquits, popped out of the tall grass like buzzing black popcorn as the ship passed. Crewmembers pointed out the sights to one another: screeching flocks of parrots bounding from tree to tree, toucans calling across the treetop canopy, an iridescent blue butterfly flitting though the dark jungles, an occasional boa constrictor hanging in sinuous loops from a tree branch.

After crossing the continental divide, the ship approached Pedro Miguel Locks. Linehandlers rowed out to the ship and clambered aboard to receive the lines from the mules. The single basin at Pedro Miguel lowered the ship 31 feet to the level of Miraflores Lake. A short traverse then took the *O'Brien* to the double basin of Miraflores Lock. Here the ship was lowered in two stages the remaining 64 feet to the level of the Pacific. The crew marveled at the massive 82-foot gates that separate the final basin from the ocean.

"That's because the tidal range here is twenty-feet," the pilot explained. "On the Atlantic side, it's only three feet, so we don't need them so big there."

After clearing the last lock, the pilot, linehandlers and Marine detail were dropped off.[6] The ship passed through the submarine nets and into the Pacific at approximately 1728, bound for Antofagasta, Chile. Secret Log: "Canal transit from 0922 to 1728. 1728 (2228 G.C.T.) departure Balboa." Then it was back to routine days at sea, zig-zagging south toward Chile.

Robert Crocker: "Our typical day was fairly quiet. The petty officer stood watch and you'd have shipboard watches. You'd make sure the men were awake and up on the guns and relieve each one for a coffee break. I'd go up on the bow and relieve both men and they'd go get coffee. Then when they came back I'd go to the bridge, and then the stern, and relieve them. And another thing, you'd have to be sure the next watch was awake. At night I'd have to make sure they had half an hour to stand outside to get their eyes adjusted so when they went on watch they could see properly.

"We had eight men, one on each of the twenties. On the three inch there was one gun captain, one sighting, one pulling the trigger and at least two loaders -- five or more. The aft gun would have five or six or even seven. The gunnery officer would be on the bridge. Then you had the signalman and the radiomen. The signalman would be up there on the bridge to handle the light and the flags. The radioman would alternate with the merchant marine in the radio room."

The voyage south was through calm, deep indigo water. The skies were pale blue with wispy white clouds. At times pelicans flew in a straight line from one end of the horizon to the other. As the *Jeremiah O'Brien* approached, the line of birds bent farther and farther in the direction the ship was travelling until finally one bird took the initiative and broke the stream, passing astern of the ship with the remainder following it. The ship crossed the equator for the first time in her career, but the traditional ceremony was ignored. Captain Gunderson was against such "foolishness."

---

[6] In the late 1960's, when the author went through the Canal on a Victory ship, the cost for the transit was approximately $14,000. Twenty-some years earlier, when the *Jeremiah O'Brien* went through, it can be assumed it was somewhat less.

As the ship passed the coast of Peru, the Andes were seen, tall, snow-covered, in the distance.

Eight days after leaving Panama, at 0425 on the morning of November 25, land was sighted off the port bow. At 0825 two patrol planes circled the ship asking for identification. The *O'Brien* answered and the planes flew off toward land. As the port of Antofagasta, Chile came into view the crew saw a barren plain beyond it that swooped quickly upward into high, scrub-covered coastal mountains and, in the distance, once again, the snow-capped Andes. By 1320 the ship was tied up fore and aft to the pier at Antofagasta.

Robert Crocker: "I wasn't too impressed with South America. You could see a lot of the German influence there. We didn't care for them and they didn't care for us. And that's the way it was."

Ted Martin: "At the time there was a lot of resentment against America in that port."

William Wallace: "I believe there was quite a few German sympathizers in South America."

Norman Robinson agreed: "There was a strong German feeling in Chile."

It took three days to load the cargo of copper and lead ingots and plates. Loading went slowly due to security measures.

Robert Crocker: "That was because the previous ships had bombs put on board. So we put a petty officer at the head of the gangway and we'd frisk the workers, the longshoremen, as they came on board. They slowed down because of that."

No one had thought to brief the crew on what to expect in South American ports. As in many other parts of the world, the local stevedores considered it their right to supplement their incomes with a "share" of the goods being loaded or unloaded. Kept within bounds, it is a tradition that most experienced foremen turn a blind eye to. The mostly young and inexperienced crew, however, feeling responsible for their cargo, tried to protect it.

Norman Robinson: "Some of the locals began stealing stuff so we took stern measures watching them."

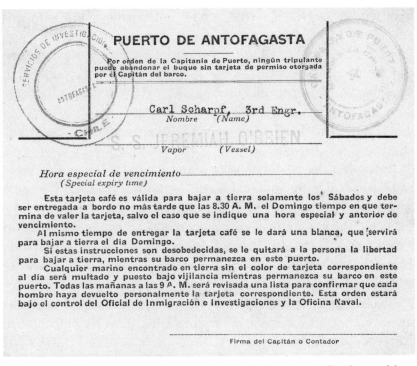

PUERTO DE ANTOFAGASTA

Por orden de la Capitanía de Puerto, ningún tripulante puede abandonar el buque sin tarjeta de permiso otorgada por el Capitán del barco.

Carl Scharpf, 3rd Engr.
Nombre   *(Name)*

Vapor   *(Vessel)*

Hora especial de vencimiento
(Special expiry time)

Esta tarjeta café es válida para bajar a tierra solamente los Sábados y debe ser entregada a bordo no más tarde que las 8.30 A. M. el Domingo tiempo en que termina de valer la tarjeta, salvo el caso que se indique una hora especial y anterior de vencimiento.

Al mismo tiempo de entregar la tarjeta café se le dará una blanca, que servirá para bajar a tierra el día Domingo.

Si estas instrucciones son desobedecidas, se le quitará a la persona la libertad para bajar a tierra, mientras su barco permanezca en este puerto.

Cualquier marino encontrado en tierra sin el color de tarjeta correspondiente al día será multado y puesto bajo vijilancia mientras permanezca su barco en este puerto. Todas las mañanas a las 9 A. M. será revisada una lista para confirmar que cada hombre haya devuelto personalmente la tarjeta correspondiente. Esta orden estará bajo el control del Oficial de Inmigración e Investigaciones y la Oficina Naval.

Firma del Capitán o Contador

Wartime regulations were strict even in South America. This brown liberty card was issued for Saturday only. A new white one was issued for Sunday. Credit Carl Scharpf

Ted Martin: "They were anti-social. In fact I pretty near got pulled off the ship because I pulled a gun on a worker. We carried forty-five automatics. I caught a guy stealing so I pulled a gun on him and they came and tried to take <u>me</u> off the ship!"

Norman Robinson: "The chief of police came aboard and started to squawk and we escorted him off. Took him ashore with an armed escort."

Ted Martin, continues the tale: "That didn't go over too good. The captain went ashore and I went ashore. They had some kind of conference and they took our guns away after that."

Norman Robinson, chuckling, "I was called ashore to Naval HQ. I received a mild reprimand for not being 'diplomatic'."

For many of the crew it was a foreign port in a strange, exotic country and, as always, the lights of the town beckoned.

Norman Robinson: "Antofagasta was a very coppery town, as far as the earth was concerned. There was a lot of red earth like you see in Georgia with copper tones, and barren. But the city itself, I liked."

Carl Scharpf: "I didn't see much of the city, it was wartime and you had to be cautious. But it was pleasant to get ashore. It was interesting to get off the ship and see a few people." There were other things to do, too.

Robert Crocker: "For recreation we went to the race track and things of that type."

Ted Martin: "I went ashore and I hired a guide and Swan and I went up in the mountains and went trout fishing. We spent some time sight-seeing around the town, too."

But there wasn't time to do much. On the morning of November 28, the ship moved out to an oiling barge for fuel. This involved dropping both anchors and tying up to buoys to take on the fuel. By noon they were underway again, bound for Callao, the port for Lima, Peru. Their cargo was copper and lead ingots and plates. A letter in the ship's file from Hugh Caldwell, Acting Chief, Insurance, Claims & Customs Branch of Reconstruction Finance Corporation states that the cargo of copper was consigned to the U. S. Commercial Company. This was a front for a government agency.

Carl Scharpf: "We made a special trip down there to get war materials. That was my understanding. What we picked up was to be used in the manufacture of ammunition."

At this point some friction developed between the military and civilian crews. Apparently the Armed Guard crew wasn't getting along very well with the ship's merchant crew. Normally the Armed Guard log is restricted to terse statements of fact. Anything else entered there is usually the result of deep-felt conviction or emotion or, in this case, frustration. It may be, too, that without the need to pull together to fight the threat of submarines, torpedoes, planes, bombs and shore fire, the men now had time to not get along. Ensign Robinson's log entry for November 29, reads. "Discussion with the Master, Captain Gunderson, concerning Armed Guard men handling the lines and swinging out the Life Boats, particularly when the Merchant crew is not doing its full duty."

But Bob Crocker remembered Robinson as "a very nice person. He was a good egg."

Sailing closer to shore now, the ship passed rugged, rocky terrain where the coastal mountains seemed to plunge into the sea. Occasional small towns were seen on high bluffs overlooking the ocean. As the *O'Brien* approached Callao, the topography leveled off, revealing a well-protected natural harbor.

On December 1, The *Jeremiah O'Brien* entered Callao, Peru and was tied up fore and aft to pier #1 before noon. The ship would be in port only a day and the crew, each in his own way, tried to make the most of the time.

William Wallace: "The American consul sent a notice down to the ship. They listed all the shops and everything that were run by the Germans and they advised us not to deal with the enemy."

Carl Scharpf: "I took a streetcar to Lima. Lima was the capital and it was about a half hour streetcar ride to Lima. I remember there was a church, the Cathedral de San Isidro and inside there was the mummified body of Pizarro. I remember seeing that."

Norman Robinson: "There were distinct Spanish influences in Lima. We only had a matter of a few hours there, just a short time ashore. I remember the flowers growing down the center dividers of the streets and there were lots of trees."

Ted Martin: "We took taxis into Lima. They had barrooms like you find everywhere else in ports. We weren't there that long."

Departure was taken at 1948 the following evening, with the ship bound for Cristobal, on the Atlantic side of the Canal Zone. Perhaps due to the quick loading, the cargo had not been well-secured.

Ted Martin: "We had a problem with the ore. The cargo was big sheets of metal ore. It broke loose in the hold and had to be re-secured. That happened almost as soon as we left port. The strapping broke loose. In fact they had to strip the canvas off the hatches and secure the cargo with four by fours and come-alongs."

The rest of the run up the west coast of South America was peaceful. The deck department took advantage of the good weather to lubricate the cargo gear and touch up some of the paintwork. The traditional poker game resumed. Some of the crew spent off-duty time on deck watching cormorants and pelicans working thick schools of anchovies. Life aboard settled into a pleasant routine.

William Wallace: "I liked Libertys. In some ways they were a lot simpler than other ships. It was a very nice trip. We had good weather."

On the morning of December 7, a small craft was sighted on the horizon that appeared to be broken down. As the *O'Brien* headed toward the vessel, it began sending light signals. The boat was to the east of the ship with the morning sun behind her and her light was too small and weak to be readable. As the ship drew closer, the mate on watch found the "distressed" craft to be a U.S. Naval Patrol vessel which asked the routine question, "What are your International and Secret Recognition signals." Once these were sent, the patrol boat signalled permission to "proceed".

Later that day, in the Gulf of Panama, a second Patrol vessel requested the ship's Secret and International Calls. Once given, the ship was ordered to hoist in place of the Ship's Call sign a two flag hoist of "Zebra-Queen." This identified the ship to Canal authorities and established her turn for transit.

The *Jeremiah O'Brien* made her second transit of the Panama Canal on December 8, 1944.

Ted Martin: "We had Marine Corps guards on board during the transit. We were under their jurisdiction going through the Canal. We were confined pretty much to the ship. I was coxswain at the time and did the watches. I think we had port and starboard liberty, so only one side got ashore this time."

The Caribbean was believed to be clear of German submarines but the war was still on and the threat was always there. Willis "Bud" Hitchcock recalled an incident in the same waters while on the Liberty *Hiram S. Maxim.*

"... we were advised that we were one of the first ships to be sent thru the Caribbean singly with no escort as German submarine activity had subsided to the point where it was considered safe. However, we were told that submarines very often tried to pick a lone ship off by surface action rather than waste valuable torpedoes, and to shoot on sight anything suspicious.

"Well, one bright sunny morning on my watch, while steaming thru the Yucatan Channel, I was startled to see the unmistakable sight of a surface-running sub coming over the horizon on a parallel approaching course.

"The general alarm was sounded and all hands went to gun stations. The sub continued on the surface and when abeam of us, and within range, changed course, turning toward us. That is all we needed, and we opened fire with our bow and stern guns. I remember thinking what a perfect straddle those first two rounds were. The 3" was just under and the 5" was just over. The sub crash-dived and disappeared from view.

"Well, the succeeding days were filled with anxiety as we thought surely we were being trailed and would eventually be torpedoed. Upon arriving at Key West, Florida for orders, our Gunnery Officer, Mr. Hansen, returned from reporting the incident and embarrassingly announced that we had fired on one of our own submarines, and came damn near sinking it. What a tragedy that would have been!"

From the Canal, the *O'Brien* headed north, toward the Mississippi Delta. The weather deteriorated and by afternoon on December 10 the ship was running into a storm wind, dead on. She was taking so much water and spray over the bow that it was necessary to move the watch from the forward gun to the wings of the bridge.

Ensign Norman Robinson: "We came back up through the Gulf of Mexico through a hurricane. The ship's bow nosed into the waves throwing off tremendous amounts of water. And at night the water was florescent. It shot up on both sides of the ship and poured over the deck like a waterfall of fire. It was beautiful. I still remember it to this day."

The storm abated during the night then kicked up again. The wind howled and shrieked. Driving rain came down from an unnaturally dark sky in heavy sheets that obliterated everything.

At 2115 that evening the watch on the stern gun was secured and sent to the bridge because of the storm. The wind blew so hard that the rain poured more horizontally than vertically. The ship heaved and rolled and pitched, its decks a constantly tilting, twisting, turning, slippery surface. Trying to get from the stern to the bridge, one man was nearly washed off the main deck. The ride was so rough the engine rpms were reduced to ease the ship in the heavy seas. The crew huddled belowdecks, some swearing, others frightened, all bracing themselves against the constant rolling and pitching. The more experienced wedged themselves in their bunks with pillows and lifejackets, their feet pushing against the bunk rail, as they read, losing themselves in a far away fictional world, waiting for the storm to abate. Throughout the ship were the sounds of breaking crockery, unfastened chairs sliding across decks, drawers crashing open, pots and pans clanging and banging and, over it all, the constant, unremitting roar of the wind.

The bad weather continued into December 12. No dawn watch was held because all the guns except those on the bridge were unusable due to the constant sea and spray on deck. Nonetheless the bridge guns were manned and forward and aft watches were still kept on the bridge. By dawn the storm was abating and the ship resumed full speed.

It was then discovered that the chain lockers contained several feet of water while the other bow areas had several inches. But the only real damage was to some winter underwear and socks stowed there belonging to the Armed Guard which were soaked in dirty salt water.

Finally, on the morning of December 14, the low, broad entrance to the Mississippi River came into view -- a welcome sight to all on board. By 1010 the pilot was aboard and the *O'Brien* was underway up river. The river delta came together in low banks dotted here and there with a ramshackle building or fishing shack. As the ship steamed farther upriver the banks became lined with vegetation and low trees hung with Spanish moss. Ships and barges passed, traveling downriver to the Gulf of Mexico and beyond. Just before midnight the *O'Brien* moored fore and aft at the docks in West Wago, Louisiana. Then she shifted to the Market Street docks in New Orleans.

William Wallace: "The joke was on me. Montgomery was right when he said we'd be back by Christmas. But the ship never came back to New York. It came into New Orleans."

For most of the crew "New Orleans" was the old French Quarter -- Dixieland jazz pouring out of every doorway and on every street corner, cajun and creole food -- crayfish, jambalaya, alligator tail, filé gumbo, pralines -- artists working at their easels, the finished paintings propped against the iron fence surrounding Jackson Square, old houses with ironwork grills, servicemen roaming the streets, noisy nights, bars everywhere, and girls, girls, girls.

Carl Scharpf: "I got off in New Orleans in December of 1944. It was a special city. I grew up in Baltimore and it was quite different from my home town. New Orleans was quite a good-time town to go to. I think I stayed there several days."

Norman Robinson: "I remember New Orleans. But it was Christmas time and I went home for the holidays. The crowded troop trains back to Massachusetts were an adventure."

William Wallace: "Some of us that were getting off the ship got hotel rooms there in Canal Street because we knew we'd be paying off and we wanted a place to bring our suitcases. We walked around a bit, I remember walking around the French quarter.

"Another fellow, Ralph Prado, the second engineer, and I had lobster at one of the restaurants. He got deathly sick, why I don't know. We were sharing a hotel room and I tried to get a doctor for him. I got one on the phone. He told me to go to a drugstore to get some paregoric and he would call them and prescribe it. I got it and started feeding it to him and the next day he was all right."

It was almost the end of the year before the last of the copper and lead were unloaded. The crew took advantage of the long layover to celebrate the holidays and relax. With great reluctance they joined the ship on December 29 as she left the Market Street dock at New Orleans and headed downriver.

Voyage 5 had been an interesting, exotic, unique adventure. Voyage 6 would be fraught with danger, not from enemy submarines or aircraft, but because of the cargo the *O'Brien* carried.

12

"ONE SHIP IN THE PACIFIC"

John L. Crosby, newly-graduated from Kings Point, joined the ship as third mate just a few days before sailing. "We loaded some ship's stores in New Orleans and sailed for Galveston, Texas."

The *O'Brien* had just cleared the dock and was partway down river when a thick fog suddenly settled in from across the bayous forcing the ship to anchor. The crew waited, listening to the river surge past, through the night and into the next day. Just before noon on December 30th the fog cleared, the ship weighed anchor, sailed downstream and cleared the Mississippi Delta a few hours later. There was no cargo on board and the only ballast was water.

After steaming a few hours in a westerly direction through the Gulf, the *Jeremiah O'Brien* anchored in Galveston Bay, Texas, on New Year's Eve. The crew was ready to celebrate, but it was not to be. Later they would find out why.

John L. Crosby: "We laid at anchor at Bolivar Roads over New Year's Eve and was not allowed shore leave for an unexplained reason."

It was January 3, 1945 before a pilot came aboard to take them in. Steaming upriver toward Houston, they tied up to the dock at the U. S. Army's San Jacinto Ordinance Base. Far downstream from the city itself, it consisted of a cluster of beige-colored wood barracks and buildings for stevedores and clerks, low warehouses just off the piers, and railheads leading from the piers to distant underground ammunition bunkers, all set on a vast, flat, well-fenced military reservation.

John Crosby remembered, "We loaded 10,000 tons of bombs, with the warheads in #3 hatch and a very high load of belly tanks on deck. During the time of loading none of the crew was allowed ashore."

Loading ammunition was a slow, careful process. First the *O'Brien's* cargo holds were cleaned of all debris. Then, in each hatch, a solid plank deck was laid over the ship's steel deck and wooden bulkheads were erected attaching them to the inner sides of the hull, creating a wood box inside the hold. There would be no steel surfaces exposed for the metal-cased bombs to rub against, eliminating the possibility of sparking.

Then the bombs, without detonators and strapped to wooden skid pallets, were loaded. The pallets were flat on the bottom surface with heavy timbers at each end. The top surfaces of the timbers were cut in a circular arc so that the cylindrical bombs fit in the cutout and wouldn't roll. The bombs were strapped to each pallet to hold them in place. As they reached a certain height a new deck would be laid to distribute the weight evenly and additional tiers were added. As each cargo space was loaded, void areas were blocked to prevent the cargo from shifting horizontally and timbers, called "toms," were wedged between the cargo and the overhead to prevent the bombs from shifting vertically.

The detonators or fuzes were loaded in a separate compartment. Because of the extreme danger involved, smoking was allowed only in the *Jeremiah O'Brien's* midship house and at designated areas ashore. Most of the stevedores chewed tobacco, rather than smoke.

The crew watched the process with increasing disfavor. They calculated the tons of explosives contained in the bombs and translated that into equivalent tons of TNT. Restricted to the ship day after day, there was nothing to distract them while the loading continued. The stories and apprehensions grew, fed on themselves, and grew some more. Tales of "ammo ships" being hit by torpedoes and vaporizing into oblivion circulated.

On January 8, one of the steward's utilitymen was logged for "failure to join," a technical term meaning he wasn't on board and hadn't reported for work. Somehow he sneaked ashore. A day later the following letter was received by the Chief Steward:

"Sir:- I have to go right back to New York because of family reasons. One relative is sick. Please transfer my pay-off to New York and the overtime.

(signed) _____, Pantry Utility.

The next week one of the oilers fell from the deck cargo, fracturing his right ankle and was hospitalized. Numerous other accidents occurred. The *O'Brien*, which had sailed through so much with a minimum of crew health problems, was suddenly becoming a floating infirmary.

According to John L. Crosby some of the injuries and illnesses were faked or deliberate. "During our stay in Houston ... several of the crew members inflicted injury to themselves by breaking an arm, etc., or causing a disability in order to get off the ship out of fear of the bombs as cargo. There was some secrecy about those bombs. We were not allowed shore leave all the time we were loading them."

On January 17, two weeks after the *O'Brien* arrived at the Ordinance Dock, her hatches were full. She sailed for Galveston to finish off with a load of deck cargo.

Consisting of airplane belly tanks and two LCM's (Landing Craft, Medium), the deck cargo would cover most of the main deck and two hatches. Because of their size and weight, the LCM's could not be positioned with the ship's jumbo gear and had to be loaded by floating crane. During the first day only one

LCM was loaded because of roughening seas and a very strong tide. On January 19, the second LCM was successfully loaded and the *O'Brien* sailed. Her cargo for voyage No. 5 was typical for wartime -- a much more typical cargo than she had carried on the South American voyage: all five hatches were full of bombs and warheads, the main decks were stacked with aircraft belly tanks and two of her hatches had LCM's on top of them. Grim jokes about instant death circulated among the crew.

Ensign Norman Robinson: "We loaded ammo, high explosives, at Houston and put two LCM's on board, on deck."

Seaman First Class Ted Martin: "They were five hundred pound personnel bombs."

The injuries and illnesses continued. Before sailing, an ordinary seaman was hospitalized with a bad strain. At sea, one of the messman had to be confined to his bunk with a swollen left testicle. He claimed it was caused by handling cases of fruit. The mate nodded skeptically as he treated the messman with hourly ice packs. When that proved insufficient, he was given 1/4 grain phenobarbital to help him sleep. Eventually he was taken ashore at Cristobal for hospitalization.

Norman Robinson: "I thought one of the boys had been drugged while he was ashore. He slept for 24 hours, between Houston and the Canal."

Late in the war as it was, caution and a sharp watch for danger continued. Sitting on top of "a million tons of TNT," the crew was especially vigilant. On January 20 a light was sighted off the starboard bow. Suspicious of everything, the crew readied the forward gun and the *O'Brien* changed course to avoid crossing the path of the other vessel. The ship turned out to be friendly and just before disappearing off the port beam it was recognized as a schooner running under jib and mainsail.

From January 21st to January 24th, as the ship zig-zagged her way south, the log recorded routine days: a patrol bomber was sighted off the port beam on January 22nd, there was no challenge by signal light or flag; on January 24th an aircraft was seen off the bow. Again there was no challenge. The ship's crew held fire and boat drills every four days.

As the *O'Brien* neared the Canal, greater security was encountered. John Crosby: "About one day out of the Panama Canal Zone we were met by two U.S. Navy destroyer escorts."

The ship arrived at Panama early the morning of January 25th and transited the Canal that afternoon with the usual Marine guard assuming watch duties.

John Crosby: "It was my first time through the Canal. I was amazed by the Canal and the engineering that went into it. But, then, I was always amazed with that place. "They [the destroyers] escorted us forward and aft through the Canal Zone, and we were given priority at all lockings due to our dangerous cargo." The crew would have gladly foregone the honor.

At 1900 the ship secured to refueling docks at Balboa, Canal Zone. As with everything else during wartime, there was an extra element of caution even in routine fueling. From the Panama Canal Orders to Merchant Vessels:

"Rule 44. VESSELS AT FUEL BERTHS: A vessel at a fuel berth shall keep up steam and be ready to move on short notice unless special authority to the contrary has been obtained from the Canal authorities."

On January 26, the *Jeremiah O'Brien* finished refueling in the early morning and cast off the last of her lines. The pilot carefully maneuvered her out of the harbor and departed at 0253. Captain Gunderson rang Full Ahead, told the engineroom to "bring her up to sea speed" and pointed the ship's bow westward, toward the far reaches of the Pacific.

John Crosby: "We were again escorted by the same U.S. Navy destroyer escorts about 300 miles into the Pacific and they waved us bye-bye and we went on alone. No one knew where we were going except the master. That was a little eerie."

The ship's crew fell into a normal routine of standing watch, maintaining the engine and cargo gear and killing off-duty time by reading, playing cards, washing clothes, telling stories and writing letters home. The Armed Guard built a target for gunnery practice. Using two metal barrels as floats, they built a wooden frame around it with a painted bull's eye on top to shoot at. Lowering it over the side, the ship continued on course as firing practice was held with the aft 3"-50. Both forward and after gun crews had a chance at the receding target on the after gun. Seventeen rounds of Common Ammunition were shot with what Ensign Robinson logged as "favorable results."

.The crossing was long, slow and relatively uneventful. The tide of the war was now in the Allies' favor. In the Pacific, the United States was driving the war onto the shores of Japan and for most of the way across the ocean was relatively secure, both on the surface and underneath. Because of incidents like the one described earlier by "Bud" Hitchcock, there was more concern about American ships not shooting at their own submarines. The following message was received by the radio operator: "Early on the Morning of Feb. 8th a friendly submarine may be sighted in the vicinity of 37.45 North and 124 West."

Some of the crew continued worrying about the cargo. Others were more fatalistic. Robert Crocker, Gunner's Mate Third Class: "We carried bombs that trip. As far as the gun crew was concerned it didn't matter. We didn't bother with lifejackets or anything, if we got hit it would all be over with anyway. We just made sure we spent all our money in whatever port we were in."

Ted Martin: "That's right, there was no sense having a lifejacket on. If we got hit we wouldn't know it anyway."

Norman Robinson did what he could to ease the tension among his Armed Guard.

Robert Crocker: "One of the funny things on the way over, since we were carrying ten thousand tons of bombs, Ensign Robinson thought it would be a good idea to have church services in the morning. So every Sunday he'd conduct church under the forward gun turret. Well, once the bombs were off we didn't do that anymore."

Norman Robinson, laughing, "It seemed like a good idea. Everyone was a little on edge because of the bombs. But once they were off the ship, that was the end of that."

In addition to the never-ending chipping and painting and maintaining the guns, the Armed Guard continued to practice. A kite was put together and flown as a target for the 20 mm machine guns. Ted Martin: "Target practice, we did that a lot, sometimes unofficially. We'd go up to the captain and ask permission. We'd say one of our guns was jammed and we'd have to shoot it to clear it. That way it didn't have to be logged."

John Crosby remembered it as a lonely crossing, "in complete blackout and radio silence to the Admiralty Islands. We were always blacked out during the war with those screens on the portholes and so forth, that was the hardest thing." But it was very comfortable, compared to his earlier trips. "My previous sea duty was in the North Atlantic where it was always cold and bad weather, in convoy, no communications. It was a given, more or less, that if we were hit by a torpedo you'd last six minutes. This was relaxing. On this ship you could wear your pajamas and take long showers and so on."

By now, with a long voyage yet ahead and no hope of malingering their way off the ship, any injuries to the crew were real. And, inevitably, they did occur.

On February 10, an Ordinary Seaman fell from the catwalk to the main deck at #3 hatch. His left eye was cut and had to be stitched, his left cheekbone was bruised and swollen, he had abrasions on both arms and he bruised his right foot. His foot was treated with hot water and epsom salts baths and by massaging it with soap liniment. The medical duties fell on Ensign Robinson because of his training as a pharmacist's mate. Assisted by the book, "The Ship's Medicine Chest At Sea," found on every merchant ship, he served as medic, giving prescriptions and first aid as needed.

After several days of lonely travel the crew of the *O'Brien* sighted their first ship since leaving Panama. It was hull down on the starboard horizon, headed east. Although they couldn't identify it, it was refreshing and reassuring to see another vessel. They didn't feel so alone on the broad Pacific. A second ship was sighted two days later. This vessel, also headed east, was sighted off the starboard bow. Apparently the *Jeremiah O'Brien's* course was converging with those of other ships sailing to the South Pacific. The crew watched with interest until it disappeared.

After more than two weeks of uneventful but dutiful zig-zagging, with but two distant ships seen in the whole time, the reality of war was suddenly brought back to the crew's attention. On February 16, two messages were received from a ship with the call letters KF2DP.

"SSSS DE KF2DP POSN 07 SOUTH 178.42 WEST TORPEDO ATTACK BT 161011Z DE ZMA (RELAYED) REC'D 1020 GMT [Greenwich Mean Time]."

Followed by:

"XXXX DE KF2DP NO FURTHER ATTACK NO DAMAGE 161225Z AR DE ZMA REC'D 1235 GMT."

John Crosby, Third Mate: "While we were out there we heard SOS's and SSS's [submarine attack] from other ships but they were out of our range so we couldn't help because our speed was too slow to reach them."

That day, at 0200 the *Jeremiah O'Brien* crossed the International Dateline for the first time in her career and February 16 became February 17. On troop ships and passenger liners, this passage into the "Realm of the Golden Dragon" was often celebrated with a ceremony and the issuing of certificates commemorating the occasion. But Captain Gunderson was not the type to indulge in such "nonsense." On February 18 the third ship of the voyage was sighted, a tanker. It rapidly overtook the *O'Brien* from the starboard quarter. As it came abeam at 1130, courtesies were exchanged via blinker.

Robert Crocker, Gunner's Mate Third Class: "It seems to me we passed a tanker or a ship and a few hours later we picked up a distress signal that the same ship had been torpedoed. We went in the opposite direction. We were too far away to be any help, so we tried to avoid the submarine."

February the 18th was a Sunday and as usual Ensign Robinson held religious services. That afternoon the wind was favorable for target practice. A kite target was sent aloft and the starboard 20 mm machine guns shot at it. The gunners' accuracy was improving. Their second magazine brought the target down.

Ted Martin: "We used to sail the kite off the fantail. It was made out of bed sheets and it was pretty big. We'd hang stuff off it, like gallon cans or something. Most of the time we'd shoot for the kite. We'd hit it and the kite would come down."

A little excitement occurred on February 20th before breakfast when an alert was sounded by the mate on watch for an unidentified plane heard off the starboard beam. The plane was seen for about one minute at a great distance as it came through the clouds and immediately disappeared.

Norman Robinson: "We were very, very fortunate. We had an airplane scare once but they turned out to be friendly."

On February 21st the ship crossed the equator for the third time in her career. On many ships this is cause for hazing and a ceremony making "polliwogs" who have not crossed before into "shellbacks." Again Captain Gunderson vetoed the "silly" ceremony.

Norman Robinson: "One of the things that has never left my mind was standing G.Q. in the early morning and late at night. There was nothing more beautiful than seeing that old sun come up and go down in a red blaze of glory. It was aesthetically very pretty."

Ted Martin: "We'd stand Condition three then G.Q. You'd have two men forward and two aft and one on the port side and one on the starboard side of the bridge. It was good duty. We didn't have to wear dress whites, there were no inspections. The only uniform we wore was dungarees and those light blue cranberry [chambray] shirts. But at sea there was no dress code. We used to cut off our dungarees and wear shorts. I can only recall one time the captain made us wear dungarees. The rest of the time we wore cutoffs."

A ship is also home for the crew while they're on board and, as with any home, it's more pleasant if it's well kept.

Ted Martin: "We always had clean sheets and we washed our own clothes. What we'd do, our washing machine was a galvanized bucket. And you'd put water and soap and clothes in the bucket and hold it under a steam line to make it hot. Then you'd take a toilet plunger and sit on the toilet working the plunger up and down and wash clothes at the same time you were taking care of your other business."

With little else to look forward to, meals are a big event on board ship. If the food is good, the crew is happy and you don't hear much about it. If not, they complain. Typically, the first few weeks of a voyage are pleasant -- until the fresh produce and milk run out.

Ted Martin: "The *O'Brien* was about equal to any other ship I was on as far as comfort goes. The food was good as a rule the first three weeks out, same as any other ship. Until you got into the powdered eggs and milk. That wasn't so good. But we did have our own messhall and had a merchant messboy."

Norman Robinson: "I had no complaints about the food. We did have plenty of liver. When we ran low on supplies that's all they served. I hate it to this day."

John Crosby wasn't so enchanted with the food. "The Steward was a hell of a nice guy, but the food was lousy."

On February 23, 1945 the *Jeremiah O'Brien* arrived at Seeadler Harbor, Manus, Admiralty Islands, New Guinea. With the excitement of arriving in port after 27 days at sea, some of the crew got careless. An Ordinary Seaman burned his entire right arm when the coffee urn in the crew pantry overflowed. In the same incident, a utilityman burned the right side of his body and his right forearm. Both men were treated with boric acid ointment and bandaged.

Manus was merely a staging area, a port of call for further orders. The next day the ship departed Manus still carrying the ammunition, airplane "belly tanks" and two LCM's.

John L. Crosby: "We anchored for a day or so and made up a convoy to Hollandia." On February 26, the *O'Brien* arrived off Humboldt Bay, Hollandia, New Guinea. This was another staging area for a yet larger convoy being made up to travel to the Philippines.

John Crosby: "There was nothing to go ashore for in Hollandia other than they had a USO there. I did take the lifeboat ashore to the USO at least once. We were anchored there and I took this lifeboat ashore with a full capacity of crew. At the USO they only allowed us two beers apiece. Well there were a lot of ships out there at anchor. So we'd go outside the place and get the fieldglasses and read the name of one of the other ships at anchor.

Then we'd change our shirts and go back in and we had all the beers we wanted."

Ted Martin: "We went into a base where they had some of them fighters with the twin tails -- P-38's. And some of us went for a ride in one. You had to sit on a box behind the pilot and hold on. That was something. I'll never do that again. I'm not sure but it might have been the 'Jolly Roger' squadron."

John Crosby: "The Jolly Roger squadron, that's right, their nickname was the Jolly Roger. I know they called it that. They had this flag, the skull and crossbones like a pirate's flag. They named it after one of the squadron heroes. Also, I remember the army did a little fishing in there with hand grenades. Any time they wanted fresh fish, they'd just toss one in the water."

By March 3 the convoy was assembled. The *Jeremiah O'Brien* left Hollandia with instructions to tow two Navy LCM's and carry their crews on board the ship, while in convoy with nine escorts and thirty-four other ships. In what the crew would soon learn was typically predictable confusion, the orders were changed a few hours later. The *O'Brien* was instructed to drop out of the convoy and release the two LCM's. Their crews were sent back aboard and instructed to return the two craft to Hollandia. It took the ship all night to rejoin the convoy and regain her position.

On March 6, without explanation, one of the escorts shot four white flares. There was no further action and, as usual, no information. Then another escort shot a single white flare and fired four rounds of anti-aircraft ammunition in the direction of the flare. Of course, the *O'Brien's* crew had no way of knowing whether this was practice or a real alert. General Quarters was sounded in preparation for possible action. When nothing else happened it was decided that the flares and firing were just for practice.

On March 7, as they passed off Palau Island, a second convoy was sighted off the port bow. By noon it had joined the *O'Brien's* group, adding twenty ships. This made a total of 70 vessels steaming together. Three days later land was raised off the starboard bow and that afternoon the "Tacloban convoy," consisting of 28 ships, one of which was the *Jeremiah O'Brien*, broke away from rest of the fleet.

There was a great deal of confusion in the South Pacific at the time. The war itself was fought bravely and effectively, but the process of supplying the machinery of war, the matériel, was chaotic. Supplies seemed to be randomly routed in all directions at once with the result that some areas were awash in materials while others operated on bailing wire and chewing gum. The *Jeremiah O'Brien* sailed directly into the middle of a figurative sea of bedlam and disorder.

As the ship entered Tacloban harbor located on Samar Island, in the Philippines, Captain Gunderson couldn't get direction from the authorities ashore where to anchor. In disgust, he finally dropped the *O'Brien's* anchor where he thought it was safest. The following day he was instructed to up-anchor and move to a specified anchorage. On March 12, the shoreside authorities suddenly realized the *O'Brien* was carrying ammunition and she was ordered to move to the explosives anchorage. One day later the ship was ordered back to the inner harbor to discharge part of her deck cargo. The deck cargo was partially unlashed when new orders came through. Captain Gunderson was told the previous order was a mistake. After spending the night re-lashing the cargo, the ship shifted back out to the explosives anchorage. And there it sat. The crew chafed, making derisive remarks about military efficiency and their chances of winning the war. A descriptive acronym had been coined, and was much used during the war, to describe normal military operations, especially as they existed in the South Pacific. The word was "SNAFU." It stood for "Situation Normal, All Fucked Up." The word was much used in crew conversation.

John Crosby recalled, "We stayed about a week and they started to unload some belly tanks from our deck load." He was more charitable than some of the crew, recalling: "There was two other "*O'Briens*" out there in the South Pacific at the same time as us. That probably explained some of the mix-up.[1]"

---

[1]   In *The Liberty Ships* Sawyer and Mitchell list the *Edward J. O'Brien* and the *Richard O'Brien*. In addition the Navy has had four successive ships (the

Someone then decided to send the *Jeremiah O'Brien* elsewhere. On March 15 the anchor was weighed and the ship began to move into convoy position but the convoy sailing was canceled and, once again, the ship returned to the anchorage.

Things finally came together on March 16 when the *O'Brien* moved out to join a northbound convoy. Thirty-three ships combined with a group of twenty-four ships coming up from New Guinea to form a convoy of 57 ships headed for the Northern Philippines. The *O'Brien* had been in the war area three weeks and still carried her cargo of ammunition, airplane belly tanks and two LCM's.

Corregidor had been retaken by American forces under General Douglas MacArthur a few weeks earlier with Manila Bay itself opening to Allied shipping only a few days before the convoy sailed. Subic Bay was recently cleared but the Japanese forces had retreated to mountain strongholds throughout Luzon and continued a determined resistance. The recent kamikaze attacks at Lingayen were a new topic of conversation and concern, as were the continual threat of attacks by air or sea.

On Saint Patrick's Day, 1945, as the convoy proceeded farther into the Philippines, there was a sudden alert. At 1110 an emergency turn to starboard was ordered. At 1115 a flag hoist (International Code Flag #2, indicating a submarine) went up on ship #21. At 1120 general quarters was called. Ten minutes later an emergency turn to port was ordered. This was followed in two minutes with another emergency turn to starboard. A few minutes after that another emergency turn to port was ordered. Nothing further happened and just after noon the ship secured from general quarters. Later that afternoon another submarine warning was hoisted. The tense alert turned into farce. Later in the day the ship heard over the TBY (radio telephone) that what the escorts thought was a submarine was in fact "Two whales and a floating swab handle".

Norman Robinson summed it up: "One day we spotted a periscope but it turned out to be a swab."

---

latest *USS O'Brien* is still active) named after Jeremiah O'Brien, the same namesake as the *SS Jeremiah O'Brien*.

This is what happened to the ship that preceded the SS Jeremiah O'Brien *carrying ammunition into Mindoro.   It was hit by a kamikaze and disintegrated. Credit National Archives*

On March 18, Mindoro was sighted just after noon. Taken by American forces in December 1944, the island had become a jungle stronghold of supplies feeding the efforts in Luzon. Suddenly, in addition to mines, submarines, depth charges, enemy bombers -- and swab handles -- the new threat of kamikaze planes became a reality.   The crew which had grown more or less accustomed to their cargo -- which they couldn't seem to get rid of -- now had their earlier apprehensions resurface.

John Crosby: "We were told that the ammunition ship going into Mindoro prior to us was hit by a Japanese kamikaze and was completely destroyed."

This was a completely new threat. In a desperate, last-ditch effort to prevent the Allies' determined advance toward their homeland, the Japanese had developed the kamikaze attack. The word means "divine wind" and stems from the 13th century when a typhoon destroyed an invading force of Mongols. The Japanese believed that the divine wind made their nation impervious to attack. To ensure their survival as the tide of war turned against them, the Japanese decided to create their own divine wind. Selecting their best pilots, the Imperial Japanese forces armed their planes with explosives and flew them directly into Allied ships. The young Japanese pilots vied for the honor of dying for emperor and country, believing such a heroic death guaranteed honor, glory and eternal life in the hereafter. The effect was dramatic but, overall, strategically ineffective. Nevertheless, if your ship was the target of a kamikaze, the danger was very real. The Liberty ship *John Burke*, fully loaded with ammunition, was hit by a suicide plane a few months earlier and vaporized, leaving not a trace of her presence when the smoke cleared. The Liberty ship *Lewis Dyche,* also loaded with ammo, suffered the same fate. According to the War Shipping Administration, merchant marine losses in the Mindoro landings were greater than those of the Armed Forces taking part in the D-Day invasion of Normandy and many of these losses were due to kamikaze attacks.

In the early afternoon the *Jeremiah O'Brien* broke away from the convoy and proceeded into the harbor area of San Jose, Mindoro. It was a small harbor with a limited work force and there weren't enough dock hands to tie her up. During the night longshoremen were located and the next day the ship went alongside the dock.

The period between March 21st and March 26th was difficult. There was a strong offshore wind and a serious concern that the pilings or dolphins the *O'Brien's* mooring lines were tied to weren't strong enough or anchored firmly enough to hold the ship. A sharp watch had to be kept to ensure that the ship wasn't blown off the dock and back into the bay. Nevertheless, by March 27 the two LCM's, all the deck cargo and some of the cargo out of No. 4 hatch had been removed. All that remained was the ammunition. The ship moved from the dock to an anchorage to await the next north-bound convoy which she joined on March 30. A day later the *Jeremiah O'Brien* and 13 ships broke off and entered Subic Bay, Luzon, with four escorts. She passed through

Left to right, George and Bob Crocker. This reunion took place in Subic Bay (the photo was taken at the O'Brien's bow gun) after being separated for 2 ½ years. Credit Bob Crocker

the submarine nets protecting the harbor and two hours later was anchored and secured.

Norman Robinson: "We pulled in Subic Bay from the States and we were told we were the first ship in there since the Japs were there, the first ammunition ship to make it. The previous one that tried got blown out of the water."

Subic Bay is a large, well-protected harbor with a narrow entrance surrounded by high, gently sloping coastal hills. The military base occupies the east end of the bay and just outside the gates lies the civilian town of Olongopo. The surrounding area was still infested with Japanese soldiers. Fighting was frequently seen and heard in the surrounding hills.

April 2 was spent discharging ammunition onto barges and mail sacks into LCM's. The discharge of the ammunition went quickly compared to the slow process of loading. The shoring and tomming were knocked out of the way and the pallets of bombs simply lifted out and set in the waiting LCM's. The ship then moved from the anchorage to the docks where cargo discharge continued.

Bob Crocker remembered a pleasant happenstance in Subic Bay because, "I signaled over to a Navy cruiser, the *Denver.* My brother was on board. I hadn't seen him for two and a half years. We met the next day on the *Jeremiah O'Brien* and had a reunion. He thought the food on the *O'Brien* was great."

John Crosby: "I did go ashore a few times in Subic Bay. The only thing that stood out was the stench in Olongopo. I know there was this air base and they were taking off from there, delivering bombs off these Mustangs. As I remember, Clark Air Force Base and Manila were still occupied by the Japanese."

Far less pleasant things happened to some of the crew in Subic Bay. Robert Crocker: "One of the bad things was one of the gun crew went ashore a couple of times and got into some bad whiskey."

Norman Robinson: "One of the boys was given this rotgut. We thought it was left by the Japs in their retreat."

Bob Crocker: "We used to call it poontang. What it was was wood alcohol."

John Crosby: "Some of the crew was drinking that bad whiskey. Some of the armed guard came back to the ship one time and they were totally drunk. Apparently they had been drinking real bad whiskey for a long time."

Ted Martin: "Actually I think there was nine of them involved in this. They went crazy. They wanted to fight everybody they saw. In fact when they came back on board, I recall whoever was on the gangway, he cried for help. These guys went in the messhall and they were just crazy. They started breaking crockery and everything. We held them down on the messroom tables until they got over it. They were berserk."

John Crosby: "They laid one of them on a table in the crews mess. He said, 'Turn on the lights.' Well, the lights were already on."

Bob Crocker: "I can remember laying him out on the gun crew mess and I don't know if he could ever see again. I forgot his name, he was usually a nice enough guy."

According to the official record, the man claimed he was blind but he was so much under the effect of liquor it was impossible to be sure if he was or not. He was removed to the Navy Dispensary in Subic.

Norman Robinson: "I stayed up there overnight with him. We could hear the Japs fighting in the background from the hospital. The kid gradually got over his blindness and then someone snuck another bottle in to him and he went blind again."

Bob Crocker: "We went up and brought him back and a few days later he went back ashore again. That was something. We pulled him out of the jungles back there. Anyway he was blind then."

John Crosby: "There were two or three of them we had to leave in the hospital, they were in such bad shape."

Three of the Armed Guard crew were detached from the ship, one suffering from blindness or "acute alcoholism."

Ted Martin: "The saddest part was when those guys drank that torpedo juice. It really set them up where they wouldn't touch anything for a long time after."

A far more serious peril was that scourge of the tropics -- malaria. The epidemic on the *Jeremiah O'Brien* began on April 13 when a gunner's mate third class was detached and hospitalized. The official diagnosis was D.U. (malaria).

Ted Martin: "Malaria was a real problem. We had some scares two or three different times. It was epidemic at the time we was in that area. They didn't have enough medicine to treat it."

Borne by the *anopheles* mosquito which flourishes in the warm humidity, malaria was common in the Philippines and much of the South Pacific. Usually occurring in three stages, it may recur for years and can stay with a person his entire life. The first, or cold, stage consists of malaise, chills, headache, aching bones, loss of appetite, nausea and vomiting. Temperature may reach 104° F. The second stage is marked by the patient feeling warm, with hot, dry skin. The face is flushed, the pulse rapid and breathing quick. The patient becomes very thirsty, his headache worsens to the point of agony, and vomiting increases. In the third stage the patient perspires freely, feels more comfortable and may sleep deeply. He will then feel fine until the next attack. If the patient's temperature gets too high he may suffer delirium followed by coma. Prescribed treatment at this time was atabrine, a quinine-based drug. It had the effect of suppressing the symptoms rather than actually attacking the parasites carried by the mosquito that cause the illness. Used as a preventative, atabrine worked very effectively. Unfortunately it was unavailable for that purpose at this stage of the war, at least to the crew of the *Jeremiah O'Brien*.

The last of the bombs was taken off and the ship moved from the cargo dock to the watering dock. All that remained on board was dunnage. The *O'Brien* rested alongside, all hatches secure, awaiting further orders. On April 17, she departed from Subic Bay to join a convoy bound for Hollandia, New Guinea, arriving there on April 27.

John Crosby: "Hollandia, it was very primitive, too. They had a lot of workers in there that were native New Guinean. They used to take their dugouts and you'd hear them rowing and singing to their families in the hills. Now I understood that none of the women were allowed in that area, although I do remember seeing a few, not that they were anything to look at. The native guys, on their lunch breaks, we'd see where one was picking at the other's hair. I understand they was getting the lice out of it."

The *O'Brien* left Hollandia for Oro Bay, New Guinea, anchored overnight, then was called into the dock to commence loading the following day. Her scheduled cargo was oil, lubricants, gasoline in drums and a deck cargo of light and medium tanks and half-tracks.

On May 8, 1945, Germany surrendered. It was noted in passing by the crew -- half the war was over, half yet to go -- as they continued with the routine but important task of getting the ship loaded. During the Battle of the Atlantic 2,603 merchant ships were sunk totalling more than 13.5 million tons. Of Allied merchant seamen, 30,248 lost their lives.

With her hatches full of lubricants and gasoline, the *O'Brien* moved to a different pier to load tanks and half-tracks. That afternoon, while lifting an Army Sherman tank, the jumbo boom collapsed. The tank crashed through the dock into deep water and the falling boom struck the No. 1 (starboard forward) gun tub and the right hand half of the gun shield. The gun tub was crushed inward on the outboard side and the gun shield bent slightly inward.

John Crosby witnessed the incident: "In Oro Bay, the Army acted as the stevedores. They were working the heavy lift, the jumbo boom. In order to do this they work on separate winches, heave on one and slack on the other. They were loading a tank and this Army stevedore was heaving on the offshore guy and the other one didn't slack the inshore guy enough and the offshore broke. It swung around and the boom with the tank on it hit a gun turret. The cargo runner broke and the tank went through the dock all the way into the water. It weighed about thirty-five tons."

The incident was dramatic and Robert Crocker remembered it, too: "A funny thing happened with one of the Sherman tanks they were loading. The line broke and the tank went right through the dock. It's probably still there. The Army, they came out and covered the hole in the pier over in no time at all and then just went right on loading. Just like it had never happened."

No one was unduly concerned. Ensign Norman Robinson: "Their attitude was the tank was government property. There were plenty more where that one came from."

With the jumbo boom broken, the remainder of the deck load had to be put aboard by floating crane. The O'Brien shifted to an anchorage to finish loading the tanks and half-tracks. Fortunately no one was injured. The gun itself was undamaged and still operated effectively even with the bent shield.

The lack of experience on the part of the military in loading ships combined with the need to do things quickly caused other problems. On May 9 as heavy cargo was being loaded on deck, the ship developed a pronounced list and Captain Gunderson ordered them to stop. The ship's engineers shifted oil and water in the double bottom tanks. The ship flopped from port to starboard and back, but wouldn't stay on an even keel. The Captain went ashore to see about correcting the loading plan while the engineers kept working on the problem. They finally filled the empty double-bottom tanks with sea water and brought the ship back almost level.   The balance remained delicate, however, and Captain Gunderson was concerned.

With the problem seemingly corrected, the military decided to load a few more tanks. Captain Gunderson was furious. He stormed back ashore.

John Crosby remembered the incident this way: "While loading the tanks on deck, we became very tender and Captain Gunderson protested the loading due to the safety of the vessel. He was advised by the Army officer in charge that these tanks were badly needed on the front, and that if he would not take the tanks he would be replaced. He conceded, and loaded the tanks under protest."

Norman Robinson: "We had maybe a ten or fifteen degree list. It seemed like it was not really terrible."

Feeling "stuck out in the jungle," the crew decided to investigate the nearest town.

John Crosby: "I was with one of the officers, probably the third engineer. And this town of Oro Bay was quite far from the dock. We were ashore there and we were walking along this uninhabited road. We looked up and coming in the opposite direction were a band of about six or eight native New Guineans. They were dressed in their loin cloths and had that fuzzy-wuzzy hair and were carrying spears and knives. They looked fierce. I said, 'What the hell are we going to do?'

"So we decided to just walk past them. Well, we were almost ready for anything. We didn't know if they were going to carve us up or what. And we got up to them and one of them says, 'Cigarette, Joe?'"

There wasn't much diversion in town for the rest of the crew. John Crosby: "Female activity was nonexistent. The only two white women I saw were two army nurses in Oro Bay and they were escorted by two armed Army M.P.'s, but that was war and war is hell."

On May 11 the ship left the dock to anchor in the bay. Despite Captain Gunderson's protests, some of the forward deck cargo was shifted and still more deck cargo was placed aboard.

John Crosby: "The vessel was very tender, but we encountered only good weather and arrived without any mishaps."

The *O'Brien* sailed on May 12, alone, to Hollandia where a convoy was being made up. Submarines were still in the area and on May 14, the following radio message was received:

"SSSS DE KQ2YY 10 deg, 08 min. North, 142 deg, 37 min. East, Vessel apparently submarine AR K. 0456 Radio message received: Cancel my SSSS of 131813 Z. "

John Crosby: "We heard several S.S.S.'s [submarine attack] from ships in the open Pacific that were sunk, but the closest was several hundred miles from us." The ship's luck was holding.

John Crosby: "We ran out of food someplace, Hollandia I think, and the army sent out some food and, boy, I think we got a few boxes intact, and the rest were all dented and broken. That's all we had after we ran out of food, Army rations, and we had powdered milk and so on. But some ships had it worse. Some of those fellows were out three or four years in the South Pacific and had to live off borrowed Army rations the whole time."

By this time the retaking of the Philippines was almost complete. Organized Japanese resistance would cease by the end of the month. As Okinawa and Iwo Jima fell, plans were made for the invasion of Japan.

May 20, found the ship preparing for another convoy. Weighing anchor, the *O'Brien* departed with 17 ships and three destroyer escorts. Her cargo was oil, lubricants and gasoline in drums and a deck cargo of light and medium tanks and half-tracks. The ship's guns were elevated and trained through the full arc of fire and firing circuits were tested.

John Crosby: "We never had any particular action where they used those guns out there. I do remember they were at gunnery practice off the coast of New Guinea and during that time or right after we received word that FDR was dead."

Many of the crew were saddened. Roosevelt had brought the country out of the Great Depression, which was still fresh in many minds, and guided it through a global war against Germany and Japan. Would his successor, Harry Truman, an unknown quantity, be equal to the task ahead? Time would tell.

The malaria epidemic continued claiming its victims. Earlier, one of the wipers was confined to the ship's hospital with a fever of 106. His temperature ranged between 102° to 104° for the next 3 days. He was treated with 15 grains of quinine bisulfate daily. Now the purser was confined to bed with a temperature, chills, a headache and muscular pains. Before leaving Hollandia, Capt. Gunderson, the ship's master, was also confined to bed on board by an Army doctor at Hollandia.

The mates took over the captain's duties and on May 21, the ship steamed in convoy position #32 toward the Philippines. As on previous convoys a message was received: "SSSS SSSS BT 10 deg. 44 min N., 144 deg, 28 min. E. Submarine sighted partly submerged. BT 210010." Again, it was over 60 miles from the *O'Brien's* position and as the convoy was well protected by escort, it was not thought to be a problem. Unfortunately, the medical problems increased.

At 1700 the *O'Brien* requested medical aid by flag hoist and blinker light. The captain, the purser and an Armed Guard crew member were ill with fever and chills. After manning the TBY (radio-telephone) the ship received directions from a doctor in the convoy and Ensign Robinson was instructed to take charge of the patients. The following day the convoy commodore sent a message requesting the condition of the patients. The purser was better, but the captain and Armed Guard crew member showed no improvement and by noon were worse. The escort Commander (aboard *DE 349*) also signaled for the condition of the men. The Captain's temperature was 103.6°, the Armed Guard crewman's, 104°.

John L. Crosby: "During the voyage Capt. Gunderson became ill with malaria and was confined to his bunk and lost plenty of weight and became very weak."

For the next twelve hours both men had violent chills. The *O'Brien* again and again requested a doctor, five of whom were known to be in the convoy, with no results. An escort (*DE 349*) ordered the vessel to fall out of position and prepare the Armed Guard crewman for transfer. He was transferred with all his gear to the escort for further medical care and hospitalization at Leyte.

Robert Crocker: "I remember a destroyer came along the port side. They shot the lines across between the two ships and took him across that way, while both ships were underway. The captain and one of the seamen got malaria. They took the seaman off but it was quite a while before the captain was treated."

Unaccountably, no doctor was sent to see the Captain, who was worse and whose temperature was 104° with a pulse of 124. His condition remained unchanged through the night then, fortunately, he made "the turn." On May 23, Norman Robinson logged his condition as "seems to have passed 'crisis'."

After breakfast Ensign Robinson signaled to the convoy commodore, explaining the captain's condition and asking for advice. The immediate reply was of little help, "Continue treatment." The convoy resumed its set speed of 9 knots, having earlier reduced speed to allow more ships to join. Thirty merchant ships were working their way north.

That evening Captain Gunderson had a relapse. More requests for a doctor were not answered. On May 24, the purser had improved and was able to be up part of the day but the captain's condition was still poor. Ensign Robinson again signaled the escort on May 25, asking for a doctor and advice. Again the response was, "Continue treatment." The escort did indicate that if the captain wished to be "high-lined" they would take him. Considering the manner in which he had been treated (or, more literally, not treated) thus far, the Captain refused, saying he preferred to stay aboard and take his chances in the next port.

Now the general uncooperative spirit manifested by the Army and the convoy escort began to spread aboard the *O'Brien*. At 0545 on May 26 general quarters was sounded. Five of the Armed Guard crew simply ignored it and stayed in bed. When called a second time, they responded, reporting fifteen minutes late. At 0900 mast was held and extra duty assigned. Four of them served their time but one refused. Upon questioning as to why he didn't turn to, he airily replied he had "other things to do." This kind of insubordination was so rare as to temporarily confuse those in charge. Was it due to boredom, or the general inactivity on board, or the many petty irritations from various sources, or the lack of recreational time? Robinson and the mates were baffled.

There may have been other causes. Bob Crocker: "We carried a lot of booze going over to the officers club in the Philippines and I think we borrowed some of it. It was all down below decks. We had to find a way through the paint locker and go down from there. So we took the door off and got some of the booze out and put the door back on. Then we repainted it so you couldn't tell it had been opened. There was an investigation but in the end I think they blamed it on the longshoremen that loaded the cargo."

Ensign Robinson held captain's mast for the recalcitrant crewman who refused extra duty. The charges were "(1) willful and premeditated refusal to follow His Commanding Officer's orders. (2) Insubordination. (3) Words and actions bordering on mutiny and to weaken the lawful authority of and respect due to Commanding officer. This man is a chronic petty offender. Disposition: Prisoner at Large until announced date to begin five (5) days on bread and water, with full ration every third day. All rights and privileges of a Petty Officer retracted and man is to stand Seaman's watches while aboard this vessel. Upon completion of this order, man is to complete the five hours duty imposed at Mast of 26 May 1945."

From time to time possible submarine contact notices were received, investigated and dismissed. These "false alarms" were becoming routine. The U. S. had almost completely secured the area but the danger from a lone Japanese submarine was still a possibility.

The convoy dispersed in San Pedro Bay, off Leyte, Philippines. All ships were ordered to proceed to their assigned destinations independently at their declared speed. It's an indication of how close to the end of the war it was and how safe conditions were considered that the ships were allowed to proceed alone and were allowed to use dim running lights at night.

On May 29, the *O'Brien* arrived at Subic Bay to await the formation of a convoy proceeding North. The ship was signaled to anchor out in the "Awaiting Convoy Anchorage Area." Captain Gunderson was still ill and very weak. As the *O'Brien* entered the harbor the mates sent a request ashore to have a doctor see the captain. After days of frustration, they finally got some action. Two Commanders, USN (Medical Corps) came aboard. They were not happy with the results of their examination and requested that the patient go ashore for hospitalization and laboratory tests.

John Crosby: "The captain was taken from the ship and was not replaced and went to the hospital. I felt that we would never see him again as he appeared extremely ill. I thought I'd never see that man again. He was nothing but skin and bones, he had a horrible case of malaria."

On May 30, Dr. O'Connell, Commander, USN, asked Ensign Robinson to come to the hospital to get results of the tests on Captain Gunderson. The Ensign was unable to get a boat from the Boat Pool and the Chief Mate refused to lower the ship's motor lifeboat. At 1345 the shore facility signaled the Armed Guard Officer to come to the Port Director for convoy conference and routing. Ensign Robinson called them again, requesting a boat. An LCVP eventually came alongside, but not in answer to the ship's request. The chief mate, Chief Radio Operator, Purser and Armed Guard Officer went in this craft to the Port Director's office. The official diagnosis was that Captain Gunderson had malaria. He would remain in the Navy medical facility until he was well enough to rejoin the ship at Lingayen Gulf.

John Crosby: "The three remaining deck officers agreed that each would take over the duties as the master on their own watch and would make any and all decisions pertaining to the operations and navigation of the ship during their watch period. Ironically we were named 'Commodore' of the convoy by the Naval Escort Commander, however we refused due to the absence of the master."

The next day, they arrived at San Fernando, Lingayen Gulf and anchored in the inner harbor. A floating crane came alongside to start removal of the deck cargo.

John Crosby: "We arrived in San Fernando during my watch and I was Acting Master and we went ashore and entered the arrival of the ship with the Captain of the Port. When they discovered our cargo they said, 'Why are you bringing more tanks here? We have enough for three wars.'" Crosby recalled with irony the problems trying to overload the ship with tanks which were "badly needed on the front." On the way back to the ship, "I was shown a sea of tanks that were inactive and their tracks were half buried in the sand."

On June 1 the ship moved in to the dock, unloaded quickly and by June 6 was empty. It was one year since the historic events of D-Day.

Norman Robinson: "The boys over there off-loaded very briskly and very casually. They bounced things off the dock and the sides of the ship and everything. After a while we got used to that."

Entertainment was hard to come by, but there was still the USO. It arranged for Hollywood to come out to the Pacific to entertain the troops. The crews aboard ship didn't often get ashore long enough to see the shows, but on at least one occasion the *O'Brien* crew had the opportunity.

John L. Crosby: "During our stay at San Fernando, I remember the great Joe E. Brown performing for the troops in a driving rain on an open outdoor stage with the roar of cannons and artillery in the background. He said, "If you troops are willing to stay in the driving rain then I will do my entire performance.' And he did. He got soaking wet like everyone else."

The farce of inter-service "cooperation" continued. Captain Gunderson was released from the hospital on June 5 in a very weak condition and set out to rejoin his ship. Again, no transportation was furnished from the Navy Hospital in Subic Bay to San Fernando so the captain had to hitch-hike his way there. He had no food for a day and a half until he reached the ship. Third Mate Crosby was so glad to see him, he reported, "Captain Gunderson returned to the ship and looked great." The epidemic on board had not abated. The purser suffered a relapse and a crew member came down with a fever, chills and a headache -- another malaria victim. His temperature was 102°, his pulse 100.

On June 8 the *O'Brien* suffered a minor mishap. A Navy tanker, *IX-179*, came alongside to refuel her. The weather was bad with a confused heavy sea and a heavy swell. In maneuvering alongside, the tanker hit the ship bending the upper deck railing and breaking the starboard gangway in two.

Empty of cargo and full of fuel, the *O'Brien* signaled ashore for sailing orders. The reply was, "To be informed later. Be prepared to sail today." A short while later an additional message from shore was sent, "Be prepared to sail at 1900. Orders en route." When the final orders came the seas were moderately heavy and it was raining hard. The *Jeremiah O'Brien* was to be Commodore of the convoy but in the dark and rain they were unable to find all the ships. Numerous exchanges of messages were sent via light with the result, "Delay until 0800, 9 June 1945."

The storm got worse. Robert Crocker: "We got hit by a couple of really bad storms. We were in one of our lifeboats coming back to the ship and it was overloaded and we hit one hell of a storm. I'll never forget it because we were trying to find our way in the dark. We'd come up to a ship and holler up and it would be the wrong one. We did that a couple of times. And the water was coming over and the motor conked out a couple of times, and we didn't have lifejackets. When we got to our ship a couple of seamen lowered a jacobs ladder over the side. The lifeboat was going up and down twenty feet at a time. We'd jump up to reach this ladder, trying to time it on the top of the swell so the boat wouldn't come up and crush us."

On June 9, a blinker message from shore was sent asking if the ship was ready to join the convoy. Four ships were scheduled with one escort. They were all outside the harbor waiting for the *O'Brien* to join up. The *O'Brien* was to be Commodore but other than that fact knew nothing of the location of the ships or the early move. Apparently the other ships had gone out on their own initiative. Snafu.

With some grousing from the crew about military orders and organization, the ship got underway at 0710 and joined the convoy leading it on a southerly course at a speed of 10 knots in very stormy conditions. The wind blew at Force 5 and the seas were confused. Visibility was about 50% of normal, but at times was down to 200 feet. The rains were torrential. That evening the convoy was dispersed with each ship proceeding independently. The *Jeremiah O'Brien* was homeward-bound, with no cargo and in ballast. Yet another member of the Armed Guard crew came down with chills and fever and was started on quinine hydrochlorate treatment for suspected malaria and the same day a second crewman reported to sick call with a fever of 102.4°.

Sailing in a northeasterly direction away from the war zone, the *Jeremiah O'Brien's* crew enjoyed a return to normal days at sea with the typical events that mark an easy passage across the Pacific. The log entries reflect the monotony of the return voyage: The Ulithi Islands were seen to starboard, showing numerous lights; on June 16, a ship was seen on the horizon travelling so fast she passed the *O'Brien*; the Armed Guardsmen with malaria returned to duty on June 18; on June 19 a Liberty ship was passed to port and exchanged signals via blinker; June 20 the *O'Brien* overtook a tug (*ARS 34*) and tow on her starboard side, blinker signals were exchanged. Passing Eniwetok Atoll on June 21st, the ship was asked by the shore tower her International Call sign and destination. This information was given and signals were exchanged until the island disappeared from sight. On the 24th of June a ship was seen approaching on the horizon on the starboard quarter; a second ship was seen approaching on the port quarter, also on the horizon. Both were running a parallel course and in the same direction as the *Jeremiah O'Brien.*

June 25th offered little more "excitement." At 1030 one of the new Victory ships passed the *O'Brien* to starboard. And at 1945 that evening a second Victory ship was seen passing to starboard.

The Armed Guard crew continued their strange behavior. A captain's mast was held, "Charge: Failure to answer General Quarters after being called three times. This is second mast for same reason. Man is a chronic offender. Punishment: To march around the deck in military manner with rifle and loaded bandoleer. Dress: Undress blues, white hat and leggings. Duration: Until further notice and at least three hours each day." Marching around the deck, as such, was not too severe a punishment, but for the offender, the embarrassment of having his amused shipmates watch was humiliating, and intended to be.

That afternoon a radio message was received of an unidentified submarine on the surface ahead. Captain Gunderson prudently changed course to go south of the position. The International Dateline was crossed that evening and the crew noted the crossing with pleasure. Now they were in the same day as "Home."

Ted Martin: "In our off time we'd play pinochle or read or play poker. Sometimes we'd just go sit with a buddy on watch and talk. There wasn't that much to do. Some of the guys played checkers, but poker was the biggest game on the ship."

John Crosby: "The ship was a happy ship. The third engineer Roy Simpson and the third radio operator, Merrill Hubbard and I would meet after our watch and talk, play cards and have fun. We were constantly playing jokes on each other."

Robert Crocker: "We expected danger constantly. We had no radar, no doctors, nothing. But it didn't seem to bother us. We were used to having very little, except ourselves. We relied on one another. The crews were good. The gun crews were very good. The merchant crews were very good.

"Sailing in the Far East didn't worry us that much. After all, one ship in the Pacific is pretty hard to find."

On June 26, a significant and very welcome message was received: "Resume traffic on 500 kcs." This is the standard calling frequency for merchant ships. For the first time since the war began it was back in use, clear proof that the war was over. V-E day had been May 8 and now this message truly marked the beginning of a return to normal. No longer would there be the fear of enemy submarines and air attacks. No longer would crews have to sleep in their clothes and lifejackets, ready to abandon ship on an instant's notice. After years of isolation, misinformation and no information, radio silence was no longer necessary and the crew would know what was going on around them and in the rest of the world. The Allies had won and the U.S. Merchant Marine had played an important part.

John Crosby: "Liberty ships, I have the greatest admiration for them. I know what they were and why they were built. I believe they were the backbone of the merchant fleet. They could get a big belly full of cargo. The engines were simple and engineers could be trained easily. The Liberty ship proved itself, the value they were in World War II in carrying supplies to the Allies. And I resent the term 'ugly duckling.'"

On July 5 they approached the West Coast of the United States and ran into fog off San Francisco harbor. Late in the afternoon a Navy patrol blimp appeared through the fog and disappeared again off the starboard bow. Forty minutes later the Farallon Island group appeared to port. A patrol vessel requested "International Call." The ship took arrival at 1650 and anchored at 1830.

John Crosby. "There was an ordinary seaman on watch with me coming into San Francisco. He says, 'You know, I have a brother that lives here.'

"I said, 'Oh, really, where?'

"And he pointed over to Alcatraz."

On July 6 the pilot came aboard, the anchor was weighed and the ship got underway. By 1016 she was secured starboard side to Pier 35, San Francisco, California.

That night one of the crew returned to the ship in a very drunken condition. He turned in and didn't make his watch that night or the next day. At morning muster the Petty Officer of the Watch reported the sailor had attempted to "roll" another crewmember for $450. As both men were in their cups, the Petty Officer took the money and gave it to the Purser to lock up. A captain's mast was held for the sailor. "Charge: Leaving the ship while on duty section without permission. Returning in an intoxicated condition so as to be unable to stand watch 2400 to 0400. Attempts to awaken him for watch were unsuccessful. Action: Seaman to be bound over to the Armed Guard Center (Pacific) for action."

Norman Robinson: "The *O'Brien* was all right. It was still dungaree Navy as far as I was concerned. We didn't have to wear uniforms except in port. I liked that. I didn't like the spit and polish of the regular Navy."

John Crosby had a good word for the Ensign: "The Ensign was a hell of a nice guy."

Ted Martin: "The merchant crew was pretty good. We used to stand wheel watch for them sometimes and they'd pay us. They'd pay five dollars to stand a watch. Of course they made a lot more money than we did. But they were pretty good. After the trip, eight or ten of them took us out in San Francisco or Alameda for a night on the town and they paid for everything."

John L. Crosby. "I remember going to a night spot in San Francisco with the chief officer and chief engineer. When we arrived, many of the crew and armed guard were there, and I noticed that I. D.'s were being checked; however, I had no fear as I was in an officer's uniform with two others fifteen to twenty years older than I. But she kept on checking and got to me and she said, 'Why you are only 20,' and they put me out. It was only then discovered by the crew that I was their third officer at age 20."

The *Jeremiah O'Brien's* first voyage to the South Pacific was over. The next voyage would go farther, to the Pacific -- and beyond.

13

DOWN UNDER AND BEYOND

July 1945. The war in the Pacific was entering its final phase. Carrier-based planes from the U.S. Pacific Fleet and U.S. Army Air Force planes from the Marianas, Iwo Jima and Okinawa pounded the Japanese homeland without let-up while Pacific Fleet surface ships with the help of a British carrier task force bombarded its eastern coast. Planes from the Philippines hit Japanese shipping in the South China Sea, Formosa and the south coast of China as General Douglas MacArthur and Admiral Chester Nimitz expanded ports and bases in the Pacific to accommodate more than a million troops from Europe, the United States, Australia, New Zealand and other areas for the invasion of Japan, scheduled for November 1.

For the *Jeremiah O'Brien* and her crew, however, 5,000 miles away from the front, July was a welcome respite. R and R were the magic letters -- repair for the ship, rest and relaxation for the crew. The last trip had been hard on both ship and crew. Yet, after six wartime voyages, battling the pounding seas of the North

Atlantic, ferrying thousands of troops, ammunition, tanks, jeeps, LCM's and other heavy cargo, and enduring the blunders of Army stevedores in the Pacific the *Jeremiah O'Brien* was still sound. A few minor repairs, some scraping and painting and the "Lucky O'Brien" was ready to go out again. It was a tribute to the skill and professionalism of the ship builders, who built the Libertys in mere days, envisioning a single voyage.

The crew's natural tendency to let go and celebrate on making home port was to be expected and some made up with a vengeance for the months of enforced abstinence and celibacy. During the next two weeks several men missed their evening watches or didn't show up for work during the day, electing to stay ashore. Some "explanations" were more elaborate than others. One of the Armed Guard crew missed several watches in succession. After being absent over leave (AOL) for more than 30 hours he came back aboard and told Ensign Robinson that his wife was in town. He offered to report aboard for duty that night if he could spend the day with her. As it had been a year since he was last in the States, the sympathetic Ensign let him go. The crewman didn't show up that night and the next day he was brought back to the ship by the Shore Patrol. He had attempted to cash a money order at the Western Union office but had no identification card. Western Union, well aware of proper procedure, called the Shore Patrol which brought the sailor to the ship for verification of his right to be ashore. Still giving the man the benefit of the doubt, a Temporary I.D. card was issued and he was allowed ashore again but Robinson noted in his log, "It is now doubtful if the woman is his wife. Man will be questioned further on his return to the ship in the morning."

Norman Robinson wasn't surprised when the man was AOL again the following morning. Having reached the end of his patience, the Ensign telephoned the Shore Patrol to issue a warrant for the sailor's arrest but while they were combing the streets of San Francisco, he wandered aboard. Broke, hungover, and subdued, he remained aboard the rest of the time the ship was in port. Before sailing he was removed and taken ashore.

That evening another member of the gun crew returned from liberty exceedingly drunk. In stumbling up the gangway he somehow lost his wallet over the side between the ship and the dock. With the help of another crewmember, almost as drunk, the inebriate went on the pier after his wallet. He fell in and disappeared from sight. He showed up a few minutes later under the dock walking on the stringers that held the pilings together. The other man managed to keep him from going between the ship and the dock but he fell in again and disappeared. This time his rescuer found him hysterically clinging to a piling far under the pier. Then, the unlucky man fell in the water yet a third time and the determined rescuer went in after him.

He was finally retrieved with an all-out effort of dockworkers, ship's crew and Armed Guard crew. With the help of a motor crane, the *O'Brien* was pushed away from the dock. A line was lowered and the drunk and his rescuer brought up. After cleaning himself up and putting on a dry uniform he left the ship with an escort of Shore Patrol. Ensign Robinson noted in the log that the man was considered "a menace to himself and others." A few days later he was detached from the ship.

On July 23, Ensign Robinson was replaced by Lieutenant Ambrose P. McGowan. Captain Gunderson left the ship to finish his recuperation.

Coxswain Ted Martin: "McGowan was a very nice guy. He just wanted to get his time in and get it over with. He was really a nice guy to work for although he was stern when he had to be."

Almost "good as new," the *O'Brien* shifted back toward Pier 35 on the morning of July 24th to load cargo. As they neared the dock, Captain Gerdes, who replaced Captain Gunderson, received word not to go alongside but to anchor where he was. Muttering "typical military maneuver," he ordered the anchor dropped and shortly after lunch received instructions to sail for San Pedro.

The run down the California coast was pleasant, offering glimpses of rugged shoreline topped with cypress and redwood forests and, farther south, low sandy beaches fringed with palm trees. The weather grew more pleasant as blue skies and sunshine replaced the grey overcast of San Francisco Bay. Arriving in San

Pedro harbor on the morning of July 26, the ship anchored briefly then went alongside Pier 176 in the early evening.

A week later the first load of cargo was taken aboard and Articles for the coming voyage were signed stating that the vessel would sail on a voyage "From the port of Los Angeles, Calif., to a point in the Pacific Ocean to the westward of Los Angeles, Calif., and thence to such ports and places in any part of the world as the Master may direct, or as may be ordered or directed by the U.S. Government, or any Department, Commission or Agency thereof." And "Back to a final port of discharge in the United States, for a term of time not exceeding twelve (12) months."

Loading was quick. On August 3 at 1900 we find the ship casting off lines and getting underway. Her cargo was listed as "general" and partially consisted of beer and a deckload of jeeps; scheduled port of discharge was Calcutta, India.

Because the war in the Pacific still on, bonuses were paid to merchant seamen. That evening the Official log noted: "Leaving San Pedro, Cal. 33 1/3% bonus effective as of 2200 hrs this date." This was followed a few days later with two entries, "August 6, 1945. At sea. 33 1/3% Bonus terminates as of 2400 hours this date," and "August 7, 1945. At sea. 136 degrees long. passed this date at 1800 hrs. 66 2/3% bonus effective at 0001 hrs this date."

On August 6, 1945 the atomic bomb was dropped on Hiroshima and three days later the second atomic bomb was dropped on Nagasaki. The Japanese Empire was defeated and the Allies, now joined by Russia, moved to finish the campaign quickly and end the war.

But this was all far away. On board the *O'Brien*, the voyage continued in much the same way as the previous one. Ships were occasionally spotted, islands appeared on the horizon ahead and disappeared astern. Minor ailments and accidents occurred. One of the wipers was burned on the right forearm. The wound became infected, with complications, including septicemia, setting in. He was treated with a full course of sulfa drugs, recovered and returned to duty in two weeks. The log noted a few incidents: on August 8 another ship was sighted; that evening a navy tug was seen four miles off the port bow; on August 11 the ship began zig-zagging; a tug towing two barges was sighted five miles off traveling away from the ship on August 12; in the afternoon of August 13, a tanker and tugboat were sighted bearing 270 degrees at a distance of five miles off going away from the *O'Brien...*

The merchant crew spent the time doing the age-old, never-ending shipboard chores -- chipping, painting, varnishing woodwork and lubricating the cargo gear while the gun crew chipped, painted, varnished woodwork and lubricated the guns. The Armed Guard stood "G.Q." at sunrise and sunset and practiced shooting the guns. On August 15, they sent aloft six helium-filled balloons for target practice. Ten rounds were fired from the two 3" guns and 360 rounds from the 20 mm. Four of the balloons were brought down.

V-J day, August 15, came and went with little notice on the ship. While back in the United States people were literally dancing in the streets, on board the *Jeremiah O'Brien* the reaction was much more blasé. Ted Martin remembered V-J day at sea this way, "We didn't believe it at first." Charles Hord, Fireman Watertender recalled: "The war ended somewhere between San Pedro and the Far East. We didn't really pay much attention to it at the time."

A radio message was received on August 17 informing Captain Gerdes that American President Lines' agents were assigned to husband the vessel while in India. The ship passed another line of demarcation. From the official log. "66 2/3% bonus terminates as of 2400 hrs this date. And on August 19: "180 meridian crossed at 0600 hrs this date. 100% + $5.00 per day effective as of (0001).

The days passed and little else happened until August 24 when the island of Guadalcanal was sighted at a bearing of 045 degrees and a distance of 10,000 yards. A day later the crew was started on atabrine (anti-malarial) pills. The misery of the epidemic on the previous voyage would be avoided, if at all possible.

A few days later when the ship crossed the equator, Captain Gerdes held a "Crossing The Line" ceremony for those who were not yet "shellbacks." With the war over some of the foolish but fun ceremonies and traditions could be resumed. The Neptune ceremony is a rite of passage that goes back several centuries to when seamen first passed into the unknown dangers that lay above and below the ocean. A sailor who hasn't crossed the equator is considered a "polliwog" and treated with disdain by the "shellbacks" who have. The process of becoming a shellback is strictly scripted and solemnly enacted. One of the crew, dressed as Davey Jones, appears on the foc'sle head and hails the bridge.

Davey Jones: "Ship ahoy."

Mate on watch: "Ahoy Davey Jones."

Davey Jones proceeds to the microphone in the wheelhouse while the mate announces, "Davey Jones has just come aboard the ship and is now talking to the chief mate. Let's listen in on the conversation."

Davey Jones: "Greetings sir. What ship is this?"

Mate: "This is the SS Jeremiah O'Brien."

Davey Jones: "Where are you bound?"

Mate: "Southwest Pacific on a War Mission."

Davey Jones: "Know ye on whose realm you are trespassing?"

Mate: "The realm of Neptune."

Davey Jones: "My congratulations to you sir. I hear you have an old friend of mine aboard, Captain George Gerdes. I first met him when he crossed the Equator and became a shellback many years ago. I have a summons for him from King Neptune."

Mate: "I will be glad to receive it for the captain."

Davey Jones: "Know All Men By These Presents: Tomorrow at five bells, His Most Titanic Majesty, Neptunus Rex, King of all the waters that cover the earth and his most gracious and lovely spouse, Queen Amphitrite, than whom there is none fairer, will deign to visit this good ship SS Jeremiah O'Brien to examine and put to the test his neophytes, those kind and good souls whom he had never seen and who he hopes will answer for themselves.

"Think well of your past sins, oh you neophytes, for King Neptune for all his graciousness is very stern with those who have transgressed against the written and unwritten laws of his realm, The Seven Seas. Think back to your days aboard this vessel and be prepared to answer for your sins tomorrow at five bells.

"Given under my hand and seal, this 28th day of August the year of our King Neptune, two million, one thousand, nine hundred and forty-five. Signed, King Neptune."

The following day at five bells Davey Jones appears and reports to the mate on watch that the Captain is to be informed that Neptunus Rex and his party have been sighted ahead. The flag of Neptune is unfurled when Neptune appears on deck. A bugle call is sounded to call all hands to attention. The royal party then proceeds slowly aft to meet Davey Jones.[1]

Neptune to Davey Jones: "Well, well. What a fine ship and what a cargo of landlubbers!"

Mate, saluting: "The captain awaits the royal party."

Captain: "A sailor's welcome to you Neptune Rex. It is a great pleasure to have you with us."

Neptune: "The pleasure is mine. I am glad to be with you again Captain. I have prepared for a very busy day in order to make your landlubbers fit subjects of my great Sea Domain."

Captain: "I am glad to hear that, Your Majesty, as I have quite a few young men of the crew aboard who have not been in the service long enough to have had the opportunity to visit your domain and become shellbacks. I beg of you to be as lenient as possible."

Neptune: "I will be as severe as I can."

Captain: "I turn my ship over to you for as long as you wish."

Neptune: "Very well, Captain, I thank you. You may direct the ship on the course assigned. All polliwogs are ordered to the after deck. Policemen, take charge of the polliwogs."

The mate escorts Neptune to a throne on number four hatch and the polliwogs are brought forth. Initiation consists of having their heads and/or eyebrows shaved, being forced to drink concoctions heavy with cod liver oil or cooking oil and tabasco sauce and running a gauntlet of firehoses or rolling in bilge water and grease while their crewmates watch with great mirth and

---

[1] Traditionally crew members dress as Neptune, Amphitrite and members of the royal party, wearing mops for hair and sheets or tablecloths for robes and gowns.

hilarity. When the rites are complete, the polliwogs are given cards certifying them to be shellbacks.

Charles Hord: "We had a ceremony. It wasn't too pleasant. They didn't do anything really bad but they rigged up some kind of terrible-tasting concoction that we had to drink. And this other kid and I shaved each other's heads. They were in such a mess we couldn't do anything with our hair the rest of the trip."

Ted Martin: "A couple of the guys got their heads shaved on top of the cargo hold. It wasn't that big a ceremony. They had a chair up there, a high-back chair that was decorated. They used a shaver on them right there. The guy that was giving the haircuts was dressed up like Neptune."

The *Jeremiah O'Brien* continued on in a southwesterly direction. As she neared Australia and the Great Barrier Reef, a stop was made on August 28 in the outer bay at Port Moresby, New Guinea, for a pilot. Extending 1,250 miles parallel to the Australian state of Queensland, the reef is thick with hull-piercing coral lying just below the surface and is considered one of the more treacherous areas of the world to navigate. The pilot guided the *O'Brien* through this obstacle and the Torres Strait and disembarked at Thursday Island.

Two days later, a second pilot came aboard to guide the ship into Darwin, and the *O'Brien* dropped anchor in Darwin harbor at 0600 the following morning. Her speed on the run from San Pedro was 11.4 knots. The propeller turned 2,749,550 times over a distance of 7,567 miles from San Francisco to Darwin during a period of 27 days, 14 hours and 35 minutes.

As often happened, the crew had very different perceptions of the city. Bob Crocker: "The first stop was Darwin. There wasn't much there. It had been bombed out."

Charles Hord: "There wasn't much to it. I don't think I got ashore there."

But Ted Martin remembered it differently. "In Darwin we had real nice liberty. The people were very friendly. You could buy about a sixteen ounce T-bone steak and a quart of Black Horse ale for $2.50. Of course it was warm ale. They kept it all at well water temperature. We were used to cold beer and you couldn't get a cold beer. I didn't like that. But it was a good liberty, they used to have dances quite often. And we used to like the Sunday afternoons when they'd go into the parks with concerts in the gazebos. Nine times out of ten, if you met somebody in the afternoon, they'd invite you to dinner. The families were all really friendly."

On September 2, Japan signed an unconditional surrender aboard the *USS Missouri* in Tokyo Bay. World War II was over. Little notice of the ceremony was taken on the *O'Brien*. As far as the crew was concerned, the war had been over for months. They lived in their own insulated, isolated world -- a cocoon crossing vast distances of ocean and time peripherally touched by the world outside. Their world, of necessity, was limited to the rails of the ship and circumscribed by the horizon of the blue sea, as Omar Khayyám called it, "that inverted bowl, the sky." Their interests were in the functioning of the ship, the lives of the people on board, and outside events, in that order. It was the only way to survive. To become embroiled in distant events over which you had no control created anxiety, stress and, in some cases, madness. The philosophy was, "do your job and let the world take care of itself. It will all work out somehow."

Sailing on September 4 at 2200 the ship continued westward, to Calcutta, India.

It was September 9, 1945 before the end of the war was officially acknowledged by the military. Late that evening a message was received from COMPHILSEAFRON (Commander of the Philippine Sea Frontier) dated 090153Z and addressed to all areas in the South Pacific. It stated that ships would no longer zigzag, blackout regulations were canceled, navigation lights were to be burned with full brilliancy, and guns no longer had to be manned. The crew listened with interest. Unlike most of the political and military information they heard, this was news that had relevance to them, on board their ship. Life really was returning to normal and they looked forward to going ashore at the next port. The vessel would load U.S. Army cargo at Calcutta for discharge at Shanghai, under the supervision of the U.S. War Department. All hands received initial immunization for Cholera.

The Indian Ocean has some of the world's worst storms and typhoons. With nothing but water between Australia and Africa, waves travel long distances, building upon themselves to great heights. The typhoon's winds, without land masses on which to expend their energy, build and sustain for long stretches of time and ocean. A major storm center in the Indian Ocean is an awesome -- and wonderful -- phenomenon, but one to be avoided, if at all possible. So, when, on September 18, Captain Gerdes received warning of a storm ahead, he immediately reversed the ship's course from north to south for eight hours. Resuming the original course the following day, he reduced the ship's speed to ensure they didn't sail into the predicted maelstrom.

Storms aside, sailing on the Indian Ocean was monotonous, hot, humid and boring. There was little entertainment other than a short-wave radio piped into the messrooms from the radio shack. The crews often gathered in the evenings on the main deck aft of the midship house to talk and tell sea stories. The officers did the same on the boat deck. The latest issues of *Saturday Evening Post, Colliers* and *Life* were read and passed around. Some might read aloud the latest adventures of Tugboat Annie or Colin Glencannon, to the delight of their gathered shipmates.

On the long voyage, the crew also got to know each other. Sometimes more than they wanted. Ted Martin: "We had one guy in the gun crew that wouldn't take a shower. I don't know why. So finally we just all ganged up on him and gave him one with a stiff brush. After that he used to take one a couple of times a week."

The *O'Brien* arrived in India on September 21. She anchored outside the Hooghly River because the tidal current was too strong for the ship to make any headway. Ten hours later she weighed anchor and proceeded upriver for 20 miles but was forced to drop anchor again to wait the turning of the tide. The following day was more of the same. The ship sailed against the current for four hours, managing to make only 20 more miles in that time, then anchored again, still forty miles from Calcutta. On September 23, she finally reached Calcutta, tying up just after supper to Berth 3 of the King William Docks.

No 178303
GOVERNMENT OF INDIA
PERMIT FOR PORT PROTECTED PLACES
SHORT PERIOD - SHIP'S CREW PASS
This pass is only valid for :-
KIDDERPORE 1.   KIDDERPORE 2.
K. GEORGE DOCK   CALCUTTA JETTIES
GARDEN R. JETTIES.   PRINSEP GHAT

No. _____ Mooring

Name _Kent, Charles_

Valid to _OCT 4 1945_

Any misuse of this pass renders the holder liable to punishment under the Defence of India Rules.

DEPUTY COMMISSIONER, PORT POLICE, CALCUTTA.

In most foreign ports the crew had to carry passes going ashore. The above belonged to Third Mate Charles Kent. Credit NLSM

The crew spent a considerable amount of time ashore, seeing the sights. As usual, perceptions varied.

Ted Martin: "I never want to go back there. It's one of the dirtiest cities I was ever in. It was bad, people sleeping in the streets, people begging continuously, everywhere you went. Even begging alongside the rickshaws as you went from one place to another."

Charles Hord: "Calcutta was very interesting. We were there long enough that I could see a lot of the city. It was bad especially going from the docks to the downtown area. We went to the Seaman's Club and they had tours that we could go on. I remember going down the river to a burning *ghat*, where they cremate their dead, and we went to see the Black Hole of Calcutta and a place called the Jane Temple. I do remember this one real fancy place we went into, Firpo's it was called, a very nice restaurant and bar. But it was only in the Seaman's Club that we would drink anything." The lessons of Subic Bay were remembered.

Ted Martin: "We got pretty friendly with people there. A couple of the women came and laundered our clothes and ironed them and everything." The poverty and misery of the people touched the crew and they tried to find ways to help. Ted Martin: "We'd take our garbage cans and instead of dumping them, we'd lower them to the dock. And the people would swarm all around the cans and pick out all the garbage, They'd be empty when they got done. Sometimes we'd take a loaf of bread or something extra and wrap it in paper and set it on top, just to give them a little more."

Remarkably, the crew generally managed to stay out of trouble, except the boatswain was slightly injured getting out of a rickshaw ashore, but one poor seaman met with a serious accident.

Charles Hord: "In Calcutta the third engineer and this young kid [an oiler] went ashore. A car hit this kid on a bicycle and the doorhandle caught him under the jaw and almost tore his chin off. This little third engineer, he was Irish and like a little banty rooster. He was cocky and outspoken. Well, the person that hit this kid was a missionary and didn't want his car messed up taking the kid to the hospital. So the engineer just told him he was going to do it. He got mean with the guy. He made him do it. They put the oiler in an army hospital and put him back together and believe it or not he tried to sail with us when we left. He had such a terrible scar on his chin."

On September 28, having completed offloading her cargo, the ship shifted to Berth 1, Garden Reach Jetties. Cargo work began the next day just after noon when dock workmen began loading gasoline drums of 100 octane aviation fuel.

The young oiler in the hospital was paid off, his clothes were packed and checked in the American Seaman's Club and a new oiler was hired to replace him.

The "gearing down" from the war process continued slowly. On October 9, 1945, at 0900, pursuant to ALNAV 248 of 8 September 1945, the censorship stamp was destroyed.

On October 10, with the cargo loaded, the mooring lines were cast off and the *Jeremiah O'Brien* proceeded upstream to the oil dock for fueling. Continuing her struggle against the tides, she eventually arrived alongside the Burmah Oil Dock No. 4, fueled and proceeded back down the Hooghly River. She anchored to await a favorable tide, got underway just before noon the following day, and cleared the river that afternoon. Her cargo was listed as: general, army vehicles and gasoline; destination: Shanghai, China.

With the war over, some sailors apparently thought they could relax. One of the A.B.s, who was supposed to be standing lookout, was found asleep on watch. The master's entry in the official log states: "Lat. 1-20 N, Long. 104-22E. On this date at 0350 hours _____, A.B. was found laying down and asleep on lookout while vessel was in dangerous waters. For this offense _____ is being fined two days' pay plus bonus amounting to $11.67. Seaman's reply: None."

The leftovers of war such as mines and uncharted wrecks were still a serious hazard. Nearing the coast of China on October 27, eight minesweepers were spotted two miles off the port quarter. Two days later a U.S. Navy patrol vessel exchanged signals and escorted the *O'Brien* through the approaches to the Yangtze River. A pilot came aboard, guided the ship into the delta and ordered the anchor dropped.

The river delta was wide and shallow with sediment in many places. Ashore could be seen low, flat farmland. In the distance was the faint skyline of Shanghai. Because of the danger of pirates, sidearms were issued to the Armed Guard on watch. There were stories of junks silently coming alongside in the dead of night, pirates slipping aboard, overpowering a ship's crew, and stealing everything of value. The comic strip "Terry and the Pirates," popular at the time, was based on fact.

Shanghai was a considerable distance from the port but some of the crew were curious and wanted to see the city.

Ashore in Shanghai, Bob Crocker of the SS Jeremiah O'Brien's *Armed Guard with a group of young admirerers. Credit Bob Crocker*

A proper visit to Shanghai can't be made without a rickshaw ride. Bob Crocker pauses before taking in the sights. Credit Bob Crocker

Bob Crocker: "A buddy of mine, Ted Martin, and I went ashore to pick up the mail when the ship was at anchor. We got a small boat to take us ashore. If you went for the mail it was an excuse to stop off at a bar and get most of the day off. Well, we walked miles and miles through the Chinese countryside trying to get to Shanghai.

Ted Martin: "We were going to get the mail, yeah. We didn't even know where we were. Jesus! We ended up going across rice paddies and everything else."

Bob Crocker: "And as we were walking we came to this huge field. We started walking through what looked like a large cultivated field. There were a lot of men working this field. So we walked across it and then I noticed these men were wearing the canvas shoes with the split between the big toe and the rest of the toes. 'These guys are Japanese,' I whispered to Martin. 'They must be prisoners.'

"As we got closer to the end of the field about 20 or 25 of them were stretched in a line across the path, blocking our way. Well I decided we'd just walk through them. So we got closer and closer and finally they parted and we walked right though the Japanese prisoners. They moved away and backed off. Then we came to a guard and he had an old rifle with the longest, sharpest bayonet on it I've ever seen. And he was Chinese and he was guarding them.

"After a while we came to a village and everyone gathered around us because they'd never seen an American before, especially in uniform. The chief of police came up to us and he had been educated in the United States. So when he found out what we were doing he arranged for a car to take us to Shanghai. The car had a charcoal burner in the back for fuel and they had to warm that up before we could go. But they drove us into Shanghai for the mail."

Ted Martin: "When we finally got to the post office in Shanghai and told them what we went across, they were just shaking their heads. 'Lucky you made it,' they said."

The next day the pilot came aboard, the anchor was raised and the ship proceeded up the Whangpoo River, the tributary to the Yangtze on which lies Shanghai. The *Jeremiah O'Brien* berthed at the military dock.

Charles Hord: "That was a pretty nice city. It was modern, like cities we were used to. The difference was really noticeable after Calcutta. They had nice department stores. We were across the river from town and had to take a sampan to get over there."

Stevedores unloaded the vehicles and the *O'Brien* then shifted to other docks to unload the general cargo. On November 3, she cast off her mooring lines to sail down river to a temporary berth at Holtz Dock, then shifted to the Hongkew Wharf to unload the fuel.

Charles Hord: "We carried aviation gas but the nice thing was we got extra money for carrying that at the time. It was considered a hazardous cargo."

Ted Martin: "That was fifty-gallon drums we unloaded in Shanghai. The pier they had us on, they had us way isolated because the whole damn dock was fifty gallon drums of aviation fuel."

From the official log, "November 15, 1945. On this date the Chief Officer Mr. Martin A. Moen was suddenly taken ill with an undetermined sickness, shortly before sailing time. He was sent to and retained on the U.S. Navy hospital ship *Repose* in Shanghai and was consequently paid off up to and including Nov. 15, 1945. His effects were sent for safe keeping to the American Seaman's Club in Shanghai. Paid $711.32."

The next day the ship sailed at 1300 for Manila. Because of the danger of mines left over from the war a mine lookout watch was set up. This would continue in force until the ship arrived at Manila.

"Gearing down" orders continued piecemeal. On November 19, the Armed Guard crew received word to get rid of their ammunition. The Navy required that it be dumped in water more than 150 fathoms deep and more than 10 miles from shore. Thousands of rounds were simply thrown over the side.

The *O'Brien* dropped anchor in Manila Bay on November 21. There was no cargo on board and the port of Manila was entered "for orders." On November 23, Capt. Gerdes was informed that they were sailing to Freemantle, Australia. The following day, when Lieutenant McGowan went ashore to report to the Port Director's Building, he learned that the ship would be placed on a maintenance status in regard to Armed Guard personnel and that the AGO and 24 enlisted men would be detached. It was another step in the process of "getting back to normal" and many of the merchant crew probably welcomed the idea of having their ship returned to them. Symbolically, the departure of the gun crew meant a sure end to the war.

Bob Crocker: "We got off in Manila. Being a gunner's mate, I had to do shore patrol. All the petty officers had to do shore patrol and the seamen had to spend their time cleaning up the barracks. And then I went back to the States again on the *USS Audobon*. So when we pulled in to Frisco what happened was they put me on shore patrol again."

This left two Navy men aboard to maintain the guns. Ted Martin: "They pulled the crew off but they kept us on the ship to maintain the guns, Swan and I. We beat them back to the States. I have a buddy I corresponded with and it turned out that by staying on the ship we beat them back by two weeks."

Ted Martin became Officer in Charge of the maintenance crew and armament aboard *SS Jeremiah O'Brien* and the ship sailed that evening for Freemantle, arriving on December 7.

Freemantle is an artificial harbor, built at the mouth of the Swan River. The river is geologically very old and consequently broad and sluggish. The harbor is virtually a tidal estuary, with brackish water backing as far upstream as Perth, twelve miles away. In the late 1800's a rock bar at the mouth of the river was blasted away, leaving a narrow entrance to the harbor, about 1/4 mile wide, and when the tide is on a strong ebb or flood a rapid current pours through the entrance. Great skill is required to maneuver a ship safely through the channel and Captain Gerdes was grateful to have a pilot familiar with the local waters guide him in. The *Jeremiah O'Brien* went straight into Victoria Quay on the south side of the harbor and tied up with her stern to the entrance.

Freemantle was a friendly port. The crew, feeling liberated from the strictly-enforced discipline of the war years, seemed to cast off all inhibitions. From the Official log: "Freemantle, Australia. On this date _____ , A.B. while on duty as watchman was ordered by the master not to allow any strangers aboard ship and to order all strangers already aboard to go ashore. Instead of carrying out these orders, _____ retained a woman aboard and later walked off the ship. For this offense he is being fined 4 days' pay for willful disobedience and 2 days' pay for neglect of duty, a total of 6 days' pay amounting to $29.00."

The next day one of the Ordinary Seamen succumbed to the blandishments ashore. He was logged for being absent without leave and fined two days' pay which amounted to $8.50. On December 15, the carpenter was found absent without leave while he was restricted to the ship. He was fined four days' pay for willful disobedience and two days' pay for neglect of duty, a total of $31.50. The same day one of the Utility Messman deserted the ship, and "thereby ceased to be a member of the crew." His clothes and pay were held over for the U.S. Shipping Commissioner at the first U.S. Port. The pay due him was $322.08. Then the first A.B. above deserted and also "thereby ceased to be a member of the crew." His clothes and pay, too, were held on board for the first U.S. port. A second A.B. was logged for being absent without leave and fined two days' pay amounting to $9.76. On the same day still another A.B. was absent without leave and fined two days' pay.

Willis "Bud" Hitchcock recalled the people of Australia as being very kind to seamen when he visited that port on the Liberty ship *SS Hiram S. Maxim.* "I remember we docked very near the American submarine base and how proud we were to see one of our subs returning from patrol displaying a broom from its conning tower, denoting a "clean sweep" in Jap waters.

"The people of Freemantle and Perth were very kind to seamen at that time and brought to our ship "care" packages of fruit and knitted cold weather gear and clothing for us. We were also invited into their homes and treated with great hospitality. Everybody hated to leave this port to return to the winter gales of the high south latitudes."

The ship took on 4,005 tons of bunker fuel during her stay in Freemantle and loaded approximately 16,500 bales of wool and skins for discharge in California. But, before sailing, there was one more special cargo: War Brides.

War brides were not uncommon in 1945. Wartime romances between U.S. servicemen and women they met while overseas occasionally resulted in marriages abroad.   English, French, Australian and others and even ex-"enemy" German and Italian women were anxious to join their American husbands and begin a new life in the U.S.   Americans often treated women more courteously than other nationalities.   Hector Miller, whose sister, Brenda, was one of the war brides scheduled for the *O'Brien*, explains how it happened.   "To start with, 98% of the population, which was just under 10 million, were of British descent (higher than Great Britain).   You can imagine the cultural shock when nearly one million Americans, whose outlook was vastly different, more like that of people from another planet, passed through Australia during '42 to '45.   However, the girls thought they were marvelous because they treated them so differently from Australian men.   No Aussie, for example, would ever think of buying flowers for a girl, let alone be seen carrying them in public when going to collect a partner on a date, nor would he think of taking them in a taxi when Public Transport was available.   When he did arrive at a dance or party they were abandoned at the door and he joined the other males, the girls being left in a separate group. The Americans did the opposite and treated them like people, not objects, and they loved it."

Thora Quackenbush: "I met my future husband, Jim, at the Embassy Ballroom.   It was a very popular dance hall for the men and women from the services.   At the time I was in the Australian Womens Army Service (AWAS).   When I was told Jim's name, Quackenbush, I thought it was a joke.   Who could have a name like Quackenbush?

"Jim was a radio operator stationed in Kings Park, Perth.   He was on the *Phoenix* at Pearl Harbor and had been sent to Western Australia for recuperation.   We were married August 12th 1944 and Jim was sent to the Philippines shortly afterward."

Some adjustments had to be made on board the *O'Brien* before the war brides embarked.   The logical place to put them was in the Armed Guard quarters aft.   But first the two remaining gunners had to be relocated.

Ted Martin: "We moved into quarters in the midship house, starboard side, main deck, next to the officer's mess."

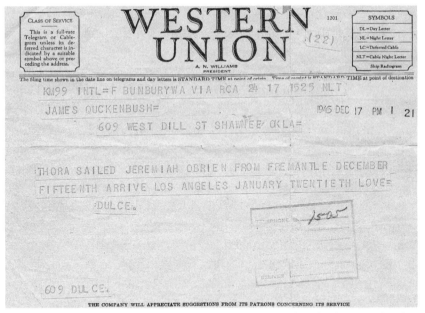

CLASS OF SERVICE		WESTERN	1201	SYMBOLS	
This is a full-rate Telegram or Cable-gram unless its de-ferred character is in-dicated by a suitable symbol above or pre-ceding the address.		UNION	(22)	DL = Day Letter NL = Night Letter LC = Deferred Cable NLT = Cable Night Letter Ship Radiogram	
		A. N. WILLIAMS PRESIDENT			

The filing time shown in the date line on telegrams and day letters is STANDARD TIME at point of origin. Time of receipt is STANDARD TIME at point of destination

KM99 INTL=F BUNBURYWA VIA RCA 24 17 1525 NLT

JAMES QUCKENBUSH=   1945 DEC 17 PM 1 21

609 WEST DILL ST SHAWNEE OKLA=

THORA SAILED JEREMIAH OBRIEN FROM FREMANTLE DECEMBER
FIFTEENTH ARRIVE LOS ANGELES JANUARY TWENTIETH LOVE=

DULCE.

609 DULCE.

THE COMPANY WILL APPRECIATE SUGGESTIONS FROM ITS PATRONS CONCERNING ITS SERVICE

This telegram was sent to Thora Quackenbush's husband after the O'Brien
sailed from Freemantle. Credit Thora Quackenbush

Nine Australian war brides, now Navy wives, and three children
came aboard.[2] They were lodged in the old gun crew quarters aft
and were but a small portion of the 15,000 Australian women who
became American war brides.

As sailing time approached on Saturday, December 15, the
women and their families said their goodbyes. It was a sad time
for many of them never expected to see Australia again. The
brides' families -- mothers and fathers, brothers, sisters, aunts,
uncles -- trudged down the gangway and stood on the dock waving.
The women stood at the ship's rail waving, shouting last messages.

Hector Miller: "The general feeling amongst the relatives
seeing the ship off was one of sadness, they assumed they were
saying good-bye forever."

Thora Quackenbush: "The first time I saw the *SS Jeremiah
O'Brien* at Freemantle Harbor was the day my family drove me
up from Bunbury, which is 115 miles south of Perth, on the coast.

---

[2] See Appendix C for a complete listing of the names of the brides and their
children.

I was surprised at the size of the ship, we expected a much larger ship, as we had seen newspaper pictures of war brides leaving from Sydney on larger passenger ships and our quarters on board was my second shock."

Hector Miller: "They were cramped and lacking in privacy."

Thora Quackenbush: "When we sailed from Freemantle there were lots of tears and sadness, leaving our family."

They had plenty of time for Captain Gerdes waited two hours but there was no sign of a pilot or tug to get the ship away from the wharf. Hector Miller watched from the dock. "It was a Saturday afternoon and weekends are sacrosanct in Australia, or at least they were at that time." Losing his patience, the captain unwisely decided to take the ship out himself. After raising the gangway, he ordered the bow lines taken in. The tide was running out and as he ordered the stern lines taken in the ship swung off the pier broadside to the current, moving sideways toward the harbor entrance. To gain steerageway he ordered full ahead on the engine so he could turn her bow toward the entrance."

Hector Miller describes what happened next. "The result was she suddenly bolted straight across the harbor towards the North Wharf on the opposite shore, like a runaway horse. Anchored there, bow to stern, were three Dutch naval ships, a frigate and two destroyers, and a collision looked inevitable. You could hear the telegraph ringing for reversing the engines across the harbor, but she had too much way on her, so taking his only alternative the skipper dropped the anchor. This action averted the collision. Then, using the anchor as a pivot, and his engines, he brought the bow around to the harbor mouth and eventually got under way."

The O'Brien was well out to sea before the captain finally let out a sigh of relief, thankful that the misadventure had not had serious consequences.

Thora Quackenbush: "It was a fine sunny day. I was standing on deck, looking out to sea when I saw Rottnest Island in the distance. Rottnest Island is only 12 miles from Freemantle, but that was as close as I got to seeing it as I became very sick immediately as we left the harbor heads and remained sick for a week while crossing the Great Australian Bight."

From left to right: Catherine Arthur, baby Maria Arthur, Grace Dexter and Thora Quackenbush. The other two brides are unknown. Credit Thora Quackenbush

Six war brides, one small infant and one crewmember enjoying the sun and sea breezes on the after deck of the O'Brien enroute to the United States. Credit Thora Quackenbush

Some of the crew posing with one of the war brides' infants. This photo was taken before arriving in San Francisco, January 1946. Credit Thora Quackenbush

Thora Quackenbush at one of the 3'-50 guns.   Her radiant smile leaves no need for words.   Credit Thora Quackenbush

The captain's next decision was what to do about all the women on board. He issued an order to the crew: "No Fraternization."

Charles Hord: "They did have the after part of the ship off limits. The captain had the bosun paint a stripe across the ship between #4 and #5 hatch. One side of the line said 'USA' and the other side 'Australia' in white letters. There were eight or nine women and some children, babies, almost."

Ted Martin: "There were nine women and three kids. They were all navy wives. Most of the guys, their husbands, worked in the fleet post office [in Freemantle]. There was no problem with them at all. Most of the time they ate in the gunner's mess with me and Swan. They kept them confined more or less from the merchant crew. It was my responsibility to keep them separate. The kids weren't a problem either. I remember seeing one of the women coming out and sitting on deck with the baby in her arms.

"They'd sunbathe while traveling. We weren't too much with them. They had the whole aft of the ship and they wouldn't come forward except to eat. We used to go out and talk to them on deck. The oldest was twenty-four or twenty-five. They were all

From left to right, Grace Dexter, Catherine Arthur, baby Maria Arthur and two unidentified crewmen.   Credit Thora Quackenbush

young like we were. Once in awhile we sneaked them up on one of the guns to take a picture."

Thora Quackenbush: "The voyage to San Francisco was most enjoyable. Calm seas, beautiful blue waters and flying fish, which fascinated me as I hadn't seen them before."

Captain Gerdes' "no fraternization" rule wasn't strictly enforced. Thora Quackenbush: "We played cards, walked the decks for exercise, chatted amongst ourselves outside our quarters and also enjoyed the ship's company who joined us to pass the time of day."

They came from all walks of life. Grace Dexter was a proof reader. Brenda Miller was educated in a convent until she was seventeen. Then she joined the Army Nursing Service where she met, nursed, and married her husband, E. Yocum. For her, the trip was a miserable one. She was ill when she boarded the ship, her cabin trunk was never put on board and never seen again and they saw no land until they reached the U.S.A. a month later. She just wanted to forget the whole episode.

Ted Martin: "One of them, I remember her name was Quackenbush, they used to kid her because she was going to a small town in Oklahoma. They'd tease her about all the hillbillies, tell her she'd better learn how to ride a horse and all that stuff."

Thora Quackenbush: "There was a Christmas celebration. I remember it well for it was the first meal in the dining room after my seasickness. The dining room had Christmas decorations, party hats and a wonderful spread of food including turkey and cranberry sauce. It was the first time I had tasted cranberry sauce.

"We did have a Crossing the Equator ceremony. It was all very fascinating because I hadn't known about it before."

For most of the women and the crew it was a long, pleasant voyage. Thora Quackenbush recalled, "I have some very warm, wonderful feelings about the captain and crew. They were so friendly and did all they could to make us feel comfortable."

Initially, the port of arrival was scheduled to be San Pedro, but two days before arrival that was changed to San Francisco. Arriving on January 16, the vessel anchored overnight.

The final entry in the captain's night order book reads: "Check anchor bearings frequently. Have passengers called at 6:30 a.m. and be ready to dock at 8:00 a.m. Call me if it gets foggy."

The ship went alongside Pier 40 the morning of January 17, 1946. Matson Navigation Company served as agents. The passengers disembarked and the *Jeremiah O'Brien* began discharging what would be her last cargo.

Thora Quackenbush: "In first seeing the U.S.A. I was so excited and greatly impressed going under the Golden Gate Bridge. It was in the evening. Many of the passengers and crew went out on the town for dinner and drinks the same night we berthed. "My husband arrived the day after we berthed. It was the first time I had seen him in civilian clothes. He had a Homberg hat on. I nearly didn't recognize him. We took a train to his home in Shawnee, Oklahoma. During the trip I saw snow for the first time."

The *O'Brien* lay idle for a few days then the last two members of the Armed Guard were taken off on January 28 and she was taken to Richmond Yard No. 2 to prepare for lay-up. There simply weren't enough peacetime cargoes for all the leftover wartime tonnage. And the Libertys, at a maximum speed of 11 knots, were far down on the "want list" when there were C-2's and C-3's that could carry the same or greater tonnages at speeds in excess of 15 knots.

Retired from service on February 7, 1946 the *Jeremiah O'Brien* entered the Reserve Fleet at Suisun Bay, California, a day later.

On February 8, 1946 the engineers rang Finished With Engines for the last time at 1153. The revolution counter showed 39,439,700 revolutions since the *Jeremiah O'Brien's* propeller was first turned over in Portland, Maine two and a half years earlier.

Most of the crew departed with a last look around, remembering shipmates, ports and adventures. The messroom, once alive with the babble of conversation, was now ghostly silent. The main deck, once vibrating with the metallic clank of steam-spewing cargo winches, was serene. The ship itself became quiet, deathly quiet, as a lone engineer shut down the plant for the last time.

From the engineer's log: "Shut down main engine at 1200 noon. Secured circulating pump and main injection valve at 1:30 p.m. Pumped up stbd setl from 6,900 gal to 13,000 gal. Secured aux. condenser, sea suction & discharge at 2.50 p.m. Shut off all fires in both boilers at 3.30 p.m. preparatory to cutting out plant. Put plant on atmospheric at 2.20 p.m. Drained main & aux condensers, hotwell and cleaned same at 3 p.m. Drained eccentric and guide pans. Pumped bilges and shaft alley well at 3.15 p.m. Shut down fuel oil service pump, sanitary pump, feed pump and all sea suction and discharge valves at 4.00 p.m. Working steam off both boilers with the generators & atmospheric valve. Opened all drains on deck machinery. Both boilers dead at 10:00 p.m. All valves connected with same shut off and all drains open on boilers. First two rows of handhole plates opened on both boilers. Water-drum manhole and mud-drum plates opened. Plant dead and work finished at 12 midnight.

(signed)

1st Asst D.E. Kranich"

Plant dead?
Work finished?
Not for the Lucky *O'Brien.*

14

INTERMISSION

W hat was believed to be the final page in the story of the *SS Jeremiah O'Brien's* active life started with a letter from the Maritime Commission's San Francisco Office to Washington, D.C., transferring title of the vessel.

March 22, 1946.

Mr. T. J. Kramer, Manager
Charters and Agreements Section
Operating Contracts Division
War Shipping Administration
Washington, 25, D.C.

Dear Mr. Kerner:

Subject: SS "JEREMIAH O'BRIEN"

The subject vessel has been placed in the Reserve Fleet at Anchorage 26, Suisun Bay (San Francisco Bay, California), and we attach hereto for your files and further disposition three copies each of certificates evidencing the redelivery by the General Agent to the War Shipping Administration and certificates evidencing the simultaneous delivery from our Operating Section to the Reserve Fleet Division of the War Shipping Administration.

Very truly yours,

(signed) L. M. Mauk, for
L. C. Fleming
Executive Assistant

The Reserve Fleet at Suisun Bay was one of eight such fleets in existence at the time. Located throughout the country, the eight fleets made up the National Defense Reserve Fleet, established so that in the next war the government wouldn't have to build shipyards from the ground up and train shipbuilders to make ships "faster than they could be sunk." They would have on hand a nucleus of ships that could provide the military a means of supply in any national emergency. So many ships were laid up after World War II that not only was there an adequate emergency fleet of Liberty ships, but there was a sizeable surplus. The government spent several years putting that surplus to good use. At first ships were sold to foreign countries including Greece, Taiwan and Panama to be used as the foundation of their post-war merchant marine. Others were sold into the U.S. fleet to companies such as Weyerhauser or Cal-Mar, and modified with longer mid-bodies for enlarged cargo capacity. Later, Libertys were taken from the fleets and used for various government projects: remade into weather ships, missile trackers, ocean radar station ships, Navy supply ships or sunk off American coasts to become fishing reefs.

The *Jeremiah O'Brien* was "in retention," tied up with several of her sisters, just one of many that were "made by the mile and cut off by the yard." Retention was the process by which ships were preserved so they would be ready for the next call-out. Inside, all the machinery, pumps, boilers, piping and equipment were opened. Cosmoline, a preservative grease that hardens into a thick protective film, was applied to boiler tubes, condensers, plumbing, valves, impellers, gears -- any surface that might rust. The underwater hull was protected against electrolysis by graphite anodes hung on each row of ships. The outside of the ship was painted, dark red at first, and later gray. Portholes were left ajar to allow air circulation and prevent mildew.

The years passed and still the *SS Jeremiah O'Brien* sat, awaiting another call to duty. Eventually the Libertys were no longer included in military plans for future wars. They were just too slow. Designed to last one voyage or, at the most, five years, the Liberty Ship had done her duty and outlived her purpose. Retention on the *O'Brien* was terminated in December of 1963 and the process of selling the Libertys out of the fleet for scrap began. One by one they disappeared.

The *Jeremiah O'Brien* languished, almost forgotten, her portholes and doors open to the wind, her superstructure providing a roost for pigeons and owls. In time her gray paint scaled off, rust corroded her decks and ran down her hull.

But the *O'Brien's* luck was not all gone. Someone remembered her, someone with an idea, a vision and "A Plan."

15

RE-BIRTH

Enter Admiral Thomas J. Patterson: "I came out here with Marad, the Maritime Administration, in 1962. I was one of two captains and two chief engineers given the job of surveying 300 Liberty Ships. They were laid up in fleets at Olympia, Washington; Astoria, Oregon; and Suisun Bay, California. Some 500 other Liberty ships were to be surveyed at the same time on the East and Gulf Coasts.

"Our task was to rank them in condition -- best to worst. The government was going to sell them. That meant most of them would go to the scrapyard. Our orders were to hold the best to the last. The reason for the exercise with these vessels was that in 1962 the Navy had informed the Maritime Administration that Libertys would not be required in their future strategy. At ten knots, they were too slow.

"The four of us 'walk-over surveyed' fifteen Liberty ships a day. We inspected the whole vessel, from the flying bridge to the engine room. We went down in every hold. Did the ship have wooden booms or steel booms? Had the ship been reinforced? What kind of ballast? Did she have any visible damage? What was the overall condition?

"I had the strongest legs I ever had in my life. Up and Down. Fifteen a day ..."

It's easy to look back from the crystal-clear perspective of the end of the century and say, "They decided to take one of the Libertys out of the fleet and make a museum out of it. So that's what happened." But before the *Jeremiah O'Brien* as a museum could happen, before there was a "they," there was one man: Admiral Tom Patterson. He had the vision and determination and, as he walked though all those Libertys, the beginning of an idea.

Admiral Patterson[1]: "One ship stood out among all the others, the *Jeremiah O'Brien*. The original doors, furniture and linoleum tables were still in place and unmarked. Where normally bored crewmen carved their initials in table tops, these were unscarred. The forward gun tub still carried traces of Miss Jerry O'Brien, a bikinied pin-up painted there by the last crew. The ship was completely unaltered except that, like all others, her guns had been removed. All World War II equipment aboard was undisturbed. All the charts were there, from Normandy to the Pacific. The glass was intact in the license frames on the bulkhead. The wartime instructions were posted alongside the Mark XIV gyro. The station bill, signed by the captain, was in place. The captain's night order book at Normandy beach was in a desk drawer. There were only minor indents in the *Jeremiah O'Brien's* plating and little hull pitting. The blueprints of the ship were mounted in the passageway abaft the wheelhouse, intact. The oak joiner work throughout her quarters was beautiful to behold. She had been kept completely original. She was just like she'd come out of the builder's yard. She'd never been used for anything other than what she was designed to do -- carry supplies to our forces -- and she'd been kept in one piece. The ship was a time capsule. I didn't know whether some way to save her could be

---

[1] Admiral Patterson was no stranger to Libertys. He sailed on them as a deck cadet during World War II and commanded them for the Navy after the war.

contrived, but something told me to try to hang on to her. We began a little exercise to keep her off the scrap list.

"The problem was that the *Jeremiah O'Brien* would have been scrapped in the first group because she was not reinforced. She did not have a 'crack arrester' -- that is a steel band riveted right around her hull at the sheer strake. A half dozen Libertys had broken up in heavy weather and finally it was decided to add a reinforcement of this sort as a precaution. The crack arrester cost about $50,000 to add to a ship during the war; it would cost more than a million dollars today.

"So the *O'Brien* was vulnerable. Some Libertys were sold for "non-transportation use" such as fish canneries, floating dry-docks, crane barges. A few were towed out and sunk for fishing reefs. But most were cut up. The price they brought the government averaged $50,000.

"We kept moving the *Jeremiah O'Brien* down the scrap list ... we kept shoving her back ... kept dropping her name down."

Harry Morgan, who became chief engineer for the project, recalled: "They kept moving that ship around because they were selling them off for scrap and she was in the best condition of them all. They kept putting her out of sight of the scrap dealers."

Admiral Patterson continues, "There was another reason. A ship on 'scrap row' was subject to being raided by the Navy. People came up from Treasure Island. The Navy still had eight Libertys on each coast, AGR's, four-hatch Libertys -- they were ocean radar picket ships. (I might point out here that I was skipper of the first of the four-hatch Liberty ships, the *USS Guardian*, AGR-1, ex-*James G. Squires.*) With some logic, a ship that was going to be broken up was picked over for equipment and furniture that would enhance the still operational AGR's. The Navy had this access. So we kept the *Jeremiah O'Brien* in another row. The game went on for years. We kept her from being raided. We also protected her from vandalism.

"Finally, like the dwindling of the ten little Indians, *Jeremiah O'Brien* was the last one. The Maritime Administration said, 'You've got to do something with that ship.' They said they had no authorization to hold her for historical purposes.

"From now on it was up to me."

It takes a unique combination of visionary, leader, arm-twister, supersalesman, money-raiser and motivator to conceive the idea of a living maritime museum, talk the government into giving up one of its ships, then convince business, industry and volunteers to contribute the time, labor and money to bring the dream to reality. Fortunately for the *Jeremiah O'Brien*, her champion was such a person.

Admiral Patterson: "I went out to industry -- the companies, the unions, the shipyards. I went to see Tom Crowley. 'What is so special about a Liberty?' he wanted to know. I tried to explain. I went to Bob Blake, Kings Point alumnus, now retired from the ship repair industry; to Admiral Jim Gracey and Captain Ernie Murdock of the Coast Guard; to Harry Morgan; to Dave Seymour. John Pottinger, who as Fleet Superintendent up at Suisun kept people off our favorite Liberty, had helped me all along in the chess game we played with the *O'Brien*. He protected that ship for years.

"The idea caught fire with people I talked to. Tom Crowley (Crowley Maritime Corporation) said, 'I guess you're right.' His help has been very important to us."

Soon there was a nucleus of enthusiasts, other people who wanted to save a Liberty ship for posterity.

Admiral Patterson: "In 1977 I went back to Washington and met Captain Harry Allendorfer of the National Trust for Historic Preservation. He told us how to get the ship on the National Register. And he told us how to apply for a grant."

With the enrollment of the ship in the National Register of Historic Places came a grant for $10,000 from the National Trust for Historic Preservation. But there was a string attached. Admiral Patterson: "We had to match it. Bob Blake did that with contributed work. We decided to overhaul the joiner work first and Bob hired a joiner just to do it."

On March 29, 1978 five volunteers logged 35 hours working on the ship, the first of more than 400,000 hours to follow in the years ahead.

This inside view of the wheelhouse is typical of the conditions the volunteers found themselves up against. Compare it to the appearance today. Credit NLSM

The National Liberty Ship Memorial (NLSM), a California non-profit corporation, was formed in 1978. The *O'Brien* was declared a National Monument and placed on the National Register as an historic object the same year.

Admiral Patterson: "So then Allendorfer advised us there would be a one-time grant for the fifty states. We asked for $550,000 for the *Jeremiah O'Brien* and explained what we were trying to do. That was in 1979. The catch was that we had to match it with funds, labor, services or material from the private sector. Barney Evans, who was then our secretary, was a big help in lining up these contributions. We made it!" The request was backed with a matching amount of more than $600,000 in services and materials from the volunteers and the maritime community.

Admiral Patterson: "Across the nation we came out #3. First was the *USS Constellation* in Baltimore. Second was the *Elissa* in Galveston. Third was the *Jeremiah O'Brien* in San

Francisco. We got $436,512." The grant actually came by way of the Department of the Interior through the California Office of Historic Preservation.

Admiral Patterson: "There were some key individuals in Marad who helped me in saving the ship and conceiving and establishing the NLSM. Samuel B. Nimerow, Assistant Secretary of Commerce for Maritime Affairs supported us. Captain Randolph Kriner, Deputy Chief of Ship Operations at Marad in Washington encouraged me. Michael McMorrow, General Counsel for Marad devised the agreement to transfer the ship from Marad to the National Park Service. Captain S. W. Galstan, Deputy Western Region Director of Marad, served as the key liaison with the maritime unions. Captain Carl Otterberg, Region Ship Operations Officer worked tirelessly on all phases of the ship's activation, restoration and operation. G.Ward Kemp, Western Region Counsel oversaw the legal issues and worked closely with other government agency counsels and the Marad General Counsel staff. Ms. Beatrice Kirschner, Region Director's Secretary, kept correspondence, messages and made all meeting arrangements. Herbert Holthoff, Marad Region Property Control Officer, saw that the ship received necessary surplus equipment from the fleet and from other government agencies. Herb personally filled out the voluminous application that resulted in the $436,512 grant.

"When we got word that we had the grant, it gave us more steam than ever before. Literally. We were up there looking the ship over, figuring how we would rig the towing bridle and Ernie Murdock says, 'Let's steam her down!'"

Bob Blake remembers the occasion, but in a different setting. "Tom Patterson had a meeting in his office at Marad. There were about ten or twelve people there from industry including Ray Ballard of Farrell Lines and Captain Ernie Murdock from the Coast Guard. At the meeting Tom said, 'We're going to tow it down and make a static display out of it.'

"So Ernie Murdock said, 'Let's sail it down.'

"Ballard said, 'I'll bet a buck you don't.'

"And I said, 'I'll bet we do.'"

Ernie Murdock: "I was the Captain of the Port when I first got involved. Tom Patterson asked me to be on the committee. At the committee meetings, as these things were winding down, we saw that we were actually going to get the ship out of the fleet and get it down here and bring it in to Fort Mason. We talked about towing it down here, but as we were leaving a meeting one day, I said, 'Why don't we go up and get the ship active or operational and run it down under its own power?' The reaction of some of them was, it couldn't be done, but there were enough there to say it could be done."

Admiral Patterson: "One of the reasons we decided to get steam up in Suisun Bay was that a diver had gone down and inspected her intakes. They had not been blanked off. She had not gone to a drydock (where this was usually done) before being towed up San Pablo Bay and through Carquinez Strait. Her last wartime crew had steamed her into the Suisun Bay Reserve Fleet for lay-up. Grace Line was her general agent for Marad back in those days and had maintained the ship properly during her wartime service.

"The other reason was the challenge. No one had ever steamed up a dead ship that had lain there thirty-four years in a reserve fleet!

"Now, the Maritime Administration had stopped all maintenance in 1963. The ship had been sixteen years with no preservation at all. But she was well preserved, just the same. There was some surface powder rust on the outside and her appearance wasn't too smart, but inside was a different matter. There was almost too much preservation. The pipelines had been flushed out with consul oil and this and other kinds of preservatives had congealed inside. One engineer I could mention had come up to Suisun Bay and after looking the situation over shook his head and told us we were nuts. He disappeared and never came back.

"But Harry Morgan came up and after also saying that we were crazy said that he would give it a go. Harry became our chief engineer."

Chief Engineer Harry Morgan: "I was approached by Bob Blake in June of 1979. He asked me to come up to the fleet with

Left to right, Harry Morgan and Ernie Murdock on the occasion of Murdock's promotion to captain in the Coast Guard. Credit Ernie Murdock

him to help restore this Liberty ship. Captain Ernie Murdock was up there also. The ship was coated with cosmoline, all the pumps were open and the cylinder heads were off, and they asked me what I thought. They said, 'We're going to steam it down.'

"I said, "All right, I think you're nuts, but let's give it a try."

Ernie Murdock and Harry Morgan go back a long way: "The first time I met Harry I was stationed in Manila and they had a big fire on the *President Madison* at the dock there. They had some cargo in number one hold that was self-oxidizing and just couldn't put it out. They had CO_2 down there by the truckload. It just kept burning and it was spreading into number two. Finally they put so much water aboard that she set down on the bottom before they finally got it out. Harry came over then to supervise the repairs. Then I met him again some years later, in '74 when I made captain in the Coast Guard. The *President Buchanan* was in Jacksonville shipyard and was being transferred to Waterman Steamship Company. Of course the American President Lines stack insignia [a spread eagle] and everything came off. I had a little party at my house celebrating making captain. And I got home that evening and here's this big eagle in my front yard with a fourteen foot wingspan out of quarter inch steel. Harry did that. One of the fellows took a picture of me in the front yard scratching my head about what to do with that eagle. And it was on the front page of the Navy Times the next issue."

Robert Blake: "We went up to the fleet a couple of days later and went aboard the ship to look it over to see what we had to do. There were five of us -- myself, a dispatcher from the Mechanics Union, Felix Childs from Farrell Lines, Harry Morgan from APL and someone whose name I forget. John Pottinger was in charge of the fleet up there and we drove up every morning and came back every night."

Harry Morgan: "We worked five to six days a week, six or seven hours a day. Of course we lost some time traveling back and forth."

Ernie Murdock: "Harry Morgan was very instrumental in getting the ship ready. We spent several weeks up there getting the boiler and the auxiliary equipment ready, the steering gear and so on."

Robert Blake: "People who are interested in ships are kind of crazy. It was a fun project. At lunchtime we'd all sit on deck and tell lies to each other, spin yarns. It was a labor of love.

"The thing I always liked about Libertys is you felt safer on them than on others. You could practically run them with your eyes closed. I think they're beautiful. I've always wanted to own one, to buy one. They were easy to run and easy to repair. They lasted for years and years."

Admiral Patterson: "We [the Maritime Administration] received a little Knot ship, a C1-M-AV1, from the Army operation up at Rio Vista. Her name was *Resolute*. We put her alongside and put aboard her some of the heavy air compressor equipment that Pottinger had for maintenance of the lay-up fleet. We got diesel oil and water off *Resolute* to light off the boilers."

Harry Morgan: "The fleet people were very cooperative. Anything we needed they'd go around to the other ships and get it. They located tools and brought us lube oil and even fuel oil. The crew up there was a great help."

It took three months in the fall of 1979 to reactivate the engine and auxiliaries.

Admiral Patterson: "Harry Morgan finally got the main engine and the windlass to turn over with air."

Robert Blake: "Pottinger put an air compressor on deck for us. We tested the systems with air pressure and everything worked fine."

Admiral Patterson: "The whole thing was a long process. There were 135 man-days put in up at Suisun Bay to get the *O'Brien* ready to steam. We could never have done it without monkey wrench engineers like Pottinger, Blake and Morgan."

Robert Blake: "There was cosmoline everywhere. Bill Harris of H and H Marine had to come up and steam-clean the ship of all the cosmoline."

Harry Morgan: "Cosmoline was our biggest problem. I'm firmly convinced that cosmoline is a great preservative, but it was everywhere, even inside the pipes and things. We steam cleaned the machinery and closed it up. To clear the cosmoline from the port boiler (the one we planned to use), we filled it to the vent cocks with water and lit a fire in the furnace. When the water became sufficiently hot, we opened all the stops and pumped the water through the main engine and auxiliaries and condensers. Hot water was also pumped through the various radiators, domestic water heaters, etc. We did this three times before we felt it was safe to begin raising steam.

"As soon as we had steam up to 150 lbs., we started blowing through the main engine and auxiliaries. When we were satisfied that we had removed as much cosmoline as possible, we closed the drains and began operating all the auxiliaries, then operating the main engine slow ahead and astern -- to avoid surging the bank of ships we were tied up to. After three hours of operating under steam, we secured for the night and advised Captain Galstan that we were ready to go when they were."

Admiral Patterson: "I might mention that the climate up there at Suisun Bay contributed to the *O'Brien's* fine state of preservation. There is a dependable prevailing westerly blowing most of the time and we had taken advantage of this over the years by leaving her portholes open and letting her ventilate inside. This kept the ship from getting musty and mildewed, particularly in her living spaces."

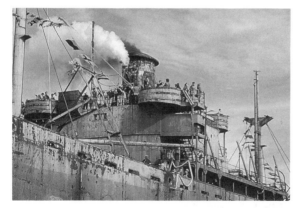

Loaded with passengers the O'Brien *steams in 1980 for the first time in 33 years. Credit George Lamuth*

Full power -- 76 revs -- from Suisun Bay to San Francisco. Credit George Lamuth

The SS Jeremiah O'Brien *proudly, eagerly steams across San Francisco Bay after 33 years of inactivity. Credit George Lamuth*

Robert Blake: "After everything was put together the only repair that had to be made was on a shuttle valve in the fuel oil service pump. We took it out and sanded it and put some oil on it and it worked fine. That was the only repair that was needed on the whole ship."

Harry Morgan: "It was an easy ship to restore. A Liberty is an easy ship to operate anyway and mechanically she was in good shape."

Admiral Patterson: "Well, meanwhile I had approached Gayne Marriner, General Manager at Bethlehem, San Francisco, and he said, 'Tom, bring her down'."

Robert Blake: "We stayed aboard all night and raised steam. Tom Crowley gave us two big launches and brought the people up. I felt exhilarated because I proved what we said we could do."

More than 500 people boarded the ship for her historic ride down the bay. Among them was Captain James Nolan, who would become the master of the *Jeremiah O'Brien* in later years. "I was a pilot and I heard they were going to restore or activate a Liberty ship. So I called down to Crowley's there and Tom Crowley says, 'Yeah, they're going to send about eight hundred people up to ride the ship down. Do you want to ride it down?' And I says, 'Yeah, sure.' So I went up there with Bill Figari, who was operations manager of Red Stack, and we rode the ship down and that was my start."

Not everyone who wanted to go, could. The number carried was limited to the number of life-jackets the ship had on board. Marci Hooper, who would later become Business Manager of the National Liberty Ship Memorial: "On October 3rd, 1979 I went to the opening session of the National Trust Conference in San Francisco. Among the speakers were Lynn Thompson and Karl Kortum, founder of the San Francisco Maritime Museum. They were talking about the Liberty ship they were going to bring out of the fleet that Saturday. And it piqued my interest because it was promoted as a very hands-on restoration thing. So after the conference session I went out to Lynn Thompson and said, 'How can I get on the ship this Saturday?'

"He said, 'Impossible.'

"So I wasn't able to join the ship until later."

On October 6, 1979 the *SS Jeremiah O'Brien* steamed out of the Reserve Fleet at Suisun Bay under her own power. For the first time since February 7, 1946 her engines were alive with fire and steam. Her machinery whirred and hummed. The entire hull once more vibrated and throbbed with life. Signal flags festooned the ship from stem to foremast to mainmast to bridge to aftermast to stern where the American flag proudly flew. Her decks were once again alive with people. Captain Samuel W. Galstan, Western Region Director of the Maritime Administration served as master.

Harry Morgan: "She performed very well. We fired up one boiler and steamed her down."

Ernie Murdock: "When it came the day that we could sail it out of the fleet, it sailed on its own power. I was on board then. A lot of us had gone up to raise steam and get everything operational. A couple of the Red and White tour boats came up with a load of people to ride the ship down. We had several hundred people on board on the way down."

"As we were coming down through Carquinez Straits, most of the engineers were busy in the engine room because things were always happening down there. You had to take care of so many things after the ship had been laid up there for more than thirty years. It kept all of us busy down below."

Robert Blake: "I was in the engine room practically all the way. Gene Gartland was down there with me as second assistant, he was the Port Director of San Francisco. But coming down we couldn't get over 70 rpm with the engines. We had the pressure wide open and that's all they would turn. I went up on deck and saw that we had two tugs alongside. I could see by the way the lines were leading we were towing them instead of the other way around.

"I told Captain Galstan, of the Maritime Administration, to let go the tugs because we were pulling them. He said, no the tugs were pulling us. I got as mad as the dickens and told him if he didn't let go the tugs I was quitting right away."

Just after haulout the crew inspects the underwater hull. Her condition was remarkably good after so many years of idleness. Credit National Park Service

Ernie Murdock: "He went up to the bridge and he was jumping up and down, shouting, 'Why is this tugboat alongside? We did all this work to get this ship down by itself, so let her travel by herself.'"

Robert Blake: "Crowley asked what was wrong and I told him. He radioed the tugs and had them throw their lines off. Well then we were able to turn full speed [76 rpms]."

Ernie Murdock: "We proceeded on down without any tugboat assistance. We were met by the San Francisco fireboats and tugboats. It was a pretty good sight to see this rusty old ship sailing under her own power down the bay into the shipyard."

Admiral Patterson was thrilled. "To take a ship that's been idle for 33 years, eight months and revive it with volunteers and load 503 people on it and steam 40 miles was in keeping with the spirit of the Liberty Ship. She was built in six weeks and here she'd lasted for all these years."

At the shipyard, the lengthy process of reconditioning began. Harry Morgan: "The boiler tubes were good. In the yard we put a hydrotest on both boilers. We had to do some minor repairs on the brickwork, but nothing major."

Admiral Patterson: "I can't say enough for the role that Gayne played in the whole thing. He and his company, Bethlehem, were the only yard that would take her. They extended credit, too!"

With the publicity attending the resurrection of the ship and her sailing into the shipyard, more volunteers began showing up. Harry Morgan: "The committee paid me a consulting fee until we went to the shipyard. I subtracted my travel expenses, donated the rest back to the project and continued the work as a volunteer. Quite a bit of the work done in the yard was by the volunteers."

Admiral Patterson: "While the ship was in Bethlehem Shipyard I appointed Captain Edward A. MacMichael as her first master. He was a 1936 graduate of the Pennsylvania school ship (the same class as Joe Rizza of the California Maritime Academy), had sailed master for United States Lines in World War II and served in the Navy on an APR. He had worked for Marad, retired after a heart attack, then came back to sea when Vietnam broke out. At that time I asked him to activate and command the *Lane Victory*. He and Harry Morgan were responsible for the excellent activation and refurbishing that occurred on the *Jeremiah O'Brien*.

Marci Hooper: "I always was a ship freak. Living in San Francisco I grew up surrounded on three sides by water. I have a picture of myself and my siblings taken on the *Balclutha* when I was eight years old. There's another picture of me when I was hanging on to something on a fishing boat coming back from Angel Island on a company picnic. My great grandmother was born on the high seas between Australia and the Sandwich Islands. So maybe it's in my blood, but I've always loved ships.

"There was an article in the San Francisco Progress saying the ship was going to come to Fort Mason and they needed volunteers. So I called the number they gave and got Captain Eddy MacMichael who gave me the telephone quiz and told me to get on my grubbies and bring some lunch and come on down to the shipyard and tell them at the gate that I was there for the

O'Brien. So I went to work on her the last week of February, 1980 and the rest is history."

Other volunteers, men and women, began to arrive -- people who had sailed Liberty ships, those who helped build them, and people who simply liked to work around ships and steam engines -- anyone interested in ships and engines and the lure of the sea. Per Dam, the *Jeremiah O'Brien's* bosun, was one of the earliest to donate his time. He found out about the *O'Brien* and went up to see Harry Dring at his house in South San Francisco. He so impressed Harry, a difficult thing to do, with his eagerness for the work and his high level of expertise and experience, that Harry took him on.

Per Dam: "First of all, I've been on seven Liberty ships myself. I was working on ships since I was 14 years old. I started out from Denmark and sailed under seven flags all together -- Danish, Norwegian, Swedish, American, Somalian, Chilean and Panamanian. I was interested and talked to the captain."

Harry Morgan: "Per Dam probably did more work than any other bosun I have known. He was paid for five days a week but he worked seven."

Joanie Morgan, Purser: "Any shipowner, then or now, would be very hard-put to find a more able, experienced, conscientious, loyal, honest and hard-working boatswain. Per was not a volunteer, but his consulting fee fell far short of any true remuneration for the work he performed (and caused to be performed)."

Marci Hooper: "Per sailed Libertys during the war. I once asked him if he remembered where all the switches and stuff were, and he said, 'Well, Captain MacMichael asked me one day to turn on the mast lights, and I said I would do it right away. When I started forward I didn't remember exactly where the box was. I got up to the spot, opened the box and hit the right switch. It comes back to you.'

"In those days you showed up and you told Per Dam you were there. You got your grubbies on and he handed you work. I did a lot of interior scrubbing and painting. I scrubbed out a number of rooms, one I remember distinctly is what we now have

The First Seamen's Memorial Cruise in 1979 and the SS Jeremiah O'Brien *looks as good as the day she was launched, 36 years earlier. Credit George Lamuth*

as the ship's office. It's the mate's room on the starboard side boat deck. And I red-leaded the chartroom ceiling.

"Harry Dring was a moving force. Harry was the head of historic ships at the San Francisco Maritime Museum. He had started in the mid-fifties restoring the *Balclutha*. So, in terms of someone who knew the territory, he was it. Harry Dring was like one of the godfathers. He would show up in the shipyard. And he always had a travel bag, a shoulder bag with room for all sorts of junk. He always had a few tools in there for something he might want to be doing and usually a lump of date nut bread already sliced up or a loaf of banana bread. If someone was new and hadn't remembered to bring their lunch, they could starve because there was no place down there to get a sandwich on a weekend. You could come down and starve the first day unless Harry showed up, with a bag with date nut bread in it. Harry was one of the major contributors. He was always there. Whatever we needed, if he didn't know where to get it he would put his head together with the other guys and they would find it. In the beginning, when things used to frustrate us, we'd go over to Hyde Street Pier to see Harry and go, 'Arrrgh' and he'd say, 'O.K. sit here. Wait a minute. Let me go fix some coffee.'

"We'd be sitting in his office and before we'd be able to weep and gnash our teeth, someone else would come in the door and we'd have to sit there and talk to them and then five o'clock would come and we'd have to leave. Walking to the parking lot, he'd say, 'I don't know what you kids are worried about. This will solve itself.'"

The goal for getting the ship out of the yard was Maritime Day, May 21, 1980. Plans were made for a Seamen's Memorial Cruise on that day to honor the merchant seamen lost at sea since the beginning of World War II. As the May deadline approached, the numbers of volunteers increased.

Marci Hooper: "There were very few women involved. There was one other girl I would say was in her early thirties, named Lillith, no last name, just Lillith. As we got closer to May, the crunch was on and instead of working just Saturday, we'd work both Saturday and Sunday. Then a few of the wives started coming down to help out. Janet Doyle was there during the week. She welded on Libertys during World War II in Richmond. She started in the shipyard restoring the painting of the ladies on the guntub."

Harry Morgan: "Even at the shipyard, the workers took a personal interest in the *Jeremiah*. I've been in a lot of shipyards and normally you have to watch them every minute. That wasn't the case at Bethlehem."

Union support was there from the outset. By the end of April, 1980 their members had logged the following hours:

National Maritime Union	630
Boilermakers, Local No. 6	180
Sailors Union of the Pacific	145
Seafarers International Union	100
Marine Engineers Beneficial Association	90

Admiral Patterson: "The Liberty ship *Jeremiah O'Brien* blossomed once again in that Bethlehem yard -- she came out of it looking like she did when she was launched. Or very close to it. We worked against a deadline of Maritime Day, 1980, and we made it."

The *SS Jeremiah O'Brien* left the yard on that day and sailed into her place in history -- the first surviving merchant marine ship of World War II to become a living museum. She was and is a tangible testimony to American shipbuilders' ability to quickly produce a quality product. Her very existence is proof positive that we <u>can</u> plan for the future and surpass our own expectations.

The *O'Brien's* future voyages would be short but full of history and memories. She was about to become a ship for all time.

16

THE SECOND TIME AROUND

B ut, first, there was one detail to be taken care of. Janet Doyle had faithfully reproduced the wartime drawings of Miss Jerry O'Brien on the forward guntub in all her bare-breasted splendor.

Marci Hooper: "Somebody said, 'We can't take the ship out with half-naked women on the guntub.' So, Doug Dickie's niece was an artist and she painted bras on. It was just for the voyage in case the T.V. cameras got a closeup of the bow. But soon afterwards that got straightened out. John Pottinger had gone up there with tracing paper and traced what they could of the original drawings before Janet put them on. After the trip she took the bras off. She did a great job, I don't think she's ever retouched them."

May 21, 1980. The *Jeremiah O'Brien* departed the shipyard at 0830 for the First Annual Seamen's Memorial Cruise. With 700 passengers she sailed out the Golden Gate, then cut the engines. In a solemn and deeply-felt ceremony wreaths were thrown into the water to commemorate the shipmates lost in so many

The figure of Miss Jerry O'Brien was given a brassiere for the first cruise but later restored to her natural appearance. Compare to the 1944 photo of the original in Chapter 10. Credit George Lamuth

wars on so many oceans. In silence the passengers watched the wreaths bob on the swells and, carried on the tide, gradually drift out to the open sea.

Admiral Tom Patterson: "That day was declared National Liberty Ship Day by the White House. We got the ship underway and proceeded out the Gate for the ceremonies; Captain E. A. MacMichael was master. The Assistant Secretary of Commerce for Maritime Affairs, Samuel Nemirow, was on board to dedicate the ship in her new role, the National Liberty Ship Memorial -- a reminder of the largest fleet of oceangoing ships of a single type that this or any country has ever launched. Those 2751 Libertys were the cargo-carrying key to winning World War II and bringing peace and liberty to the world."

Harry Morgan, chief engineer, in a typical understatement: "The next May we went on the first cruise. We put both boilers on the line and everything went all right."

It was a very special event and everyone wanted souvenirs of the occasion. The volunteers had been so busy getting the ship ready there wasn't time to stock the ship's store.

Marci Hooper: "When we left the pier and went out for the day, the Women's Propeller Club came and sold patches. That was all they had at that time. The patches were made by 'Coke' Schneider who was cadet on the ship during the war."

That afternoon, after completing her second "maiden voyage," the *O'Brien* arrived at her new home berth, Pier 3 East, Fort Mason, in the Golden Gate National Recreation Area. A luncheon was held in the pier shed. All her workers, volunteers and passengers were jubilant at their success.

The power of determination and the effectiveness of volunteerism were contagious and more volunteers began to appear. There was still plenty to be done. Phil Sinnott: "I'd been sailing boats and one thing and another since I was twelve years old. And after the war, I was very much around the water, I love ships. In fact, I once thought that I'd stay at sea, but I knew that I'd get married some day, and it's a hard life for somebody with children. So this seemed like of one of the best ways to split the difference.

"I was sailing my own boat right there under the stern of the *Jeremiah O'Brien* at the end of May in 1980. And I said, 'Gee, I've got to get on board.'

"This was about a week after that first cruise. I came down to the pier and there was a 'Government Property, Keep Off' sign on the fence there. I climbed over it and came aboard and there was nobody around. I came back later and found the bosun, Per Dam, who was also the shipkeeper. I asked him if there was anything I could do. He said, 'Well, I don't know.'

"Finally he asked me if I could paint and I said yes I could paint, and he said well, O.K. He gave me a brush and a can of black paint and he had me paint all the bitts on the main deck. So as I was painting he would come back every five minutes and check on me. What I was tempted to do, was paint a skull and crossbones or a heart on it or something to screw him up. But I didn't and that's how I got started."

Joanie Morgan (neé Redington): "The first time I saw the *Jeremiah O'Brien,* I was having lunch at the Mission Rock Resort, across the way from the Bethlehem yard. That must have been mid-October of 1979. The sight really took me back. As a little kid in New York I had learned to identify Libertys. The stack covers made it easy -- I would see a ship with a black hat on the stack and ask my father, 'Is that a Liberty?' So when I saw the *Jeremiah* at Bethlehem, thirty-four years later, I said, 'My God, that's a Liberty!'

"Then a piece came out in *Motorland* about the attractions at Fort Mason. That's how I found out where the *Jeremiah* was and went to visit her. Then I found out she was a Grace Line ship. My father had been medical director for Grace Line and Panagra so Grace was an additional attraction. They wanted volunteers and I decided to volunteer. That was in February of 1981.

"We started by doing the most unattractive jobs. We began by scraping the paint under the sink in the pantry, something that no one else wanted to do. And one of my friends swabbed the deck in two of the mess rooms."

"Years ago, I worked for the old man on board Grace ships and did some of the purser's jobs, things they didn't want to do like typing voyage letters on stencils. As soon as Captain MacMichael discovered I could write and type he became very interested in having me help him. He asked me if I would like to be secretary and then appointed me purser. Later I was selected to be secretary of the board."

The volunteer crew grew slowly at first. Phil Sinnott: "At first there just wasn't a deck gang. About the time I got there, old Charlie Something showed up. He was absolutely deaf as a post. He worked on board for a little while. Then I tried getting Ralph Stevens to come in. He lives over my way, so we rode together. So we became the deck department. Little by little we got bigger. For a long time it was just the old man, the bosun and us."

In the early days the ship often lay unattended in her berth. There just weren't enough people to "stand watch." Phil Sinnott: "About the second or third time I came over it was on a Monday. I came down to turn to and there was nobody on board. I figured that the bosun was gone ashore to get something. I had my lunch and my coffee and I said, 'Well, I'll hang around awhile.'

"So, after awhile, I look up on the boat deck and I saw the exterior door was open, so I went inside. It was kind of dark but

I went all over the ship, even down in the engine room. For me it was a good opportunity to spend some time just looking at it. I finally came up and nobody was around so I left.

"I came back the following week, and Jesus, this bosun, Per Dam, he gave me the strangest look. He asked if I had been on board. I said, 'Yeah, I was on board.' He said, 'Somebody was here and he was lighting pieces of newspaper inside the exterior door.' I hadn't done anything wrong, but somehow I knew I was in trouble. You get that feeling. About ten-thirty that morning, the captain comes up. I'm still painting bitts black. He says, 'I understand you were on board.' He's giving me the grilling, so I'm thinking I'm in big trouble. Well, it was about two weeks later I came on and Per says, 'Oh, I got the guy.'

"It turned out this guy climbed in a scuttle someplace back aft and went down, pitch black, no lights on. He was lighting things to see with. There was a cigarette lighter and fluid. The guy was lighting rags and pieces of paper down in the engineroom. Then he came up topside and spent the night in there. So the bosun caught him in the morning. And the guy said he was from the FBI or the police. Well, as it turned out, he wasn't, he was just a derelict. But the captain was furious because he kept a bottle of scotch in his desk drawer for dignitaries and apparently the fellow had drunk all the remainder of his whiskey and then urinated in the bottle. The old man was more angry about the bottle than he was the fact that the guy got on board."

As more volunteers came aboard, there were fewer such incidents. By the following year the ship was well cared for with either someone on board all the time or the entrance to the pier locked.

Gene Anderson: "The first ship I sailed was out of San Francisco and it was a Liberty. That was just after the war.

"Then in 1981 a fellow came in the office at work and said he saw a Liberty ship over the weekend. I said, 'Where is it?' So he told me and the next week I was down and talked to Harry Morgan. I started right away and made all the annual cruises except that first one."

The second cruise attracted the interest and admiration of a grateful nation. On Maritime Day, Thursday, May 21, 1981, President Ronald Reagan issued the following proclamation:

The maritime industry has been a key contributor to our economic strength and security since our Nation was founded. Its continued growth and prosperity is necessary for the economic renewal we all seek.

As leader in world trade and the principal military power of the free world, the United States conveys goodwill through its Merchant Marine, serving the cause of international peace. The Merchant Marine also stands ready to provide logistical support in military emergencies.

In recognition of the importance of the American Merchant Marine and the men and women serving aboard our merchant ships, Americans have observed National Maritime Day on May 22 for the last 49 years.[1] This observance commemorates the same date in 1819, when the *SS Savannah* began the first steamship, transatlantic voyage from the port of Savannah, Georgia.

NOW, THEREFORE, I, RONALD REAGAN, President of the United States of America, do hereby urge the people of the United States to honor our American Merchant Marine on May 22, 1981, by displaying the flag of the United States at their homes and other suitable places, and I request that all ships under the American flag dress ship on that day.

IN WITNESS WHEREOF, I have hereunto set my hand this twenty-second day of April in the year of our Lord nineteen hundred and eighty-one, and of the Independence of the United States of America the two hundred and fifth.

This was accompanied by a Proclamation from [U.S. Senator] Dianne Feinstein, then Mayor of San Francisco:

---

[1] The actual date is May 21.

WHEREAS, The S.S. Jeremiah O'Brien, one of the 2,751 Liberty Ships built and sailed during the Second World War and the last unaltered Liberty Ship in existence, had the signal honor of making 11 round trips between United Kingdom shores and the Normandy Beachhead on D-Day; and

WHEREAS, The S.S. Jeremiah O'Brien was anchored in Suisun Bay from 1946 to October 1979 when one boiler was fired up by volunteers, and she steamed down to Bethlehem Shipyard and was refurbished; and

WHEREAS, On May 21, 1980, the S.S. Jeremiah O'Brien was dedicated by the President of the United States and the First Annual Seaman's Memorial Services was held on Board; and

WHEREAS, The ship is now tied up at Fort Mason and available for viewing by generations of Americans unfamiliar with Liberty Ships; now

THEREFORE, BE IT RESOLVED THAT I, DIANNE FEIN-STEIN, Mayor of the City and County of San Francisco, do hereby proclaim May 21, 1981, the date of the Second Annual Seaman's Memorial Service, as NATIONAL LIBERTY SHIP DAY in San Francisco, honoring the 2,751 Liberty Ships built and sailed during the Second World War and commend the observance of this most worthy occasion to all San Franciscans.

On board were a full complement of dignitaries: Admiral Thomas J. Patterson was the master of ceremonies on the second cruise; William Whalen, General Superintendent of the Golden Gate National Recreation Area was on board representing the National Park Service; Captain Harry C. Allendorfer, Jr., who was so instrumental in pointing the NLSM in the proper direction for funding, represented the National Trust for Historic Preservation; The California Maritime Academy was represented by RADM Joseph P. Rizza, its President; RADM David G. Ramsey, Commander, Amphibious Group Eastern Pacific, was also aboard as was Thomas B. Crowley, National Chairman of the National Liberty Ship Memorial.

Admiral Thomas J. Patterson, the man who made it all happen, at the podium during one of the many Seamen's Memorial Cruises.   Credit Don Watson

Again the ship went outside the Golden Gate, stopped inside Mile Rock and held a ceremony commemorating departed seamen. Twenty-eight wreaths from maritime and military organizations were thrown into the sea in their honor. The cruise was sponsored by the Propeller Club of the United States, Port of the Golden Gate. A buffet luncheon was provided and the ship's store did a brisk business.

Marci Hooper: "The next May the Women's Propeller Club came in, so we had t-shirts, key rings, bumperstickers and patches. And some Lyle Galloway Christmas cards. The Women's Propeller Club arranged that with the Old Man. I was still in the painting, chipping and scraping business."

One of the biggest problems in the fledgling organization was keeping track of everything. What started as a fun project for a few friends and acquaintances was quickly becoming a business with hundreds, and eventually thousands, of people involved.

Joanie Morgan: "When I started in April of '81 there were very few names on the mailing list. There was no accounting system. The accounts were kept in a ruled notebook. What was needed was systems: filing, communications, historical reference, accounting and volunteer record-keeping. One of the first things I did was set up a cruise sheet. I was very concerned with the cruises and correspondence and the details, parking, transportation, and so on. Captain Wilson set a limit of 850 souls on board. I set up a chart of accounts and arranged the book-keeping accordingly, quarter to quarter, year to year.

"Practically every week I would add names to the mailing list. I used to keep spreadsheets for the cruise passes. Why, how, who, comps, et cetera."

On September 27, 1981 Liberty Fleet Day was celebrated on board the *Jeremiah O'Brien*. It was the 40th anniversary of the launching of the first Liberty ship, the *SS Patrick Henry*.

Visitors began coming to see the ship. Many were ex-merchant marine, men who had sailed Libertys during the war to North Africa, Murmansk, Normandy, the South Pacific and the far corners of the world. They would pause in a doorway, looking into a room. "I spent six months in a room just like this," the veteran would tell his wife or grandchild. "Slept in that bunk right there." Or they would step gingerly across the floorplates of the engineroom, looking everywhere, recalling incidents and events of long ago.

Gene Anderson: "When I started, I worked on the warping winch aft, took it apart, cleaned it and got it operating. So I got my two boys interested and we tore all ten winches down and reset valves and pistons and rebuilt them all. They learned a little about steam and broadened their knowledge about the world. We worked together and it was a good experience for us."

Marci Hooper: "I came on board a few months later and we were starting to do 'Steaming Weekends' -- getting steam up to show the world we're here. Eddy MacMichael sent for me and I went up there and he gave me a key. He said, 'The stuff's in the room next to the saloon, start selling it.' So that was the beginning of my career as a Storekeeper. I did that for a long

Wreaths line the deck on the morning of the Seamen's Memorial Cruise. They will be cast into the Pacific in honor of America's merchant seamen who gave their lives answering the call of duty. Credit Don Watson

time until the opportunity presented itself to be the business manager."

Saturday, May 15, 1982 was the Third Annual Seamen's Memorial Service, the first of the cruises to be held on a weekend, a tradition that continues. The 35-member volunteer crew took 970 passengers from as far off as Rhode Island. The *O'Brien* was assisted by the tugs *Catano* at the bow and *Sea Hawk* at the stern, their services donated by Red Stack, a Thomas B. Crowley company, while the fireboat *Phoenix* provided the water serenade. The *SS Jeremiah O'Brien's* builder's plate was presented to the ship by Captain S. W. Galstan, Western Region Director of the Maritime Administration.

Master of Ceremonies on this trip was Gayne Y. Marriner, General Manager of Bethlehem Steel Corporation of San Francisco, who had done so much to help the *Jeremiah O'Brien* in its drydocking. The Reverend John P. Heaney, Director of the

Apostleship of the Sea provided the invocation. Dignitaries on board were John H. Davis, General Superintendent of the National Park Service, Captain Galstan, John Henning, Secretary of the California State Federation of Labor, RADM Joseph P. Rizza, and VADM James P. Stewart, Commander, Pacific Area of the U.S. Coast Guard Twelfth District.

Thirty-two wreaths were thrown over in memory of deceased seamen.

During that year 30,000 volunteer hours were contributed by 334 volunteers ranging in age from 18 to 78.

Harry Morgan: "It was a fun job and we had excellent volunteers. Most of them had no previous experience. They'd do anything you'd ask them to. We'd just take everything apart and put it together again."

In June 1982 the first Women Shipbuilders Reunion Reception was held on board. "Rosie the Riveter" and "Wendy the Welder" were common nicknames in the group. Among them were the staunch women who made up a significant percentage of the workforce that built Libertys and other ships during the war. Long before the battle for "equal rights" became a *cause célèbre* they had proved their worth and won that battle.

During this year Captain MacMichael stepped down for health reasons. Captain Ralph "Buck" Wilson replaced him as master of the vessel. Joanie Morgan: "Captain Wilson was fantastic. He was an experienced Liberty ship master and he had sailed in convoys during the war. He also had a spirit which I think you simply have to say was inspiring, and he was experienced in public relations. One of the first things he said about working on the *Jeremiah O'Brien* was, 'They are volunteers. You don't have a crew, you have volunteers. You can't order them around.'"

The Fourth Annual Seamen's Memorial Service was held on Saturday, May 14, 1983. Mayor Feinstein issued another proclamation (the same as the one for the second cruise with slight modifications and the date changed). Master of Ceremonies was Captain Galstan. The invocation was given by Reverend John P. Heaney. Representing the National Liberty Ship Memorial was Lynn H. Thompson, Executive Director. John H. Davis, General

Superintendent of the Golden Gate National Recreation Area represented the National Park Service. W. B. Hubbard was aboard. A Senior Vice President of American President Lines, he spoke on behalf of the American steamship operators. RADM Joseph P. Rizza once again represented California Maritime Academy as did VADM Charles E. Larkin the United States Coast Guard. For the first time, the *Jeremiah O'Brien* made two cruises, one on Saturday and one on Sunday, a practice which continues.

The ship was now open to the public almost every day of the year with the engines operating on "steaming weekend," the third weekend of each month. With greater access came more interest and with more interest came a need for information about the ship. Joanie Morgan: "I championed the idea of getting a tape tour. I wrote all the material used on the ship: brochures, handouts, information sheets. I also wrote hundreds of letters, public service announcements, press releases and press kits and distributed them."

June 19, 1983 was the 40th anniversary of the *O'Brien's* launching. The event was marked with a gala reception and dinner on board. The Second Women Shipbuilders Reunion Reception was held on board the next day.

Bob Burnett, one of the early volunteers, is now Shipkeeper on the *Jeremiah O'Brien*: "I was living in Portland, Oregon in the middle-late sixties when some of the Libertys were being scrapped. My knowledge about them was fairly dim but I did know something of them. As a child, I remember one night over in Sausalito, driving by the shipyards and seeing the illuminated scaffolding. So, one Monday morning a guy came into my office at work, and he said, 'Oh, I had a neat weekend. I did something I really enjoyed doing.'

"I asked what was that, and he said, 'Oh, wow! I went on this World War II Liberty ship.'

"'Oh, yeah?' I said, 'I want to do that.' It was several months before I came up and visited. I spent four and a half hours on board the first time. It was just so fascinating. And the engine was operating. I spoke with the chief engineer, Harry Morgan, for about an hour, and the bosun, Per Dam. Then I came

The completely restored engine room of the SS Jeremiah O'Brien, *taken from the fire room looking aft. Credit Russell Fraser*

up for a Fleet Week and I drove into Fort Mason and parked inside the warehouse on Pier 3. In going back to my car, the door to the warehouse was rolled up and I saw the gangway down and there was a table out there. Joanie Morgan, or Joanie Redington at the time, was manning the gangway and I chatted with her. The following Tuesday night I set my alarm and just decided that Wednesday I was going to come up and be here. I was bitten before I got here and I was bitten on that first day working ... I just wanted to get involved with ships. I never had a chance to play on ships before so this was an opportunity to play on a ship and learn a great deal about one type. I started in October of eighty-three."

The master's stateroom after restoration. Thousands of hours of volunteer labor went into making the ship look better than new. Credit NLSM

The Fifth Annual Seamen's Memorial Service was held on Saturday, May 19, 1984. Again, Mayor Dianne Feinstein proclaimed it National Liberty Ship Memorial Day in San Francisco. Once again Captain Galstan served as master of ceremonies. Representing the National Liberty Ship Memorial was Joanie Redington, Secretary and Acting Executive Director. John H. Davis again represented the National Park Service. American steamship operators were represented by Capt. R. J. Murray, General Manager of the Marine Operations Department of Matson Navigation Company, Inc. Paul Dempster of the San Francisco Maritime Trades Port Council was on board as was Capt. K. F. Bishop, Jr., Captain of the Port of San Francisco for the United States Coast Guard. Music of the thirties and forties was provided by the Unicorns.

In her remarks during the cruise, Joanie Redington enumerated the accomplishments of the volunteers since the ship's

Two of the ship's volunteers, Bill Williams and Adrian Ruddell, discuss future projects at the engineer's log desk. Credit NLSM

reactivation. "The engine room is completely restored and restoration of the midship house is very nearly complete. The domestic refrigeration system and cargo gear are operative. Defensive weapons (demilitarized) typical of the period are in place in the bow and stern gun tubs. A machine shop has been created in #5 'tween deck to facilitate ongoing restoration and preservation of the vessel. Toward the goal of a live, operating, historically-accurate museum-ship (which contains maritime display galleries but remains seaworthy), we have developed #2 'tween deck into a multi-purpose room for displays, classes, meetings, film screenings and receptions. The area will be available to the public on a rental donation basis, providing an all-weather facility for groups seeking a unique meeting space, and bringing in funds for the continuing preservation of the ship."

On September 18, the ship's engine became America's 72nd National Historic Mechanical Engineering Landmark under a program offered by the American Society of Mechanical Engineers. The engine was honored because "it represents a progressive step in the evolution of mechanical engineering, and reflects its influence on society." A brass plate with the designation was presented to the ship and is affixed to the bulkhead of the fidley, just inside the main entrance to the midship house.

During the previous year 220 volunteers had donated their efforts to refurbishing the ship. But it wasn't all just chipping paint, oiling engines and swabbing decks. Between chores, the volunteers gathered in the mess for coffee and doughnuts -- someone was always bringing a box of doughnuts or danishes -- and swapped sea stories or exchanged ideas on some pet project for the ship. Friendships blossomed. In some cases, friendship developed into something more significant.

Two months after the Engineering Landmark ceremony Harry Morgan and Joanie Redington were married. Joanie Morgan: "We were married in the wheelhouse on Thanksgiving Day, 1984. My Mom gave us a splendid reception breakfast in #2 'tween deck.' Attendance exceeded expectations, but Chief Steward Joe Tex and Chief Cook Dorothy Alexander managed beautifully. It was one great party."

Ernie Murdock: "There have been several marriages on board. A girl named Suzette came aboard as a volunteer. She had worked for Delta Line, I think, ashore. When they closed up shop she had some time on her hands so she volunteered. One of her first assignments was in one of the lifeboats, to clean that up. Then she became an oiler. We had a young man who was doing some engine work. They got introduced and several months later got married aboard the ship. The steward got married on here, one of our engineers got married on board and the chief engineer got married too."

Gene Anderson: "Myron Alexander was one of those that got married. That was spectacular! They held the ceremony on number 4 or 5 hatch. Ernie Murdock was the engineer on the fire boat *Phoenix*. The fire boat pulled close alongside the *O'Brien* and the moment they said, 'I do,' they fired off all the nozzles. What a show!"

The Sixth Annual Seamen's Memorial Cruise, on May 18, 1985 was another National Liberty Ship Memorial Day by proclamation of Mayor Feinstein. Captain Galstan was again master of ceremonies. The United States Department of the Interior was represented by W. Lowell White, Associate Regional Director for Management and Operation for the National Park Service. Maritime Labor was represented by Clarence E. Briggs, Executive Secretary-Treasurer of the Pacific Coast Metal Trades District Council. Capt. Warren G. Leback, Deputy Administrator to the Maritime Administration was on board representing the United States Department of Transportation. Music was provided by the Richard A. Martini Band. They played "big band" music reminiscent of the swing sound of Glenn Miller and Benny Goodman in the war years. Their arrangements were excellent and the passengers listened with great enjoyment. Impromptu dancing broke out on the main deck as, for a few hours, the swing era came back to life.

Len Sawyer, co-author of the book *The Liberty Ships*, was on board. He has thousands of pictures collected over years of photographing every ship he has ever seen. The book encompassed only a small part of his collection of ship pictures. His enthusiasm for the ship and Libertys in general brought him from his home in England to make the trip. With him was Vic Young, a ship photographer from New Zealand and, if such a thing is possible, even more enthusiastic than Mr. Sawyer. They roamed the ship with delight, taking pictures, talking to everyone, their enthusiasm infectious to all who spoke with them.

In the previous year 216 volunteers had donated their time to the ship. With so many offering their services, some of the positions became "filled."

Bob Burnett: "My interest originally was in the engineroom. When I spoke with Harry Morgan he said that there were thirteen chief engineers down below acting as wipers and there wasn't a real need for an inexperienced outsider. So I wound up on deck." No one minded. Working on a ship was the main objective, and they gladly did whatever they could.

The most common misconception on the part of the general public is that the *Jeremiah O'Brien* is a Navy ship. This may stem from the fact that the ship is painted grey and the public associates grey ships with the United States Navy. Joanie Morgan is passionate on the subject. "We had so many people walk aboard off the dock who thought the ship had something to do with the Navy. These are not war ships, they are merchant ships -- manned by civilian officers and crews. They were part of the mainstream of American commerce lending itself to the war effort. They are NOT NAVY!"

Another reason for the misconception may be that the *Jeremiah O'Brien* frequently participates in Navy events. For example, in August the U.S. Navy invited the *O'Brien* to participate in the V-J Day "Peace in the Pacific" parade of ships on San Francisco Bay. This was presided over by then Vice-President George Bush and Secretary of State George Schultz. Helicopter carriers, cruisers, destroyers and supply ships, all painted gray, passed in review along San Francisco's Embarcadero, sailors in dress uniforms lining their decks.

All government-owned cargo ships, such as the *Jeremiah O'Brien,* serving in World War II, Korea, Vietnam and Saudi Arabia were painted grey. The Preamble to the Merchant Marine Act of 1936 states, in part, that the nation shall have a merchant marine capable of serving as a military or naval auxiliary when required. The *Jeremiah O'Brien,* government-built and owned, manned by American merchant seamen, operated by a U. S. steamship company for the account of the government, under the operational control of the Navy was such a ship. Today, as a National Memorial, she operates with Navy ships during the annual Fleet Week ceremonies in San Francisco.

In September 1985, the ship was drydocked at Continental Maritime. It had been more than five years since the previous drydocking and her hull badly needed scraping and repainting. John Pottinger: "She risked major corrosive damage to her aging hull. In salt-water that comes from staying too long in one place. Ordinarily, we take her out only for the two annual memorial cruises around the bay."

One of the 20 mm's after restoration, as pristine as the day it was made and a tribute to the effort and skill of the volunteer crew. Credit Russell Fraser

Maneuvered into place over the bottom of a floating drydock, the water was pumped out of the dock causing it to rise until the *Jeremiah O'Brien* rested on previously-positioned bilge and keel blocks. Then the drydock with the ship on it rose until both the ship and the working surface of the dock were out of the water. A ship out of water is a very impressive sight. The true scale of it is realized when one sees each blade of the propeller is bigger than a man, or walks under it between dark bilgeblocks dripping water. Yard workers set to work with long-handled scrapers and jets of water to remove barnacles and marine growth from the ship's underwater hull. Intake screens, which prevent the ship's pumps from sucking in debris, were cleaned.

Per Dam: "Near the stern we found rivets eaten away and had to ring-weld them. She needed a patch job on her rudder too."

The *Jeremiah O'Brien* had her bottom sandblasted free of marine growth and coated with anti-corrosive and anti-fouling

Although the O'Brien *was one of the few ships to have a 3"-50 at the stern, she now carries a 5"-38 in that location.   Credit Joanie Morgan*

paint. The brass propeller was buffed until it shined. Continental Maritime generously waived the costs of lifting the ship, charging only for labor and materials for the repairs and painting.

At first the *O'Brien* had difficulty locating guns to faithfully recreate her World War II armament. Eventually Captain John Donahue, U.S. Navy, found enough 20 mm guns to give the ship a full complement at the Navy's facility in Cairns, Indiana. With the help of Norman Burke, a NLSM director who provided the transportation, the seven tons of armament were transported to the ship, reassembled and mounted in the proper guntubs.

Captain James Nolan is an avid military memorabilia enthusiast. He has a museum-quality collection of uniform patches, buttons and insignia, and has restored several World War II and Korean War jeeps: "...so I was kind of interested in those twenty millimeters. They said I could pick my piece and I could field strip it or do whatever else I wanted." He was soon fully involved.

Working together week after week, the volunteers' comaraderie grew. They got to know about each other's families, their hobbies, vacations and, first, last and always, their sea stories. As they chatted and joked, the humor occasionally took a macabre twist. Marci Hooper: "There was the time they talked about using the boilers for cremation. Doug Dickie had just finished rebricking the starboard boiler. The engineers were talking about degrees of temperature and in the conversation someone mentioned that somebody had passed away. Doug said, 'Well, you know, I think when I die I'd like to be cremated in the starboard boiler.'

"Harry Morgan said, 'I had a talk with the crematorium guys a few months ago about temperatures and cooking times and I think we could get it up to the right temperature.'

"Myron [one of the volunteer engineers] thought Doug should go out holding a Foster-Wheeler[2] certificate in his hand.

"Doug told me I couldn't look because he heard the body just curled up and that would be not a tasteful sight. I told him I had no intention of looking.

"Then Harry Dring shut them all up with this statement. He goes, 'Oh, great -- then -- they -- will -- call -- it -- The -- Death -- Ship.'

"So after that they shut up and we didn't hear much more about it. Another one of their more innovative ideas: How to raise money? We'll do cremations. Somehow I think the Board of Health would be on our case."

The Seventh Annual Seamen's Memorial Cruise took place on Saturday, May 17th, 1986 with a San Francisco Bay Cruise the following day. Again, Mayor Feinstein proclaimed the day National Liberty Ship Memorial Day in San Francisco. In a departure from previous years, in which the National Anthem was played by whatever band was on board, this year it was sung by David Malis, a baritone from the San Francisco Opera. Special guest for the day was James F. Goodrich, Under Secretary of the Navy. VADM John D. Costello, Commander, Pacific Area and Twelfth Coast Guard District was on board. So was John Gaughan

---

[2] Foster-Wheeler is a major manufacturer of marine boilers, for which Doug Dickie worked many years.

Captain James Nolan, who served as master of the SS Jeremiah O'Brien, *with a couple of future Liberty ship sailors. Credit Don Watson*

of the Maritime Administration. Special guests were Albert Haas, who had been purser on the ship from January to October, 1944, the Normandy voyages, Coleman "Coke" Schneider, the ship's first deck cadet, and Robert Milby, one of the *O'Brien's* World War II radio operators.

In a unique ceremony, Captain James Nolan, a San Francisco Bar Pilot, received the Merchant Marine Distinguished Service Medal presented by John Gaughan on behalf of Elizabeth Hanford Dole, Secretary of Transportation. Captain Peter Crowell, Master of the Pilot Boat *San Francisco* received the Merchant Marine Meritorious Service Medal and the Pilot Boat *San Francisco* was awarded the Gallant Ship Unit Citation Bar. They had been involved in a dramatic disaster on San Francisco Bay a few months before -- the explosion of the tanker *Puerto Rican.*

Captain Nolan had piloted her out and was preparing to go down the pilot ladder to the waiting boat when, without warning, the ship exploded. He and the ship's third mate were blown

Just a small part of the bountiful buffet served on each of the Seamen's Memorial and Bay cruises.   Credit Don Watson

several hundred feet into the air, landing in the water a quarter mile away. Several people were killed as the main deck peeled back and the ship was consumed in flames. According to Captain Nolan, accumulated gasses in the ship's cargo tanks were ignited by the pilot boat's exhaust as she came alongside. The Pilot Boat *San Francisco* picked up Nolan and the third mate and brought them to an ambulance on the pier. The third mate was burned over most of his body, but recovered. Captain Nolan's legs were broken in several places. To this day he walks with a slight limp.

Captain Nolan replaced Captain Ralph Wilson as master of the *O'Brien* on June 13, 1986. James Nolan: "Tom Patterson asked me, he says he would take the Chairman of the Board on the Jeremiah -- the National Liberty Ship Memorial Inc. -- if I would be the executive director and the captain. 'Well,' I says 'I worked with you many years, Tom. I enjoy it, so let's give it a try.' So that's how we got started on it."

The Marine Corps color guard is a standard feature on the Annual Seamen's Memorial Cruise.   Credit Don Watson

Ernie Murdock: "He was a good skipper and had a good handle on things. He was young and energetic."

On Friday, May 23, 1986 there was a special cruise for the US Navy Armed Guard Veterans who were holding their National Reunion in San Francisco. More than 600 Armed Guard veterans from all over the United States were on board.

Bob Burnett: "They chartered the ship for the first charter cruise ... and this was a joyful cruise. These people really enjoyed it. As I walked around, I'd ask several of the Armed Guard, 'Are you having a good time?'

"'Why, son, I'm having a great time.   I remember when I was right there and those guys were up there and we were shooting at them and ... '

"And I asked this one woman, 'Are you having a good time?'

"She said, 'Oh, yes. I'm having a wonderful time. For the first time in forty years I know what my husband did during the war.'

"How important this was for her. Because for forty years she'd been hearing these stories and not being able to relate to: What's a 441 and a half foot ship -- a football field and a half? Twenty millimeter -- that's bigger than five inch, right? It's very interesting."

From June until the end of the year there were more changes. Thomas B. Crowley, Chairman of the NLSM, resigned and was succeeded by RADM Thomas J. Patterson, who was elected by unanimous vote. Harry and Joanie Morgan left the ship.

Joanie Morgan: "It was getting to be too much time. I had spent five and a half years, some seven thousand hours, at it and I was looking for time to do other things."

Harry Morgan: "Once we got to Pier Three we started working on cosmetics and I began to lose interest. We were at the point where we did just routine maintenance and kept working on it until everything was spit-and-polish. Finally I lost interest altogether. Harry Dring had been after me for years to help with the steam tug *Hercules* and I decided there was nothing else left for me to do on the *O'Brien*. The *Hercules* was more of a challenge." Ernie Murdock became chief engineer on the *O'Brien*.

"Routine maintenance" is not necessarily easy to accomplish. On a large ship, even simple tasks take on an exponential increase in difficulty. For example, when the *Jeremiah O'Brien* is at her permanent berth at Fort Mason, in addition to her mooring lines she is secured with heavy anchor chain to the shore and an offshore buoy. The anchor chains act as springs, holding the ship away from the dock and preventing her from rubbing up and down on the pilings. This preserves the hull and the external appearance of the ship. In preparing for the annual cruise, the heavy offshore "winter moorings" must be readied for a quick departure. Bob Burnett explains the process: "One thing that's evolved over the years is preparing the ship for a cruise. When we first started we evolved a method of changing over from our heavy permanent winter moorings to our lighter mooring. It used to take about two and a half days, getting the lines out, handing the lines over. As the work has gone on and the team has developed, we've gotten it down to about a four-hour event. We have sophisticated the changeover to where we use shackles instead of having to drag an entire chain back using the ship's mooring gear. We have shackles and little segments of chain around each of the bitts.

"The most difficult ones are the two offshore lines. This used to entail a tugboat to lower to and retrieve from, and now what we do is attach a long wire cable to the chain, lower it into the water and then walk that wire all the way around the stern of the ship. Then we take it to shore and drop it and just put it over the wire. We recover it in the opposite direction.

"For a while we would disconnect the port anchor chain at the rocks and haul the anchor chain all the way back on the ship. Then to send it back ashore we would have to get a large snatch block out on our anchoring anchor chain that's embedded in the rocks out there and with a very long, about a one and a quarter inch diameter nylon braided rope, we'd take a bite out to the snatch block and then one end would lead to the anchor chain and the other end would come back to the windlass and we would essentially pull the anchor chain out there, hoping that nothing would break. That was the most difficult, that would take a couple of hours of preparation and of course you want it at low tide. But then about three years ago we decided to do the same thing with the forward offshore we were doing with the after. We break the chain now and drop a wire into the mud and retrieve it. That causes another problem. As the wire stretches it starts to twist the chain and we have to figure how to get rid of all these twists. But it's saved us a lot of time." That's just one facet of work aboard the *O'Brien.*

In 1987 the ship cruised (Eighth Annual Cruise) on May 16, 17 and again on the 24th because of popular demand. The cruise on the 24th was in honor of the 50th anniversary of the Golden Gate Bridge. A Transportation Parade of Ships took place to celebrate the day. The *Jeremiah O'Brien* was the only merchant ship in a parade of Navy and Coast Guard vessels.

Governor George Deukmejian issued a special proclamation to honor the occasion of the Maritime Day cruise:

On behalf of the State of California, it is my sincere pleasure to convey my warm regards to all setting sail aboard the SS

JEREMIAH O'BRIEN on the occasion of the 8th Annual Seamen's Memorial Cruise.

As the last unaltered American Liberty Ship still in operating condition, the SS JEREMIAH O'BRIEN stands as a symbol of the strength of America as well as the dedication and devotion of her proud people. The exceptional work of all involved in the preservation and restoration effort of this national memorial is indeed a tribute to the revered American spirit and is deserving of our deepest gratitude and highest commendation.

This year, you gather to honor America's Merchant Seamen and, in particular, the men killed by enemy action serving aboard the SS BATON ROUGE VICTORY. These brave seamen gave their lives to ensure that our soldiers serving nobly in Vietnam would be provided with arms to defend themselves and their country. As the first United States cargo vessel to sink in the Vietnam conflict, I am honored to join these brave Americans whose devotion and love of America will serve as a legacy to us all.

On this very special occasion, please accept my best wishes for a most enjoyable cruise. May our reflection on our nation's triumphant past serve as an inspiration as we prepare for our future challenges.

RADM Thomas J. Patterson was the master of ceremonies, representing the United States Coast Guard was Vice Admiral John D. Costello. Mr. Brian O'Neill, Superintendent of the Golden Gate National Recreation Area presented a plaque designating the *SS Jeremiah O'Brien* as a National Landmark.

Typically, cruise day begins with hot coffee and pastry for the passengers as they come on board. From 0730 to 0930 they walk up the gangways in ever-increasing numbers, bundled warmly for the typical San Francisco summer -- cold, overcast and/or fog. The ship's store is open from 0800 to 1600 and seasoned *Jeremiah O'Brien* aficionados stop there first to see what new items are on hand and make their purchases before anything is sold out. At 0930 the gangways are raised and at 1000, with whistle blowing

Songs of the thirties and forties were the forté of the "Girls Night Out," here harmonizing for an appreciative audience. Credit Don Watson

and tugs chuffing, and most of the passengers lining the rails to watch, the ship backs away from the pier. The band, set on number three hatch, strikes up popular music, usually of the thirties and forties. The ship cruises leisurely out the Golden Gate, passing under the bridge, and stops her engines, drifting just outside the main ship channel. Prayers and remembrances are said honoring departed seamen and one by one the wreaths are thrown over. Each garland of flowers slowly drifts alongside the ship, past the rudder and out to sea, carrying with it the gratitude of its patron and the memory of lost shipmates. Marine guards snap to attention and fire a salute with their rifles. On occasion, ashes of departed seamen are scattered. (The ashes of Captain Southerland, the ship's first master, were cast during an Armed Guard cruise in 1987.) When the ceremonies are over, the propeller turns again, gently pushing the ship back inside San Francisco Bay where she passes under both the Golden Gate and Oakland Bay Bridges. By now the band has resumed playing and buffets are set for lunch.

One of the more fascinating aspects of the annual cruise is passing under the Golden Gate Bridge. Most people drive <u>over</u> it but few pass <u>under</u> it. Credit NLSM

As the passengers file past, filling their plates with chicken, ham, roast beef, salads, vegetables, bread and dessert, the ship enters the Oakland Estuary. This narrow ship channel is carefully navigated by Captain Jahn, who has piloted the *Jeremiah O'Brien* on every trip she has made since leaving the Reserve Fleet, except one, until she is adjacent to Jack London Square. There the captain delicately turns the ship, in an area so narrow it wouldn't seem possible, and points her toward the Bay again. Leaving the estuary, the *O'Brien* steams east and north of Treasure Island, past Angel Island and through Raccoon Straits, and finally returns to her berth at Pier 3. The passengers disembark after making arrangements for next year's cruise and a final stop at the ship's store.

This May 16 it was cold, overcast and windy. One wreath was donated by Pierre Layec of France, who sailed in French-flag Libertys during World War II. His wreath was thrown by Air

Just a few of the almost 300 volunteers that annually devote their time to the preservation and maintenance of the SS Jeremiah O'Brien. *Credit Wes and Bev Masterson*

France Executive Pierre Lebris. Three small French flags were donated to the ship on the occasion. A rifle squad was provided by the U.S. Marine Corps from the Marine Barracks, Naval Air Station, Alameda. Entertainment on this cruise was provided by the Girls Night Out singing trio and a four piece band. The trio wore flowing Veronica Lake 40's hair styles, dresses with long hemlines and the open-toed, thick, high-heeled shoes of the era. Their selections ranged from "Boogie-woogie Bugle Boy of Company B" to "You Belong To Me." Oscar Niemeth Towing of Oakland provided two tugs, the *American Eagle* and the *Sea Eagle* to assist the ship on all three cruises.

Father John Heaney held a special ceremony for the late Captain John M. O'Brien [no relation to Jeremiah], the well-loved and well-known former master of the *Permanente Silverbow*, a San Francisco-based ship. This was followed by the spreading of Capt. O'Brien's ashes on the outgoing tide (the cremation was done ashore). In a sudden gust of wind, the ashes were blown back over those gathered on the foredeck. People were momentarily taken aback, at first unsure how to react. Then someone said, "If Captain John is up there somewhere watching, he's probably laughing his head off." Then everyone laughed and brushed the ashes off. Those who knew him began reminiscing -- how he started on fishing boats in Santa Barbara as a boy, how well-liked he was, how, after retiring as a ship captain, he went back to running fishing boats.

The Ninth Annual Seamen's Memorial Cruise was held on Saturday, May 21, 1988 and commemorated the 45th Anniversary of the *Jeremiah O'Brien*. Mr. John W. Borden, Chairman and CEO of the NLSM, Inc. was the master of ceremonies. Carl Scharpf, who was third assistant engineer on voyage 5 to South America was on board as a special guest. Capt. Robert A. Bryan, Western Region Director for the Maritime Administration represented that agency and Brian O'Neill represented the Golden Gate National Recreation Area (GGNRA). Music was provided by Dick Saltzman. The 170 volunteers had contributed more than 25,000 hours of labor during the previous year. Their hours counted toward complimentary cruise passes of their own.

Visitors donate a small sum to see the ship but the cruises generate most of the ship's operating income and are the glamour event of the year. The *Jeremiah O'Brien* "shows" well -- her brass polished, her woodwork gleaming, or, in the language of seafarers, "everything ship-shape in Bristol fashion." Visitors are pleasantly surprised at "How good she looks."

As mentioned earlier, it takes a lot of work to keep a ship looking good. Although the ship is open every day except Thanksgiving and Christmas, the public seldom sees what must be done to keep the *O'Brien* the showpiece she is. One day a week is set aside for the deck department, another for the engine department. This lets each group work on projects that need the labor of more than one person and keeps them out of each other's way. There is a traditional rivalry between the "deck" and "engine" departments on any ship and good-natured jibes come out at the slightest provocation.

Engineer: "You'd never get anywhere without us."

Mate: "You'd never know where you were without us."

In 1988 the O'Brien *returned to the Suisun Bay Reserve Fleet, her home for thirty-three years. This time she stayed just a week, long enough to gather spare parts. Credit Wes and Bev Masterson*

The volunteers enjoy the time together and, as always, tell their sea stories.

"I was on a ship one time..."

"You know, that Murmansk run was something..."

Tales of romance and adventure in strange lands abound.

"There was this girl in Valparaiso..."

"I was in Hong Kong at the Red Lion, and...

"We pulled in to Naples, just after the war, and you could..."

Strange sights on the world's oceans are described.

"Dutch Harbor was so cold that night..."

"You might not believe this, but..."

"This is no shit..."

Then coffeetime is over and the volunteers get back to the process of restoration and preservation that never ends. On any given day you will find volunteers chipping, painting, scraping, polishing, sweeping, cleaning. They are a resourceful group and often come up with creative and inventive ways to use what they can "scrounge up" to accomplish some project. The *Jeremiah*

The cake honoring the "1st Official Looting Expedition" was provided by the Fleet Superintendent. Credit the author

In the spirit of the occasion the ship flew a pirate flag. Never were so many spare parts transported by so few for such a good cause. Credit the author

O'Brien presents a better appearance today than when she was launched because of the volunteers and their tireless energy and devotion.

Captain James Nolan is a history buff: "The more I studied the history of Jeremiah O'Brien and his six brothers up in Machias Maine, all the way from there to South Portland, Maine where they actually built this thing in 1943, the more fascinating it got. Roosevelt calling these things the 'ugly ducklings' -- they only made them for one trip -- but twenty-seven hundred and fifty-one were built and there's not a one left [in its original condition] except for the *Jeremiah O'Brien* and I thought to myself, I can't believe this. I started searching around for spare parts and I couldn't find a spare stub-shaft, I couldn't find a spare this and a spare that. I kept thinking, isn't that amazing."

But spare parts were available at the Suisun Bay Reserve Fleet. During the war the Maritime Commission wisely designed its vessels so that many of the parts were interchangeable from one class to another. Fittings, fixtures, parts and pieces are common to Libertys, Victorys, C-2s, C-3s, etc.

With permission from the Maritime Administration [successor to the Maritime Commission], which still technically owned the ship, the *Jeremiah O'Brien* sailed back to the fleet on May 23, 1988 on an official "raiding expedition." No pirate crew ever tackled a treasure ship with more delight and spirit than the *Jeremiah O'Brien's* as they fell on the *Pacific Victory* on scrap row. Even before all lines were fast, the *O'Brien's* engineers were cutting an access to the emergency generator on the adjacent ship. Gold ingots and Spanish doubloons did not shine more brightly to the buccaneers than those old nuts and bolts and valves and hatch boards did to the crew who swarmed aboard and hauled away everything they could move, heave or winch aboard the *Jeremiah O'Brien.* In the spirit of the occasion, a pirate flag was flown from the truk and the Superintendent of the Fleet sent out a sheet cake decorated with a skull and crossbones.

Alongside scrap row for a week, the *O'Brien* crew finally found the no-longer-manufactured supplies and parts they had desperately needed. As a government-owned ship the *O'Brien* is entitled to receive government surplus material and equipment through the use of a property transfer notice. No longer would they have to scrounge and invent and make-do. They could lay in enough to supply their ship for years to come. At week's end, a very tired but still enthusiastic crew proclaimed the "raid" a great adventure and a great success. On May 27, the precious spare parts safely stowed, the *O'Brien* sailed back to her berth at Fort Mason.

By this time chief engineer Ernie Murdock had other commitments and was relieved by Allan A. Rynberg, Captain Nolan was replaced by Captain George M. Tuttle, Jr.

The steam-powered steering gear of the SS *Jeremiah* O'Brien, *now like new and operating perfectly, thanks to the efforts of the ship's many volunteers. Credit NLSM*

Captain James Nolan: "I just loved working with the people. When I first started there were so many people I couldn't remember their names and who was who. I tried to make it a point to take at least a minimum of an hour each working day to walk around and talk to each individual, at least to say hello, even if it was just eye contact. Each single individual volunteer. Over a couple of years' time I got where I knew everybody. I knew their name, I knew where they were coming from, I had heard the same story at least twice. I just really loved the volunteers. They don't have to be there. I asked one guy, I said, 'You're the president of your own company, you're very successful. What do you come down here for?' And he says, 'Well, Jim, I come down here and I oil and I clean up and I fire and I don't have the pressure that I have at work.'

"I spent 27 months on the *Jeremiah O'Brien* and it was just a wonderful, wonderful learning experience. Very, very positive. I felt like a salesman, really. Just selling cruises. Sell, sell, sell.

Tickets were the main thing, the main source of revenue was tickets on the *Jeremiah O'Brien* cruise."

Bob Burnett: "Per Dam was originally hired as the bosun and the restoration supervisor. And Per is a man that has been around ships and shipping for forty some-odd years and knows his way around and knows all the tricks of the trade. He's just a wonderful person. He retired and the board was looking for a replacement. I had been very interested in the ship and so I was asked if I would take his position as acting bosun for maybe two months until they found somebody permanent. I just wound up staying on the job."

Marci Hooper became the ship's business manager, giving up her position with a large legal firm. Rita Bertillion, an executive with Wells Fargo Bank, replaced Marci as volunteer storekeeper. With the death of Captain Tuttle, Captain George Jahn, San Francisco Bay Pilot, became master of the *Jeremiah O'Brien.*

The Tenth Annual Seamen's Memorial Cruise was held on May 20, 1989 with a Bay Cruise the following day. Robert E. Blake acted as master of ceremonies. The invocation was given by Reverend John Bosch. RADM Thomas J. Patterson was guest of honor providing a commentary on the history of the American merchant marine and the *Jeremiah O'Brien.*

While many of the ship's volunteers are former Liberty ship sailors or merchant seamen, some are neither. Barry Bertillion is one example. Although he has never sailed, he is a "natural" when it comes to mechanics. As owner of his own racing auto shop, he constantly repairs, tinkers with, and adjusts engines. On the *O'Brien* he brings his mechanical talent to the refrigeration machinery, steering gear or anywhere else needed. An enthusiastic World War II buff, he provides period training films, movies and even old phonograph records for music and dancing on steaming weekend when the crew gathers after dinner on Saturday night.

The Maritime Industry Reunion was held on board September 22-24, 1989. Co-chaired by Admiral Thomas Patterson of the NLSM and Frank O. Braynard of the American Merchant Marine Museum Foundation, it brought together Liberty ship sailors and others from around the United States. Attending the reunion were

Congresswoman Helen Bentley of Maryland, VADM Paul Butcher, COMSC, Adolph Kurz, Mike Sacco of the SIU, Arthur Moore and Joe Ekelund of the California Maritime Academy. Friday night and Saturday were devoted to meetings, with a Bay cruise on Sunday. During the cruise the "Confederate Air Force" flew some of its vintage aircraft over the ship and a Navy Riverine Force displayed its prowess for those on board.

The Eleventh Annual Memorial and Bay Cruises were held on May 19 and 20, 1990. The printed program included a letter from President Bush:

> As a Naval veteran, I know firsthand the heroic contributions of our Nation's maritime industry to the Allied victory in World War II. America's extraordinary maritime build-up was essential to the war effort and was one of the most remarkable feats ever accomplished by any nation. All who took part--our merchant marine veterans, associated military service veterans, shipbuilders, port managers, longshoremen, and others--have earned our Nation's eternal gratitude.
>
> I congratulate the officers and members of the National Liberty Ship Memorial for their wonderful efforts to bring together the seafarers and other maritime industry personnel who took part in that great endeavor. The Liberty Ship was the workhorse of World War II, and the SS JEREMIAH O'BRIEN provides a fitting location for this reunion. I join with you in honoring the memory of the more than 6,000 civilian seafarers who gave their lives so that others might live in freedom, and I salute all of you for your unselfish service to the United States.
>
> Barbara joins me in sending our very best wishes. God bless you, and God bless America.

Robert E. Blake was master of ceremonies. RADM Thomas J. Patterson introduced RADM John W. Bitoff, Commander of the Naval Base San Francisco, who gave a talk on maritime heritage highlighting the importance of the merchant marine in naval strategy.

More than 170 volunteers contributed in excess of 25,000 hours to the restoration and operation of the ship since the last cruise.

The job of shipkeeper requires a great degree of versatility. Bob Burnett: "At a minimum it's just opening and closing and acting as security and then performing work. Going beyond that, it is also the person who has a day-to-day idea of what's going on and what had gone on or what needs to go on. For example, when a volunteer comes aboard and needs to have a job assignment, then, based on what was done yesterday and what needs to be done tomorrow, I'm able to guide them in a certain direction. There are other times when I'm called upon as a tour guide or docent because there's no one here and a large group arrives. So I take people around. I have also some wonderful opportunities, not enough, but wonderful opportunities to talk to people and enjoy some of their experiences. And I've been fortunate enough to make contact with several people who have identified themselves as having been ex-*Jeremiah O'Brien* sailors."

Keeping up the *O'Brien* isn't all painting, oiling and working on the engine.

Bob Burnett: "You learn some interesting skills on a ship. There aren't many places other than a ship like this that you can climb up the mast. We have to top the mast now and then to overhaul the topping blocks. About every two years we lower all the booms and overhaul all the headblocks and the heelblocks and paint them, but normally we don't have to go up there. We used to have to sweep the pigeons out of the crow's nest every now and then, it would fill up with their leftovers. But we've since put up a little bit of screen to keep them out."

Phil Sinnott: "Every other year we drop all our booms down and work our way from bow to stern. We take everything apart, heel blocks and everything and then we put 'em back up. It's dirty, heavy work and seems to go on forever." Laughs.

The Twelfth Annual Memorial Seamen's and Bay Cruises took place on May 18 and 19, 1991. Capt. C. O. Otterberg was master of ceremonies. Monsignor John Heaney gave the invocation. RADM Thomas J. Patterson was the guest speaker.

A visiting sailor demonstrates the technique of stoking the coal-fired stove in the galley. Coal and air-flow are the only temperature controls. Credit NLSM

Music was provided by the Unicorns. On board both days were two authors, Captain Walter Jaffee, author of *The Last Mission Tanker*, and Justin Gleichauf, author of *Unsung Sailors*. They signed copies of their books and shared stories with interested merchant marine veterans.

On Saturday a group of U.S. Army sailors were on board. They were part of the 35th Army Transportation Corps and had been responsible for moving Army troops and supplies in the Southwest Pacific Theater. They were in San Francisco holding their first reunion.

Exactly 31,534 hours were contributed by volunteers that year.

In addition to the once-a-week gathering of departments, steaming weekend is a major event for the crew. Held on the third weekend of each month, it is devoted to the operation of the ship's main engine. Douglas E. Dickie, survivor of an old-name

One never appreciates the true size of a ship until it's out of the water.
Barry Bertillion, who is well over 6', stands under the stem.   Credit
Barry Bertillion

Under the supervision of a Southwest Marine worker, the rudder is lowered into place after being reconditioned. Credit Barry Bertillion

After reconditioning and polishing, the ship's propeller is swung into place. Credit Barry Bertillion

San Francisco ship design firm, is the present chief engineer. Many volunteers show up on Friday night and sleep on board, all the better to get an early start in the morning. The galley crew sets out dinner prepared on the ship's coal-fired stove. During the night the engineroom fires are lit and steam is raised. In the morning everyone turns to and after a hearty breakfast prepared by the volunteer cook, visitors are allowed on board and taken on tours of the engineroom. They see the massive gleaming piston rods of the ship's steam reciprocating engine powerfully pumping up and down. It is an impressive sight. Noise fills the air -- the constant hiss of steam, the roar of fires in the boilers, pumps spinning, compressors building air -- making it difficult to talk. The more daring look in the shaft alley where the massive steel propeller shaft slowly turns. In the engineroom are volunteers oiling, cleaning, tending fires, watching gauges. They range in age from octogenarian chief engineer Dickie to California Maritime Academy Cadet Brian Goldman, in his early twenties. Occasionally an engineer will climb to the main deck to get away from the heat, but soon returns to the "excitement" of the engineroom.

In another part of the ship the radio room will be open, radio operators sending and receiving messages or just listening. Occasionally a sea story comes out. "I was on a ship once..."

The ship's store is open for the weekend, offering everything from books to sweatshirts to refrigerator magnets. Rita Bertillion presides over it, her infectious smile making everyone smile back. Only two or three of her staff of half a dozen may be there on any given day, but the fortunate visitor may find Janet Doyle, also known as "Wendy the Welder." In her youth she welded on these ships. You can buy a postcard with her picture on it dressed in full welding gear. She will gladly autograph it for you.

In the purser's office you may find Bob Imbeau or Homer Winter collecting and cataloging stories from Liberty Ship sailors who come on board. The *O'Brien's* files contain hundreds of adventures. Or you may find Homer manning the information booth at the foot of the gangway.

Saturday night dinners are the highlight of steaming weekend, something everyone looks forward to. The galley crew works

*The propeller shaft housing or stern tube without the propeller shaft.   Credit
Barry Bertillion*

*The ship was in such good condition the new shaft wasn't needed.   In this
photo it's lowered into the 'tween deck for stowage.   Credit Barry Bertillion*

most of the day keeping the big coal-fired stove stoked, preparing the meal. There may be up to half a dozen volunteers working in this small hot space. Typical of them is Stella Chin, who manages to keep everything clean and anticipate the cook's next need, all the while smiling cheerfully. Or Ron Robson, who will patiently peel crayfish for hours at a time or Bill Smith, who cheerfully helps wash the kettles and pans, or Laura Tordson who rolls out pie crusts or Irene Williams who willingly serves the hungry volunteers.

Cooking for up to sixty hard-working volunteers requires quantities of food and cooking equipment far larger than most people ever see. The mixer for the galley, located on the deck below, is industrial-sized, able to handle batter for a cake for a hundred people. The adjacent storerooms and refrigerated spaces hold meat by the hundredweight, cans by the carlot, eggs by the gross and produce by the case. Imagine stirring filé gumbo for sixty in a thirty-gallon pot with a paddle the size of an oar. Envision making twelve large loaves of bread at once. A meal might include salad, roast ham, celery with pecans, corn on the cob, homemade bread and cherry pie. All done "from scratch" on a range whose only temperature control is the judicious balance of hot coals and ventilation. When the meal is ready -- breakfast is served at 8 a.m., lunch at noon, dinner at 5:30 p.m. -- Ron or Stella or Marci will take an old xylophone and go around the ship from engineroom to bridge deck, the melodious notes calling everyone to the galley.

"She's still a good feeder," is an appreciative remark often heard.

From January 9-29, 1992 the ship underwent major repairs at Southwest Marine, a San Francisco shipyard. This drydocking was unusual in that the propeller shaft was drawn or removed and the shaft bearings renewed. To do this the rudder was dropped and pulled aside, the propeller taken off, part of the shaft pulled out and part pulled into the shaft alley. The bearings were renewed and, like a Chinese puzzle, everything was put back in place.

The "Lucky 13th" Annual Memorial and Bay Cruise took place on May 16 and 17, 1992. The volunteers called it lucky because the ship had successfully completed its dry-docking and the spare propeller shaft, which it was thought would be needed in the drydocking, was still in number 3 hold as a spare. On board were Captain Walter Jaffee, author of *The Last Victory*, and William Kooiman, author of *The Grace Ships 1869-1969 (The Illustrated History of the W.R. Grace Shipping Lines)*. They signed their books for all purchasers, with profits from sales going to the *O'Brien*. Music was provided by the Unicorns who mixed wartime classics with modern music. Capt. C. O. Otterberg was master of ceremonies. Monsignor John Heaney gave the invocation. RADM Thomas J. Patterson introduced Capt. Warren Leback, Maritime Administrator for the Maritime Administration.

The volunteers worked a total of 32,801 hours during the previous year.

On October 10, 1992 the ship took part in Fleet Week on San Francisco Bay. The only merchant ship in a flotilla of Coast Guard and Navy vessels, the *Jeremiah O'Brien* proudly represented the American merchant marine -- the ships and sailors long gone but not forgotten, and the hopes of the future. The passengers enjoyed a passing parade of Navy and Coast Guard ships and a stunning air show put on by the Blue Angels.

The fourteenth Annual Seamen's Memorial Cruise also marked the 50th anniversary of the ship. Joining the *SS Jeremiah O'Brien* for the cruise on Saturday, May 22, 1993 were seven of her original crew members: Rosario Carista, Charles Hord, Daniel Bandy, Carl Scharpf, Morgan Williams, Hank Kusel and Robert Milby. Captain C. O. Otterberg was master of ceremonies and the principal speaker was RADM Merrill W. Ruck, USN. The weather was perfect and the food excellent.

But the real life of the *O'Brien* is personal, a special feeling -- different in each case to those who are on intimate terms with her.

Per Dam: "It's a pleasure to be down here. I've always liked the ship and I enjoy seeing visitors come on board. It's nice to see they appreciate it."

Shipkeeper Bob Burnett: "There are times when the ship and I have a little conversation. Those are the wonderful times early in the morning or late in the afternoon and we are alone, the ship and I. There are times when I romanticize and try to place it fifty years ago and be present. But mostly the people are the ones who provide the personality. And many of the crew, when they are in an expansive mood, share some of their experiences and that makes this ship come alive."

Marine Superintendent Ernie Murdock: "It has a personality, but the volunteer crew on here that had been on ever since the ship came out also affects my feeling toward the ship 'cause they're such a great group of people and they maintain the ship so well. In fact I think it operates better now than it did when it was new. And probably looks better than new in a lot of places."

Phil Sinnott: "I think all ships have a personality. Yeah, they really do. This one has a rather perverse personality at times, I might say. Of course I feel that way 'cause I put so much into it. I feel very comfortable with what I do. One reason is I love the work, it does a lot for a person. I'd really like to take it out to sea 'cause that's where you really get the feel of what she's like. Some of them [ships] have that cranky motion, some of them have kind of an easy-going comfortable lift and roll."

The *Jeremiah O'Brien* is unique in her persona. Some ships have a distinct personality. People sense it, they can identify it, they develop an affection for it. The *Jeremiah O'Brien* is not one of those. She reveals almost nothing of herself. Sturdy, capable, dependable, with no eccentricities or peculiarities, she presents a bare face, a *tabula rasa*, to her crew and keeps her secrets. She does not intrude her "personality" on others; she lets people build theirs on her. Whatever they need to see, to feel, to find, to remember or imagine, they can do it on the *Jeremiah O'Brien*. She becomes all things to all people. They walk her broad decks or run their hands along the brass instruments or caress the deck rails and think their own thoughts, remember their own dreams, do what they want to do.

More than with most ships, then, the story of the *Jeremiah O'Brien* is the story of those who sailed on her, who worked on her, and who have preserved her. Because of them the *Jeremiah O'Brien* endures. Alone, among her 2,751 sisters, she endures.

Alone, from the 5000-ship Armada, she endures. And, as a living museum ship, she will carry the history of the twentieth century into the twenty-first.

Bob Burnett: "We're all here for different reasons. Many of us are here to relive our youth. People come here and they're twenty years old again. They're on a ship and they're on something that represents some of the most exciting periods of their life. The adventure that was available during that period is a once-in-a-lifetime opportunity. There are some horrors of war but there are also some major adventures. For many of them it was their first job, and first jobs are especially exciting. As a seaman you see foreign and exotic places and you have adventure and sometimes stark terror.

"People come here for comaraderie. Most of these folks are retired. Instead of sitting around home they come out and they hang around on the ship and they meet with some friends one day a week and do some work. Our average age right now is about seventy-one. We have had people get physically exhausted on a hot day working down in the lower hold and you're almost convinced that you'll never see them again. Some of them go home and they have to put on their back braces and rest for several days but they're back the next work day because one day a week they feel whole, that they've really done something.

"Some people just really enjoy working with their hands. We have a lot of people who've worked in an office most of their lives. We also have a lot of ex-manual workers. These folks like to get their hands dirty and it's a lot of fun. I've talked to some people who are sailing currently as chief engineers and they're not allowed to touch a tool. But they can come down here and they can lift a wrench."

Phil Sinnott: "What we do here, what the workers do on board here, is real sailors' work. We just don't get much pay. The other important thing is the great guys you work with. They're all volunteers and it's such a fraternity, especially when you work on heavy gear, stuff that's really life-threatening. We trust each other's knots and you trust each other with your life. There's a

The SS Jeremiah O'Brien *at home, Pier 3, Fort Mason. Here she will always be for Liberty ship sailors past, present and future. The tugs are* Catano *and* Sea Lark II. *Credit George Lamuth*

fraternity there that you don't get much elsewhere. Kind of like the military in combat."

Per Dam: "What got me is they're not seamen I'm working with, they're from all walks of life. But they're so dedicated."

Marci Hooper: "Some people come down here for fun, some people come down here 'cause it's the only place they can take apart a steam engine and put it back together. The ship probably has a hundred and ninety-eight different uses, one for everybody. Some people are here because they feel it keeps their war alive, not the bad part about it, but the good part about it. Some people are here because their wives are very happy to see their back on Wednesday or Thursday. I have had wives come up to me and thank me for having a place for their husband to go one or two days a week."

The ship has the effect of making people feel young again. Working on board gives them a sense of accomplishment and a feeling of fulfillment.

Captain James Nolan: "These guys worked so hard, I had them come up to me, the old timers, after the end of the day, guys that were in their eighties, saying, 'You know, captain, I feel like I put ten more years on my life just coming up here. And I can't tell you how tired I am, but I just want to keep doing this.'"

Bob Burnett: "Other people are learning new skills. Not that they hope to use them in a professional way, but it's fun to learn. So people will come down and learn to fire if they've never learned to fire before, or oil, or handle lines. A lot of modern working sailors don't know about stick ships or ships with booms. They sail on box-ships and tankers. We have a lot of amateurs on this ship who have never sailed and never will sail that know how to sail this and they know how to assist in the rigging of some of our equipment."

Phil Sinnott: And another part of it is, and maybe it's just as good as anything else, when you're finished, here's the ship that people can come on board and enjoy. I find every time I meet people from all over the world, you learn things from them."

Marci Hooper: "The people are remarkable. The average person on this ship would come and help you if you get a flat tire. They might ask you why you didn't keep up your three A membership but they would come and help you. That's part of the spirit. We could not have done this without the help of a great number of people. Some of the more sterling ones are on the Board, and some of the people that were very important to our basic beginning are shy and retiring and you won't see them. They're just not around a lot, but they were very important.

"It's like a giant extended family. It's a place to accomplish what I think I do best. The company is usually pretty good and the help is certainly good. You couldn't pay some of these people what they're worth for the work they do for us.

"Everybody has a reason for coming here and that's become more and more obvious to me over the years. One volunteer, I've known him for years and one day somebody told me that six months before we got the ship underway, his daughter had killed herself. He'd been devastated. He was in his late fifties or early sixties and his career was such that he didn't need to drown himself in his work. He needed some place to go where he could be useful and work out his problems. He's more than done it.

Some people come here with problems you never even know they have. They're looking for a place to do what they enjoy, they're looking for comaraderie.

"My chief thrill is getting people who don't know each other working together and having fun and going home afterward. That's the best part about it. I don't care if what you've done is break out a very complicated piece of machinery and put it back with no spare parts left over or paint the deck, you walk down the pier feeling satisfied with what you've done that day. That's a successful day, as long as you go home happy, that's all that matters."

Bob Burnett: "We have visitors that are so joyful, so excited to be here. And you can just see this fifty-year stare on their face. They're just so happy. These are wonderful people to talk to. Then there are those who become very sad, very thoughtful, when they're on board because they remember some other experiences."

Marci Hooper: "Almost everybody's left a little piece of themselves here, whether it's the booby hatches into number two or if it's that reefer on number four that we got as a loan and the company went out of business and no one ever asked for it back. There's a little piece of everyone left here."

Admiral Tom Patterson: "Long may this splendid ship float. And steam. And to her volunteer crew ... Bravo Zulu! They are the best."

EPILOGUE

June 6, 1994, will be the fiftieth anniversary of the Allied landings at the Normandy beachheads. There will be a great celebration in Europe in the weeks surrounding the anniversary, focused on the landings at Normandy, with the participation of fleets of ships from many countries. The United States Navy will play a major part in the celebration. Plans are underway for the *Jeremiah O'Brien* to return to Normandy. Traveling in tandem with the *Lane Victory* and the *John Brown*, also World War II survivors, the *O'Brien* will sail to England and France. But of all the ships from all over the world that participate in that event, the *SS Jeremiah O'Brien* will be the only ship that took part in the original invasion.

It's not an easy task to take a fifty-year-old ship crewed with volunteers halfway around the world. Preliminary planning began years in advance with a $2 million budget but the logistics of the planned six-month voyage are daunting. Where to get the fuel, stores, and supplies are only a few of the things to anticipate.

A major portion of the budget involves drydocking the vessel. It must be brought up to Coast Guard standards for the long ocean voyage. Will the volunteer crew, with an average age of 71, be up to the voyage? Will the country's leaders support this historic voyage? What ports of call should be made along the way and on the return trip? Certainly, Portland, Maine, where the ship was launched is a must. But what about other ports the O'Brien went to in her career: Antofagasta, Callao, Panama, New Orleans, Galveston, Houston, New York, Southampton, Halifax, Loch Ewe, Methil, Gourock, Belfast? And then there are the ports that would like to have the O'Brien visit: Rouen, Calais, Brest, London, Baltimore, Philadelphia and Charleston are interested.

The task ahead is formidable but the SS Jeremiah O'Brien, her friends and her volunteers are up to the challenge. Over and over they have proved their perseverance and determination. Like the namesake who brandished his sword in the War of 1812, ready to do battle again, the ship will sail to Normandy and once more do her part. But this time the cause is not war but a celebration of the triumph of freedom and liberty. Jeremiah O'Brien would be proud.

APPENDIX A

TONNAGE

There are several types of tonnage used when referring to ships. In hopes of clearing up some of the confusion for the non-seafarer, the following definitions are offered.

DEADWEIGHT TONNAGE. Expresses in long tons[1] the amount of cargo, stores and fuel a vessel can carry. It is the difference between the number of tons the ship displaces when light, or not carrying these commodities, and the number of tons it displaces when loaded to the load line. The terms "deadweight tonnage" and "deadweight carrying capacity" are interchangeable.

CARGO TONNAGE. This term is expressed as either weight or measurement tonnage. A weight ton is a long ton of 2,240

---

[1] The long ton is the traditional measurement used at sea on British and American ships and consists of 2240 pounds. In the very early days of seafaring, wine casks, called "tuns" weighed this amount when full. The measurement and the term "ton" come from that cask.

pounds. In France and other countries using the metric system a weight ton is 2,204.6 pounds. This is sometimes referred to as a metric ton or tonne. A measurement ton is usually 40 cubic feet.

GROSS TONNAGE. This refers to a vessel's internal volume in terms of cubic feet. A gross ton is 100 cubic feet. All the internal spaces of a ship are measured and divided by 100 cubic feet to determine a vessel's gross tonnage.

NET TONNAGE. This is also a measurement of internal volume of a vessel. By taking a ship's gross tonnage and subtracting the volume of the crew accommodations, machinery spaces, navigation areas and engine room and fuel tanks (all in terms of 100 cubic feet), one arrives at the vessel's net tonnage.

DISPLACEMENT TONNAGE. The weight of a vessel and its contents in terms of tons of 2240 pounds. If the vessel is light, that is, without stores, bunker fuel or cargo, the term used is "light displacement tonnage." If loaded, then "loaded displacement tonnage." The term comes from calculating how much water the ship would displace in either of these conditions.

REGISTERED TONNAGE. Normally this is given in terms of both gross and net tonnage. The term simply means that the vessel's certificate of registration shows these tonnages.

PANAMA CANAL TONNAGE. Ships that travel through the Panama Canal are measured in terms of gross tons and given a special "Panama Canal Tonnage," which is used as a basis for determining the fee for transiting the canal.

SUEZ CANAL TONNAGE. The concept is the same as Panama Canal Tonnage, but the numbers come out slightly differently.

Appendix B

Manufacturers of Materials and Equipment for Liberty Ships

A listing of the businesses that supplied the parts and equipment for Liberty ships reads like a cross-section of American Industry. From the far corners of the country came bearings, bells, davits, engines, fittings, floodlights, propellers, pumps and the thousands of other inert objects that, when put together, brought life to a Liberty ship.

Airports[1]
   Oil City Brass Works, Beaumont, TX

Anchors
   Baldt Anchor Chain & Forge Co., Chester, PA
   Columbia Steel Co., San Francisco, CA
   Pittsburgh Steel Foundry Co., Glassport, PA

---

[1] A mechanism through which air flows, not a place for landing aircraft.

Annunciators
>Graybar Electric Co., Inc., New York, NY

Asbestos Board
>Johns-Manville, New York, NY

Batteries
>Philco Radio & Television Corp., Philadelphia, PA
>U.S.L. Battery Corp., Oakland, CA

Bearings, Line Shaft
>Bangor & Aroostook Railroad, Bangor, ME
>Helser Machine and Marine Works, Inc., Portland, OR
>W.A. Jones Foundry & Machine Co., Chicago, IL
>Lynchburg Foundry Co., Lynchburg, VA
>Millinocket Foundry & Machine Co., Millinocket, ME

Bearings, Thrust
>Kingsbury Machine Works, Philadelphia, PA

Bedplate Section
>Troy Foundry Co., Inc., Troy, NY

Bells, Electric
>Graybar Electric Co., Inc., New York, NY

Bells, Ship's
>Bevin Brothers Manufacturing Co., East Hampton, CT
>M. Greenberg's Sons, San Francisco, CA

Bitts
>American Well & Prospecting Co., Corsicana, TX
>Beaumont Iron Works, Beaumont, TX
>Dibert, Bancroft & Ross Co., Ltd., New Orleans, LA

Blocks

>   Boston & Lockport Block Co., Boston, MA
>   W.H. McMillans' Sons, New York, NY
>   Henry Stewart & Co., Philadelphia, PA
>   Western Block Co., Lockport, NY

Boilers

>   The Babcock & Wilcox Co., New York, NY
>   Combustion Engineering Co., New York, NY
>   Edge Moor Iron Works, Edge Moor, DE
>   Foster Wheeler Corp., New York, NY
>   Puget Sound Machinery Depot, Seattle, WA
>   Staples Engineering Co., Houston, TX
>   Henry Vogt Machine Co., Louisville, KY
>   Western Pipe & Steel Co., San Francisco, CA
>   Wickes Boiler Co., Saginaw, MI

Bolts

>   Hubbard and Co., Oakland, CA
>   Oliver Iron and Steel Corp., Pittsburgh, PA

Booms

>   Berkeley Steel Construction Co., Inc., Berkeley, CA
>   Bethlehem Steel Co., Bethlehem, PA
>   Enterprise Wheel & Car Corp., Bristol, TN
>   National Tube Co., Pittsburgh, PA
>   North American Iron & Steel Co., Inc. Brooklyn, NY
>   Portland Spar Co., Portland OR

Bulkheads, Expanded Metal

>   Consolidated Expanded Metal Companies, Wheeling, WV
>   Expanded Metal Engineering Co., New York, NY

Buoyant Apparatus

>   Colvin-Slocum Boats, Inc., New York, NY

Canvas

Ames, Harris, Neville Co., San Francisco, CA
Brooks Tarpaulin Co., Inc., New Orleans, LA
Foster Manufacturing Co., Framingham, MA
Harbor Sailmakers, Wilmington, CA
W. E. Palmer Co., Boston, MA

Chain

American Chain & Cable Co., Inc., American Chain
Division, New York, NY
Cleveland Chain & Manufacturing Co., Cleveland, OH
The Hodell Chain Co., Cleveland, OH
The McKay Co., York, PA
Portland Chain Manufacturing Co., Portland, OR
Round California Chain Corp., Ltd., South San
Francisco, CA
S. G. Taylor Chain Co., Hammond, IN

Chain, Anchor

Baldt Anchor Chain & Forge Co., Chester, PA
National Malleable & Steel Castings Co., Cleveland, OH

Chocks

Alloy Steel & Metals Co., Los Angeles, CA
American Well & Prospecting Co., Corsicana, TX
Dedman Foundry & Machine Co., Houston, TX
Electric Steel Foundry Co., Portland, OR
Enterprise Wheel & Car Corp., Bristol, TN
Texas Electric Steel Casting Co., Houston, TX
Vulcan Steel Foundry Co., Oakland, CA

Circuit Breakers

I-T-E Circuit Breaker Co., Philadelphia, PA

Communication Equipment

Henschel Corp., Amesbury, MA

Compass Platforms
>   Chicago Hardware Foundry Co., Chicago, IL

Compasses
>   Kelvin & Wilfred O. White Co., Boston, MA

Condensers
>   Condenser Service & Engineering Co., Hoboken, NJ
>   Foster Wheeler Corp., New York, NY
>   Heat Transfer Products Inc., New York, NY
>   M.W. Kellogg Co., Jersey City, NJ
>   Struthers-Wells, Warren, PA
>   The Turl Iron and Car Co., Newburgh, NY
>   Worthington Pump & Machinery Corp., Harrison, NJ

Conduit
>   Graybar Electric Co., Inc., New York, NY

Convectors
>   The Trane Co., LaCrosse, WI

Copper Sheets and Tubing
>   American Brass Co., Waterbury, CT
>   C.G. Hussey & Co., Pittsburgh, PA
>   New Haven Copper Co., Seymour, CT

Crow's Nests
>   American Machinery Corp., Orlando, FL
>   J.L. Austin Sheet Metal Works, Portland, OR

Davits
>   Welin Davit and Boat Corporation, Perth Amboy, NJ

Deck Covering
>   National Tile & Marble Corp., New York, NY
>   William Lee Co., San Francisco, CA
>   Selby, Battersby & Co., Philadelphia, PA

Deck Plates
    Richmond Foundry & Manufacturing Co., Richmond, VA

Desuperheaters
    Dri-Steam Products, Inc., New York, NY

Doors
    Commercial Shearing & Stamping Co., Youngstown, OH
    Heintz Manufacturing Co., Philadelphia, PA
    Morton Manufacturing Co., Chicago, IL

Engine Cylinders
    Cooper-Bessemer Corp., Mt. Vernon, OH

Engines
    Alabama Marine Engine Co., Birmingham, AL
    American Ship Building Co., Cleveland, OH
    Clark Bros. Co., Inc., Olean, NY
    Ellicott Machine Corp., Baltimore, MD
    The Fiber & Stowell Co., Milwaukee, WI
    General Machinery Corp., Hamilton, OH
    Joshua Hendy Iron Works, San Francisco, CA
    National Transit Pump & Machine Co., Oil City, PA
    Toledo Shipbuilding Co., Toledo, OH
    Willamette Iron and Steel Corp., Portland, OR
    Worthington Pump & Machinery Corp., Harrison, NJ

Engines, Auxiliary
    B.F. Sturtevant Co., Boston, MA

Engines, Turning
    Ready Machine Tool and Die Co., Inc. Connersville, IN

Evaporators
    Davis Engineering Corp., Elizabeth, NJ
    Heat Transfer Products, Inc., New York, NY

Struthers-Wells, Warren, PA
The Turl Iron and Car Co., Inc., Newburgh, NY

Fairwaters
American Manganese Bronze Co., Philadelphia, PA
Cramp Brass & Iron Foundries, Philadelphia, PA
Doran Co., Seattle, WA

Fathometer Equipment
Bludworth, Inc. New York, NY
Submarine Signal Co., Boston, MA

Fire Buckets
Crunden-Martin Manufacturing Co., New York, NY

Fire Extinguishers
Walter Kidde & Co., New York, NY

Fire Extinquishers, Portable
The General Detroit Corp., Detroit, MI

Fittings
Acme Brass Foundry, San Francisco, CA
Alamo Iron Works, San Antonio, TX
Alhambra Foundry Co., Ltd., Alhambra, CA
W.D. Allen Manufacturing Co., Chicago, IL
American Chain & Cable Co., American Chain Division,
     New York, NY
J.B. Astell & Co., New York, NY
Atlas Brass Foundry, Inc., Los Angeles, CA
Barco Manufacturing Co., Chicago, IL
By Products Steel Corp., Coatesville, PA
Central Forging Co., Catawissa, PA
The Cosgrave Corp., Baltimore, MD
Crane Co., Chicago, IL
Culbert Pipe & Fittings Co., Jersey City, NJ
Davidson Manufacturing Co., Los Angeles, CA

Detroit Brass & Malleable Works, Detroit, MI
Electric Steel Foundry Co., Portland, OR
The Fairbanks Co., New York, NY
The Farnan Co., Cleveland, OH
Flori Pipe Co., St. Louis, MO
Grinnell Co., Inc., Providence, RI
Gustin Bacon Manufacturing Co., Kansas City, MO
Harrisburg Steel Corp., Harrisburg, PA
Houston Pipe & Steel Co., Houston, TX
Illinois Malleable Iron Co., Chicago, IL
Imperial Brass Manufacturing Co., Chicago, IL
Chas. S. James Co., San Francisco, CA
Jefferson Union Co., Lexington, MA
Johnson Pump Co., Los Angeles, CA
Kingwell Bros., Ltd., San Francisco, CA
Lacy Manufacturing Co., Los Angeles, CA
Lee Brothers Foundry Co., Anniston, TX
Lenape Hydraulic Pressing & Forging Co., West Chester,
    PA
Link-Belt Co., Chicago, IL
Los Angeles Steel Castings Co., Los Angeles, CA
Lovell-Dressel Co., Inc., Arlington, NJ
McGowen-Lyons Hardware & Supply Co., Mobile, Al.
Mendell Electric Manufacturing Co., Inc., New Bedford,
    MA
Metal Fabricators, Inc., New York, NY
Metropolitan Electric Manufacturing Co., Long Island
    City, NY
Midwest Piping & Supply Co., St. Louis, MO
Newman Bros., Inc., Cincinnati, OH
Olympic Foundry Co., Seattle, WA
Lloyd E. Oncal, Jersey City, NJ
Pacific Body Rebuilders, Portland, OR
Parr Electric Co., Newark, NJ
Patterson Plumbing Supply Co., New Orleans, LA
Peck Spring Co., Plainville, CT
Peden Iron & Steel Co., Houston, TX

Phoenix Brass Fittings Corp., Irvington, NJ
Prier Brass Manufacturing Co., Kansas City, MO
Seattle Brass Co., Seattle, WA
Security Engineering Co., New York, NY
Semler Co., Jeannette, PA
H.B. Sherman Manufacturing Co., Battle Creek, MI
Skookum Co., Portland, OR
Standard Brass & Manufacturing Co., Port Arthur, TX
Chas. C. Steward Machine Co., Birmingham, AL
Taylor Forge & Pipe Works, Chicago, IL
Topping Bros., New York, NY
Tube-Turns, Inc. Louisville, KY
U.S. Pipe Bending Co., San Francisco, CA
Upson-Walton Co., Cleveland, OH
Valley Steel Products Co., St. Louis, MO
Van Brunt Electric Manufacturing Co., Brooklyn, NY
Victualic Co. of America, New York, NY
Walsh-Holyoke Steam Boiler Works, Inc., Holyoke, MA
Warren Foundry & Pipe Corp., Phillipsburg, NJ
The Watson-Stillman Co., Roselle, NJ
Wm. E. Williams, New York, NY
E. J. Willis Co., New York, NY

Floodlights
General Electric Co., Schenectady, NY

Funnels[2]
Boyle Manufacturing Co., Los Angeles, CA
Butler Manufacturing Co., Kansas City, MO

Furniture
Geo. H. Buckler, Portland, OR
Hopeman Bros., Inc., New York, NY
John C. Knipp & Sons, Baltimore, MD
W. & J. Sloane Manufacturing Co., New York, NY

---

[2] The ship's smokestack is technically referred to as a funnel.

Steven Sash & Door Co., San Antonio, TX
Western Hardwood Lumber Co., Los Angeles, CA

Gages
Belnap Manufacturing Co., Bridgeport, CT
Energy Control Co., New York, NY
James P. Marsh Corp., Chicago, IL
Penberthy Injector Co., Detroit, MI
Pneumercator Co., Inc., NY
Reliance Gauge Column Co., Cleveland, OH

Galley Equipment
Bastian-Blessing Co., Chicago, IL
Dohrmann Hotel Supply Co, San Francisco, CA
Marlboro Wire Goods Co., Marlboro, MA
L.A. Young Spring & Wire Corp., Detroit, MI

Galley Ranges
Malleable Steel Range Manufacturing Co., South Bend, IN
John Van Range Co., Cincinnati, OH

Gaskets
Garlock Packing Co., New York, NY

Generators
General Electric Co., Schnectady, NY

Generator Sets
Pierce, Butler & Pierce Manufacturing Corporation, Ames
Iron Works Division, Oswego, NY
Troy Engine & Machine Co., Troy, PA

Governors, Pump
Hammel-Dahl Co., Providence, RI

Grease Extractors
Andale Co., Philadelphia, PA

Grips
>R.J. Atkinson, Inc. Brooklyn, NY
>The Harris Co., Portland, ME

Hardware
>Sargent & Co., New York, NY
>The Stanley Works, New Britain, CT

Hatches
>Birmingham Fabricating Co., Birmingham, AL
>Enterprise Wheel & Car Corp., Bristol, TN

Hawse Pipes
>Beaumont Iron Works, Beaumont, TX
>Bethlehem Steel Co., Bethlehem, PA
>Cunningham Steel Foundry, Seattle , WA
>Dibert, Bancroft & Ross Co., Ltd., New Orleans, LA
>Electric Steel Foundry Co., Portland, OR
>Enterprise Engine & Foundry Co., San Francisco, CA
>Newport News Shipbuilding and Dry Dock Co., Newport
> News, VA
>Washington Iron Works, Co., Seattle, WA

Heaters
>Davis Engineering Corp., Elizabeth, NJ
>Heat Transfer Products, Inc., New York, NY
>Richmond Engineering Co., Richmond, VA
>Southwestern Engineering Co., Los Angeles, CA
>Struthers-Well, Warren, PA
>The Turl Iron and Car Co., Inc., Newburgh, NY
>Zallea Bros. & Johnson, Wilmington, DE

Hose
>Goodall Rubber Co., Philadelphia, PA
>Goodyear Tire & Rubber Co., Milwaukee, WI
>U.S. Rubber Co., New York, NY

Hose Racks
    American Machinery Corp., Orlando, FL

Injectors
    Manning, Maxwell & Moore, Inc., Bridgeport, CT

Instruments, Portable Electric
    Westinghouse Electric & Manufacturing Co., East
        Pittsburgh, PA

Insulation, Pipe and Boiler
    Philip Carey Manufacturing Co., Cincinnati, OH

Insulators
    Porcelain Products, Findlay, OH

Joiner Work
    Geo. H. Buckler Co., Portland, OR
    Hopeman Bros., Inc., New York, NY
    John C. Knipp & Sons, Baltimore, MD
    McPhillips Manufacturing Co., Mobile, AL
    P.J. Walker Co., Los Angeles, CA
    Western Hardwood Lumber Co., Los Angeles, CA

Kettles, Steam Jacketed
    Groen Manufacturing Co., Inc., Chicago, IL

Kingposts
    American Locomotive Company, Alco Products Division,
        New York, NY
    Bethlehem Steel Co., Bethlehem, PA

Ladders and Gratings
    Thos. Devlin Manufacturing Co., Burlington, NJ
    A.J. Fritschey Corp., Brooklyn, NY
    Monarch Forge & Machine Works, Portland, OR
    Reliance Steel Products Co., McKeesport, PA

Southern Engineering Co., Charlotte, NC
Southern Ornamental Iron Works, Arlington, TX
L. Theiss & Sons Corporation, Maspeth, NY
Vulcan Rail & Construction Co., Maspeth, NY
Whaley Engineering Corp., Norfolk, VA

Lamps
Koehler Manufacturing Co., Inc., Marlboro, MA
Perkins Marine Lamp & Hardware Corp., Brooklyn, NY
Wolf Safety Lamp Co. of America, Inc., Brooklyn, NY

Lifeboats
Globe American Corp., Kokomo, IN
Imperial Lifeboat Equipment Corp., New York, NY
Neptune Boat & Davit Corp., New Orleans, LA

Life Buoys
Atlantic-Pacific Manufacturing Co., Brooklyn, NY

Life Rafts
C.C. Galbraith & Son, New York, NY

Lifting Gears
Lord & Burnham Co., Irvington, NY
National Greenhouse Manufacturing Co., Pana, IL
Warner Machine Co., Passaic, NJ

Lighting Fixtures
Beranck & Erwin, Los Angeles, CA
Dayton Manufacturing Co., Dayton, OH
Russell & Stoll Co., New York, NY
Sterling Bronze Co., Long Island City, NY

Lighting Panels
Electric Switchboard Co., New York, NY
General Electric Supply Corp., Bridgeport, CT
Kinney Electrical Manufacturing Co., Chicago, IL

Lockers

> Republic Steel Corp., Berger Manufacturing Division, Canton, OH
> Falstrom Co., Passaic, NJ
> Pacific Gas Radiator, Huntington Park, CA

Locks

> Independent Lock Co., Fitchburg, MA
> Norwalk Lock Co., New York, NY
> Slaymaker Lock Co., Lancaster, PA
> Wilson Bohannon Co., Marion, OH

Log Desk

> Globe-Wernicke Co., Cincinnati, OH

Manhole Guard Plates

> Babcock-Davis Corp., Boston, MA
> Bethlehem Steel Co., Bethlehem, PA
> California Cornice, Steel & Supply Corp., Los Angeles, CA

Manifolds

> H. Belfield Co., Philadelphia, PA
> Homestead Valve Manufacturing Co., Coraopolis, PA
> Ludlow Valve Co., New York, NY
> National Radiator Co., Johnston, PA
> Warren, Killion & Clark, NY

Masts

> American Chain & Cable Co., Inc., American Chain Division, New York, NY
> American Locomotive Co., Alco Products Division, New York, NY
> Bethlehem Steel Co., Bethlehem, PA

Mitre Gears

Foote Bro. Gear & Machine Corp., Chicago, Il
Western Gear Works, San Francisco, CA

Motors, Electric
Westinghouse Electric & Manufacturing Co., East
Pittsburgh, IL

Name Plates
American Name Plate & Manufacturing Co., Chicago, IL
Colonial Brass Co., Middleboro, MA
Etched Products Corp., Long Island City, NY
L. P. Grammes & Sons, Inc., Allentown, PA
Kaag, Inc., Los Angeles, CA
Kennedy Name Plate Co., Los Angeles, CA
United States Bronze Sign Co., New York, NY

Nuts and Bolts
Milton Manufacturing Co., Milton, PA
Oliver Iron and Steel Corp., Pittsburgh, PA

Packing, Metallic
C. Lee Cook Manufacturing Co., Louisville, KY

Paint Equipment
Western Block Co., Lockport, NY
Wyatt Metal & Boiler Works, Houston, TX

Pipe, Anchor Chain
Cornell & Underhill, Inc., New York, NY

Pipe, Brass and Copper
Bridgeport Brass Co., Bridgeport, CT
Chase Brass & Copper Co., Waterbury, CT
National Copper & Smelting Co., Cleveland, OH
Revere Copper & Brass, Inc., New York, NY

Pipe, Mooring

Beaumont Iron Works, Beaumont, TX
National Erie Corp., Erie, PA
Texas Electric Steel Casting Co., Houston, TX
Warman Steel Casting Co., Los Angeles, CA

Pipe, Steel

Albert Pipe Supply Co., Inc., Brooklyn, NY
Albro Metal Products Co., Bronx, NY
J. B. Astell & Co., New York, NY
Bethlehem Steel Co., Bethlehem, PA
Crane Co., Chicago, IL
Ducomnun Metals & Supply Co., Los Angeles, CA
Globe Steel Tube Co., Milwaukee, WI
Hajoca Brass Works, Philadelphia, PA
Jones & Laughlin Steel Corp., Pittsburgh, PA
George E. Keenan Co., Bayonne, NJ
National Tube Co., Pittsburgh, PA
Noland Co., Newport News, VA
North American Iron & Steel Co., Inc., Brooklyn, NY
South Chester Tube Co., Chester, PA
Spang, Chalfant & Co., Inc., Pittsburgh, PA
Youngstown Sheet & Tube Co., Youngstown, OH

Pipe, Wrought Iron

A. M. Byers Co., Pittsburgh, PA

Piston Rings

Kearfott Engineering Co., New York, NY

Plumbing Fixtures

American Radiator & Standard Sanitary Corp., Pittsburgh, PA
Crane Co., Chicago, IL

Propeller Shaft Sleeves

Sandusky Foundry & Machine Co., Sandusky, OH
Shenango-Penn Mold Co., Dover, OH

Propellers
>American Manganese Bronze Co., Philadelphia, PA
>Bethlehem Steel Co., Bethlehem, PA
>Cramp Brass & Iron Foundries, Philadelphia, PA
>Doran Co., Seattle, WA
>Koppers Co., Bartlett Hayward Division, Baltimore, MD
>Newport News Shipbuilding and Dry Dock Co., Newport
>News, VA

Pump Liners
>Sandusky Foundry & Machine Co., Sandusky, OH

Pumps
>W. B. Conner Engineering Corp., New York, NY
>Dean Brothers Pumps, Inc., Indianapolis, IN
>The Deming Co., Salem, OH
>Duro Co., Dayton, OH
>Frederick Iron & Steel Co., Frederick, MD
>Goulds Pumps, Inc., Seneca Falls, NY
>Morris Machine Works, Baldwinsville, NY
>The F. E. Myers & Bro, Co., Ashland, OR
>Worthington Pump & Machinery Corp., Harrison, NJ

Pyrometers
>The Brown Instrument Co., Philadelphia, PA

Radiators
>U.S. Radiator Co., Maspeth, NY

Radio Direction Finders
>Federal Telegraph Co., Newark, NJ

Reels
>Continental Bridge Co., Chicago, IL
>Lookout Boiler & Manufacturing Co., Chattanooga, TN
>Wirt & Knox Manufacturing Co., Philadelphia, PA

Refrigerating Equipment
>Carrier Corp., New York, NY
>Eastern Cold Storage Insulation Co., New York, NY
>York Ice Machine Corp., York, PA

Regulators, Pressure
>Mason-Neilan Regulator Co., Boston, MA

Rescue Breathing Apparatus
>Mine Safety Appliances Co., Pittsburgh, PA

Rigging Fittings
>The Thomas Laughlin Co., Portland, ME
>Main Steel, Inc., South Portland, ME
>Arthur J. O'Leary & Son Co., Chicago, IL
>Texas Electric Steel Casting Co., Houston, TX
>L. Theiss & Sons Co., Maspeth, NY
>Wilcox Crittenden & Co., Inc., Middletown, CT

Rope, Cotton
>Seaboard Twine & Cordage Co., New York, NY

Rope, Manila
>Plymouth Cordage Co., Plymouth, MA
>Tubbs Cordage Co., San Francisco, CA

Rope, Wire
>American Steel & Wire Co., New York, NY
>Bethlehem Steel Co., Bethlehem, PA
>Pittsburgh Steel Co., Pittsburgh, PA

Rudder Fittings
>American Well & Prospecting Co., Corsicana, TX
>International-Stacey Corp., Columbus, OH
>Oil Center Tool Co., Houston, TX
>Premier Gear & Machine Works, Portland, OR

Schmitt Steel Co., Portland, OR
South Portland Shipbuilding Corp., Portland, ME
Wilson Manufacturing Co., Inc., Wichita Falls, TX

Rudders
Bethlehem Steel Co., Bethlehem, PA

Salinity Indicators
McNab of Bridgeport, Inc., Bridgeport, CT
The Instrument Laboratory, Inc., Seattle, WA

Searchlights
Crouse-Hinds Co., New York, NY

Separators
Wright-Austin Co., Detroit, MI

Shafting
Allis-Chalmers Manufacturing Co., Milwaukee, WI
American Forge Co., Berkeley, CA
Arms-Franklin Corp., Franklin, PA
Bethlehem Steel Co., Bethlehem, PA
Bevis Machine Co., Middletown, OH
Black Clawson Co., Hamilton, OH
Broadfoot Iron Works, Wilmington, NC
Camden Forge Co., Camden, NJ
Carnegie-Illinois Steel Corp., Pittsburgh, PA
Erie Forge Co., Erie, PA
International Derrick & Equipment Co., Beaumont, TX
Isaacson Iron Works Co., Seattle, WA
E. D. Jones & Sons Co., Pittsfield, MA
Pennsylvania Forge Corp., Philadelphia, PA
Pusey & Jones Corp., Wilmington, DE
Rice Barton Corp., Worcester, MA
South Portland Shipbuilding Corp., Portland, ME
Standard Steel Works, New York, NY
Sheets, Copper

C. G. Hussey & Co., Pittsburgh, PA
New Haven Copper Co., Seymour, CT
Revere Copper & Brass, Inc., New York, NY
Standard Brass & Manufacturing Co., Port Arthur, TX
Wolverine Tube Co., Detroit, MI

Shipyards

Alabama Dry Dock & Shipbuilding Co., Mobile, AL
W. A. Bechtel Co., San Francisco, CA
Bethlehem-Fairfield Shipyard, Inc., Baltimore, MD
Brunswick Marine Construction Corp., Brunswick, GA
California Shipbuilding Corp., Wilmington, CA
Delta Shipbuilding Co., Inc., New Orleans, LA
Higgins Industries, Inc., New Orleans, LA
Houston Shipbuilding Co., Houston, TX
Kaiser Co., Inc., Vancouver, WA
North Carolina Shipbuilding Co., Wilmington, NC
Oregon Shipbuilding Co., Portland, OR
Permanente Metals Corp., Richmond, CA
Rheem Manufacturing Co., Providence, RI
Richmond Shipbuilding Corp., Richmond, CA
St. John's River Shipbuilding Co., Jacksonville, FL
Southeastern Shipbuilding Corp., Inc., Savannah, GA
South Portland Shipbuilding Corp., South Portland, ME
Todd-Bath Iron Shipbuilding Corp., South Portland, ME

Sounding Machines

John E. Hand & Sons Co., Philadelphia, PA

Sounding Rods and Rules

The Lufkin Rule Co., Saginaw, MI
Pacific Marine Supply Co., Seattle, WA
J.C. Petterson Co., Los Angeles, CA
L. Theiss & Sons, Corp., Maspeth, NY

Stanchions

Hawley Forge & Manufacturing Co., San Francisco, CA
Mulford Manufacturing Co., Los Angeles, CA
Redman Bros., Beaumont, TX
Silver Engineering Works, Inc., Denver, CO

Steel, Hull
Alan Wood Steel Co., Conshohocken, PA
Bethlehem Steel Co., Bethlehem, PA
Carnegie-Illinois Steel Corp., Pittsburgh, PA
Colorado Fuel & Iron Corp., Denver, CO
Granite City Steel Co., Granite City, IL
Inland Steel Co., Chicago, IL
Jones & Laughlin Steel Corp., Pittsburgh, PA
Lukens Steel Co., Coatesville, PA
Otis Steel Co., Cleveland, OH
Phoenix Iron Co., Phoenixville, PA
Republic Steel Corp., Cleveland, OH
Sheffield Steel Corp., Kansas City, MO
Truscon Steel Co., Youngstown, OH
Weirton Steel Co., Weirton, WV
Worth Steel Co., Claymont, DE

Steel, Sheets
Armco Railroad Sales Co., Inc., Middletown, OH
Carnegie-Illinois Steel Corp., Pittsburgh, PA
Wheeling Steel Corp., Wheeling, WV

Steering Columns
The Dake Engine Co., Grand Haven, MI
Oregon Brass Works, Portland, OR

Steering Gear
Arms-Franklin Corp., Franklin, PA
Sumner Iron Works, Everett, WA
Webster-Brinkley Co., Seattle, WA

Stems

Bethlehem Steel Co., Bethlehem, PA
Newport News Shipbuilding and Dry Dock Co., Newport
News, VA

Stern Frames
Bethlehem Steel Co., Bethlehem, PA
Columbia Steel Co., San Francisco, CA
Penn Steel Castings Co., Chester, PA

Stern Tube Bushings
Sandusky Foundry & Machine Co., Sandusky, OH

Stern Tubes
Dodge Manufacturing Co., Mishawaka, IN
Helser Machine and Marine Works, Inc., Portland, OR
South Portland Shipbuilding Corp., Portland, ME
Union Machine Co., San Francisco, CA
Vulcan Iron Works Co., Denver, CO

Strainers
American Bronze Co., Chicago, IL
The Coen Co., San Francisco, CA
Henry Valve Co., Chicago, IL
Johnson-Chapman Co., Chicago, IL
Nadler Foundry & Machine Co., Inc., New York, NY
Purolator Products, Inc., Newark, NJ
Warren, Killion & Clark, New York, NY
Yarnall-Waring Co., Philadelphia, PA

Studs
Oliver Iron and Steel Corp., Pittsburgh, PA

Stuffing Boxes
Albro Metal Products Co., Bronx, NY
Alamo Iron Works, San Antonio, TX
Dodge Manufacturing Co., Mishwaka, IN
Enterprise Wheel & Car Corp., Bristol, TN

Helser Machine and Marine Works, Inc., Portland, OR
Thomas F. McGann & Sons, Boston, MA
South Portland Shipbuilding Corp., Portland, ME
Union Machine Co., San Francisco, CA
Vulcan Iron Works Co., Denver, CO
Wilson Manufacturing Co., Inc., Wichita Falls, TX
Z.A. Zurn Manufacturing Co., Erie, PA

Switchboards
Electric Service Control, Inc., Newark, NJ
Plainville Electric Products Co., Plainville, CT

Switches
Betts & Betts Corporation, New York, NY
Cutler-Hammer, Inc., Milwaukee, WI

Tanks
The Bigelow Co., New Haven, CT
Graver Tank & Manufacturing Co., East Chicago, IN
Hunt Tool Co., Houston, TX
Pennsylvania Range Boiler Corp., Philadelphia, PA
Richmond Engineering Co., Richmond, VA
Warren Brothers Roads Co., Cambridge, MA
D. D. Wessels & Sons Co., Detroit, MI

Tape, Lagging
Gustin Bacon Manufacturing co., Kansas City, MO
Owens-Corning Fiberglas Corp., New York, NY

Telemotors
Arms-Franklin Corp., Franklin, PA
Lidgerwood Manufacturing Co., Elizabeth, NJ

Telegraphs, Mechanical
Bendix Aviation Corp., Marine Division, New York, NY
Jos. Harper & Son, Inc., New York, NY
Telephones, Sound Powered

American Automatic Electric Sales Co., New York, NY
Henschel Corp., Amesbury, MA

Terminal Strips
Burndy Engineering Co., Inc., New York, NY

Thermometers
C. J. Tagliabue Manufacturing Co., Brooklyn, NY
Taylor Instrument Companies, Rochester, NY

Tools, Machinists
The Lufkin Rule Co., Saginaw, MI

Torch Rods
Allen & Son, San Bernardino, CA
J.P. Hanson & Son, New York, NY

Traps, Steam
The Trane Co., LaCrosse, WI
Yarnall-Waring Co., Philadelphia, PA

Trick Wheel Stand
Arms-Franklin Corp., Franklin, PA

Trolleys
Conco Engineering Works, Mendota, IL

Tube Cleaners
Thos. C. Wilson, Inc., Long Island City, NY

Universal Joints
Bellingham Iron Works, Inc., South Bellingham, WA
Blood Brothers Machine Co., Allegan, MI
Brooks Equipment Corp., New York, NY
Earle Gear & Machine Co., Philadelphia, PA
Foote Gear Works, Chicago, Il
New England Auto Products Co., Pottstown, PA

Valves

    Albro Metal Products, Bronx, NY

    Alpha Steam Specialty Co., New York, NY

    American Chain & Cable Co., Reading-Pratt & Cady
        Division, Bridgeport, CT

    Chapman Valve Manufacturing Co., Indian Orchard, MA

    Columbia Machine Works, Inc., San Francisco, CA

    Crane Co., Chicago, IL

    Darling Valve & Manufacturing Co., Williamsport, PA

    Detroit Lubricator Co., Detroit, MI

    The Edward Valve & Manufacturing Co., Inc., East
        Chicago, IN

    Everlasting Valve Co., Jersey City, NJ

    The Fairbanks Co., New York, NY

    Fulton Sylphon Co., Knoxville, TN

    Henry Valve Co., Chicago, IL

    Jenkins Bros., New York, NY

    Kerotest Manufacturing Co., Pittsburgh, PA

    Kieley & Mueller, Inc., New York, NY

    Lawler Automatic Controls, Inc., Mt. Vernon, NY

    Le Valley, McLeod & Kinkaid, Co., Elmira, NY

    J.E. Lonergan Co., Philadelphia, PA

    The Lunkenheimer Co., Cincinnati, OH

    Manning, Maxwell & Moore, Inc., Bridgeport, CT

    Mason-NeiLan Regulator Co., Boston, MA

    The McAlear Mfg. Co., Chicago, IL

    A.Y., McDonald Mfg. Co., Dubuque, IA

    Ohio Injector Co., Wadsworth, OH

    Okadee Co., Chicago, IL

    Pittsburgh Valve & Fittings Co., Barberton, OH

    The Wm. Powell Co., Chicago, IL

    Price Pfister Brass Manufacturing Co., Inc., Los
        Angeles, CA

    Reed Roller Bit Co., Houston, TX

    Rockford Brass Works, Rockford, IL

Ruggles-Klingeman Manufacturing Co., Salem, MA
Star Brass Manufacturing Co., Boston, MA
Stockhan Pipe Fittings Co., Birmingham, Al.
Robert H. Wager, New York, NY
Walworth, Inc., New York, NY
Williams & Wells Co., New York, NY

Ventilators
American Casting Co., Birmingham, AL
Rudman & Scofield, New York, NY

Vises
R. J. Atkinson, Inc., Brooklyn, NY

Winches
American Hoist & Derrick Co., St. Paul, MN
Helser Machine and Marine Works, Inc., Portland, OR
Hesse-Ersted Iron Works, Portland, OR
McGann Manufacturing Co., Inc., York, PA
W. A. Riddell Co., Bucyrus, OH

Windlasses
American Hoist & Derrick Co., St. Paul, MN
Arms-Franklin Corp., Franklin, PA
Hesse-Ersted Iron Works, Portland, OR
Street Bros. Machine Co., Chattanooga, TN
Sumner Iron Works, Everett, WA

Wire fabric
The Gilbert & Bennett Manufacturing Co., Georgetown, CT
Wickwire Spencer Steel Co., New York, NY

Wire and Cables, Electric
General Cable Corp., New York, NY
Okonite Co., Passaic, NJ
Simplex Wire & Cable Co., Cambridge, MA
Work Benches

Falstrom Co., Passaic, NJ

Wrenches
   Allen & Son, San Bernardino, CA
   Owatonna Tool Co., Owatonna, MI
   Trojan Metal Works, New York, NY

APPENDIX C

THE VOYAGES OF THE
SS JEREMIAH O'BRIEN

Voyage 1 -- July 10, 1943 to September 11, 1943

Ports of Call: Portland, Maine
                           Boston, Massachusetts
                           Halifax, Nova Scotia
                           Aultbea, Loch Ewe, Scotland
                           Methil, Firth of Forth, Scotland
                           London, England
                           Southend, England
                           Methil, Firth of Forth, Scotland
                           Aultbea, Loch Ewe, Scotland
                           Gourock, Firth of Clyde, Scotland
                           New York, New York

Crew:[1]

Oscar Southerland	Master
Charles A. Christenson	Chief Officer
Frank Pellegrino	2nd Officer
Oliver Morgan	3rd Officer
Robert C. Morgan	Radio Operator
Thomas J. Ender	Senior Purser
Theodore Samaras	Carpenter
John C. Gird	Boatswain (Bosun)
Mario Di Lorenzo	AB (Able-Bodied seaman)
Leo Doyle	AB
Charles McCarthy	AB
William Fallon	AB
Manuel Dias, Jr.	AB
Thomas Sullivan	AB
Sebastian De Manuel	OS (Ordinary Seaman)
Donald Corbett	OS
Signumd Rudnitsky	AB
Coleman Schneider	Deck Cadet
Richardson Montgomery	Chief Engineer
William J. Shields	First Asssistant Engineer
Donald Morrison	Second Assistant Engineer
Leo G. Halpin	Third Assistant Engineer
Thomas J. Gill	Junior Engineer
Herman C. Bryce	Oiler
Frank Smith	Oiler
William J. McCarthy	Oiler
Lester C. Card	FWT (Fireman WaterTender)
Timothy E. Harrington	FWT
Joseph E. Charleton	FWT
Tom C. Hall	Wiper
Richard Lannan	Wiper
James D'Andrea	Engine Cadet

---

[1] Because the ship made a coastwise voyage and then signed foreign articles there are additional crew listed, i.e. Two Chief Stewards, Two Chief Cooks, and so on. This reflects changes in crew after the ship reached Boston.

William C. Austin	Oiler
Ricardo Briones Zapata	Chief Steward
L. F. Fillmore	Chief Cook
Ormon T. Bibbs	Second Cook
Donald T. Vaughan	Third Cook
Vincenzo Carista	Messman
Nicholas Carista	Messman
Rosario Carista	Crew Messman
Francis McCormick	OS
Lam Spark	Chief Cook
Tee Kai	Second Cook
Ow Tong Gee	Third Cook
Lee Ah Nyok	Utility
Albert K. Bernardo	Chief Steward
Edmond Botelho	Utility
Joseph J. Brown	Utility
Louis Lambert	Utility
Vincenzo Patrinzi	AB
Joseph Cadogan	AB
Frederick C. Warren	FWT
John Float	Wiper

Armed Guard:

Charles L. Foote	Ensign
Robert Nelson Caron	Seaman 1/c
Herbert Emmett Landrum	Coxswain
James Francis Godsell	Gunner's Mate 3/c
Morgan Casto Williams	Gunner's Mate 3/c
Charles Robert Garbett	Seaman 3/c
Harmon Eugene Morick	Radioman 3/c
Lewis Edwin Hudson	Radioman 3/c
Howard Leon Campbell	Seaman 1/c
William James Chisolm	Seaman 1/c
Armando Frank Felci	Seaman 1/c
Philip Frederick Gould	Seaman 1/c
Thomas W. Hodgson, Jr.	Seaman 1/c

Kenneth Lloyd Holsapple	Seaman 1/c
John Joseph Hunt	Seaman 1/c
Henry Douglas Pinkerton	Seaman 1/c
Georges Jack Serra	Seaman 1/c
Jerome Edgar Shaw	Seaman 1/c
Edward Jardine Smedley, Jr.	Seaman 1/c
Raymond Smith	Seaman 1/c
Ludwig Joseph Stojek	Seaman 1/c
Alvis Franklin Straughan	Seaman 1/c
Gildo Ralph Surdi	Seaman 1/c
Clarence Swisher	Seaman 1/c
Edward Anthony Sznukowski	Seaman 1/c
Charles Talyai	Seaman 1/c
James Carwile Thomas	Seaman 1/c
Herbert Leslie Tyler	Seaman 1/c

Voyage 2 -- September 14, 1943 to November 3, 1943

Ports of Call: New York, New York
                                        Jersey City, New Jersey
                                        Liverpool, England
                                        New York, New York

Crew:[2]

Oscar Southerland	Master
Charles Christenson	Chief Officer
Frank Pellegrino	Second Officer
Oliver Morgan	Third Officer
Thomas J. Ender	Purser
Thoedore Samaras	Carpenter
Donald Corbett	AB
Joseph Cadogen	AB
Donald L. Moors	AB
Francis McCormick	OS
Coleman Schneider	Deck Cadet
Richardson Montgomery	Chief Engineer
James D'Andrea	Engine Cadet
Lee Ah Yok	Third Cook

Armed Guard:

Charles L. Foote	Ensign
Herbert Emmett Landrum	Coxswain
James Francis Goodsell	Gunner's Mate 3/c
Morgan Casto Williams	Gunner's Mate 3/c
Charles Robert Garbett	Seaman 3/c
Harmon Eugene Morick	Radioman 3/c
Lewis Edwin Hudson	Radioman 3/c

---

[2] Because the official log for voyage #2 is not available there is no source of merchant crew names for voyage #2. The names listed are those who made voyages 1 and 3 and logically would have been on voyage 2 also.

Howard Leon Campbell	Seaman 1/c
William James Chisolm	Seaman 1/c
Armando Frank Felci	Seaman 1/c
Philip Frederick Gould	Seaman 1/c
Thomas W. Hodgson, Jr.	Seaman 1/c
Kenneth Lloyd Holsapple	Seaman 1/c
John Joseph Hunt	Seaman 1/c
Georges Jack Serra	Seaman 1/c
Jerome Edgar Shaw	Seaman 1/c
Edward Jardine Smedley, Jr.	Seaman 1/c
Raymond Smith	Seaman 1/c
Ludwig Joseph Stojek	Seaman 1/c
Alvis Franklin Straughan	Seaman 1/c
Gildo Ralph Surdi	Seaman 1/c
Clarence Swisher	Seaman 1/c
Edward Anthony Sznukowski	Seaman 1/c
Charles Talyai	Seaman 1/c
James Carwile Thomas	Seaman 1/c
Herbert Leslie Tyler	Seaman 1/c
Robert Nelson Caron	Seaman 1/c

Joined in New York on September 13, 1943:

William James Rose	Seaman 1/c
Robert Martin Howell	Seaman1/c

Voyage 3 -- November 19, 1943 to March 24, 1944

Ports of Call: New York, New York
                        Loch Ewe, Scotland
                        Methil, Firth of Forth, Scotland
                        Immingham, England
                        Methil, Firth of Forth, Scotland
                        Loch Ewe, Scotland
                        St. John, New Brunswick
                        Halifax, Nova Scotia
                        Oban, Scotland
                        Leith, Scotland
                        Loch Ewe, Scotland
                        New York, New York

Crew:

Oscar Southerland	Master
Charles Christenson	Chief Officer
Frank Pellegrino	Second Officer
Oliver Morgan	Third Officer
Robert Milby	Radio Officer
Louis Harris	Purser
Theodore Samaras	Carpenter
Alton Cook	Boatswain (Bosun)
Terry Trendell	AB (Able-Bodied Seaman)
Walter Weingaertner	AB
Sherman Valentine	AB
Donald Corbett	AB
Daniel Bron	AB
Joseph Cadogan	AB
Joseph Cioffi	OS (Ordinary Seaman)
Sebastian DeManuel	OS
Francis McCormick	OS
Coleman Schneider	Deck Cadet
Richardson Montgomery	Chief Engineer
Donald Morrison	First Assistant Engineer

Walter Whitney	Second Assistant Engineer
William Watson	Third Assistant Engineer
Carlos Pinheiro	Junior Engineer
Tom Hall	Oiler
Michael Wasko	Oiler
Clarence Bonem	Oiler
Vernon Joell	FWT (Fireman WaterTender)
Henry Ruppert	FWT
Martin Twiggs	FWT
Isaac Cuevas	Wiper
Jose Tiban	Wiper
James D'Andrea	Engine Cadet
Percy Martin	Chief Steward
Ming Wee Sung	Chief Cook
Yeu Wee Hie	Second Cook
Lee Ah Yok	Third Cook
George Quistgaard	Utility
Francis Start	Saloon Messman
Noel Cramer	Messman
Jose Dias	Utility
Dong Ah Wee	Utility
Yeo Sung Hai	Utility
Albert E. Haas	Purser
Russell J. Smith	Third Officer

Armed Guard:

Charles L. Foote	Ensign
Robert Nelson Caron	Seaman 1/c
Herbert Emmett Landrum	Coxswain
Morgan Casto Williams	Gunner's Mate 3/c
Charles Robert Garbett	Seaman 3/c
Harmon Eugene Morick	Radioman 3/c
Lewis Edwin Hudson	Radioman 3/c
Howard Leon Campbell	Seaman 1/c
William James Chisolm	Seaman 1/c
Armando Frank Felci	Seaman 1/c

Philip Frederick Gould	Seaman 1/c
Thomas W. Hodgson, Jr.	Seaman 1/c
Kenneth Lloyd Holsapple	Seaman 1/c
John Joseph Hunt	Seaman 1/c
William J. Rose	Seaman 1/c
Georges Jack Serra	Seaman 1/c
Jerome Edgar Shaw	Seaman 1/c
Edward Jardine Smedley, Jr.	Seaman 1/c
Raymond Smith	Seaman 1/c
Ludwig Joseph Stojek	Seaman 1/c
Alvis Franklin Straughan	Seaman 1/c
Gildo Ralph Surdi	Seaman 1/c
Clarence Swisher	Seaman 1/c
Charles Talyai	Seaman 1/c
James Carwile Thomas	Seaman 1/c
Herbert Leslie Tyler	Seaman 1/c

Joined in New York on November 8, 1943:

Buford Veitch Mitchell	Seaman 1/c
Edwin Lewis Williams	Seaman 1/c
Jack William Roberts	Radioman 3/c
Daniel Glendyn Bandy	Seaman 1/c
Robert Noble Mason	Seaman 1/c

Joined Halifax on January 27, 1944:

Allen R. Memhard, Jr.	Lieutenant
Alfonse Adolph De Smedt	Master

Joined in Halifax on February 6, 1944:

Joe Emmett Morris	Seaman 1/c

Voyage 4 -- March 25, 1944 to October 12, 1944.

Ports of call:		
		New York, New York
		Brooklyn, New York
		Newport, Wales
		Gourock-the-Clyde, Scotland
		Southampton, England
	1	Omaha Beachhead, Normandy
		Southampton, England
	2	Omaha Beachhead, Normandy
		Southampton, England
		Belfast, Ireland
	3	Utah Beachhead, Normandy
		Southampton, England
	4	Utah Beachhead, Normandy,
		Southampton, England
	5	Omaha Beachhead, Normandy
		Southampton, England
	6	Omaha Beachhead, Normandy
		Southampton, England
	7	Utah Beachhead, Normandy
		Southampton, England
	8	Utah Beachhead, Normandy
		Southampton, England
	9	Utah Beachhead, England
		Southampton, England
	10	Utah Beachhead, Normandy
		Southampton, England
	11	Utah Beachhead, Normandy
		Cherbourg, France
		Mumbles Point, Swansea, England
		Milford Haven, England
		New York, New York

Crew:

A. A. DeSmedt	Master
Frank Pellegrino	Chief Officer
Oliver Morgan	Second Officer
Edward Seymour	3rd Officer
Robert A. Milby	First Radio
Gerrit deWaard	Second Radio
Albert E. Haas	Purser
Thomas McGeehan	Cadet
Henry Kusel	Cadet
Theodore Samaras	Carpenter
Alton Cook	Boatswain (Bosun)
Trendell L. Terry	AB (Able-Bodied seaman)
Sherman A. Valentine	AB
Daniel Bron	AB
Donald H. Corbett	AB
Henry Klittsgaard	AB
James Rudesill	AB
Louis S. Garcia	OS (Ordinary Seaman)
Osborne P. Jones	OS
Emil Bennes	OS
Richardson Montgomery	Chief Engineer
Ludvig Lauritsen	First Assistant Engineer
Walter C. Whitney	Second Assistant Engineer
William L. Watson	3rd Assistant Engineer
Harris Wentworth	Junior Engineer
Vernon R. Joell	Oiler
Francis E. Erdmann	Oiler
Herman H. Kuber	Oiler
Martin J. Twiggs	FWT (Fireman WaterTender)
Ernest A. Ooghe	FWT
Jose C. Tibau	FWT
Hubert Miller	Wiper
Olaf M. Saxvik	Wiper
Lo Kite	Steward
Ming Wee Sung	Chief Cook

Geo Wee Hie	Second Cook
Foo Hee Song	Third Cook
Noel Cramer	Messman
John Yacynik	Messman
George M. Wray	Messman
Jose N. Dias	Utility
Dong Ah Wee	Utility
Yeo Sung Hai	Utility
Herbert Doyle	AB

Armed Guard:

Allen R. Memhard, Jr.	Lieutenant
Daniel Glendyn Bandy	Coxswain
Robert Noble Mason	Seaman 3/c
James Jones	Gunner's Mate 3/c
James Davis Potts	Gunner's Mate 3/c
Morgan Casto Williams	Gunner's Mate 3/c
Wallace James Hardin	Seaman 3/c
Joseph William Bires	Seaman 1/c
Samuel Clifton Christian	Seaman 1/c
Luther Wetzel Counts	Seaman 1/c
Stanley Morrell Cunningham	Seaman 1/c
Fred Dennison	Seaman 1/c
Alvin Leroy Huffstetler	Seaman 1/c
William Robert Gorman	Seaman 1/c
Albert Frederick Helbling	Seaman 1/c
James Lamonica	Seaman 1/c
John Thomas Murphy	Seaman 1/c
Robert Roy Pilcher	Seaman 1/c
John Paul Planeta	Seaman 1/c
Robert Jerome Robichaud	Seaman 1/c
Melvin David Rubin	Seaman 1/c
Richard Paul Savering	Seaman 1/c
Elbert Ray Sharpe	Seaman 1/c
John Edwin Sirrine	Seaman 1/c
Donald Harvey Slaight	Seaman 1/c

| Clarence Alvin Swanson | Seaman 1/c |
| Donald Oirse Weeks | Seaman 1/c |

Voyage 5 -- October 14, 1944 to December 15, 1944

Ports of call:

Hoboken, New Jersey
Cristobal, Canal Zone
Antofagasta, Chile
Callao, Peru
Balboa, Canal Zone
West Wego, Louisiana
New Orleans, Louisiana

Crew:

Arthur J. Gunderson	Master
R. H. Scott	Chief Officer
R. N. Cruickshanks	Second Officer
W. J. Ganley	Third Officer
G. J. de Waard	Radio Operator
Joao Thiago	Bosun
T. Samaras	Carpenter
Arthur Graham	AB (Able-Bodied seaman)
Trendell Terry	AB
Louis Salas	AB
Manuel Lopez	AB
Angel Targa	AB
William Roper	AB
Robert W. Glasgow	OS (Ordinary Seaman)
Cornelius Duffy	OS
Louis Larouche	OS
R. Montgomery	Chief Engineer
W. Wallace	First Assistant Engineer
Ralph Prado	Second Assistant Engineer
Carl A. Scharpf	Third Assistant Engineer
Joseph Leifken	Jr. Engineer
Richard Bush	Oiler
Paul Kemper	Oiler
V. Joell	Oiler
M. Twiggs	FWT (Fireman WaterTender)

J. Tiban	FWT
E. Ondesko	Wiper
R. Camelo	Wiper
J. H. Zoetjes	Wiper
Philip Hegarty	Ch. Steward
Tela Owens	Second Cook
Low Bow Eng	2nd Cook
Jose Dias	3rd Cook
David C. Smith	Messman
D.D. Magers	Messman
J. Esposito	Messman
Redames Arias, Jr.	Utility
W. S. Halliday	Utility
H. Wentworth	Oiler
E. A. Haney	Purser

Armed Guard:

Norman Evans Robinson	Ensign
James Joseph Doyle	Coxswain
Robert Arthur Crocker	Gunner's mate 3/c
Henry Walter Morieko	Gunner's mate 3/c
Louis Bator	Seaman 1/c
LeRoy George Bartels	Seaman 1/c
Clarence Earle Barnett	Seaman 1/c
Earl Roy Carver	Seaman 1/c
James Daniel Casey	Seaman 1/c
Charles Grant Conklin	Seaman 1/c
Orval Franklin Crumley	Seaman 1/c
Johnny McDonald Curtis	Seaman 1/c
John Wesley Davis	Seaman 1/c
Marion LaVerne Henzen	Seaman 1/c
Cleveland Joseph Hassler	Seaman 1/c
David Bicking Kennedy	Seaman 1/c
Charles Edgar Lewis	Seaman 1/c
Theodore S. Martin	Seaman 1/c
Albert Joseph Ogonowski	Seaman 1/c

George Joseph Poskie	Seaman 1/c
Joseph Peter Salandino	Seaman 1/c
Robert James Swan	Seaman 1/c
Vernon Earl Williams	Seaman 1/c
Robert Lee Wilson	Seaman 1/c
Kermit Lee Roy	Seaman 1/c
William Clayton Kuhlman	Seaman 1/c
Joseph Walker	Seaman 1/c
John R. Andrews	Seaman 1/c
Wesley R. Armour	Seaman 1/c
Louis Elmer Veatch	Seaman 1/c

Voyage 6 -- December 16, 1944 to July 10, 1945

Ports of call:	New Orleans, Louisiana
	Houston, Texas
	Balboa, Canal Zone
	Manus, Admiralty Islands
	(Seadler Harbor)
	Hollandia, New Guinea
	Tacloban, Philippine Islands
	San Jose, Philippine Islands
	Subic Bay, Philippine Islands
	Hollandia, New Guinea
	Oro Bay, New Guinea
	Hollandia, New Guinea
	Subic Bay, Philippine Islands
	San Fernando, Philippine Islands
	San Francisco, California

Crew:

Oscar J. Gundersen	Master
Arthur Antony	Chief Mate (Acting)
William Ganley	Second Mate (Acting)
John Crosby	Third Mate
Edwin Haney	Purser
Gerritt de Waard	Chief Radio Operator
John Callahan	Second Radio Operator
Merill Hubbard	Third Radio Operator
Theodore Samaras	Carpenter
William Sterling	Boatswain (Bosun)
Louis Salas	AB (Able Seaman)
Manuel Lopez	AB
Paul Stallings	AB
Spellman Patterson	AB
Vincent Sunday	AB (Acting)
Max Carman	AB (Acting)
Paul Kinesiak	OS (Ordinary Seaman)

David Daly	OS
Carroll Douglas	OS
Richardson Montgomery	Chief Engineer
John Tagert	First Assistant Engineer
John E. Torppa	Second Assistant Engineer
Roy E. Simpson	Third Assistant Engineer
Harris Wentworth	Junior Engineer
Paul Kemfer	Oiler
Clinton Lanier	Oiler
Melton Brooks	Oiler
John Wright	Oiler
Harold Anderson	FWT (Fireman WaterTender)
Louis Ordonez	FWT
Wilbert Morris	FWT/Wiper
Malcolm Louney	FWT
Jose Tiban	FWT
Billie Hemphill	Wiper
Stanislaus Wajdo	Wiper
Howard Edwards	Steward
Philip Hegarty	Chief Cook
Edward Denny	Second Cook
Charles Mestoyen	Assistant Cook
Jose Dias	Utility
John Louse	Utility
Ivan Vozquez	Utility
Carlos Mora	Utility
Emmette Thomas	Messman
Robert Surmall	Messman
Jeff Fragler	Messman
Don Vaughn	Messman
Joseph Martin	OS
Thomas Carter	Boatswain

Armed Guard:

Norman Evans Robinson	Ensign
Robert Arthur Crocker	Gunner's mate 3/c

Henry Walter Morieko	Gunner's mate 3/c
Louis Bator	Seaman 1/c
LeRoy George Bartels	Seaman 1/c
Clarence Earle Barnett	Seaman 1/c
Earl Roy Carver	Seaman 1/c
James Daniel Casey	Seaman 1/c
Orval Franklin Crumley	Seaman 1/c
Johnny McDonald Curtis	Seaman 1/c
Marion LaVerne Henzen	Seaman 1/c
Cleveland Joseph Hassler	Seaman 1/c
David Bicking Kennedy	Seaman 1/c
Theodore S. Martin	Seaman 1/c
Albert Joseph Ogonowski	Seaman 1/c
George Joseph Poskie	Seaman 1/c
Joseph Peter Salandino	Seaman 1/c
Robert James Swan	Seaman 1/c
Vernon Earl Williams	Seaman 1/c
Robert Lee Wilson	Seaman 1/c
Kermit Lee Roy	Seaman 1/c
William Clayton Kuhlman	Seaman 1/c
John R. Andrews	Seaman 1/c
Louis Elmer Veatch	Seaman 1/c

Joined May 18, 1945 at Hollandia.

Ballard Lee Howell, Sr.	Gunner's Mate 3/c
Henry H. Dent, Jr.	Seaman 1/c
Eryl B. Dickinson	Seaman 1/c

Voyage 7 -- July 11 1945 to January 17, 1946

Ports of call:

San Francisco, California
San Pedro, California
Port Darwin, Australia
Calcutta, India
Shanghai, China
Manila, Philippine Islands
Freemantle, Australia
San Francisco, California

Crew:

George Gerdes	Master
Martin C. Moen	Chief Mate
David Holmes	Second Mate
Charles R. Kent	Third Mate
Roy E. Petherbridge	Chief Radio Operator
Edward L. Hanyak	Second Radio Operator
Bruce S. Meador	Purser/Pharmacist
Robert Gallagher	Boatswain (Bosun)
Carlos Q. Kellner	Carpenter
Frank Novick	AB (Able Seaman)
Phillip J. Brox	AB
Robert J. Pardy	AB
George Cicic	AB
William C. Coats	AB (Acting)
Roy Anderson	AB (Acting)
Pedro A. Delgado	OS (Ordinary Seaman)
Layton E. Branson	OS
Oscar D. Pearson	OS
Carl B. Weyls	Chief Engineer
George A. Swanson	First Assistant Engineer
Donald E. Kranich	Second Assistant Engineer
Charles N. McGrinty	Third Assistant Engineer
Theodore J. Pennington	Deck Engineer
Thomas L. Schinskey	Oiler

Robert H. Anderson	Oiler
Harold W. Wolfe	Oiler
Manuel Taibo	FWT (Fireman WaterTender)
Charles E Hord	FWT
Howard W. Fogle	FWT
Albert Giaccki, Jr.	Wiper
Edward A. Burtch	Wiper
Juanito P. Lazano	Steward
Joseph Candias	Chief Cook
Robert C. Flowers	Second Cook and Baker
Jose D. N. Dias	Third Cook
Aloys F. La Gates	Utility Messman
Morris Shaw	Utility Messman
Richard C. Tozer, Jr.	Utility Messman
George E. Ward, Jr.	Utility Messman
Joseph T. Sizemore	Utility Messman
Roy O. Mason	Utility Messman
Francis D. Porter	Utility Messman
Rafael Santos	Oiler
Eimar Argerup	Chief Mate
J. Clarke	Galleyman
Kennedy Watt	AB

Armed Guard:

Ambrose Patrick McGowan	Lieutenant
John R. Andrews	Signalman 3/c
Louis Bator	Gunner's Mate 3/c
Robert Arthur Crocker	Gunner's mate 3/c
James Joseph Doyle	Coxswain
Ballard Lee Howell, Sr.	Gunner's Mate 3/c
William Clayton Kuhlman	Signalman 3/c
Theodore S. Martin	Coxswain
Henry Walter Morieko	Gunner's mate 3/c
George Joseph Poskie	Gunner's Mate 3/c
Robert Lee Wilson	Coxswain
LeRoy George Bartels	Seaman 1/c

Clarence Earle Barnett	Seaman 1/c
Earl Roy Carver	Seaman 1/c
James Daniel Casey	Seaman 1/c
Orval Franklin Crumley	Seaman 1/c
Johnny McDonald Curtis	Seaman 1/c
Henry H. Dent, Jr.	Seaman 1/c
Eryl Dickinson	Seaman 1/c
Marion LaVerne Henzen	Seaman 1/c
David Bicking Kennedy	Seaman 1/c
Albert Joseph Ogonowski	Seaman 1/c
Joseph Peter Salandino	Seaman 1/c
Robert James Swan	Seaman 1/c
Louis Elmer Veatch	Seaman 1/c
Vernon Earl Williams	Seaman 1/c

Joined July 16, 1945 in San Francisco:

Bert Erwin, Jr.	Gunner's Mate 3/c

Joined July 23, 1945 in San Francisco:

Ambrose Patrick McGowan	Lieutenant

Joined July 28, 1945 in San Francisco:

Ira Jim Cook	Seaman 1/c
Clifford Francis Bartel	Seaman 2/c
Charles Thomas Cunningham	Seaman 1/c
Joseph Sherlock Davey	Seaman 1/c
Yeon Flores	Seaman 1/c
Paul Peter Lafave	Seaman 1/c
Thomas Frederick Kelly	Seaman 1/c
George A. Toalson	Seaman 1/c
Casey Lonzo Walker	Seaman 1/c
Frankie Lee Lucas	Seaman 1/c

Armed Guard on board after Manila:

Theodore S. Martin	Coxswain
R. J. Swan	Seaman 1/c

Passengers boarded in Freemantle:

Arthur, Catherine Lilliam
Arthur, Maria Florence (daughter) age 6 months
Benesh, Edith Florence
Benesh, Robert Antone (son) age 2 years, 2 months
Czatynski, Doris Lesley
Dexter, Grace
Guillemette, Dorothy Leslie
Konkel, Doreen
Konkel, Elsworth Leroy (son) age 8 months
Marks, Patricia
Quackenbush, Thora Venetia
Yocum, Brenda Kathleen

APPENDIX D

GENERAL ORDERS FOR USN GUN CREW

GENERAL ORDERS

DUTY

   a) You are assigned to this ship for <u>military duties only.</u>

   b) Read and understand the Navy Dep't order of July 1942 which states: "...the members of the Armed Guard will not be required to perform any ship duties except their military duties and these will be performed invariably under the direction of the Commander of the Armed Guard."

PORT WATCHES

   a) Port watches are stood by the Armed Guard <u>only</u> to prevent sabotage of Navy material.

   b) Uniform for the watch will always be undress blues, leggings, watch caps or white hats and sidearms. (any change in the uniform will be announced)

c) The watch will be stood in a military manner - smoking or eating not allowed.

d) In case of fire:
1. Ring the general alarm.
2. Notify the bridge and engine room
3. Prepare to throw ammunition over the side; if necessary, flood magazines.

e) Each sentry will know location of magazine flood valve and have key for it with him.

f) The PO of the watch will have keys to all magazines with him.

g) A sentry will never leave his post without being properly relieved, except in the hours of darkness to call his relief.

h) You will salute all officers of the Armed Services.

SEA WATCHES

a) Lookouts will always be alert and responsible for a definite area.

b) Unnecessary talk, smoking or eating while on station is not permitted.

c) Lookouts will never leave their assigned stations without approval of the PO of the watch.

d) Report to the bridge at the beginning of each watch.

e) Report all objects seen: ships, lights, floating objects, slicks, etc.

f) At night the relief watch will be called 30 minutes before watch is to be relieved. Each member of the new watch will be on deck 10 minutes before he goes on watch and will wear dark adaptation glasses for 30 minutes before his watch. Anybody going below while on watch will wear dark adaptation glasses.

GENERAL

a) Keep your life jacket near you in the quarters; always wear it on sea watch and GQ.

b) Salute military officers who come aboard, and when they go ashore when on gangway duty.

c) Drinking wines, beers or liquor aboard or having same in your possession is prohibited.

d) Gambling is not permitted.

e) Nobody with sidearms is allowed in the mess halls.

MAINTENANCE OF QUARTERS

a) Bunks will be made up each day before breakfast.

b) Bunks will be made up after use later in the day and kept neat.

c) Decks in the quarters and heads will be swabbed by the cleaning detail daily.

d) Keep the gear you are using from day to day in your lockers. Keep the rest of your gear in your sea bag.

e) No gear will be left on top of lockers, under pillows or adrift elsewhere in the quarters.

f) Clean the wash basin each time after you use it.

(signed) A.R. Memhard, Jr.
Lt. A.R. Memhard, Jr., USNR
Armed Guard Commander
SS JEREMIAH O'BRIEN

APPENDIX E

WARTIME INSTRUCTIONS TO MASTERS FOR THE PORT OF SAN FRANCISCO

The following abstract is from the instructions issued on June 1, 1942 in the Port of San Francisco to masters of merchant ships. It is typical of the shipboard precautions taken in every American port during the war.

It is expected that company officers and representatives who are on and around the docks and ships will be on the alert at all times for any potential instruments of sabotage, for any potentially mischievous personnel in the crew of vessels in and departing from our ports, and for any unusual circumstances which might be of interest or concern.

Close Watch will be kept for all stragglers and wanderers and all such persons will be excluded.

Efficient continuous watches aboard ship will be maintained both day and night by a deck officer and an engineer officer. The night relieving officer will remain actually on watch and make tours of the decks, superstructure, cargo spaces where cargo is being worked, boiler rooms, engine rooms, and machinery spaces at irregular but sufficiently frequent intervals to check on conditions and actions of ship and shore personnel. The deck officer will keep himself informed of the approach of all small boats, barges and other shipping.

Continuous gangway watch will be maintained by reliable watchmen, who will require recognition of all persons boarding the ship. All packages, containers, and bags or baggage carried by ship or shore personnel will be opened and inspected both at the head of the pier and at the ship's gangway. Night watchmen and officers on watch will be provided with powerful flashlights.

Cargo hold watchmen will be on duty in each cargo compartment where cargo is being loaded. Stevedores and longshoremen will not be permitted to visit other cargo spaces unless watchmen are present.

Before closing cargo spaces or hatches at the end of the shift or when securing for sea, a thorough search will be made by officers and ship's personnel to guard against sabotage, fire, stowaways, etc.

The cargo space will be well lighted while cargo is being worked so that watchmen may observe the actions of all personnel. This applies to spaces as well in which cargo is not being worked, but to which men might wander. Decks, cargo hatches, gangways, alleyways and all spaces which are always accessible will be illuminated at night and also by daytime if necessary.

Crew quarters, storerooms, galleys, interior of life boats, and all deck lockers, mast houses, and other parts of the ship will be thoroughly inspected at least daily by ship's officers to prevent possible sabotage arrangements from being carried out. While a minimum of one inspection daily is recommended, more frequent inspections at irregular and surprise times, are to be preferred.

Steam will be maintained on at least one boiler on steam-powered ships to provide light and fire protection. Fire pumps, fire mains and fire detection equipment will not be dismantled or disabled without the permission and knowledge of the officer in charge of the ship and the engineer on duty. If, for any reason, the ship's fire-fighting equipment is out of service, arrangements will be made to provide water under pressure from shore fire mains, if vessel is alongside a dock, or from a towboat or other powered vessel, if the ship is at anchor. Similar precautions will be taken on Diesel-powered ships.

Strong wire screens will be securely fastened in the tops of ventilator pipes to prevent the dropping of incendiary bombs into cargo spaces and other unwatched compartments.

Pilot houses, chart rooms, radio rooms, store rooms, paint and lamp lockers, magazines, steering engine rooms, and unused crew quarters and passenger accommodations will be kept locked to prevent unauthorized entry. The keys, properly labeled, must be readily accessible to the officer in charge at all times.

Ships alongside of docks will be moored in such a way that lines may be slipped or cut from either the ship or the dock in case of necessity. It is undesirable to have anchors down unless definitely required by the circumstances.

At all times when vessels of 1000 gross tons or over are moored to docks, piers or wharves they shall have available on deck, fore and aft, hawsers capable of being used for emergency towing. The eye of such hawsers shall be extended beyond and outboard of the chock about five feet and ready to run and the ship's end shall be stopped off on the bitts to permit reasonable scope of hawser for towing. A heaving line made up and secured to the rail by rope yarn shall be bent to the eye of each hawser.

Barges, lighters, and other craft should not be permitted to come alongside or remain alongside the ship except when necessary. The possibility of sabotage arrangements being carried out from craft alongside must be borne in mind, and the necessary precautions observed.

The water supply will be checked to determine that pure drinking water and satisfactory boiler and washing water are obtained.

Provide ample illumination over the side on offshore side of ship.

The exterior of the ship's hull, rudder, propeller, overboard discharge, and hull appendages will be examined when the ship is in light condition and frequently while being loaded, to prevent sabotage and the attachment of equipment to the vessel.

Effective action will be taken to prevent the use of short-wave or secret radio equipment carried by the crew or passengers for receipt or transmission signals.

APPENDIX F

THE SECRET LOG

The *S.S. Jeremiah O'Brien* carried Secret Log No. 23466 issued by the United States Navy. The cover carries the title, "Secret Log for a UNITED STATES MERCHANT VESSEL." Under the title is the seal of the Navy Department and under that the sub-title, "United States Fleet, Headquarters of the Commander in Chief, 1943. In the lower right corner of the cover is a line, "S.S._____" for the vessel's name.

Page (II) contains a statement by R. S. Edwards, Vice Admiral, U.S. Navy, chief of Staff.

1. The secret log for United States Merchant Vessels shall be issued by routing officers to all United States owned and controlled vessels and shall be kept and handled in accordance with the instructions contained herein.

The instructions begin on page 1 and carry over to page 2.

INSTRUCTIONS FOR KEEPING THE SECRET LOG

1. The following extract is quoted from section 2, article 11109 (p. 16) of the WARTIME INSTRUCTIONS FOR UNITED STATES MERCHANT VESSELS:

(c) A deck log and engine log may be kept but shall *not* contain, under any circumstances, any record of, or information relative to, the following particulars:

    (1) Latitude and longitude.

    (2) Courses steered.

    (3) Bearings or distances of land, lights, or other marks.

    (4) Names or positions of any ships sighted.

    (5) Movement in convoy.

(d) The secret log is to be kept by the master in which he is to record such information (enumerated in (c) above) as is necessary. When not in use, this secret log shall be kept in the overboard bag with the master's confidential books.

(e) The various log books, both secret and otherwise, are to be produced for inspection when required by naval authorities and extracts are to be supplied to them if requested.

Note: Officers examining this log must indicate fact by signing in appropriate space provided. If any excerpts are copied from log, the fact must be indicated.

(f) On completion of a voyage at a port in continental United States the master shall turn over to the U.S. Navy routing officer his *secret logs*. At this time copies of the deck log and engine log, which comply with paragraph (c) above, may be furnished the owners and the War Shipping Administration, if desired.

Note: No record shall be furnished owners or the War Shipping Administration which contains information relative to:

    (1) Latitude and longitude.

    (2) Courses steered.

    (3) Bearings or distances of land, lights, or other marks.

    (4) Names or positions of any ships sighted.

    (5) Movement in convoy.

2. The purpose of supplying the master with this secret log book is twofold:

(1) To keep under one cover all secret information.

(2) To provide the master with a note book in which to record all events or observations of naval interest.

3. With regard to paragraph 2 above, masters are requested to enter in the Remarks section information relative to:

(a) *Sightings of enemy submarines, surface ships, or aircraft.*--Include (1) time of sighting, (2) exact position, (3) estimated course and speed of advance of enemy craft, and (4) a description of enemy craft.

(b) *Port Information.*--Include statements as to congestion of port, facilities available for loading and discharging, difficulties experienced in stevedoring, in obtaining bunkers, water, supplies, and pilotage.

(c) *Crew discipline.*--Include statement as to general efficiency and discipline of crew. When a member of the crew is logged in the standard deck log, the fact should also be recorded in the secret log.

(d) *Convoy and routing procedure.*--Include constructive comments relating to United Nations' convoy or routing administration. Suggestions for improvements will be welcomed.

4. In connection with paragraph 3 (c) above, the following extract from Section 333, NAVAL COURTS AND BOARDS, is quoted below for information of masters:

The officers, members of crews, and passengers on board merchant ships of the United States, although not in the naval service of the United States, are under the laws of the United States, the decisions of the courts, and by the very necessities of the case, subject to military control while in the actual theater of war.

While vessels are in the actual theater of war, or are part of military missions, all breaches of discipline by members of the crew which jeopardize the safety of the vessel, or tend to obstruct the prosecution of the war, should be referred to the nearest naval authority without delay. The actual theater of war is defined as all waters excepting the territorial waters of neutral or unoccupied countries.

5. Compliance with these instructions will ensure a definite contribution by the master toward winning the war.

The remaining pages contain lines for Record of Examinations by Naval Authorities, Date, Time, Latitude, Longitude, Base course, Distance and remarks.

APPENDIX G

CANAL ZONE WARTIME RULES AND REGULATIONS

The rules and regulations for the Canal Zone during wartime reflect the intense concern for the safety and security of the "Crossroads of the World." The following were given to ships transiting the Canal during World War II.

Codes and publications.

It is directed that you bring your inventory list of publications and <u>all the codes and publications held by your ship</u> to the Publication Officer for a complete check-up."

Order #4.

Boarding officers are directed to advise masters of all merchant ships calling at Cristobal and Balboa that they must bring their radio operator with them when they call at Port Director's Office for routing interview, and that the radio operator must have with him at that time a copy of the radio log covering the period since leaving last port.

Alert Notice.

   Full Alert. A full alert will be ordered in the event of an impending attack. Notice of "Full Alert" will be given through normal communication channels.

   Air Raid Alarm. Indicates that an immediate air attack is expected.

   The signal for an Air Raid Alarm in the outer anchorages will be a series of approximately five <u>red smoke grenades</u> during daylight and a series of approximately <u>five green stars</u> at night, fired at approximately 30 second intervals. The signal for "All Clear" will be <u>one black smoke grenade</u> during daylight and three long dashes on a signal light, repeated at one minute intervals, at night. These signals will be given by the station ship on the Pacific Side and at Fort Sherman on the Atlantic Side.

   The signal for an Air Raid Alarm in the inner harbors and the Canal itself will be a series of (5 second) blasts sounded on air raid sirens repeated at five second intervals. The "All Clear" will be three long blasts (1 minute blasts at 1 minute intervals). This "All Clear" signal will be repeated 15 minutes after first sounding.

   At "Full Alert" or "Air Raid Alarm" all vessels in the anchorages or at the docks within Canal Zone waters are to be in a state of readiness for such action or operations as may be ordered by the Commander Panama Sea Frontier.

   On the Air Raid Alarm signal all naval vessels in the harbor and armed merchant vessels man anti-aircraft installations and prepare for instant action to repel attack. Naval vessels with gun crews open fire on any enemy aircraft within range. Other vessels in the harbor will use their defensive armament and searchlights only if directly attacked.

   When the "All Clear" signal is sounded, remain at "Full Alert" status until further orders. The Blackout status changes from a "Complete Blackout" to an "Alert Blackout."

   How does one blackout a ship? The Navy supplied the answer.

TYPES OF BLACKOUTS

a. <u>Normal Blackout.</u> This will be the normal status of light control. During the Normal Blackout period:

    (1) Electric power circuits remain energized, Light control will be exercised by individuals.

    (2) Interior lighting is authorized until 2300, but shades, screens and low intensity bulbs must be used to keep the glare to a minimum. Between 2300 and 0545 essential interior lights must be shielded so that no light is visible outside.

    (3) Except as authorized in (4) below, all exterior lights will be extinguished.

    (4) Exterior lights are permitted at essential defense projects, at locks for construction work and transiting of ships, at piers for loading and unloading cargo and supplies. The number and brilliance of lights in use will be held to a minimum.

    (5) All authorized exterior lights must be shaded so the beams follow the horizontal.

    (6) Motor vehicles are authorized to travel with headlights painted to conform to current instructions.

b. <u>Alert Blackout.</u> This will be the status of control when an attack is imminent. It will be effective when ordered by Commanding General, Panama Task Force. During an Alert Blackout:

    (1) Electric power lines remain energized. Control of lights will be by individuals.

    (2) Motor vehicles are authorized to travel with headlights painted to conform to current instructions.

    (3) All exterior lights will be extinguished except those absolutely necessary to prepare for the pending attack.

    (4) Essential interior lights will be shielded so that no light is visible from the outside.

c. <u>Complete Blackout.</u> This will be the status of light when enemy aircraft are approaching. It will be effective when ordered by the Commanding General, Panama Task Force, or when the "Air Raid Alarm" is sounded. During a Complete Blackout:

    (1) Electric power circuits to essential defense activities only will remain energized. All other circuits will be deenergized.

    (2) All exterior lights will be extinguished.

    (3) Essential interior lights will be shielded so that no light will be visible from the outside.

    (4) (a) The following motor vehicles will be permitted to travel without lights or with the approved blackout guide lights:

        Army and Navy official vehicles.
        Vehicles carrying alert passes.
        Police and fire department vehicles.
        Ambulances.

    (b) All other motor traffic will pull off the road, stop, and extinguish lights.

And:

In the interest of security every vessel at any dock or mooring within Canal Zone waters shall be ready to move at all times on a moment's notice. At least one third of the ship's officers and crew must be kept on board at all times so that the ship may be ready to move on a moment's notice. The captains and crews of vessels should be on board at least 12 hours prior to going to sea or transiting the Panama Canal.

APPENDIX H

NUTS AND BOLTS

Name: *SS Jeremiah O'Brien.*
Keel Laid: May 6, 1943.
Launched June 19, 1943.
Builder's dock trial: June 26, 1943.
Official Dock Trial: June 29, 1943.
Delivered: June 30, 1943.
Type: Steam screw.
Hull: Steel
Built for: United States of America represented by the
United States Maritime Commission.
Decks: 2
Masts: 3
Stem: Raked
Stern: Cruiser-elliptical.
Length between perpendiculars: 416' 0".
Length overall: 441' 6"
Beam molded: 56'10 3/4"

Breadth: 57'

Depth molded to upper deck: 37' 4"

Depth: 34' 8.5/10

Draft, keel loaded: 27' 6 7/8"

Displacement tonnage, at loaded draft: 14,245.

Cargo and fuel tonnage: 9,146.

Gross Tonnage: 7176.49

Net Tonnage: 4380.41

Deadweight tonnage: 10,735.

Engine: Reciprocating (triple expansion), built at Hamilton, Ohio by General Machinery Corp., Steam powered.

Fuel consumption: 170 barrels per day at 11 knots giving a range of 19,000 nautical miles.

Normal IHP: 2,500.

MCE Hull No. 806

Yard Hull # 230.

CARGO

Compartment	Grain Cap. Cu. Ft.	Bale Cap Cu. Ft.
No. 1 Hold	41,257	36,083
Tween Decks	42,924	39,322
No. 2 Hold	98,860	92,008
Tween Decks	46,744	42,630
No. 3 Hold	68,459	59,793
Tween Decks	27,970	23,904
No. 4 Hold	58,620	51,571
Tween Decks	34,570	30,864
No. 1 Deep Tank, Port	3,639	2,729
" " Stbd.	3.639	3,004
No. 2 Deep Tank, Port	7,473	5,294
" " Stbd.	7,473	5,578
No. 3 Deep Tank, Port	13,674	12,506
" " Stbd.	13,188	12,024
Total	562,608	499,573

WATER BALLAST

Tank	Cu. Ft.	Tons at 35 Cu. Ft.
Fore Peak	4,845	138
No.1 Water Ballast	5,045	144
No 2 Water Ballast, Port	6,041	173
" " Stbd.	6,041	173
No. 3 " " Port	4,453	127
" " Stbd.	4,453	127
No. 5 " " Port	4,485	128
" " Stbd.	4,485	128
No. 6 " "	4,191	120
After Peak Culinary Water	5,318	152
No. 1 Deep Tank, Port	3,983	114
" " Stbd.	3,983	114
No. 2 " " Port	7,427	212
" " Stbd.	7,427	212
No. 3 " " Port	13,583	388
" " Stbd.	13,101	374
Total	98,861	2,824

FRESH WATER

Tank	Cu. Ft.	Tons at 35 Cu. Ft.
No. 4 Reserve Feed, Port	18,042	67
" " Stbd.	18,042	67
F. W., Fr. 108-113, Port	7,387	27
" " , Fr. 108-113, Stbd	7,387	27
Total	50,858	188

FUEL OIL

Tank	Gals.	Tons at 37.23 cu. ft.
No. 1 Fuel Oil Tank	37,038	133
No. 2 Fuel Oil Tank, Port	44,278	159
" " " Stbd.	44,278	159
No. 3 Fuel Oil Tank, Port	32,582	117
" " " Stbd.	32,582	117
No. 5 Fuel Oil Tank Port	32,861	118
" " " Stbd.	32,861	118
No. 6 Fuel Oil Tank	30,633	110
Total	287,113	1,031
F.O. Settling Tank Fr. 88-96 Port	13,924	50
F.O. Settling Tank Fr. 88-96 Stbd.	13,924	50
Total	27,848	100

Cargo Oil or Fuel Oil

	Gals.	Tons
No. 3 Deep Tank, Port	99,696	358
" " Stbd.	96,076	345
Total	195,733	703
Total (all F.O.)	510,733	1,834

STORE ROOMS

Space	Cu.Ft.
Bos'n stores on 2nd deck F.P. to Fr. 12	3,034
Bos'n stores on flat bet. 2nd & upper decks	3,492
Cabin Stores 2nd deck (Frs. 88-106)	4,329
Linen Locker	585
Bonded Stores	186

Refrigerated Stores:	Gross Cu. Ft.	Net Cu. Ft.
Meat	801	628
Fish	173	128
Vegetables	768	765
Dairy	176	154

NARRATIVE DESCRIPTION

Hull construction.

Of a single-screw, full scantling type, with raked stem and cruiser stern, the hull is subdivided by seven transverse bulkheads, watertight to the upper deck, providing five cargo holds. The engines and boilers are located amidships in a single compartment.

There are two complete decks, the upper and second with a flat forward of the fore peak bulkhead between these decks. Deep tanks are provided for water ballast or dry cargo in No. 1 hold and for water ballast, oil or dry cargo in No. 4 hold.

The hull is transversely framed and in most cases completely welded. The stem above the load waterline is a heavy formed plate; the stern frame is of cast steel in three pieces. The rudder is of contra form, with the rudder top post of forged steel. A gland packed rudder head carrier takes the whole weight of the rudder. The rudder neck bearing is of cast steel, lined with lignum vitae. The gudgeons are brass bushed and lined with lignum vitae. Bilge keels, 10 inches deep, extend from frame 54 to frame 105.

The double bottom, extending from peak to peak, is welded and made suitable for carrying fuel oil or salt water ballast, except for the portion under the engines, which is designed for carrying reserve feed water, and that under the boilers which is a dry tank.

All main bulkheads below the upper deck are watertight except those bounding oil tanks which are oiltight. Steel centerline bulkheads are arranged in the holds clear of hatches. The centerline bulkhead in the after deep tank is oiltight and that in the forward deep tank is watertight. Details of the framing, shell plating and decks are shown on the midship section.

The deck houses are of steel, of watertight construction. All bulkheads dividing staterooms, passages, offices, etc., are of plywood 1 1/8 inches thick.

All hatches, except in way of deep tanks on the second deck and in No. 1 hold are fitted with wooden covers. On the upper deck they are covered with tarpaulins. Douglas fir ceilings are laid on the tank top and deck under the main cargo hatches Nos. 2, 3 and 4, extending 1 foot beyond the hatch line, beyond which a steel covered brow is fitted all around.

The deck areas exposed to the weather are covered with paint. In the accommodations the passages, staterooms, offices, messrooms and hospital are covered with magnesite, the toilets and showers with ceramic tile or cement, the galley and pantry with commissary tile and the various storerooms with paint.

Cargo Handling. The vessel has three cargo masts located at frames 39, 68 and 134. The mast at frame 68 is designed for a safe working load of 10 tons with shrouds but without preventer stays. The mast at frame 39 is designed for a safe working load of 30 tons with shrouds and three preventer stays. The mast at frame 134 is designed for a safe working load of 15 tons with shrouds and a centerline preventer stay.

Five cargo booms are installed on the mast at frame 39, four of them are 5-ton booms and one is a 30-ton boom. Two 5-ton booms are installed on the mast at frame 68, and four 5-ton booms and one 15-ton boom are installed on the mast at frame 134.

All boom and mast fittings are for 5-ton booms and are designed for a safe working load of 10 tons to permit the installation of 10-ton booms and rigging, if desired. All cargo-handling gear for 5-ton booms is designed for a boom angle of 25 degrees with the horizontal, and for 15-ton and 30-ton booms for a boom angle of 35 degrees.

There are ten steam-driven cargo winches, five right hand and five left-hand, installed as indicated on the general arrangement plans. Each winch consists of a wirerope drum and a gypsy head driven through spur gearing by 8 by 8-inch cylinders. The drum is 16 inches diameter and 20 inches long, and the gypsy head 14 inches diameter and 14 inches long. The gypsy head is mounted on the drum shaft. The winches are fitted with foot brakes.

Deck Machinery. In addition to the cargo winches the deck machinery includes a windlass, warping winch and steering gear.

The windlass is a 10 inch by 12 inch steam-driven unit with quick-acting warping heads, capable of hoisting two anchors simultaneously from a 30-fathom depth of water at a chain speed of 30 feet per minute. The windlass is capable of hoisting each anchor and the maximum scope of chain under all service operating conditions. There are two wildcats on the main horizontal shaft and two warping heads on the intermediate shaft ends, all driven by spur gearing. Each wildcat is fitted with a hand operated brake of sufficient capacity to stop and hold the anchor and chain when let go under control of the brake.

The warping winch, installed aft, is of the horizontal reversible steam spur-gear type, capable of handling a load of at least 2500 pounds at a speed of 75 feet per minute for taking slack lines. The maximum pull at the gypsy heads is from 23,000 to 26,000 pounds. The gypsy heads are 18 by 18 inches.

The steering gear is of the 2-cylinder type with an 8-inch by 8-inch steam engine controlled by telemotor from the wheel house and an extension from the steering wheel to the flying bridge. The engine is operated condensing.

The steering gear is capable of moving the rudder from hard-over to hard-over (70 degrees) in 30 seconds when the vessel is going ahead full speed at full load draft. For emergency operations, tackle is arranged for connecting the quadrant to the after winch. A trick wheel is fitted to the engine for emergency local control, and is connected by shafting to the wheel at the aft steering station. A mechanical rudder-angle indicator is installed in the steering gear room.

Ground Tackle. Hawse pipes, of cast steel, are provided for two stockless bower anchors and welded chain pipes lead from the windlass bedplate to the chain locker.

The anchor chains are cast of forged steel in 15-fathom lots. The stream line and towlines are of 6/24 plow steel wire rope. The hawsers and warps are of manila.

Ventilation and Heating. Natural ventilation is carried to the holds, machinery spaces, shaft tunnel and accommodations through cowl or mushroom head ventilators, coamings and trunks. A 6-inch ventilator is fitted to each storeroom, a 9-inch ventilator to the galley and a 10-inch ventilator to the steering gear room. The main machinery space has four ventilators, each 30 inches in diameter, carried well above the weather deck and fitted with movable cowl heads arranged for operating from below.

The ventilation air is not heated, the quarters being heated by steam radiators supplied with steam at 15 pounds gage pressure at the reducing valves.

Fire Protection. The fire main system is equipped with hydrants of hose outlets so arranged that any point on the ship can be reached by a single 50-foot length of hose. Steam smothering is provided for all cargo holds, paint and lamp room lockers, etc. As required for all oil-fired vessels, the machinery spaces are protected by an adequate CO_2 smothering system. Portable fire extinguishers are distributed throughout the vessel as required.

No fire detection system is provided, but a system of 8-inch alarm gongs, operated from the wheel house, is installed. Electrical current for this system is obtained from the 20-volt interior communication circuit.

Navigating equipment.   Standard magnetic compasses and binnacles are installed in the wheel house, on the wheel house top and at the after steering station. The navigational equipment also includes a 12-inch searchlight, a sounding machine, mechanical engine-room telegraphs, fog horn, voice tubes, clocks, bells and gongs.

Lifesaving equipment.   Each vessel is equipped with four steel lifeboats, stowed under davits on the boat deck, two on each side. Each lifeboat is of 31 person capacity and one of the boats on each vessel is equipped with a motor for propulsion. All the boats are completely equipped with sails, gear, first-aid equipment, water and provisions.

Additional buoyant apparatus is provided, sufficient to accommodate all on board, as well as life preservers and life buoys.

Accommodations.   Accommodations for the full complement of 44 officers and crew are provided in the deck house amidships. The captain's stateroom and office is on the bridge deck, starboard side, with the radio operator's on the port side. The quarters for the deck officers and engineers are on the boat deck, and for the crew on the upper deck. The officers' mess and lounge is at the forward end of the deck house on the upper deck, while the petty officers' and crew's messrooms are on the port side. The galley is amidships between the boiler and engine casings. The hospital is aft on the upper deck.

The quarters for both the officers and crew are comfortably and conveniently arranged. Built-in berths are provided in the officers staterooms and pipe berths in the hospital and crew's quarters. The floors are covered with Selbalith, the bulkheads are of gray tint and the doors light gray. The officers furniture is upholstered in brown leather and the crew's in dark tan Pantasote.

The galley is equipped with a 2-oven center-fired coal range, a 25-gallon steam-jacketed stock kettle and other necessary appliances. In each mess there is an electric hot plate and an electric toaster.

Propelling Machinery.

Propulsion of the vessel is by a single screw driven by a direct-acting, condensing, 3-cylinder, triple-expansion reciprocating steam engine, operating normally at 76 revolutions per minutes, supplied with steam of 200 pounds gage pressure and 440 degrees F. temperature at the throttle by two cross-drum sectional sinuous header straight-tube oil-fired boilers. The main engine, designed by the General Machinery Corporation, Hamilton, Ohio, is designed to exhaust at 26 inches vacuum to a surface condenser bolted to the back columns of the engine.

The cylinders of the main engine are 24½, 37 and 70 inches in diameter and have a stroke of 48 inches. The cylinders are of cast iron and the high-pressure cylinder fitted with a high grade cast-iron liner suitable for superheated steam. A liner is also fitted in the high-pressure valve chest. All of the cylinders are cast individually and bolted together, forming a unit block. The cylinders are covered with magnesia protected by sheet iron lagging. The top of the engine has a mat covering with sheet iron, so split that sections can be easily removed. Relief valves are provided on all cylinders and on the intermediate and low-pressure valve chests.

The cylinder arrangement from forward to aft is as follows: High-pressure, intermediate-pressure, and low pressure. The direction of rotation of the engine, looking forward, is clockwise, with the crank sequence as follows: High-pressure, low-pressure, intermediate pressure.

The steam chests are cast integrally with the cylinders, thus eliminating interconnecting steam pipes. The high-pressure cylinder is fitted with a piston valve, and the intermediate and low-pressure cylinders with double-ported box-type balanced slide valves. The valve gear is of the Stephenson link type with double bar. The eccentric rods are crossed and attached to the eccentric strap at the bottom and to the link bars on top. The valve stems bolted to the valves are attached to the link blocks with brass bushings and shims for adjustment for wear. The link blocks are of forged steel fitted with bronze gibs.

The valves admit steam as follows: High-pressure inside steam, intermediate and low-pressure outside steam. Lockwood and Carlisle rings are fitted to the high-pressure piston valve and to the high and intermediate-pressure pistons. The low-pressure piston has a Ramsbottom ring with coach springs. Metallic packing is used throughout for all piston rods and valve stems.

The eccentrics and straps are of cast iron, the straps being lined with babbitt metal and the eccentrics keyed to the crankshaft. The eccentric rods are of forged steel and are bolted to the eccentric straps. The upper part has bronze boxes for attaching to the link bar pins. One set of link bar pins is extended to take the drag rod bronze bearings.

The bedplate is of cast iron in three sections held together by fitted bolts. Cross girders provide flat bottom recesses for the main bearings. The bottom of the bedplate is flat, but slightly tapered, and is bolted to the tank top through chocks with holding-down bolts. The columns are of box section, there being three front and three back columns. The lower ends of the columns are bolted to the bedplate and the upper ends to the cylinder feet. To the back columns are bolted cast-iron crosshead guides provided with water cooling. The astern guides are of cast iron bolted to the ahead guides.

The crankshaft. of forged steel, is of the built-up type, 14¼ inches in diameter, made in two sections with the high-pressure and intermediate-pressure forming the forward section and the low-pressure the after section. The crankpins and shafts are shrunk into the crankwebs. All eccentrics are bolted to the forward shaft section. The low-pressure section carries the turning gear worm wheel. Coupling flanges are forged integral with the shaft and are held by fitted bolts.

The main bearings consist of upper and lower cast-iron babbitted boxes, fitted into a recess on the bedplate and held in one place with a flat steel bearing cap. The main bearing bolt extends through to the bottom of the bedplate with shims for taking up wear.

The crossheads are of the single slipper type of forged steel. The crosshead slipper is of cast iron and is bolted to the crosshead. The go-ahead side is babbitted. A comb is attached to the crosshead slipper, dipping into the trough at the bottom of the crosshead guide, providing lubrication for the ahead guide, in addition to two feeds from a syphon box on the cylinders. The astern guides are provided with cups for hand lubrication.

The connecting rods are made of forged steel, with cast-steel babbitted boxes on the crank and bronze boxes for the crosshead end. Laminated brass shims are provided for taking up wear.

The pistons are made of cast iron of box section and are provided with follower rings. The piston clearances are 3/8 inch at the top and 1/2 inch at the bottom. The piston rods are of straight cylindrical construction, with tapered ends for securing the pistons and crossheads.

Relief valves are fitted on the top and bottom of all cylinders and on top of the steam chest covers. Drain valves are mounted on the bottom of all cylinders and steam chests. The throttle valve is of the single seat, balanced poppet type. The body is a steel casting, while the valve and seat are of Monel metal. There is a pilot valve for relieving the pressure on the balancing piston for easy operation of the valve. A butterfly valve for quick throttling is built into the extension neck of the throttle valve to the high-pressure steam chest.

The reverse shaft, 6½ inches in diameter, is of steel. The reverse levers are keyed to the reverse shaft and slotted with the screw arrangement to permit a change in the cut-off of the individual cylinders. The reversing gear is of the all-around type operated by a single-cylinder reversing-valve engine, 6 inches diameter by 7 inches stroke, located on the after side of the high-pressure front column. Reversing is accomplished through a worm attached to the reversing engine crankshaft driving a worm wheel. The pin on the worm wheel connects to the reverse arm on the reverse shaft through a drag rod. A pointer is located on the worm wheel indicating the ahead or astern position of the engine.

The turning engine consists of a single-cylinder, steam-driven unit, 8½ inches diameter by 7 inches stroke, mounted on the after end of the bedplate of the engine. It operates through two sets of worm gears to the crankshaft of the engine. This engine is reversible so that it may be used for setting the valves or making repairs.

The other auxiliaries mounted on and driven off the main engine are the air pump, two bilge pumps and the evaporator feed pump.

The air pump is of the Edwards single-acting type, 24 inches in diameter by 26 inches stroke, bolted to the bedplate and the after column. The pump body is of cast iron, with removable bronze liners and cast-iron bucket rim. The lower end of the liner has cast ports through which condensate is admitted to the pump cylinder. This type of pump requires no suction valves. The discharge valves, of the bronze Kinghorn type without springs, are located on the headplate, bolted to the top of the liner. The valves are accessible through an inspection door on the side of the pump body. The bucket rod is of Muntz metal, the upper end being secured to the air pump crosshead. The air pump discharge chamber is provided with an overflow pipe discharging into a funnel, draining to the bilge.

Attached one on either side of the air pump are two bilge pumps, each 4½ inches diameter by 26 inches stroke, driven from the air pump crosshead. The bilge pumps are of cast iron with bronze plungers of the vertical ram type. The after bilge pump suction chest is of the manifold type, with suction shut-off chest and safety valve. The discharge valve has a quick closing non-return check valve. The forward bilge pump suction valve is also of the manifold type and is provided with double suction, one with direct suction from the sea and the other suction from the bilge. Each bilge pump is provided with cast-iron air chambers. A switch valve in the discharge is provided for discharge either overboard or to the deck.

The evaporator feed pump is attached to the forward side of the low-pressure column. It is of the single-acting plunger ram type, 2 inches in diameter by 9 inches stroke, and is driven from the air pump beam through links. The suction and discharge valve box is bolted direct to the pump. The box is of cast iron and the valves and seats are of bronze.

Water-cooling service is provided for the eccentrics, main bearings and crankpin boxes. The nozzles connect to the main service piping through a swivel joint, with necessary valves to be used on individual points when required. The crosshead guides are provided with continuous cooling, and a connection is make for the cooling coil in the thrust block. The cooling piping is connected to the sea water piping in the vessel.

The main steam pipe is 8 inches in diameter and the exhaust pipe is 25 inches in diameter. To permit admitting high-pressure steam to the various cylinders, a bypass starting valve is bolted to the throttle valve, and pipe connections made to the intermediate and low-pressure cylinders as well as to the reversing engine.

Forced lubrication is provided for the high-pressure cylinder by a nozzle connection in the throttle valve and to the high-pressure piston rod metallic packing. Also special leads are provided on each side of the intermediate-pressure slide valve. Tallow cocks are used for lubricating the low-pressure slide valve and for the domes of the intermediate and low-pressure valve stems.

For main engine lubrication, brass oil boxes are located at the top of the cylinders, with syphon feeder wicks and pipes leading to the individual running parts of the engine. The eccentrics are lubricated by individual cups on the eccentric rods, these being hand lubricated. On each main bearing is located an oil box with wicks for lubrication of the bearings. Individual lubricating oil boxes are also located on the air pump beam links and the air pump crosshead.

The thrust bearing, of the Kingsbury type, consists of a semi-steel housing with two journal bearings, a thrust shaft, 14¼ inches diameter, with integral forged collar and two pairs of thrust shoes, two for ahead and two for astern thrust. Each shoe covers about 60 degrees of arc. They are individually adjustable fore and aft by jack screws. The journal bearings have removable lower half shells lined with babbitt metal. The upper half bearing babbitt is cast in the housing cover, leaving large pockets for oil. The thrust bearing is bolted to the tank top independent of the engine bed-plate.

Lubrication is automatic, being accomplished by a metal scraper riding on the collar and distributing oil to the collar surfaces and the journal bearings. Ordinarily, the bearing will cool itself by radiation, but a small copper cooling coil is provided in the oil bath for emergencies. The thrust shaft collar is 33 inches in diameter and 5 inches thick. The ends of the bearing are sealed by stuffing boxes around the shaft.

The weight of the main engine, complete with attached auxiliaries is approximately 271,000 pounds.

Shafting and Propeller. The line shafting is of forged steel 13½ inches in diameter. The journals for steady bearings are about 16 feet 6 inches apart. The steady bearings, of cast iron with the bottom section lined with bearing metal, are of the wick-oiled type with reservoirs for solidified grease. The after bearing is fitted with bearing metal on both top and bottom.

The bulkhead stuffing boxes and glands are of cast iron with brass bushings. The propeller shaft, of forged steel with a diameter of 15¼ inches, is fitted with a composition liner extending the full length of the shaft except in way of the coupling and the propeller taper. The after end of the liner is carried into the recess in the propeller hub where it is made watertight by means of a rubber ring. The after end of the shaft is tapered to fit the bore of the propeller. The forward end of the shaft has a coupling forged integral with the shaft and is arranged for withdrawal inboard.

The stern tube is of cast iron, in one piece, secured by a flange to the bulkhead at the forward end. The after end of the tube is fitted into the stern frame and locked by a steel nut. The tube is fitted with a composition bushing lined with sectional lignum vitae staves.

Water service pipes supplied from the circulating system are fitted along the shaft tunnel for emergency cooling of the steady bearings and lubrication of the stern tube bearings.

The propeller is a right-hand, 4-bladed, manganese bronze or cast steel, solid wheel about 18 feet in diameter. The blades are of airfoil section.

Boilers. Steam is supplied at 220 pounds per square inch gage pressure and 450 degrees F. total temperature by two oil-fired watertube boilers arranged with a fore and aft firing aisle at the forward end of the machinery space amidship. The boiler is of the Babcock & Wilcox section-header, 2-inch tube design, with oil-burning refractory furnace and overdeck superheater.

The boilers are of the conventional 3-pass, straight-tube cross-drum type, with 22 sections each having one lower row 4-inch tube and seven groups of 2-inch tubes 13 feet long between tube plates, designed to evaporate 24,000 pounds of steam per hour with 230-degree feed temperature. The boilers are capable of sustained operating at 30 percent excess evaporation. They are fitted for burning bunker C fuel oil under forced draft at a normal rate of evaporation of 5 pounds per square foot and at a sustained overload of 6.5 pounds per square foot of boiler water heating surface. They are equipped with steam soot blowers.

Each boiler is fitted with a convection-type superheater located after the first gas pass of the boiler in a separate casing on top of the main boiler casing and arranged so that all the steam generated in the boiler will pass through the superheater. No air heaters or economizers are fitted.

Each boiler is fitted with four oil burners working under forced draft. Two fuel-oil transfer pumps draw from high and low suctions in the settling tanks, and in an emergency from the transfer suction main through a duplex suction strainer, and discharge to the boiler service main through a duplex discharge strainer. Each fuel oil service pump is arranged to discharge into a single header and led, via duplex strainer and oil heater, to the burner header on each boiler front. A combined ballast and fuel-oil transfer system is installed and arranged so that either ballast water or fuel oil can be transferred from any one fuel oil and ballast tank to any other fuel oil and ballast tank, and vice-versa. Two fuel-oil heaters are installed, each of which has a capacity to heat 3500 pounds per hour of bunker C fuel oil from 100 degrees to 230 degrees F. when supplied with steam at 125 pounds gage pressure.

The boiler feed system is of the open feed type, consisting of feed pumps, feed and filter tank, exhaust heater, grease extractor and traps. The suction sides of the feed pumps are connected to the feed and filter tank and the reserve feed tanks. The feed pumps discharge to the boilers via the grease extractor and exhaust feed heater. The feed pumps are also arranged to discharge through the grease extractor, thence through an auxiliary feed line to the boilers. Feed pump suction and discharge connections are so arranged that either pump may be overhauled while the other is in service. A connection is led from the reserve feed tank to the main and auxiliary condensers for emergency feed make-up. The exhaust feed heater is supplied with steam at 10 pounds gage from the auxiliary exhaust line and drains are led to the feed and filler tank.

The feedwater heater is of the multi-pass closed type capable of heating 48,000 pounds of feedwater per hour from 125 degrees to 230 degrees F. when using exhaust steam from the auxiliary exhaust system.

The filter and grease extractor installed in the feed line between the feed pumps and feed heater is of the twin type, each unit of which is capable of filtering the entire amount of boiler feedwater. The feed and filter tank is designed to filter all of the condensate and to provide storage capacity for the boiler feed.

Auxiliaries.

Vacuum Equipment. The main condenser is of the 2-pass surface condensing type of about 3000 square feet of cooling surface, designed to maintain a vacuum of 26 inches when the main engine is developing normal full power ahead. At sea the main condenser also handles any excess auxiliary exhaust. The condenser is bolted to the back columns of the main engine.

The auxiliary condenser is also of the 2-pass type, containing about 700 square feet of cooling surface, capable of condensing the exhaust from one generator plus the exhaust from winches and other auxiliaries during port operations. The condenser is mounted directly over a reciprocating combined auxiliary circulating and wet air pump.

Evaporator Plant. The evaporator plant consists of a vertical submerged-type salt water evaporator with a capacity of 20 short tons per 24 hours. Steam is supplied to the coils at 125 pounds gauge pressure. Vapor is generated at 5 pounds gage and is discharged to the distiller and from there through a 60-gallon test tank to the distilled water and drinking water storage tanks, reserve feed tanks and to the bilge. Cooling water to the distiller is supplied by the salt water service pump.

Salt Water Systems. The vessel is provided with the following salt water system: main circulating, auxiliary circulating, water service, bilge, fire and clean ballast.

Circulating water for the main condenser is supplied by a centrifugal pump driven by an enclosed reciprocating engine. Cooling water for the shaft alley water service and main engine service is supplied from the main circulating system. Circulating water for the auxiliary condenser is supplied by the auxiliary circulating and wet air pump.

An independent steam-driven salt water service pump takes suction from the sea and supplies water for the distiller, refrigerator condenser, sanitary system and on emergency connection the shaft alley service. One of the attached bilge pumps is arranged to serve this system when the main engine is in operation at sea.

The bilge system is arranged to permit pumping from all of the holds, machinery space, and all void compartments in contact with the inner bottom and to take care of all drainage between deck spaces under all practical conditions. The arrangement of the bilge system is such as to prevent the possibility of water or oil passing into the cargo and machinery spaces, or from one compartment to another.

The fire main system is served by the fire pump, with the general service pump as a standby.

For the clean ballast system a ballast main runs between the peak tanks with suction and discharge connections in the engine room to the general service pump and to the bilge and ballast pumps.

Fresh Water Systems. Fresh water for drinking and wash basins, showers and baths is carried in tanks located amidships above the second deck.

The potable and washing water system consists of a motor-driven pump complete with automatic control devices, a standby hand pump and a pressure tank. The fresh hot washing water system consists of a storage tank with heater coils and necessary equipment, functioning as a thermo-syphon system. A similar smaller system is supplied aft for the hospital.

Refrigeration for Ship's Service. A freon direct-expansion refrigerating system supplies refrigerant to the ship's refrigerated stores, to the scuttlebutt and to an ice-making tank. The Freon-12 refrigerating unit comprises a vertical, air-cooled, multi-cylinder, single-acting compressor; a horizontal condenser; a liquid receiver, strainers and dryer; controls and piping. Circulating water is supplied from the sanitary system.

Pumps. The following pumps are installed for the various services on the vessel:
- 1 horizontal centrifugal main circulating, 3650 gallons per minute, 40 feet head, driven by steam engine.
- 1 horizontal duplex plunger potable water, 5 gallons per minute, 60-pound head, ½ horsepower motor.
- 1 potable water, 5 gallons per minute, manually operated.

Steam Reciprocating Pumps
- 2 vertical simplex double-acting, fire and bilge, 12 by 8 by 12 inches, 300-pound head.
- 1 vertical duplex double-acting, fire and bilge, 10 by 11 by 12 inches, 560 gallons per minute, 125 pound head.

1 vertical duplex double-acting fuel-oil transfer, 10 by 11 by 12 inches, 320 gallons per minute, 50-pound head.

2 vertical simplex double-acting fuel-oil service, 7½ by 4 by 10 inches, 8 gallons per minute, 250-pound head.

1 vertical simplex double-acting salt-water service, 6 by 8 by 8 inches, 140 gallons per minute, 50-pound head.

1 horizontal simplex double-acting auxiliary circulating and air, 10 by 12 by 12 by 12 inches.

Attached Pumps
1 Edwards air.
2 ram bilge
1 ram evaporator feed.

All of the steam reciprocating pumps operate on boiler pressure with about 10 pounds back pressure. For an auxiliary means for feeding the boilers and also for use in washing down, etc., there is provided a 2½-inch double-tube injector, taking suction from the hotwell tank or reserve feed tank and discharging to the auxiliary feed line.

Electrical Plant. The electrical plant consists of two 20-kilowatt generators driven by direct-connected reciprocating, forced-lubricated steam engines, supplying 120-volt direct current. The main switchboard is of the live-front type with panels for the control and protection of the generators and the power and lighting circuits. A battery charging panel is provided for charging the interior communication batteries. The lighting circuits are operated on the 115-volt two-wire system.

All telephones are of the sound powered type. The call bell annunciator is operated on a 20-volt circuit, as is the general alarm system. Duplicate sets of 12-cell 24-volt storage batteries are installed for the 20-volt interior communication system. Separate batteries are provided for the radio equipment.

APPENDIX I

PLANS AND DRAWINGS

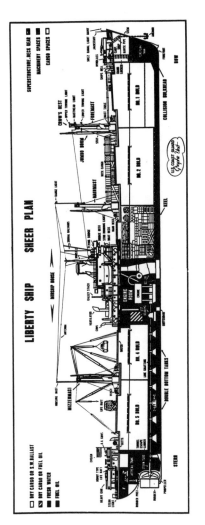

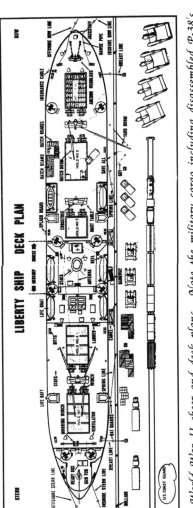

World War II sheer and deck plans. Note the military cargo including disassembled P-38's.

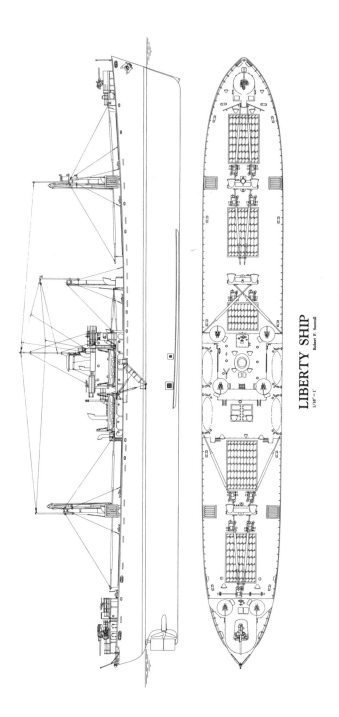

LIBERTY SHIP

1/16″ = 1′   Robert F. Sumrall

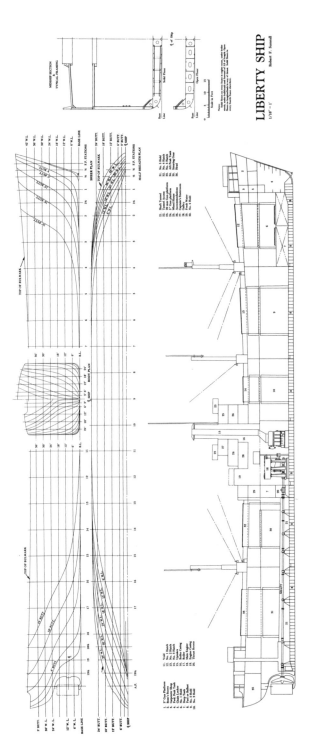

LIBERTY SHIP
Robert F. Sumrall

APPENDIX J

THE PRESENT (1993) CREW OF THE
SS JEREMIAH O'BRIEN

BOARD OF DIRECTORS

Audett, Charles
Blake, Robert E.
Booth, John
Burke, Norm
Chiles, Capt. John
Crowley, Thomas B. Jr.
Dickie, Doug
Duncan, William
Gedney, Capt. C. E.
Harris, Sr., William J.
Haskell, Arthur J.
Hayman, Marc
Hopkins, Warren
Jahn, Capt. George
Johnston, Francis X.

Jones, Capt. S. A.
Lundeberg, Gunnar
Moore, Thomas R.
Murdock, Ernest
Nardi, Ugo
Patterson, RADM T. J.
Simonsen, Capt. H. W.
Thomas, William G.
Turner, Ed
Vaughan, William E.
Watson, Don
Willard, Walt

STAFF

Hooper, Marci
Burnett, Bob

VOLUNTEER CREW

Abela, Anthony
Adkins, David C.
Alexander, Myron
Alexander, Phyllis
Alexander, Tom
Anderson, Gene
Anderson, Kristen
Anderson, Nils
Armijo, Sam
Auble, Michael
Audet. Charles
Avery, Mikel
Bell, Russell A.
Bennett, William
Berge, Kathleen
Berger, Lars A.
Bertillion, Barry

Bertillion, Rita
Best, Otto G.
Blanchette, Ed
Borowiec, John
Boroweic, Betty
Bowers, Kenneth
Brannon, Richard
Brown, Charles
Brown, Susan
Bulkley, David
Burke, Patrick
Campbell, Del
Carrier, William
Carroll, John
Chin, Stella
Cilia, William
Conrady, Raymond F.

Conwell, Jim
Currie, Richard
Cuzens, Bill
Dam, Per
Darms, John
David, Charles
Davidson, Robert
Detels, Jeff
Dewing, Fred
Doyle, Janet
Dunbar, Dick
Duncan, Dorothea
Dunn, John F.
Fairfield, William
Fenton, William
Fernandois, Luis
Fitzgerald, John D.
French, Corky
Gillis, James
Gisslow, Bob
Goldman, Brian
Guipre, Lyle
Harris, Sr., William J.
Haskell, Arthur J.
Hayman, Marc
Henry, M. L.
Higgins, Paul
Hill, Richard A.
Hiller, Bob
Hobbs, George
Imbeau, Bob
Imbeau, Cora
Immisch, George B.
Jackson, Daniel
Jacobson, Alberta
Jacobson, Bob
Jaffee, Capt. Walter W.

Jasen, George
Jasen, Rudolph
Jellinek, Arleen
Jellinek, Steven
Jenkins, Chuck
Jones, Buzz
Jones, Capt. S. A.
Kaddas, Kimon
Kaufman, Fred
Kiesling, Roy
Kilduff, Kevin
Kramer, Bill
Kreidler, Jr., Carl
Lawrence, Jo
Le Pendu, Francois
Lebeau, Gabriel
Lingenfeld, Edgar
Lodigiani, Capt. Ed
Loomis, Jack
Lorini, John
Malone, Ruth
Masterson, Bev
Masterson, Wes
Mayer, William D.
McGee, William
McKenzie, Thomas
Meyer, David
Milcic, Joe
Miller, Hans
Miller, Jim
Millspaugh, Herbert
Montano, Javier
Mooney, Charles
Mooney, Gene
Moore, J. E.
Moore, Thomas R.
Morgan, Kay

Moser, Brandon
Mowat, David
Murray, Adele
Murray, Ken
Nelson, Bob
Nelson, Milo
Nevermann, Alice
Newbold, Alexander
Nilan, Carmela
Nilan, Clifford
Olijaynyk, Stephen
Oliveri, Bill
Oppenheim, John
Otterberg, Capt. Carl
Otterberg, Nell
Palacin, Ray
Palange, Tim
Paul, John
Pottinger, John
Radovich, Ray
Rapp, Tony
Reed, Rich
Regal, Charles
Remus, Andrew
Rettig, James B.
Rivers, John
Roberts, Ed
Robson, Ron
Rocha, Clarence
Rowlands, Bill
Ruddell, Adrian
Ruegg, Lawrence
Russell, Herb
Salerno, Mark
Sawyer, Bill
Schoenstein, Norman
Sears, Arnold

Secondari, Elliott
Secondari, Richard
Sinnott, Jr., Philip
Skelly, Sam
Smith, Bill
Smith, Edward
Smith, Ronald C.
Smith, Warren
Sommerauer, Otto
Speight, Jeff
Stark, Christian
Steinberg, Mary
Stevens, Ralph
Stout, Alma
Sturken, Ed
Switz, Lou
Thompson, James
Tolliday, Muriel
Tordsen, Ernest
Tordsen, Laura
Torres, Moe
Tostanoski, Edward
Turner, Ed
Turning, Michael
Verhalen, Joe
Von Der Porten, Edward P.
Walsh, Jim
Watson, Terence
Wefald, Martin
Westerfield, Richard
White, K. Margaret
Williams, Greg
Williams, Irene
Williams, W. F.
Wilson, Roy
Winter, Homer
Wood, Sam D.

Woodward, Mary
Yates, Jean
Yellin, Elliott

The NORMANDY '94 Committee:

    Robert Blake, Chairman, NLSM
    Gerald Bowen, Military Vehicle Collectors' Club
    Norman Burke, Corporate Finance
    Douglas Dickie, Chief Engineer
    William P. Duncan, Crewing Committee
    Capt. C. E. Gedney, Industry & Union
    Arthur F. Haskell, Budget
    Marci Hooper, Business Manager, NLSM
    Capt. Walter W. Jaffee, Historian
    Capt. George Jahn, Master
    Fred Kaufman, Naval Architect
    Frank Martell, Insurance Representative
    E. L. Murdock, Vice Chairman
    Ugo Nardi, Treasurer
    CDR Franklin S. Nelson USN, Medical
    Capt. Carl Otterberg, Chairman, Fundraising, Scrap Ship
        Committee
    RADM Thomas J. Patterson, Chairman
    John Pottinger, Crew Representative
    Charles Regal, Publicity Chairman
    Capt. Paul Reyff, Washington Representative
    Ed Roberts, Military Vehicle Collectors' Club
    Capt. Hank Simonsen, Legislative Chairman
    BGEN Robert C. Tripp, U.S. Army Liaison
    William E. Vaughan, Legal Chairman
    Lt. Col. William Voortmeyer, U.S. Army Liason
    CDR Don Watson, Medical Department

APPENDIX K

CONTRIBUTORS TO THE NLSM

The following is not meant to be a complete listing of contributors, but is a sampling based on those individuals and organizations whose names were printed in each of the annual cruise programs. The author apologizes in advance to anyone whose name is omitted.

The below-listed organizations have generously contributed food, supplies, services and funds throughout the volunteer years to make the *Jeremiah O'Brien* the success it is. It could not have been done without their help and the help of many who are not listed.

A. Paladini Seafood Co.
A & M. Service Co.
Able Ship
Allied Business Machines Co.
Allied Packers, Ltd.
Allied Packing & Supply Company, Inc.

Allied Tax Service
Allied Taxicab Company
American Marine Fumigating Co.
American President Lines, Ltd.
American Society of Mechanical Engineers
Antenna Theater
Argo International Corp.
Argo Marine
Auction Outlet, Inc.
Captain Olav Aune
The Aune Family
Automotive Engineering Co.
Ray A. Baker
Bar Pilots Association
Bay Port Supply, Inc.
Beale Air Force Museum
Bearing Agencies
Beck Electric Supply
Beck's Brewing Co.
Berkeley Farms Dairy
Joseph Benjamin
Bethlehem Shipyard
Bethlehem Steel Corporation
Birite Company
John Boroweic
Brennan-Hamilton Corporation
Charles Brown
Buckles-Smith Electric Co.
Bull & Roberts
Burke Industries
Cal 20 Association
California Council for the Humanities
California Maritime Academy and Alumni
California Stevedore & Ballast Co., Inc.
Calistoga/Perrier
Calistoga Water Company
Captain Wallace Campbell

Carpenter Rigging & Supply Co., Inc.
The Centennial Foundation
The Charles Lowe Company
Chevron Oil Company
Chevron Shipping Co.
Chevron U.S.A., Inc.
Coast Marine & Industrial Supply
Coast Marine Engineering Co.
Coast Marine Supply
Coastal Marine Engineering Co.
Commercial Tire Company
Confederate Air Force
Continental Maritime of San Francisco, Inc.
Council of American Master Mariners
Steve Crawford
Crowley Maritime Corporation
Crowley Maritime International
Dahl Beck Electric Company
George Damveld, Director, Pabst Brewing Co.
The Darrow Foundation
Delta Steamship Lines, Inc.
Denver Meat Company
Dick Derby
Dockside Machine & Ship Repair
John Donnelly
Eagle Marine Services
Kate Ellis
Equadorian Line, Inc.
Exxon Company, U.S.A.
Exxon Oil Company, U.S.A.
Farrell Lines
Jim Ferrigan, The Flag Store
Florence Ravioli & Distributing Co.
Susan Forsythe
Fort Mason Center
Furuno, U.S.A., Inc.
Gallo Salami

General Engineering & Machine Works
George E. Butler Company
Ghiselli Bros., Inc.
W. R. Grace Foundation
H & H Ship Service Company
Harbor Ship Service
Harbor Ship Supply
Harrison & Bonnini
Hewitt Marine
Holland-American Society of California
Capt. George Hollinger
IBM
IT Corporation
Inland Boatman's Union
International Longshoremen and Warehouseman's Union
International Organization of Masters, Mates and Pilots
International Paint
J & H Marine
J. L. Henderson Co.
Captain George Jahn, S. F. Pilot
JAMCO Marine
Johnson & Higgins of California
Kaiser Cement Corporation
Kaiser Electric
Kansas Packing Company
Kansas Packing Company of California, Inc.
Fred Kaufman, naval architect
Wilma F. (Mrs. Charles) Kent
KFRC-AM
William H. Langenberg
Levin Metals Corporation
D.N. Lillevand
Lockheed Shipbuilding and Construction Company
Louis Mayer, Ham & Hot Dogs
Louis Mayer/Rich Turkey
Luce and Co., Inc.
Lykes Brothers Steamship Co., Inc.

Mr. & Mrs. Herb Maletz
Marin Tug and Barge, Inc.
Marine Cooks and Stewards
Marine Engineer's Beneficial Association
Marine Firemen's Union
Marine Staff Officers
Maritime Administration
Maritime Couriers, Inc.
John W. Massenberg
Masters, Mates and Pilots
Matson Navigation Co.
Philip Mattingly
Al Mesitas, Crown Electric
Bob Meyer, Group 4 Marketing
Donna Middlemist
Military Vehicle Collectors Club, Northern California
Joanie Morgan
Morgan Marine & Chemical Inc.
National Maritime Museum Association
National Maritime Union
National Maritime Union Job Corps
National Park Service
National Trust for Historic Preservation
New York Brands Seltzer
Nolan Associates, Inc.
NuLaid Eggs
Olympia Brewing Company
Olympia-Hamms Brewing Company
Oscar Mayer/Louis Rich
Pabst Brewing Co.
Pacific Bell
Paladini Seafood Co.
Parisian Bakeries, Inc.
RADM Thomas J. Patterson
Perrier Group
Quality Fresh Produce, Inc.
Quality Produce

Quality Refrigeration
Redi-Marine Electronics Co.
Rich's Turkey
Roberton & Schwartz, Inc.
Roberton & Schwartz, Mfg.
Roberton & Schwartz, Sales
Roberton & Schwartz Sales Co., Inc.
Clarence Rocha
Roth Electricians
John Roveda, President, United Beverages, Oakland
Sailors' Union of the Pacific
San Francisco Bar Pilots
Seafarers International Union
Sea-Land Service, Inc.
Service Engineering Co.
Ship's Laundry of North America
Society of Port Engineers of San Francisco
Special Boat Unit 11, U.S. Navy, Treasure Island
Spentonbush Red Star Companies
Stan Flowers Co., Inc
Stroh's Beer/United Beverage Dist.
Thomas A. Short, Company
Thomas Hydraulic & Hardware Supply, Inc.
Trans-Bay Electronics, Inc.
Bill Trenam
Triple A Shipyard
Capt. George M. Tuttle, Jr.
U. S. Coast Guard
U. S. Naval Hospital, Oakland, CA
U. S. Navy
U. S. Navy Armed Guard Veterans of World War II
U. S. Navy Band, Treasure Island
U. S. Navy Color Guard, Treasure Island
U. S. Navy Medical Command, NW Region
U. S. Park Police
United Beverage Distributors
United Maritime Ship Suppliers, Inc.

United Maritime Ships Chandlers
United Peoples Laundry, Inc.
United States Merchant Marine Academy Alumni Association
William Vaughan, Attorney-at-Law
W & O Supply, Inc.
Waldron, Duffy, Inc.
Watson & Watson Enterprises, Inc.
Wente Winery
West Coast Ship Chandlers, Inc.
West Winds, Inc.
Western Marine Suppliers of California
Western Marine Supply of California, Inc.
Willard Marine Decking, Inc.
Wilsey Bennett Co.
Women's Propeller Club, Port of the Golden Gate
Alan Young
YYK Enterprises

APPENDIX L

WREATHS

Through the years many wreaths have been cast upon the ocean in honor of the memory of departed seamen. They have come through the generosity and compassion of the following organizations, clubs, unions, associations and individuals, many of whom have contributed a wreath on every voyage:

American Legion Port #144
American Merchant Marine Veterans, Golden Gate Chapter
American President Lines, Ltd.
Apostleship of the Sea
Barney Evans Public Relations
Bay Counties District Council of Carpenters
Bethlehem Steel Corporation
California Maritime Academy
California Maritime Academy Alumni Association
California Stevedore & Ballast Co.
Capasso's Marine Marketing

Chevron Shipping Co.
Civilian Officers Military Transport Retiree Association
Clair Marine Corp.
Coast Marine & Industrial Supply, Inc.
COMTRA
Council of American Master Mariners, S.F.B.A. Chapter
Crowley Maritime Corporation
Daggett Plumbing, Inc.
The Darrow Foundation
Delta Steamship Lines, Inc.
District No. 1, MEBA/NMU, Fremont Street
District No. 1, MEBA/NMU, Mariposa Street
District No. 1, PCD, MEBA
Eagle Marine Services, Ltd.
Exchange Club of Alameda
Exxon Shipping Company
Federal Maritime Commission
William B. Fortune Family
Fred J. Noonan Company, Inc.
Gallups Island Radio Association
Gallups Island Radio Association Region 9
H & H Ship Service Company
Hands of Friendship Organization
Harbor Tug & Barge
Frank B. Hugg
I.B.E.W. Local Union 6
International Longshoremen and Warehousemen's Union
International Organization of Masters, Mates & Pilots
Islam A.R.C. Club
Islam Radio Club
Islam Temple Guard
Pierre Layec of Arzon, France
Lillick, McHose & Charles
Lykes Bros. Steamship Co., Inc.
Capt. E. A. MacMichael Family
M. A. Notch Corporation
Maine Maritime Academy

Marin Tug & Barge, Inc.
Marine Engineer's Beneficial Association
Marine Engineer's Beneficial Association, District No. 1
Marine Fireman's Union
Marine Square Club, Port of San Francisco
Marine Staff Officers
Maritime Administration
Matson Navigation Company, Inc.
MEBA/NMU District No. 1
MEBA/NMU District No. 1 -- Unlicensed Division
Military Sealift Command, Pacific
National Liberty Ship Memorial, Inc.
National Maritime Union of America
National MEBA/NMU
Norman S. Kurtz & Associates, Inc.
Oceanroutes, Inc.
Pacific Maritime Association
Pacific Merchant Shipping Association
Panama Canal Pilots Association
RADM and Mrs. T. J. Patterson, Jr.
Pennsylvania Schoolship Association
Port of Oakland
Port of San Francisco
Port of San Francisco/Marine Square Club
Propeller Club of the U.S., Port of the Golden Gate
Sailor's Union of the Pacific
San Francisco Bar Pilots
San Francisco Maritime Trades Port Council
Schnitzer-Levin Marine Co.
Seafarers International Union of North America
Sea-Land Service, Inc.
Service Engineering Company
Albert C. Smith, S.U.P. (Ret.)
Society of Port Engineers of San Francisco
Southwest Marine, Inc.
Southwest Marine of San Francisco, Inc.
Sperry Corporation

Sperry Corporation, Sperry Electronic Systems
Sperry Marine Systems
Todd Shipyards Corporation (San Francisco Division)
U. S. Merchant Marine Academy Alumni Association
U. S. Public Health Service Hospital
United States Coast Guard
United States Lines, Inc.
United States Merchant Marine Academy Alumni
    Association, S.F. Bay Chapter
United States Transportation Command
Waterman Steamship Corp.
Willard Marine Decking
Women's Propeller Club of the U.S., Port of the Golden Gate.

BIBLIOGRAPHY

Anderson, Robert Earle. The Merchant Marine & World Fron-
tiers.

Bunker, John Gorley. Liberty Ships, The Ugly Ducklings of
World War II. Annapolis: U.S. Naval Institute, 1972.

Cohen, Susan. Historic Preservation. "World War II Ugly Duckling Comes Home." March-April 1980.

Hahn, Herbert Paul. American Mariner, A Documentary Biogra-
phy. Kings Point, New York: American Merchant Marine
Museum Foundation, 1990.

Hughes, Terry and John Costello. Battle of the Atlantic, The.
New York: The Dial Press/James Wade, 1977.

Jones, Herbert G. <u>Portland Ships Are Good Ships</u>. Portland, Maine: Machigonne Press, 1945.

Kooiman, William. <u>The Grace Ships, 1869-1968.</u> Point Reyes, California: Komar Publishing, 1990.

Kortum, Karl and Adm. Thomas J. Patterson. "How We Saved the *Jeremiah O'Brien*." <u>Sea History.</u> Winter 1988-89.

Ladd, J. D. <u>Assault From the Sea 1939-45.</u> New York City: Hippocrene Books, Inc., 1976

Levingston, Steven E. <u>Historic Ships of San Francisco</u>. San Francisco: Chronicle Books, 1984.

Maclay, Edgar S. <u>History of American Privateers, A.</u> 1899.

Mangone, Gerard J. <u>Marine Policy For America, The United States At Sea</u>. Lexington: D.C. Heath and Company, 1977.

Mitchell, C. Bradford. <u>Every Kind of Shipwork.</u> New York: 1981

Morison, Samuel Eliot. <u>Invasion of France and Germany, 1944-1945, The</u>. Boston: Little, Brown and Company, 1957.

Palmer, M.B. <u>We fight With Merchant Ships.</u> Indianapolis: Bobbs Merrill Co.

Pitt, Barrie and the editors of Time-Life Books, <u>Battle of the Atlantic, The</u>. Vol. 5 of the series <u>World War II</u>. Alexandria, Virginia: 1977.

Rubin, Hal. "The Last of the 'Libertys'." <u>Oceans.</u> March 1979.

Ryan, Cornelius. <u>Longest Day, June 6, 1944, The.</u> New York: Simon and Schuster, 1959

Sawyer, L.A. and W. H. Mitchell. The Liberty Ships, Second Edition. London: Lloyd's of London Press Ltd., 1985.

Schofield, William G. Eastward the Convoys. Chicago: Rand McNally & Company, 1965.

Sherman, Rev. Andrew M. Life of Jeremiah O'Brien. Morristown, N. J.: Jerseyman Office, 1902.

Steinberg, Rafael and the editors of Time-Life Books. Island Fighting. Vol. 10 of the series World War II. Alexandria, Virginia: 1977.

Taylor, J. E. Last Passage, The. London: George Allen & Unwin Ltd., 1946.

United States. Advisory Committee on the Merchant Marine. Report Of The President's Advisory Committee On The Merchant Marine. Washington: GPO, 1947.

World War II, A Concise Military History of America's All-Out, Two-Front War. Matloff, Maurice. Editor. New York City: Galahad Books, 1982.

Zich, Arthur and the editors of Time-Life Books. The Rising Sun. Vol. 4 of the series World War II. Alexandria, Virginia: 1977.

INDEX